ADVANCE PRAISE FOR *Beaver, Bison, Horse*

"R. Grace Morgan's important study of the impact of beaver, bison, and horse on the lifeways of Indigenous people of the Northern Great Plains remains relevant in our times. Morgan deftly analyzes the long-term ecological history of this region, where animals, humans, fire, water, and drought have struck important interrelationships. Her insights can significantly influence our assessments of the economic trajectories and environmental sustainability of the Great Plains in the modern age." —GEORGE COLPITTS, author of *Pemmican Empire: Food, Trade, and the Last Bison Hunts in the North American Plains*

"Morgan's *Beaver, Bison, Horse* is a brilliant, thorough investigation of the powerful ties that bind humans to their wild brethren on the Northern Plains. In synthesizing traditional knowledge with her own groundbreaking fieldwork, Morgan's book serves as both a meticulous reconstruction of the precolonial world and a road map to the restoration of North America's keystone species. Like a beaver pond spilling its banks, this book overflows with ecological insight and wisdom." —BEN GOLDFARB, author of *Eager: The Surprising, Secret Life of Beavers and Why They Matter*

"An important book. The detail on beaver habitat manipulation . . . is rich and nuanced and cannot be found elsewhere." —NORMAN HENDERSON, author of *Rediscovering the Great Plains*

"A fascinating analysis of the ecological knowledge and religious practices of Indigenous people." —ROSALYN LAPIER, author of *Invisible Reality: Storytellers, Storytakers, and the Supernatural World of the Blackfeet*

"Morgan's work takes archaeological interpretations beyond basic descriptions of past technologies and foodways to considerations of how Indigenous Plains Peoples interacted with and maintained their lands and why they occupied their lands as they did." —DAVID MEYER, author of *The Red Earth Crees, 1860–1960*

(dg)

University of Regina Press designates one title each year
that best exemplifies the guiding editorial and manuscript
production principles of long-time senior editor Donna Grant.

BEAVER
BISON
HORSE

THE TRADITIONAL KNOWLEDGE AND
ECOLOGY OF THE NORTHERN GREAT PLAINS

R. GRACE MORGAN

University of Regina Press

COVER ART: "Beaver" by Szymon Bartosz; "Bison Walking Out of the Mist" by Effect of Darkness; and "White horse, black and white portrait" by Laure F. / all Adobe Stock.

COVER AND TEXT DESIGN: Duncan Campbell, University of Regina Press
COPY EDITOR: Alison Jacques
PROOFREADER: Kendra Ward
INDEXER: Patricia Furdek

Library and Archives Canada Cataloguing in Publication
TITLE: Beaver bison horse : the traditional knowledge and ecology of the Northern Great Plains / R. Grace Morgan.

NAMES: Morgan, R. Grace, 1934-2016, author.

DESCRIPTION: Includes bibliographical references and index.

IDENTIFIERS: Canadiana (print) 20200301438 | Canadiana (ebook) 20200301500 | ISBN 9780889777880 (softcover) | ISBN 9780889777941 (hardcover) | ISBN 9780889777903 (PDF) | ISBN 9780889777927 (EPUB)

SUBJECTS: LCSH: Grassland ecology—Great Plains. | LCSH: Traditional ecological knowledge—Great Plains.

CLASSIFICATION: LCC QH104.5.G73 M67 2020 | DDC 508.315/30978—dc23

10 9 8 7 6 5 4 3 2 1

University of Regina Press, University of Regina
Regina, Saskatchewan, Canada, S4S 0A2
TEL: (306) 585-4758 FAX: (306) 585-4699
U OF R PRESS   WEB: www.uofrpress.ca

We acknowledge the support of the Canada Council for the Arts for our publishing program. We acknowledge the financial support of the Government of Canada. / Nous reconnaissons l'appui financier du gouvernement du Canada. This publication was made possible with support from Creative Saskatchewan's Book Publishing Production Grant Program.

Canada Council   Conseil des Arts   Canada   creative
for the Arts   du Canada   SASKATCHEWAN

CONTENTS

Publisher's Note on Terminology **VII**

Foreword by James Daschuk **IX**

Acknowledgements **XIII**

Introduction **3**

CHAPTER 1   The Regional Setting **21**

CHAPTER 2   Human-Animal Relationships **33**

CHAPTER 3   The Ecological Evidence **69**

CHAPTER 4   The Historical Evidence **101**

CHAPTER 5   The Archaeological Evidence **115**

CHAPTER 6   Changing Lifeways on the Northern Plains **145**

Conclusion **175**

Afterword by Cristina Eisenberg **185**

Figures **205**

Appendix: "Dynamics of Fire and Grazing by Bison on Grasslands in Central Alberta" by R. Grace Morgan and R.J. Hudson **219**

Notes **259**

References **293**

Index **317**

Publisher's Note on Terminology

In 2018, the publishing industry saw the release of Greg Younging's influential text *The Elements of Indigenous Style: A Guide for Writing by and about Indigenous Peoples.* In this 2020 publication of R. Grace Morgan's important research into the ecological impacts of beaver, bison, and horse on the Indigenous populations of the Northern Great Plains, the publisher has endeavoured to reflect the current preferred terminology in Younging's guide where it was deemed possible, while at the same time trying to maintain the integrity of the author's original text and her voice as it was at the time of writing.

FOREWORD

James Daschuk

race Morgan has written an ecological lament for a lost way of life in an environment that no longer exists: the prairies of western Canada prior to contact. The relationships that she illuminates among humans, beaver, bison, and later horses are key to understanding the ancient ecology of the Northern Great Plains. They also shed light on our current and precarious occupation of the prairies in this age of climate uncertainty. Today our political leaders debate the true impacts of climate change as we continue headlong with industrial farming using genetic modification and other scientific methods to buffer the impacts of drought and other climatic anomalies in the 21st century. This book points to both what was and what might have been, to sustainable land management practices that kept Indigenous communities protected for thousands of years from climatic variability. This is the story of traditional environmental knowledge at its most elegant.

As with so much Indigenous knowledge and so many ancient practices, the balance among species was forever lost as the modern world economic system took the North American Plains into its grasp. In a real sense, this is the story of an extinct ecology that can never be remade. The disappearance of the bison, the defining species of western North America, is widely recognized as the greatest environmental catastrophe to befall the continent. Almost a century earlier, at the turn of the 19th century, the extirpation of the beaver from the grasslands not only signalled the loss of a commercially valued species but also marked the end of a truly Indigenous way of life that used the species as the centre of an ancient system of water management in an arid and potentially dangerous environment.

By the 20th century, not only had the plains environment been irrevocably changed but also Indigenous institutions of governance, religion, and education had endured decades of state-sponsored attacks against what Canadian authorities called "tribalism." The forcible relocation of Treaty Indians to and their confinement on reserves through the pass system, along with the establishment of Indian residential schools, in many cases broke the connections among Indigenous people, the land, and the animals that had endured since time immemorial. So complete was the assault on Indigenous ways of knowing that, for some, their traditional practices and even their histories were suppressed.

For much of the 20th century, scholars were even uncertain about the historical occupation of the prairie region. Were the Plains Cree the ancient inhabitants of the region, or did they come west as agents of the nascent global economic system? In the 1930s, American anthropologist David Mandelbaum was among the first to consider the westward migration of the Cree in a scholarly monograph.[1] Earlier writers, notably surveyor and mapmaker David Thompson, argued for the historical arrival of the Cree in the west.[2] In the 1970s, historical geographer Arthur J. Ray used evidence from the Hudson's Bay Company Archives, which had recently been brought to Winnipeg from London, where they had been stored for almost three centuries.[3] His was a pioneering work in the field of "ethnohistory," a hybrid focus that blended ethnography with historical research, the first Western scholarly practice to recognize and concentrate on the historical development of Indigenous societies. Ray's work firmly ensconced the westward-migration thesis as the standard interpretation of Indigenous territoriality on the eastern plains.

In the decades that followed the publication of Ray's *Indians in the Fur Trade*, the prevailing view of the westward movement of the Cree came under increasing criticism. The new interpretation—one that stressed the long-standing occupation of the region by the

Cree—gained momentum as the political and legal conflict over Indigenous rights took hold in the wake of the Constitution Act, 1982, which recognized the inherent rights of Indigenous Peoples. At the time, it was thought that the longer an Indigenous group occupied its territory, the stronger the group's claim to the land. By the 1980s, a growing chorus of scholars argued that the Cree were the long-standing inhabitants of the region, that the westward movement of fur traders themselves had created the erroneous impression that the Cree had moved west.[4] By the end of the 1990s, the contention that the Cree had moved west was so beleaguered that Ray, the champion of the migration interpretation, was forced to revisit the issue in the introduction to the second edition of *Indians in the Fur Trade*, published in 1998. Addressing his critics, Ray asserted that "there is overwhelming evidence in the documentary record to support my conclusion that significant population relocations took place before the early nineteenth century." He added that "new conceptual approaches" and further research were needed to go beyond the "simplistic notion that population movement took place in a wave-like fashion."[5]

Grace Morgan's research put an end to the debate. Her meticulous work—combining scientific fieldwork, archaeological analysis, and investigation of historical documents—proved beyond a doubt that the long-time inhabitants of the grasslands did not hunt beaver prior to European contact and refused to do so when the commercial economy pressured them to do so. Many, such as the A'aninin–Gros Ventre, maintained the tradition to their peril; they were exiled from Canadian territory by the turn of the 19th century, driven from their homeland by newcomers motivated by the quest for furs.

Although the dissertation version of this book was completed in 1991, this study remains as important today as when it was defended. Morgan's scientific observations on the impact of drought on prairie streams were undertaken during the severe drought of the 1980s. As I write this in the summer of 2017, we have experienced the driest July in 130 years.[6] No doubt there have been advances in specific aspects of the story told below. Yet its core findings are so important that they are worthy of publication a quarter century after the completion of Morgan's PhD and after her unfortunate death in February

2016. My own publications on the environmental history of the plains are derived from Morgan's insights.[7]

Despite her brilliance, Morgan did not have a traditional academic career, as was the case with many female scholars of her generation. The pressures of marriage and parenthood forced so many women to put their own aspirations on hold until an opportunity presented itself. The current generation of active scholars would be so much richer if Morgan and her peers had had the chance to teach and mentor them. In addition to challenging gender roles, she pushed traditional academic boundaries with her work. As an archaeologist, her emphasis on ecology rather than excavation was controversial since her study did not include a long list of uncovered remains, thought by some to be the measure of her discipline.

Grace Morgan was my friend and my teacher. Reading her work changed the way that I understand the prairies. After reading this work, you will never look at the plains in the same way.

James Daschuk
Lumsden Beach, Saskatchewan
September 2017

ACKNOWLEDGEMENTS

This book is the realization of a life project for its author, Dr. R. Grace Morgan, who died of ovarian cancer on February 2, 2016, in Regina, after many years of determined resistance. Grace, our mother, most certainly would have dedicated this book to her children, Brian, Jerry, Michael, and Kim, and their families. We now have the opportunity and great pleasure to dedicate this book to her and to acknowledge those whose encouragement and support helped bring her innovative, transdisciplinary scholarship to a wider audience. It was always Grace's intention to influence how we live in the present—which we do irresponsibly, in her view, no longer guided by the experiential knowledge and ecological wisdom that sustained early Plains Indigenous Peoples. In this sense, her unique ethnohistorical and anthropological reconstruction of the past was increasingly informed, in later life, by a growing concern over climate change and the persistent environmental errors she gave voice to when family and friends gathered.

These gatherings at Grace's home were often spontaneous and always animated, fuelled in part by her ability to conjure up a sumptuous buffet for guests at any time of the day or night. It was at one of these occasions that we first met James Daschuk, author of *Clearing the Plains*. We are incredibly indebted to James for encouraging Grace to complete her manuscript for publication and for writing the beautiful preface that introduces this book. Grace was immensely proud to have James recognize the original and visionary significance of her research and to be cited by him in several of his own publications. Also, at one of Grace's impromptu gatherings, we first met Karen Clark, scholarly acquisitions editor at the University of Regina Press. Karen's ongoing support throughout the publication process has been invaluable, especially in helping navigate the challenges of a posthumous publication. Several others at the University of Regina Press are also deserving of our thanks: managing editor Kelly Laycock, copyeditor Alison Jacques, cover designer Duncan Campbell, and former director Bruce Walsh. We'd also like to acknowledge the editorial work of Dallas Harrison in the early preparation of the manuscript. We are most grateful to Dr. Cristina Eisenberg for writing a wonderful afterword that illuminates and contextualizes the importance of Grace's work for a more contemporary readership. We also wish to thank Yasmin Hudson, widow of the late Dr. Robert J. Hudson, for permission to publish the co-authored paper "Dynamics of Fire and Grazing by Bison on Grasslands in Central Alberta" as an appendix in this book.

Our mother's research was a huge part of our lives, with each of us having our own relationship and commitment to it. Mike and Kim often served as unpaid research assistants in the field collecting data. Jerry provided generous support that enabled her time and space to work on her research. Having followed in Grace's academic footsteps, Brian was often seconded for lively and sometimes contentious editing duties, which have continued through to the completion of this project. Grace was a scientist, an environmentalist, and an artist—an accomplished violinist and opera singer, in earlier times. She was also a perfectionist. All of these qualities find their place within this book. We invite readers to share in our delight and pride in its publication.

The Morgans
April 2020

BEAVER, BISON, HORSE

THE TRADITIONAL KNOWLEDGE AND ECOLOGY OF THE NORTHERN GREAT PLAINS

INTRODUCTION

There is a prevailing perception in North America that, during the historical period, Indigenous groups were mainly responsible for the destruction of fur and game animals.* However, the advent of the fur trade brought into focus an interesting paradox. While

---

* The terms *prehistorical, protohistorical,* and *historical* referring to chronological periods have been conventional indicators of contact stages between colonizers and Indigenous Peoples in archaeology and anthropology since their disciplinary beginnings. Though these problematic terms have since been contested for their devaluation of oral traditions and literacies (see Trabert 2018; Younging 2018), Morgan used them in part for their unique relevance to the evolving conditions her study describes. Regarding the non-beaver-hunting communities of the Northern Plains (i.e., the Blackfoot), Morgan applies a protohistorical timeframe beginning in the late 17th century and ending in the mid- to late 18th century based on indirect contact with European fur traders and goods through the intermediation of Indigenous middlemen, mostly Cree and Assiniboine (Ray 1978). Several factors contributed to the end of this protohistoric period: inland expansion of the fur trade, westward migration of Woodlands Indigenous groups, overhunting, and a devastating smallpox epidemic in the early 1780s. All of these led to direct contact with and increased dependence on European goods (Daschuk 2012).

In Morgan's study, the historical period comprises two parts: the first begins with the cession of lands now known as Canada to Great Britain

the early inhabitants of the woodlands actively participated in the beaver fur trade, those inhabiting the Northern Plains—according to first-hand accounts by European explorers and fur traders—were generally reluctant to hunt riverine animals, in particular beaver, and sometimes even prohibited it, even though doing so often resulted in political and economic disadvantages. A paucity of beaver remains in the archaeological record of the latter group suggests that the origin of this aversion was ancient.

Fur traders were emphatic in their complaints about this aversion and its detrimental effects on their trade. While trading at Fort Vermilion in 1808, Alexander Henry (the Younger) noted that "beaver are numerous, but they [Blackfoot] will not hunt them with any spirit, so that their principal produce is dried provisions, buffalo robes, wolves, foxes and other meadow skins, and furs of little value."[1] John McDonnell, a North West Company (NWC) trader, stated that "the Assiniboils of the Red [Assiniboine] River are . . . the worst hunters of any Indians in the North-West who have traders amongst them. Their whole hunt consists of wolves, foxes, kitts and buffalo robes; for beavers, otters and other good furs they seldom take any."[2] The explorer Alexander Mackenzie similarly distinguished the Assiniboine and Gros Ventre in the vicinity of the Red and Assiniboine Rivers as non–beaver hunters.[3] While in charge of an NWC post on the North Saskatchewan River (1784–87), Edward Umfreville also observed the reluctance of Blackfoot and Gros Ventre to hunt beaver, but he was particularly adamant about the negative influence on the Sarcee, complaining that "these Indians are lazy and improvident; they bring us very few peltries, and those ill drest. Wolves skins are their

through the signing of the Treaty of Paris in 1763 and culminating in the merger of the Hudson's Bay Company with the North West Company in 1821; and the second starts soon after with the end of the bison-hunting tradition followed by the eventual destruction of the bison herds in the late 19th century. Throughout this book, Morgan's original timescale terminology has been maintained when referencing the specific contexts of her study (i.e., protohistorical and historical periods, as described above).

The term *precontact* has been used to replace *prehistory*, to reflect evolving standards of appropriate language use when describing Indigenous content (Younging 2018).

chief commodity."[4] Duncan McGillivray, in charge of Fort George (also an NWC post) on the North Saskatchewan River, grouped non-beaver hunters in the category *gens du large*, including the Blackfoot, Gros Ventre, Blood, and Piegan, who, compared with beaver hunters (Woodlands Cree and Assiniboine), were received with much less enthusiasm at the fort, as they lacked beaver furs as a trading commodity.[5]

Farther south, as noted by fur trader Jean Baptiste Trudeau, though beaver and otter were numerous on the Cheyenne River, the nations in its vicinity—Kiowas, Arapahoes, Pawnees, and Cheyenne—never hunted them prior to contact with Europeans.[6] Joseph Jablow also noted that the Cheyenne did not know how to trap or dress beaver.[7] Another fur trader, Charles MacKenzie, observed that the village tribes—the Hidatsa—were emphatic about their dislike of hunting beaver, even though while travelling with a group of Hidatsa he saw that beaver were numerous in their lands.[8] In 1805, while travelling with the Crow and a group of Shoshone (Snake) to their wintering areas, François Larocque found that his attempts to persuade the Crow to hunt beaver and his offers of instruction in trapping them were generally unsuccessful, and he was able to purchase beaver only from the Shoshone.[9]

The evidence from these areas is inconclusive and often contradictory, mainly because the American fur trade—particularly during its early stage—was carried out primarily by white trappers. Indigenous groups were generally bypassed and thus played little or no role in trapping fur-bearing animals. One of the earliest traders arrived in 1809 on the Missouri River with 300 men to trap beaver.[10] Trade goods were likely used as gifts to obtain the right to trap on Indigenous lands. Trappers were often intrusive, though, which led to violent confrontations.[11] In 1837, Alfred Jacob Miller, a trader, estimated that between 40 and 50 beaver trappers were killed per season.[12] Moreover, it was frequently difficult to determine how the Indigenous Peoples procured furs for European traders, for they often acted as middlemen or obtained furs by robbing or killing white trappers. Charles MacKenzie noted that the Assiniboine had killed several white men and carried away their effects.[13]

Ethnographers such as Edward Curtis, John Ewers, and Frank Secoy, as well as the historian Arthur Silver Morton, have also pointed out different approaches among various Northern Plains groups to hunting riverine animals.[14] According to J.G. Nelson, these groups did not appear to hunt small fur-bearers before the coming of Europeans.[15] Ewers has stressed that the non-use of beaver resources did not appear to be a response to scarcity: "If the traders anticipated a rich harvest of beaver in the Blackfoot trade, they were soon disillusioned. There were plenty of beaver in the creeks and rivers. A good hunter could have killed a hundred of them a month with his bow and arrows. . . . The Blackfeet were generally not beaver hunters."[16]

Geographical and/or environmental distinctions between Woodlands and Plains Indigenous communities** have been identified to explain differences in attitude toward beaver hunting. Mackenzie pointed out such distinctions between beaver hunters and non–beaver hunters: "Of all these different tribes, those who inhabit the broken country on the North-West side, and the source of the North branch [of the Saskatchewan River], are beaver-hunters; the others deal in provisions, wolf, buffalo, and fox skins; and many people on the South branch do not trouble themselves to come near the trading establishments."[17] Ethnohistorical documentation by Morton and Nelson has also pointed out a broad geographical distinction with regard to beaver hunting.[18] Nelson has also claimed that differences in attitude toward beaver hunting affected relationships between Indigenous Peoples and fur traders: "The Indians of the North became dependent on the trader much more quickly than the people of the plains. One reason was their lack of any apparent phobia against the hunting of riverine animals."[19]

**   Morgan used the terms *Woodlands Indians* and *Plains Indians* throughout the original text to refer generally to the variety of communities or groups that inhabited those regions. More specifically, Morgan used the term *Woodlands* to refer to those groups who hunted beaver, and *Plains* to refer to those who did not hunt beaver. In this text, the term *Indians* has been replaced with current preferred terms, such as *Indigenous Peoples, communities, groups,* or *inhabitants.* When specific communities within those regions are referenced, the names of those groups have not been changed from the original text.

These environmental differences brought about intratribal distinctions with regard to beaver hunting, strongly evident among the Assiniboine since contact. Ray notes that in 1685 the Assiniboine were recognized as one of the primary suppliers of furs to the Ottawa Indian–French trading system.[20] Contacts were made at the eastern margin of their territory, specifically in the Rainy Lake region. However, as early as 1739–40, Joseph La France, during his explorations in the interior, distinguished the "Assiniboine of the Meadows" from the "Assiniboine of the Woods."[21] Also during this period (1738), La Vérendrye, while travelling through the parklands, was informed by a group of Cree "that we were going among people [Assiniboine] who did not know how to kill beaver, and whose only clothing was buffalo skin, a thing we did not require."[22] It is therefore highly likely that the Assiniboine whom Ray mentions were from the Woodlands division. Earlier references to the non-use of beaver by the Assiniboine reflected the behaviour of those occupying the Northern Plains. Both divisions were observed to trade at Fort George on the North Saskatchewan River, the Strong Wood Assiniboine being the beaver hunters.[23]

Whereas the Blackfoot Nation as a whole manifested the strongest aversion to hunting beaver, a similar dichotomy of beaver hunters and non–beaver hunters was found among the Piegan. Again, the distinguishing factor was environmental conditions. Alexander Henry observed that

> there are 30 or 40 tents [of the Piegan] who seldom resort to the plains. . . . This small band generally inhabit the thick wood country along the foot of the mountains, where they kill a few beavers, and being industrious, they are of course better provided for than those Piegans who dwell in the Plains. The latter despise labor, and will not kill a beaver or any other fur animal to enable them to purchase an axe or other European utensil, though beaver are numerous in every stream throughout their country.[24]

There is also documentation confirming that several groups became averse to beaver hunting as they moved onto the Northern Plains during the historical period. Henry commented that the Sarcee, before they moved from the north side of the Saskatchewan River to the south side, "were excellent beaver hunters . . . but from intercourse with the Slaves [Blackfoot] have become fully as lazy and indolent." He observed the same phenomenon among the Cree: "Those only who frequent the strong wood country can purchase liquor and tobacco. Those who inhabit the plains are a useless set of lazy fellows. . . . Buffalo is their only object. Although passionately fond of liquor and tobacco, still they will not resort to the woods where they could procure furs to purchase those articles."[25]

The archaeological record of the Northern Plains supports the non-utilization of beaver resources. At several sites in Saskatchewan— including the Garratt site, the Long Creek site, and the Lebret site— extremely low frequencies of beaver remains suggested minimal use of this resource or none at all.[26] Faunal analyses of seven archaeological sites excavated in the Bighorn Canyon of Montana and Wyoming revealed no evidence of beaver use.[27] In analyses of faunal remains from approximately 20 sites ranging from the early precontact period to the late precontact period, and located predominantly in the Northern Plains, beaver was identified in only one site.[28]

Attempts have been made to explain the perceived aversion to beaver hunting by appealing to the cosmology of Plains Indigenous communities. While travelling with a group of mainly Blackfoot and Piegan, Peter Fidler, on observing their lack of experience in beaver hunting, commented that "several of them are so full of superstition as even not to touch one and a great many of them will neither eat of them nor suffer one of them to be brought to their tents."[29] Ewers implied that among the Blackfeet the non-hunting of beaver might have been related to its being considered a sacred animal, and Umfreville noted that the Blackfeet did not eat amphibian animals, which he specified as beaver and otter.[30] In a similar vein, Richard Lancaster's Blackfoot informant in Montana stated that Blackfoot never trapped beaver on a commercial basis because of a religious prohibition against trapping underwater persons, of which beaver persons were the leaders.[31]

Traditional stories and rituals associated with medicine bundles often portray the beaver as a protector and imply cultural prohibitions against killing it. Clark Wissler considered the Blackfoot beaver bundle ritual as one of the oldest and most sacred, and a Blood version implies supernatural benevolence or power if beaver were protected.[32] In a similar vein, Curtis noted that Blackfoot traditional stories stressed dire consequences if beaver were harmed.[33]

A Cheyenne traditional story discouraged harming beaver to the extent that one band never ate beaver or touched it for fear of becoming sick.[34] An Osage origin story stated that "a snail living on the banks of the Arkansas River married a beaver's daughter. They became the ancestors of the Osages living on that river. Therefore, until the very late days of the beaver trade the Osages had no part in it."[35]

Religious prohibitions were clearly related to ecological factors, though, as evident in the different beliefs and practices of Plains and Woodlands Indigenous groups. Marvin Harris has stressed that taboos or prohibitions can serve ecological functions.[36] More specifically, George Bird Grinnell has related the sacred status of the beaver to its role in conserving surface water: "The beaver was reverenced to some extent . . . no doubt because of the intelligence which was attributed to it, from the fact that beaver built dams to raise waters in streams, and houses to live in. It is said that in very old times beavers were not often killed, and that no Cheyenne woman would dress or even handle a beaver-skin."[37] Charles MacKenzie, while on the Missouri River, likewise observed the beaver's ability to conserve water in smaller waterways.[38]

The Comanche were among those least tolerant of trappers or traders in their territories. I have included them in this study because their Beaver Ceremony emphasized the fundamental relationship between the beaver and surface water resources. Comanche religious beliefs were almost completely individualized, and only two group rituals were recognized: the Beaver Ceremony (a healing rite) and the Eagle Dance.[39] The former, performed under the direction of a powerful Beaver Medicine Man, involved a reconstruction of the beaver's habitat, including ponds, effigies, lodges, and so on.[40] Fehrenbach also observed that the Comanche had a taboo against eating water creatures.[41] Given that the Comanche were located in some of the most arid regions in North America, the importance attached to the beaver-water relationship is understandable.

Understanding the different responses of Plains Peoples to beaver hunting in the historical period requires an interdisciplinary approach using archaeology, ecology, ethnohistory, and contemporary studies of beaver populations. The only way to understand the complex range of cultural characteristics is through an integration of ethnohistorical and ecological approaches. Given the beliefs and practices regarding exploitation or non-exploitation of beaver by Plains communities, a broad ecological-anthropological framework can help us to understand human ecology prior to the fur trade and arrival of the horse. The model represents gathering available facts and ideas and moulding them into a pattern or perceiving patterns in previous observations and integrating them. Historical and ethnographic records provided the initial clues, both ecological and cultural, in formulating the model. An understanding of the ecological dynamics of a particular time and/or area, especially in defining human-animal relationships, was useful in providing contextual meaning to the ethnohistorical information and in resolving conflicting views or opinions.

Briefly, the model perceives the plains ecosystem as a unique combination of components and corresponding interrelationships in contrast to the ecological dynamics in the surrounding woodlands environment. One of the most important and abundant components was the bison; vast numbers occupied the area, attesting to the ideal habitat of the grasslands. My theoretical approach was first formulated in my studies of bison migrations. I concluded that bison behaviour during migrations allowed for maximum resource utilization with the least detrimental effect on associated vegetation.[42] Eugene Odum similarly pointed out the advantages, noting that migrations allowed bison to maintain higher average forage density.[43] For example, migrations between winter and summer ranges (a two-field rotation) occurred when grasses could still undergo regeneration. During times of drought, the return to the winter range would be earlier since water resources would be scarcer, whereas under favourable moisture conditions the return would be delayed since the curing stage would be postponed and the grasses on the summer range would remain highly nutritious. In addition, movements between ranges were staggered so that overgrazing was prevented. An essential attribute of grazing is that most plant matter consumed by herbivores is returned to the soil in forms easily used by plants and micro-organisms, and the rate of nutrient recycling compared with that of litterfall is greater.[44] Specifically, between 80% and 85% of forage nitrogen ingested by grazers is excreted, 85% of it in urine. The higher nitrogen values provided by urine patches benefit herbivore populations and explain the attraction of bison to these areas.[45] In my research in Elk Island National Park in 1991, I found that bison selected urine patches and these areas were heavily grazed.

The bison was the basic economic unit in the subsistence strategies of early occupants of the Northern Plains. Their annual life cycle and movement were thus closely correlated with migrations of bison herds. Within the plains biome lie the Valley Complex (river/stream) systems, the major source of surface water. Its scarcity, both seasonally and, particularly, during major climatic fluctuations (e.g., droughts), strongly highlighted the ability of the beaver to conserve and stabilize this crucial resource through the storehouse effect of dam-pond systems. Within the broader framework of bison migrations (winter and summer ranges), human settlements were strongly influenced by the availability of surface water, determined to a large extent by beaver activity.

The primary hypothesis to be tested is this: the non-use of beaver resources by early occupants of the Northern Plains was a response to limited water resources and a recognition of the beaver's role in maintaining these resources in Valley Complex systems. Stabilizing surface water by not hunting beaver was a crucial survival strategy for pedestrian peoples with limited mobility. Studies of the sacred cow of India provide an important theoretical link between beaver and taboo. Harris notes that the sacredness attributed to cattle in India, and proscriptions against their use as food, reflected their value as traction power and the importance of their dung as fuel.[46] In a roughly similar fashion, the value of beaver in conserving and maintaining a critical resource (surface water) would have far outweighed its value as food. Supernatural control was invoked through the mechanisms of story, ritual, and ceremony.

Low populations on the plains, combined with a highly visible and stationary lifestyle, made beaver especially susceptible to human overkill. Because of its susceptibility to human predation, the beaver had to be protected. During the early 1800s, David Thompson, a trader-explorer with the NWC, attributed the rapid destruction of the beaver to its peculiar lifestyle: "As the Beaver is a stationary animal, it could be attacked at any convenient time in all seasons, and thus their numbers soon became reduced."[47] Terminology used by the Woodlands Cree in taking animals also reflected the beaver's lifestyle. Thompson observed that "the term 'hunting' they apply only to the Moose and Rein Deer, and the Bear; they look for and find the Beaver."[48]

In my earlier research, I stated that the success of bison hunting on the Northern Plains depended largely on the ability of early occupants to predict processes (in particular, bison behaviour) in their environment. They were able to assess, with high degrees of accuracy, the potential of essential resources, thus increasing their availability. This advantage was maintained by the development of hunting techniques that did not disrupt ecological processes and by the non-exploitation of components (e.g., beaver) that guaranteed the availability of a precarious resource (surface water), particularly during periods of drought. This advantage was also enhanced by using fire to predict the behaviour/movement of bison, thus further optimizing the availability of this resource. My study of bison herds in Elk Island National Park found that 46.7% of the burned grassland areas were grazed, whereas only 19% of the unburned grassland areas were grazed, representing a significant preference.[49]

The importance of Valley Complex systems to the survival of human populations on the Northern Plains cannot be overemphasized. In my earlier research, I found that "factors influencing the selection of the Valley Complex as a preferred winter camp are multiple: adequate water supplies, alternate food resources, shelter, the availability of wood, and of greatest importance, the abundance of bison."[50] However, resource distribution (particularly surface water) within a Valley Complex network is not uniform. Differences in the availability of surface water are most commonly related to the size of the waterway. Ewers has stated that Indigenous Peoples of the plains preferred the valleys of the larger tributaries for their winter camps.[51] By fall, even under normal climatic conditions, surface water is restricted to the Valley Complex systems. As human populations moved from bison summer ranges to winter ranges, the small to medium tributaries functioned as migration corridors. In these areas, any appreciable amount of surface water was restricted to beaver ponds.

Other researchers have also concluded that hunter-gatherers were highly perceptive of networks of cause and effect in particular environments and that this knowledge was important in their resource procurement. Robin Ridington describes environmental knowledge as a fundamental means of production in hunting and gathering societies.[52] Henry Lewis stresses that "hunting-gathering adaptations involve extensive and detailed understanding of natural phenomena."[53] More specifically, in his ethnographic studies of the Indigenous Peoples in northern Alberta, Lewis concludes that their use of fire was based upon sound ecological principles.[54]

Since this book deals with ecological conditions as they would have existed prior to human intervention, the concept of uniformitarianism—that is, that processes operative in the past can still be operative today—becomes highly relevant. Lewis Binford states that ecological studies can support this notion since many of the species with which humans interacted in the past are still available for observation today.[55] Clearly, the tradition of bison hunting is long gone, but the species—notably bison and beaver—that fundamentally influenced the lifeways of Plains Peoples are still here and can be studied. Uniformitarian principles are given further credibility because, for most animal species other than humans, innate or genetically programmed behaviour predominates. According to Michael Treshow, patterns of behaviour among animals are highly resistant to environmental modification or perturbation.[56] Therefore, if processes that operated in the past are still operating today, then the activities of, say, beavers should still have similar ecological effects, such as water conservation.

Yet, when we speak of programmed behaviour, it is only in the broadest sense. For example, if we consider the distribution of beaver across several environmental zones, then we must assume a high degree of flexibility or opportunistic behaviour. The beaver is extremely successful in adapting to its local environment. It has a restricted foraging radius but uses almost every plant growing within that radius.[57]

Such a degree of adaptability to various food resources allows it to satisfy its food needs in a wide range of regional biomes.

A fundamental rule, given the nature of living systems, is that ecological knowledge can never be exact. As John Livingston notes, "no two springs are ever alike; things change in nature, and flux does not end with the circling seasons."[58] Human and animal migration, drought, flood, fire, and so on can cause imbalances in ecological systems. Humans are an especially important factor nowadays, of course, for they have unprecedented power to exploit the environment to their advantage and thus modify it.[59] However, another fundamental aspect of an ecosystem is that energy and matter maintain highly ordered and therefore predictable interrelationships.[60]

Early occupants of the Northern Plains were aware of—had ecological knowledge of—the broadly fluctuating but predictable patterns of bison migration:

> The migration [of bison] into the parkland in winter was initiated by the need for shelter. The specific temporal and spatial manifestations of this general movement, however, were conditioned from year to year by a variety of factors whose effects were largely predictable to both the aboriginal and non-aboriginal residents of the region. Most important among these factors were winter mild spells, heavy snow, hunting pressures and fires.[61]

Similarly, occupants of the Northern Plains were aware of the habits of beaver and their importance for water conservation. Environmental studies show that on the Northern Plains (see Figure 1), even under average climatic conditions, water resources limited both human and animal populations; by the fall, water was restricted mainly to the main streams of the Saskatchewan and Qu'Appelle Rivers.[62] The presence of beaver in these streams would have helped to maintain their levels and thus enhance the potential for survival of nearby human populations.[63] During times of drought, beaver ponds might have been the only sections of streams containing water.[64] The larger tributaries also promoted the growth of trees, used by beaver for their lodges and dams and by humans for their shelter and firewood. Beaver populations thus reached their highest densities in these tributaries. Ewers has stated that the Northern Plains tribes preferred the valleys of the larger tributaries for their winter camp sites, and archaeological evidence should indicate that large winter camp sites and pounds were most often located along them.[65]

In smaller tributaries, in which treed areas and water supplies are in even closer proximity, during periods of drought, human and/or beaver populations would have been more ephemeral. The archaeological record should therefore reflect such ecological instability, showing temporary camp sites to be the most common in such areas.

In main waterways, the extent of floodplains would make treed areas less accessible and would generally have acted against their suitability as wintering areas for human populations. Yet, because of the greater stability of water in them, main waterways would have been important wintering areas (perhaps crucial during droughts) for beaver populations. Again, the archaeological record should indicate temporary camp sites in such areas. Because the main rivers were seasonal sources of supplementary food resources such as fish, the record should also indicate special-purpose sites reflecting seasonal use.

A detailed ecological analysis of the entire Great Plains of North America would be prohibitive. I have chosen instead to examine the Northern Plains. This area reflects a relatively contained ecological unit in regard to migrations of the northern bison herds. The specific area that I have selected to test the above hypotheses is the Qu'Appelle River Valley of southern Saskatchewan (see Figure 1). Historical documentation has established that the Qu'Appelle River Valley Complex was an important wintering area for both bison and human populations. Of equal importance was the profound effect of bison migrations on the settlement patterns of the associated Northern Plains Peoples. Mandelbaum states that

> the migrations of the herds regulated the tribal movements. When the buffalo, drifting southward, crossed the South Saskatchewan In June and July, the Plains Cree gathered in large encampments along that river. During the summer months many buffalo roamed the open plains between the

Grand Coteau of the Missouri (roughly, the international boundary line) and the Qu'Appelle and Saskatchewan rivers. At that season many of the tribal camps were located in those plains. In the autumn when the herds moved northward into the woods along the Saskatchewan and Qu'Appelle valleys and into the hilly regions, most of the Cree camped in the wooded country.[66]

I have selected for analyses, within the Qu'Appelle River Valley Complex, the following waterways, categorized by decreasing size: (1) Qu'Appelle River (the main waterway), (2) Wascana Creek and Moose Jaw River (large tributaries), and (3) Cottonwood Creek (a medium-sized tributary).

To provide a more specific analysis of the contrasts and similarities between woodlands and plains ecosystems and the resulting effects on human-animal relationships, beaver in particular, I also carried out ecological studies in Elk Island National Park, east of Edmonton, categorized as part of the Parkland–Boreal Forest transition zone (see Figure 1).[67] In northern areas, more favourable moisture conditions lead to a predominance of trees, lakes, and rivers, which in turn provide an abundance of habitat for beaver populations. For the Indigenous groups who occupied these areas, the beaver was a major resource, providing both food and clothing. As noted above, Nelson, upon observing differences in response to the beaver among Plains and Woodlands communities, concluded that the latter became more dependent on the fur trade than the former because they were not averse to hunting riverine animals.[68]

I will determine the validity and/or utility of the theoretical model by examining three separate data sets: modern beaver ecology in a specific setting relevant to the entire Northern Plains ecosystem; records of the earliest contact period before the fur trade and horse; and the precontact record of the specific setting in which the beaver study was conducted. I will then build upon this analytically supported model of precontact/protohistorical Northern Plains human ecology to explain the changes that occurred as a result of the fur trade, introduction of the horse, and consequent population movements. I will show how different groups reacted to these factors depending on their previous, and variable, relationships with specific resources such as the beaver.

Chapter 1 describes the regional setting, the Northern Plains, prior to European contact and introduction of the horse. Bison migrations and corresponding human movements are regional in scope. An accurate ecological perspective cannot be gained without a preliminary analysis of this larger environmental zone.

Drawing on the historical record, ethnographic studies, previous ecological investigations, and my own fieldwork, chapter 2 develops the theoretical model: that is, the traditional relationships between Indigenous Peoples and the Northern Plains environment operative at the time of contact. Specifically, the chapter examines how human needs, such as the availability of surface water, shelter, and firewood, were related to the presence of beaver. The annual cycle of human activities is reconstructed under both normal and drought conditions. To emphasize the differences between contrasting ecological systems (i.e., woodlands and plains), I formulate a less detailed model of human-beaver relationships for the woodlands environment.

Chapter 3 provides the initial test of the theoretical model from an ecological perspective. The study of the Qu'Appelle River Valley Complex, specifically, Cottonwood Creek and Moose Jaw River, examines how environmental conditions in waterways of different sizes reflect or contrast with each other and how these conditions affect beaver habitat and population size. The main focus is on determining the effects of beaver activities on the environment, especially in maintaining surface water. However, since beaver activities in different environmental zones have different ecological consequences, less detailed ecological studies carried out in a woodlands environment— Elk Island National Park—are also presented.

Chapter 4 tests the theoretical model from a historical perspective. The study of the protohistorical and early contact periods attempts to establish the origins and territorial/political alignments of the various tribal groups. However, the chapter is concerned mainly with testing the assumption of the model that aversion to beaver hunting was strongest among groups entering the Northern Plains as pedestrian peoples.

I have chosen as representative of Northern Plains groups the Blackfoot Nation—consisting of three divisions: Piegan, Blood, and Blackfoot proper—and the Gros Ventre (allies of the Blackfoot). These groups are generally considered to be the earliest inhabitants of the Northern Plains. Alice Kehoe notes that the Blackfoot lived on both sides of the Alberta-Saskatchewan border from at least 1400 CE, while the Atsina (Gros Ventre) occupied south-central Saskatchewan and adjacent northwestern North Dakota in the late precontact period.[69] With the exception of part of the Piegan division, these groups had the strongest aversion to beaver hunting. Another group examined are the Sarcee, who, as they moved from the woodlands to the plains in the historical period, became allies of the Blackfoot tribes and appeared to have developed an aversion to beaver hunting. I discuss as well the Cree and Assiniboine, major antagonists of the Blackfoot tribes, since they also exhibited the intratribal dichotomy of beaver-hunting and non-beaver-hunting groups.

Ray distinguishes the protohistorical period as a time of transition between the initial receipt of European goods by Indigenous Peoples and the actual arrival of Europeans.[70] Here this period refers mainly to the time when the Blackfoot communities were beginning to experience the events noted above. By this time, both the Assiniboine and the Cree were well into periods of more direct and sustained contact.

The archaeological analysis in chapter 5 is the final test in that it predicts what precontact settlement patterns ought to look like in the Qu'Appelle River Valley Complex if the hypothesis is essentially correct. I selected Cottonwood Creek (a small to medium-sized tributary) and Wascana Creek (a large tributary) as research areas in this system. The focus is on determining whether the archaeological record supports the assumption that large tributaries provide the most favourable habitat for human populations. The analysis includes definitions of several site types—in particular, a winter camp site—and a study of their frequency of distribution along waterways of different sizes.

Chapter 6 presents a more developed model of relationships among beaver, geography, and humans, and it examines how changing conditions in the protohistorical and historical periods altered traditional relationships, specifically among non–beaver hunters. Although the historical period witnessed many changes, such as the influx of new populations and the development of new hunting techniques, an acceleration of changes occurred in the protohistorical and early contact periods. The most important of these earlier events was acquisition of the horse, which significantly altered pedestrian lifeways. The first section of the chapter analyzes the increasing role of the horse in transformations during the historical period. The remainder of the chapter examines some assumptions:

1. Preferential treatment of beaver hunters by fur traders significantly altered territorial alignments and increased animosities toward traders and among various Indigenous groups.

2. Some Northern Plains groups, particularly Blackfoot tribes, made concerted efforts to keep fur-trading establishments out of their territories. They also attempted to prevent trapping in their areas.

3. A gradual erosion of the prohibition against beaver hunting occurred among some of the Northern Plains Peoples, for several reasons, including changing ecological conditions, increased animosities between Indigenous groups (which necessitated acquisition of trade goods such as guns and ammunition), and psychological and financial pressure by fur traders combined with the addictive nature of alcohol.

The following propositions are also discussed in chapter 6: first, that some Northern Plains groups were able to maintain the prohibition against beaver hunting until the end of bison hunting; second, that Northern Plains communities were not responsible for destruction of the beaver populations in their territories; and third, that before destruction of the bison herds, many Northern Plains communities were relatively independent of the fur trade and participated mainly in the provisions market (e.g., pemmican) and bison robe trade.

This book aims to provide an integrated view of the changing relationships between people and the environment on the Northern

Plains in precontact, protohistorical, and historical times. It makes an original contribution to this field of study in that it views ethnographic and historical descriptions of Northern Plains Peoples from both developmental and ecological points of view.

So, contrary to the views of early European explorers and fur traders, the Indigenous Peoples of the plains had sound ecological reasons for not killing or otherwise harming beaver, with which they shared a life-sustaining habitat on the arid plains. An underlying, though undeveloped, theme of this book is that their intimate ecological knowledge stands in contrast to Judeo-Christian cosmology and Western scientific tradition in stressing human connection to rather than separation from the natural world around us. The latter have been criticized for their rendering of nature into discrete units, which stymies a holistic view of ecological dynamics and leads to a remoteness from natural phenomena. The result is the loss of a sense of place within our natural world. This was not the case for hunter-gatherers on the Northern Plains, whose subsistence activities and ecological practices integrated them, from generation to generation, into their environment. Their very survival depended on their experiential knowledge of the ecological dynamics of their environment; our very survival today across the globe also depends on such knowledge, which many of us no longer seem to have.

CHAPTER I

THE REGIONAL SETTING

An important step in my analysis is reconstruction of the plains environment as it might have been just prior to contact. To do so, I rely on contemporary climatological data and vegetative studies. The validity of inferring precontact environmental conditions from contemporary data is based upon several assumptions and conditions. First, paleontological data and radiocarbon dates from several Saskatchewan sites indicate that after 10,000 years BP (before present) a change from spruce-dominated to grassland-dominated biomes occurred.[1] This dominance of grassland vegetation continued into the present. Although the climatic sequence for the late Plains Indian period (2000 BP to 170 BP) indicates periodic fluctuations from warmer dry conditions to cooler moist conditions and vice versa, pronounced climatic fluctuations are a characteristic of the plains environment that persist today, and their effects have been incorporated into many ecological studies.[2] My main concern here is with the effects of drought on this environment and the role of the beaver in helping to conserve surface water for both bison and human populations. Given the notion of uniformitarianism, we can assume that processes operating in the past are still operating today and that beaver activity in contemporary Valley Complexes should result in ecological conditions like those in the past.

Historically, the Valley Complex has been the preferred habitat of both human and beaver populations and the major source of surface water.[3] To test this hypothesis, I have selected the Qu'Appelle River Valley Complex of southern Saskatchewan (see Figure 2), at the southern periphery of the bison winter range, as a suitable wintering area for early human populations. An accurate ecological assessment of the Valley Complex cannot be gained without a preliminary analysis of its significance or role within the larger framework of the plains ecosystem, in this case the Northern Plains and, to a lesser degree, some associated peripheral areas. For this information, I draw on my earlier research in the study area.[4]

Although the analysis concentrates on the Valley Complex–beaver-human ecological relationship, the importance of the grassland-bison-human subsystem in the plains ecosystem cannot be overemphasized. It is within this larger framework, the bison life cycle, that I consider the lifeways of early human populations of the area.

NATURAL VEGETATION

The Northern Plains include almost all of the grasslands east of the Rocky Mountains and north of the Canadian-American boundary (see Figure 3). From an ecotone (or boundary zone between different plant communities) with the True Prairie in southwestern Manitoba, this area extends to the aspen forest in the foothills of the Rocky Mountains, and in the north it is bounded by the boreal forest.[5]

Robert Coupland distinguished five vegetative communities or types in the Mixed Prairie, which I have grouped, for the purpose of analysis, into two categories: the Mesic Mixed Prairie, which includes the *Agropyron-Koeleria* and *Stipa-Agropyron* vegetative types, and the Xeric Mixed Prairie, which includes the *Stipa-Bouteloua*, *Bouteloua-Agropyron*, and *Stipa-Bouteloua-Agropyron* vegetative types (see Figure 3).[6] Xeric Mixed Prairie is associated with more arid conditions in which a shortgrass is co-dominant with midgrasses. In Mesic Mixed Prairie, dominance is restricted to midgrasses. Xeric Mixed Prairie occupies southeastern Alberta, southeastern Saskatchewan, and eastern Montana. Mesic Mixed Prairie forms an arc west, north, and east of Xeric Mixed Prairie and occupies Alberta, Saskatchewan, and North and South Dakota. According to Coupland, the mesic types (containing a moderate amount of water) *Agropyron-Koeleria* and *Stipa-Agropyron* are distinctive to the Canadian Plains.[7] Henry Wright and Arthur Bailey, however, have observed that the *Stipa* and *Agropyron* co-dominants in the Canadian Plains are also present in North Dakota but in combination with a range of other grass species.[8] The Fescue Prairie—the most mesic grassland community—occupies the northern boundary of the Mesic Mixed Prairie from central Saskatchewan west to the foothills of the Rocky Mountains (see Figure 3).

Within the grassland zone, where moisture conditions are favourable, small stands of aspen are found. When such stands occur with sufficient frequency, the area is classified as the Aspen Grove Region (see Figure 3). This region is situated primarily near the forest margin.[9] In Alberta, the Aspen Grove Region is associated with the Fescue Prairie; in Saskatchewan, only the northern part of the Aspen Grove Region is associated with the Fescue Prairie, while east and south it is associated with a transitional type between the Fescue Prairie and the *Stipa-Agropyron* type of the Mesic Mixed Prairie (see Figure 3).[10] The True Prairie, or Tall Grass Prairie, region occupies the eastern edges of North and South Dakota and extends into southern Manitoba.[11]

The habitats associated with river valleys and old drainage channels have been defined as the "Valley Complex."[12] Since the Valley Complex is my focus here, I discuss it in greater detail later under a separate heading.

CLIMATE

The climate of the Canadian Plains "is characterized by low precipitation, the relative effectiveness of which is increased by low temperatures and the short growing season and is reduced by the high drying power of the wind. Deficiency of precipitation is usually a greater hazard to plant growth than either the deficiency of heat or shortness of the frost-free season."[13] The Rocky Mountains, acting as a barrier to the flow of warm and humid air from the Pacific Ocean, create drier conditions on the Canadian Plains, causing marked temperature differences between summer and winter.[14] According to E.A. Christiansen, temperatures in the Regina–Moose Jaw area have ranged from 38°C (100°F) to −48°C (−56°F).[15] Significant temperature differences also occur among various areas. The mean annual temperature is highest in southern Alberta (Xeric Mixed Prairie), reaching 6°C (43°F), but it progressively decreases to about 1°C (34°F) at the boundary between the dark-brown (Mesic Mixed Prairie) and black (Fescue Prairie) zones.[16]

Richmond Longley has calculated that in southeastern Alberta and southwestern Saskatchewan (Xeric Mixed Prairie), the mean annual precipitation rate was 33.5 cm (13.2 in).[17] In southeastern Saskatchewan (Mesic Mixed Prairie), which includes the Qu'Appelle River Valley research area, the mean annual precipitation rate was 41 cm (16.2 in). In central Alberta (Aspen Grove Region), which includes the Elk Island National Park research area, the mean annual precipitation rate was 43 cm (17 in). Marked variations in annual precipitation have also been noted. For example, in the Regina–Moose Jaw area, annual precipitation has ranged from 16 cm (6.25 in) to 60 cm (23.73 in), with variations between successive years as high as 35 cm (14 in).[18] Nearly half of this precipitation occurs during the summer months. About a quarter of the remaining precipitation falls from August to October, while the rest occurs as snow.[19] The period of snow cover lasts up to five months, starting generally in November and ending in April.[20] More precisely, the period of reliable snow cover has been defined as the first and last snow cover lasting seven days or longer; in the Edmonton area, this period averages from November 17 to March 27.[21] This period is significantly shorter farther south on the open prairie.

The winds are mainly westerly: Chinook winds from the southwest, and colder winds from the northwest, are the most typical.[22] Chinook winds from the southwest can be felt as far away as Regina.[23] They are associated with dryness, the dissipation of clouds, and a rise in temperature. Winds reach their greatest intensities—from 19 km (12 mi) to 26 km (16 mi) per hour—in the Mixed Prairie association. Forest cover reduces velocities in the Aspen Grove Region from 14 km (9 mi) to 19 km (12 mi) per hour.[24]

Blizzards are also highly variable. Storms that generally develop in the Calgary–Red Deer area register 60 hours per winter there. They move southeast into Saskatchewan, where they reach their highest frequencies: 150 hours per winter in Moose Jaw and 120 hours per winter in Regina. Moving north, the frequencies drop to 30 hours per winter in Edmonton and 11 hours per winter in North Battleford.[25]

DROUGHT CONDITIONS

The main hypothesis of my study stresses the importance of beaver activity in maintaining surface water, particularly during times of drought. It was thus fortuitous that I undertook fieldwork for this study during a time period—the late 1980s—said to have experienced the most intense drought conditions of the 20th century. Which conditions constitute drought? Since summer precipitation normally evaporates, the prairie region is highly dependent on fall rain and winter snow. When these are lacking, drought usually occurs. On the Canadian Plains, the worst years in a drought cycle usually had dry falls and winters.[26]

Comparisons of meteorological conditions during the droughts of the 1930s and 1980s attest to the severity of the latter. Precipitation totals over the 10-year periods from 1929 to 1938 and from 1979 to 1988 were almost identical. In the 1930s, the worst precipitation deficits were in 1936 and 1937; in the 1980s, they occurred in 1986, 1987, and 1988, with precipitation in autumn 1987 and winter and spring 1988 being the lowest on record. Temperatures in the period from 1986 to 1988 were much warmer than in the period from 1936 to 1938, indicating that evaporation was higher in the later drought.[27] The area most affected by drought in the 1930s was southern Saskatchewan, whereas the area in the 1980s was more widespread; by 1988, the area below 70% of normal precipitation covered the southern two-thirds of all three prairie provinces, while an area below 50% of normal precipitation covered half of the agricultural area of Alberta and Saskatchewan. Moose Jaw was one of the areas most seriously affected by the drought.[28]

Drought conditions were also strongly reflected in the amount of spring runoff during this period. Runoff, primarily from snowmelt, provides most of the surface water in the Qu'Appelle River Valley Complex. In Cottonwood Creek, the mean discharge from 1974 to 1986 was 0.452 cms (cubic metres per second). During the drought cycle (1986–88), the mean discharge in 1986 was 0.087 cms; in 1987, it was 0.037 cms; and in 1988, at the height of the drought, it was 0.000 cms, giving a mean of only 0.041 cms for the entire period, or 9% of the overall mean.[29] On the Moose Jaw River, a large tributary, the mean discharge from 1910 to 1986 was 2.64 cms. The mean discharge for 1986 was 1.40 cms, for 1987 it was 0.099 cms, and for 1988 it was 0.001 cms, giving an overall mean of 0.50 cms for the drought cycle, or 19% of the overall mean.[30]

Interestingly, for the equivalent drought years in the 1930s (1936–38), for 1936 the mean discharge was 3.34 cms, for 1937 it was 0.003 cms, and for 1938 it was 0.749 cms, giving an overall mean of 1.36 cms. Spring runoff was thus much higher during the drought of the 1930s than during the drought of the 1980s.

WATER RESOURCES

Two major drainage systems, the Saskatchewan and the Qu'Appelle-Assiniboine, have networks extending into the study area. The southwest is drained by the Milk and Frenchman Rivers. Large areas of southern Saskatchewan are poorly integrated into the major drainage system and tend to have internal drainage. Melting snow and spring and summer rains provide local water surpluses, which collect in local depressions but usually evaporate during the summer. Surface water is thus limited mainly to the main streams of the Saskatchewan and Qu'Appelle Rivers and shallow saline sloughs. In northern areas of the province, more favourable moisture conditions allow a predominance of treed areas and numerous lakes and rivers. In fact, most of Saskatchewan's surface water supplies are concentrated in the north.[31]

THE VALLEY COMPLEX

As previously noted, the term "Valley Complex" denotes the habitats within river valleys and old drainage channels, and "where factors other than the zonal climate are more important in determining the character of the native vegetation, the plant cover is more variable and must be considered as a complex. These complexes are most commonly associated with differences in local availability of moisture and tend to be conspicuous features in the grassland rather than the forest zone."[32] Habitat variability is so great, Coupland and Rowe stress, that vegetative descriptions must be kept general. However, they do distinguish several factors that affect vegetation, such as aspect of slope, steepness of slope, depth of valley, character of substratum, and degree of salinity.[33]

Ayyad and Dix also stress the importance of aspect and position but in terms of their effects on soil moisture and temperature, which they suggest are the major factors determining the vegetative character of prairie slopes.[34] They note that, on north-facing slopes, soil temperatures are lower and soil moisture conditions are significantly higher than on south-facing slopes. Also, soil moisture shows a gradual and constant change from lower values at upper elevations to higher values at lower elevations; upper and middle elevations are warmer than lower ones. The differences in microclimatic conditions between north-facing and south-facing slopes are explained by the fact that south-facing slopes receive more solar radiation and are exposed more frequently to prevailing winds than north-facing slopes.[35]

In the main research area, the Qu'Appelle River Valley Complex, these dynamics are evident in vigorous stands of trees and shrubs on north-facing slopes and lower ends of tributary valleys. Such areas support dense stands of aspen, poplar, chokecherry, snowberry, saskatoon, elderberry, and rose. On southern-facing slopes, the vegetation is primarily grasslands. Major grass species include northern wheat grass, western wheat grass, porcupine grass, blue grama, June grass, and forbs such as pasture sage. Shrubs such as snowberry, saskatoon, and chokecherry are also found, with stands of poplar and rose occurring in gullies. The vegetation on the floodplains, a mosaic of trees, shrubs, and grasslands, also indicates favourable moisture conditions. Tree species include aspen, poplar, Manitoba maple, ash, elm, and birch. More mesic grass species predominate. Also present are species such as wild licorice, sunflower, and wild barley, usually associated with moist habitats and deep coulees. At the stream edge, where moisture conditions are most favourable, willow and red osier dogwood are found. Coupland also includes rose and western snowberry as riparian species.[36]

In the Valley Complex, then, a range of local factors constant in nature and independent of zonal climatic conditions markedly affects the vegetative nature of the area. One effect is a gradient of increasing soil moisture that begins at the boundary with the Mixed Prairie uplands and terminates at the stream edge. Notable differences in microclimatic conditions between north-facing and south-facing slopes comprise another effect. One consequence of the above is that a wide range of habitats occurs within a relatively limited area. In addition, most of the habitats within the Valley Complex, with the exceptions of upper and possibly middle portions of southern-facing slopes, exhibit more favourable soil moisture conditions than those on the adjacent Mixed Prairie uplands.[37]

ECOLOGICAL DYNAMICS

On the Mixed Prairie uplands, soil moisture is the limiting factor for plant growth.[38] I concluded that, from a focal point in the Xeric Mixed Prairie of southeastern Alberta and southwestern Saskatchewan, a gradient of increasing soil moisture radiates west, north, and east to the Aspen Grove Region. Increasing soil moisture is the result not only of more favourable precipitation rates but also of factors that increase the effectiveness of available precipitation: decreasing temperatures, different soils, and the sheltering effect of aspen groves. In response to the above dynamics, the grasslands exhibit a progressive increase in vigour and percentage composition of higher-yielding midgrass species, causing a corresponding increase in grassland productivity.[39] The result of these ecological conditions is an arched geographic placement of major grassland communities around a core area: the Xeric Mixed Prairie (see Figure 3).

Pronounced climatic fluctuations occur in the study area, causing significant changes in the vegetative nature of the grasslands. Variations in height, with a corresponding effect on productivity, are the initial responses of grass species to changes in moisture. If climatic fluctuations are prolonged, then changes in the density of cover occur, further affecting productivity.[40] During times of drought, the most pronounced productivity losses occur in the Xeric Mixed Prairie since little adjustment to decreases in density can be made. In the Mesic Mixed Prairie, the exposed areas of the Aspen Grove Region, and the Fescue Prairie, density/productivity losses are partly reduced by an increase in xeric grass species.[41] In the treed areas of the Aspen Grove Region, the sheltering effect of aspens modifies the effects of drought. The Valley Complex is least affected by drought since the beaver and a range of local physical features independent of zonal climate modify its effects on the majority of habitats. The Valley Complex thus reflects the highest degree of stability in the study area.[42]

THE QU'APPELLE RIVER VALLEY

The Qu'Appelle River Valley in southern Saskatchewan is the area that I have selected to represent the Northern Plains environment (see Figure 2). The main feature of the basin, which encloses an area of approximately 52,000 km² (20,000 sq mi), is a flat, mostly treeless plain. It extends 400 km (250 mi) from the headwaters of the Qu'Appelle River near Lake Diefenbaker in south-central Saskatchewan to its confluence with the Assiniboine River in Manitoba.[43] The Qu'Appelle River, the main waterway draining the basin, flows through seven major lakes and has 10 major tributaries, including the specific study areas: Moose Jaw River, Wascana Creek, and Cottonwood Creek, a tributary of Wascana Creek.

The upland vegetative communities in the western and southwestern portions of the Qu'Appelle Valley are the *Stipa-Agropyron* and *Agropyron-Koeleria* types of the Mesic Mixed Prairie. More specifically, Wascana Creek and Cottonwood Creek are also associated with the *Agropyron-Koeleria* vegetative type of the Mesic Mixed Prairie. The Moose Jaw River primarily lies along the southwestern periphery of the *Agropyron-Koeleria* type. The northern and eastern parts of the basin are found in the Aspen Grove Region; here the associated grassland community is primarily a transitional type consisting of both rough fescue and the *Stipa-Agropyron* type of the Mesic Mixed Prairie.

The present topography of the Qu'Appelle River Valley is largely the result of two factors: the most recent glacial advance (Wisconsinan) and the preglacial topography (the Missouri Coteau), which confined the meltwaters that formed glacial Lakes Regina and Moose Jaw during the glacial retreat. During the final phase of glacial history, drainage of Lake Regina occurred first through Moose Jaw Creek and then through smaller channels such as Cottonwood, Wascana, and Boggy Creeks. The Qu'Appelle Valley was the main glacial spillway for these waters.[44] Eventually, retreat of the Qu'Appelle Valley glacial meltwaters left many dry valleys with underfit streams. The Qu'Appelle River Valley itself is entrenched from 30 m (100 ft) to 91 m (300 ft) into the surrounding plains, with a floodplain width varying from 1.6 km (1 mi) to 3 km (2 mi). A significant postglacial modification in the Qu'Appelle Valley was the formation of alluvial floodplains. Alluvial sediments in the Qu'Appelle Valley range in thickness from 6 m (20 ft) to 12 m (40 ft).[45] The Qu'Appelle Valley was further modified by the formation of alluvial fans at the mouths of tributaries flowing into the main valley; sometimes the fans coalesced to form natural dams providing lakes.[46]

Climatic conditions in the basin generally conform to those discussed earlier for the Canadian Plains. Average annual precipitation ranges from 35.5 cm (14 in) in the western part of the basin to 43 cm (17 in) in the eastern part, with snowfall accounting for about 25% of the total annual precipitation. Net annual evaporation in the basin ranges from 0.45 m (1.5 ft) of water in the west to less than 0.3 m (1 ft) in the east. However, evaporation from a free water surface averages from 0.6 m (2 ft) to 0.9 m (3 ft) of water annually to extremes of over 1.2 m (4 ft).[47]

In regard to surface water, the major characteristic of the tributaries is that high volumes of flow occur during spring runoff but that little or no flow occurs during the rest of the year. Of the total volume of water contributed to the Qu'Appelle River by its tributaries, 90% originates from snowmelt and occurs from March to May; therefore, spring runoff is the major determinant of surface water supplies for the year.[48]

ANNUAL BISON MOVEMENTS

The annual bison cycle, which I reconstructed in my earlier research, indicates that most of the herds could be found during the summer and early fall primarily in the Xeric Mixed Prairie, defined as their summer range (see Figure 4).[49] Their winter range included geographic areas where most of the herds could be found during the late fall, winter, and spring. The major vegetative communities associated with this area are the Mesic Mixed Prairie, the Fescue Prairie of the Aspen Grove Region, and the transitional grasslands of the Aspen Grove Region. As previously noted, on the Canadian Plains these vegetative communities have an arched geographic placement around a core area, the Xeric Mixed Prairie. This pattern established a central positioning of the summer range, with the winter range generally located along its periphery (see Figure 4).

Bison movements varied considerably, depending on where the herds wintered. The vegetative communities committed the seasonal movements of the Saskatchewan herds to a north-south orientation. This pattern generally involved a southward movement to the summer range and a northward movement to the winter range (see Figure 4). As noted earlier, the Qu'Appelle River Valley Complex lies at the southern periphery of the bison winter range. Herds wintering in the foothills of the Rocky Mountains moved east to the summer range and west to the winter range.[50] The Manitoba herds were also committed to a general east–west orientation, wintering in the woodlands in the eastern part of the province and summering on the grasslands in the western part.[51] Historical documentation indicates that the summer range was also shared with some of the Montana herds.[52] Therefore, the Montana herds would move north to the summer range and south to the winter range, the reverse of the Saskatchewan herds.

Bison migrations on the Northern Plains reflect a symbiotic relationship between herbivores and grasslands. The shift to the summer range occurred when the heavily utilized grasslands of the winter range could still undergo regeneration. Movement to the summer range coincided with the emergence of *Boutela gracilis* (a highly nutritious shortgrass) a month later than the midgrasses.[53] By late summer on this range, the grasses had been heavily grazed and cured, resulting in a marked decrease in their nutritional value.

Adverse climatic conditions in the fall forced herds to seek sheltered areas, where they tended to form sedentary groups for most of the winter. The return of the herds to the winter range occurred when the normal growth of grasses was complete, guaranteeing the availability of sufficient forage. On this range, because of more favourable climatic conditions, the curing stage was postponed, so grasses were still partially green, thus retaining more of their nutritional value. The sheltered grasslands, with forage capacities four to five times greater than those of the summer range, were able to accommodate the large sedentary herds. In the spring, when forage was in limited supply, the gradual dispersal of the herds from the winter range to the summer range allowed both areas to be used simultaneously and thereby reduced grazing pressure significantly.[54]

So, during the yearly cycle, the availability of superior forage was the major stimulus of herd movements, and the annual bison migrations allowed the maximum resource utilization with the least detrimental effect on the associated vegetative communities.[55] The movement of the herds within a two-field rotation system optimized their survival.

Having briefly outlined the characteristics of the regional setting, the Northern Plains, I turn next to a discussion of human-animal relationships more specifically during the time periods under study. Once again, these relationships indicate a holistic view among Plains Indigenous communities of the natural environment, in that both humans and animals were dependent on the same habitat to sustain them in a region that at times could be harsh.

CHAPTER 2

HUMAN-ANIMAL
RELATIONSHIPS

The importance of the bison to the Indigenous Peoples of the plains cannot be overemphasized. According to Michael Kennedy, the bison was "the staff of life" that provided them with most of their food and material needs.[1] The migrations of the herds thus strongly influenced the movements of the people, who developed spiritual relationships with the bison because of their dependence on them. Documentation by George Arthur indicates that a bison drive and its associated ceremonies were managed by a poundmaster (shaman) who had supernatural power to bring in the herds.[2] David Mandelbaum made the interesting observation that, as the Cree became more plains oriented, "the ease with which buffalo could be secured probably caused the atrophy of the Eastern hunting magic and hunting observances."[3] Frank Roe described a pervasive belief among the Plains communities that bison herds were an inexhaustible resource, emerging each spring in countless numbers from the earth.[4] In other words, such a predictable phenomenon required much less reliance on ceremony and the supernatural.

Equally important was the beaver, at the core of a more profound and/or encompassing traditional framework for Plains communities. The taboo among certain groups against hunting beaver has its closest parallel in the sacred cow of India. Harris stresses the ecological underpinnings of taboos, pointing out that

the case of the sacred cow of India conforms to the general
theory that the flesh of certain animals becomes very expensive as a result of ecological changes.... With the rise
of the state and of dense rural and urban populations, however, cattle could no longer be raised in sufficient numbers
to be used both as a source of meat and as the principal
source of traction power for pulling plows.[5]

Harris concludes that the value of cattle as traction power, and the
importance of their dung as fuel, greatly outweighed their value as
food, and therefore they had to be protected. Hinduism thus began
to stress that to refrain from killing cattle or eating beef was a sacred duty. Yet there were avenues through which the taboo could be
circumvented. Harris observed that, despite the ban on slaughtering
cattle, Hindu farmers culled their herds and adjusted sex ratios indirectly through various forms of neglect. In addition, cattle that died
of natural causes could be eaten by certain outcastes. In a roughly
similar fashion, the value of beaver on the plains in conserving and
maintaining a critical resource (i.e., surface water), and in providing a
major source of firewood and construction material, would have far
outweighed its value as a food resource. Low beaver populations also
acted against using the animal as a food source.

The importance of beaver in Plains Indigenous worldviews has
often been noted. Some groups believed that the world was originally made by giant beaver, and other groups claimed to have de-
scended from beaver. Among the Blackfoot, the beaver bundle was
the most sacred ceremony.[6] Ewers noted that among the Blackfoot
"the most important of these animal cults ... [in pedestrian days] was
that of the beaver, for it was the Beaver Medicine Men whose rituals
charmed the buffalo into the corral and brought food to their people
in time of need."[7] Ethnographers also observed that religious beliefs
associated with the beaver suggested a prohibition against killing it.[8]

There also appears to have been a taboo against the consumption
of beaver flesh. The traditional knowledge surrounding the name of
one of the divisions or clans of the Northern Cheyenne, "closed gul-
let," refers to the "killing by a man of a medicine beaver, the eating of
which caused all who partook of it to choke and thereafter made the

flesh of the beaver, a beaver-skin, or anything pertaining to a beaver ... taboo to these people and to their descendants."[9] As noted earlier, Fidler observed a similar taboo among his Blackfoot and Piegan travelling companions, who were "very little acquainted with killing the Beaver in their houses"; he wrote that they would not touch the animal and further that "a great many of them will neither eat of them nor suffer one of them to be brought to their tents."[10]

The means by which a beaver bundle could be acquired also reinforced the cultural taboo against killing the beaver. Edward Curtis established that the various skins and objects in a beaver bundle could be acquired only by purchase since Indigenous people were not allowed to kill the beaver.[11] However, as with the sacred cow, the prohibition was circumvented at times. Richard Lancaster observed that "on occasion the Blackfoots would take the pelt of an Underwater Person [beaver] for employment in religious ritual, but they did not trap beaver on a commercial basis." The Blackfoot also apparently had no aversion to trading beaver pelts trapped by other groups: "Those beaver pelts that were brought in by the Blackfoots for purposes of trade with the White Man invariably had been captured from White trappers or from the Crees or from other tribes that had no religious prohibitions with regard to trapping the Underwater Persons."[12]

Ethnographic sources show that traditional stories surrounding beaver bundles reinforced the aversion to beaver hunting. According to a Piegan version, one man killed every kind of animal to obtain skins for his medicine bundle so that his medicine would be powerful.[13] One summer he was camped by a stream in which there was a beaver dam. He immediately decided to obtain a beaver skin because he did not yet have one in his bundle. The old beaver, having supernatural powers, became aware of his intention and was angered. As revenge, the beaver persuaded the man's wife to come live with him in his lodge. The man was so unhappy about his wife's disappearance that the beaver finally relented. He sent the wife and the young beaver, her son, back, stating that if her husband treated the child with kindness, he would give him a gift. The husband accepted the child, and the beaver gave him the gift of the tobacco plant. This traditional story and a Blood version of it stress dire consequences if beaver are destroyed or harmed. Another Piegan interpretation of the above story emphasizes the role of the beaver as a protector or guardian of human life.[14]

In his studies of the Cheyenne, George Bird Grinnell found that beaver were regarded as sacred because of their intelligence in building dams and thereby raising water levels.[15] Other contemporary ecological studies also emphasized the importance of beaver in stabilizing surface water for humans and animals on the plains:

> Thousands of western streams that arise in the high mountains regularly become torrential soil-eroding floods in the lowlands during the spring runoff and then subside to leave dry creek beds during the heat of summer. Since the reestablishment of beaver, many such streams have been altered so fundamentally that their waters rarely attain flood stages in the spring and they have a stabilized flow through the driest summers.[16]

Dorothy Bergstrom found that beaver dams reduce runoff fluctuations, and the ponds store water during dry periods. More specifically, beaver ponds provide increased water surface area, water current deceleration, and regulation of stream flows. During times of drought, beaver ponds might be the only sections of streams containing water.[17]

As noted in the previous chapter, on the plains the amount of surface water is not only limited but also variable—crucial limiting factors for human and animal populations. Even under normal climatic conditions in Saskatchewan, surface water is generally restricted by the fall to the main streams of the Saskatchewan and Qu'Appelle River Valley Complexes, and pronounced climatic fluctuations such as drought seriously affect the availability of surface water. Therefore, the stabilization of surface water by beaver was crucial for pedestrian peoples, and areas with beaver populations were an important consideration in their annual movement and settlement patterns.

Just as surface water was limited on the plains, so too were suitable beaver habitats and thus beaver populations. Limited water volume in small and medium tributaries would have restricted the number of beaver in them. In a main waterway like the Qu'Appelle River, because of limited food supplies, beaver populations might be only 0.61 colony per kilometre of river.[18] Larger tributaries generally supported higher densities. For example, the beaver population in Pheasant Creek, a large tributary of the Qu'Appelle River, was 1 lodge per kilometre of creek.[19] Arthur Ray made similar observations for several fur-bearing animals in the parklands, including beaver: "Since their habitats were concentrated in a few areas, these animals were quickly discovered and destroyed, and by the 1820s they had been largely exterminated from the middle and upper portions of the Assiniboine River valley."[20]

Moreover, as indicated above, beaver were extremely vulnerable to human predation, and even limited hunting could disrupt the critical relationship between beaver and surface water. Traditional hunting techniques documented among Woodlands Indigenous communities prior to the fur trade and the introduction of steel axes included breaking apart beaver dams in the summer and thereby draining ponds, so that beaver became easy prey.[21] It is highly unlikely that Plains communities would have similarly destabilized beaver dams so crucial for maintaining surface water resources. The beaver thus had to be protected through mechanisms of traditional story, ritual, and ceremony. These interacting forces underlay the aversion to beaver hunting among certain Plains communities strongly brought into focus by the advent of the fur trade.

Drawing in this chapter on the historical record, ethnographic studies, and previous ecological investigations, I reconstruct models of traditional relationships between Plains and Woodlands Peoples and their environments operative at the time of contact with Europeans. More specifically, I analyze how the presence and protection of beaver met human needs such as the availability of surface water, shelter, and firewood. Studies of human-animal relationships in the woodlands are not detailed and centre on the effects of beaver-induced flooding and the importance of beaver as a resource for food and clothing. Studies of such relationships on the plains are more comprehensive and are central in establishing my primary hypothesis: the non-hunting of beaver by early occupants of the Northern Plains was a logical response to the limited availability of surface water in the ecosystem and a clear recognition of the role of beaver in maintaining this resource in the Valley Complex.

Using the Qu'Appelle River Valley as a focal point, I follow a hypothetical precontact human population through an annual life cycle. In an earlier publication, I reconstructed such a cycle for the human populations in southern Saskatchewan, which I use here as a framework.[22] In turn, recognizing the close relationships of early occupants of the Northern Plains with bison herds, and the corresponding effects of bison migrations on the movements and settlement patterns of these peoples, I also correlate the annual human cycle with the annual bison cycle. Because of pronounced climatic fluctuations in the plains ecosystem, and their marked effects on the availability of surface water, I reconstruct the annual cycles under both drought and average climatic conditions.

THE PLAINS

Average Climate

Spring runoff in the region under study can result in flooding, making most low-lying areas uninhabitable. Indeed, during spring runoff in the main Qu'Appelle River Valley, water levels can be 2.4 m (8 ft) higher than during the summer.[23] Human populations wintering on the valley bottoms of the large tributaries would have been forced to move to higher ground. Major movements of herbivores, particularly bison, out of the Valley Complex and sheltered areas of aspen parklands would also have been influenced by the emergence of spring grasses on the exposed prairie uplands. Such herd movements would have led to a sudden scarcity of essential resources near winter camps. However, if upland grasses near camps were burned in late winter or early spring, then large herds tended to aggregate in these areas.

Several investigators have documented the attraction of bison to grass on burned areas on the plains.[24] Contemporary studies of the effects of fire on ungulates (hoofed mammals) have similarly established the attraction to them of burned areas.[25] Ethnohistorical documentation also indicates that the burning of grasslands by Plains communities occurred primarily in autumn or early spring and occasionally in winter.[26] By controlling herd movements through the use of fire, traditional hunting techniques could be maintained during this time period. According to Arthur, the northern tribes also used fire in the initial phase of the bison drive to herd or manipulate the animals (up to 64 km, or 40 mi) to the pound or processing area.[27]

The summer pattern of small grazing herds dispersed over the range contrasts sharply with the winter pattern of large sedentary herds aggregated near sheltered areas. Differences in forage capacity were the major influence on these patterns. The annual forage capacity of the grasslands on the summer range was about half that of the grasslands on the winter range, necessitating the more nomadic and dispersed grazing pattern.[28]

Major human movements to the summer range would have begun after the first week in May. During these movements—that is, until the herds were located on the summer range—dried provisions were an important staple of the human diet. The historical record indicates that a major activity associated with winter drives was the production of dried provisions. While wintering with the Piegan, David Thompson observed that herds were driven into pounds from the middle of January to the middle of March and that "during this time the women are busily employed in splitting the flesh into thin pieces and hanging it over the smoke to dry, and when dried [it] is a favorite food to all people."[29]

Human populations would probably have travelled cross-country since surface water from melting snow and spring rain would generally have been available. Waterways would generally have been avoided for two main reasons: first, most of the large faunal species (deer, elk, and bison) that were sources of food would have left the valleys, attracted by the new spring growth of grasses on the uplands; second, following the tributaries would have entailed an unnecessary expenditure of energy. John McDonnell, in describing the Assiniboine River, noted that it was "one of the most crooked that fancy can conceive. A man on foot, who marches straight through the plains, in three hours' time can go as far as the canoes in a day."[30] Henry Youle Hind indicated that canoe travel on the Qu'Appelle River posed similar problems: "The tortuous character of the stream before we took the canoe out of the water, may be imagined from the

fact that eleven hours constant, steady tracking enabled us to progress only five miles in a straight line through the valley, and not less
than 200 courses and distances were recorded in the canoe."[31] Such
conditions indicate why the canoe, as a vehicle of transportation, did
not gain much favour on the plains.

Human populations following the herds to the summer range
were thus faced with a critical resource dispersed over a wide area.
However, if areas particularly suited for summer residence (i.e., treed,
with sufficient surface water) were burned in the fall, prior to human
movements to the winter range, then a convergence of large herds
would occur in these areas. Given the above dynamics, it would have
been possible for human populations on the summer range to continue communal hunting techniques and to remain relatively sedentary.
I have estimated occupancy of the summer range at up to three and
a half months.[32]

During the rut, which peaked sometime between mid-July and
mid-August, the behaviour of bison changed; they became not only
more unpredictable but also more aggressive. Manipulation of the
herds (based upon predicted behaviour), so important to the successful operation of a pound, was no longer feasible and even dangerous. George Frison also noted that, "lacking horses, it would be
extremely difficult to successfully execute a buffalo drive if young
calves or cows in rut were present in a herd."[33] Given this situation,
I have estimated that human populations abandoned the bison summer range by about mid-August.[34] Complementary factors also initiated these movements: water resources on the summer range were
more limited, and alternative sources of food—elk, deer, berries, and
so on—were abundant in the valleys of the winter range. The limited
availability of surface water was particularly critical. Even during average climatic conditions, with the exception of early spring, surface
water on the open plains is not abundant. Isaac Cowie, a trader in the
Qu'Appelle River district, noted that "in summer, too, there was [the]
greatest dearth of water, and when it was to be had at all it was often
horribly alkali, or, if the buffalo were numerous, tainted with the foul
excretions of the wallowing herd."[35] By fall, the situation would have
been critical. The area associated with the summer range is not well
integrated into the major river systems, and local water resources

evaporate by fall, leaving surface water generally restricted to the Saskatchewan and Qu'Appelle Rivers. Therefore, the return to the winter range would essentially have entailed moving into the Valley Complex networks. The small to medium-sized tributaries would primarily have served as migration corridors as the groups moved inward to their wintering areas on the larger tributaries. More specifically in the study area, the Moose Jaw River, with its tributaries projecting into the summer range, would have played an important role in these movements.

The role of the beaver in maintaining surface water was thus crucial in the fall, by which time any appreciable amount tended to be confined to and/or maintained in beaver-populated areas. However, the distribution of surface water in Valley Complex systems is highly variable, with the least abundance in small to medium-sized tributaries. For example, in Cottonwood Creek (a small tributary), the mean discharge rate during the 13-year period from 1974 to 1986 was 0.452 cms, whereas in the Moose Jaw River (a large tributary), the mean discharge rate for the 76-year period from 1910 to 1986 was 2.64 cms.[36] In the main waterway, the Qu'Appelle River, even during a drought year (1987), the mean discharge rate was 4.32 cms, substantially higher than in its tributaries. In addition, small tributaries tend to be intermittent. In Cottonwood Creek, the stream flow generally ends by July; the mean number of days of flow per year is 81.6. In a small tributary, compared with a large one, suitable beaver habitat would be restricted and consequently so would surface water, perhaps even relegated to beaver ponds.

Therefore, as the human populations moved back to the bison winter range, beaver-occupied areas on smaller tributaries would have been crucial sources of water, and they would have attracted alternative food species such as elk and deer. George Knudson noted that beaver-influenced areas show "marked density increases for many animals and substantial increases in the number of species using most of the ponds and meadows and their environs as compared to the density and variety of species using the stream above and below the beaver pond and meadow."[37] These areas, with their availability not only of water but also of superior forage, would have attracted herbivores. Moreover, beaver dams raise water tables so that nearby grasslands continue to grow and remain green longer, whereas forage elsewhere cures and becomes less palatable.[38] Beaver activity also provides firewood (discussed in a later section).

Which specific factors influenced the choice of a wintering area? I indicated in previous research that the "factors influencing the selection of the Valley Complex as a preferred winter camp are multiple: adequate water supplies, alternate food resources, shelter, the availability of wood, and of greatest importance the abundance of bison."[39] Several other authors have also attempted to determine these factors. For example, David Bushnell noted that the permanent camping grounds of the Cree were always near a supply of fuel.[40] For the Assiniboine, Kennedy observed, "after roaming the prairie from early spring until late in the fall, the tribe, when the winter came, camped along the large, heavily wooded rivers, where there was fuel and shelter."[41] Comanche and Kiowa allies preferred to camp "along meandering creek valleys toward the headwaters of larger streams, where there were adequate canyons, arroyos, and breaks for protection [i.e., some form of wall], abundant grass for the large horse herds, ample buffalo and antelope for food, wood for the camp fires, and sweet water for drinking."[42] Richard Dodge mentioned the presence of trees as a significant factor in providing shelter and noted that in choosing a stream for a winter camp the Indians specifically looked for attributes such as "the shelter furnished by the bluffs on each side of the stream, . . . the amount of timber and wooded thickets along its valley, [and] . . . the sufficiency of grass or cotton-wood to keep ponies alive."[43] In describing the winter camps of the historical Plains Peoples such as the Gros Ventre and Blackfoot, Ewers gave perhaps the most comprehensive and precise assessment of what constituted a good wintering area in the Valley Complex:

> It would have been suicidal for these Indians to have remained on the open plains in the treacherous winter season of intense cold, high winds, heavy snows and blizzards. In late October or early November each band sought the shelter of a river valley where they could pitch their lodges among the trees and obtain shelter from the elements.

They preferred winter camp sites where high banks afforded protection from winds, and required locations which would provide not only good drinking water but sufficient wood for their campfires and grass to pasture their horses. Not all river valleys met these requirements. Generally, it was only the valleys of the larger tributaries that did. So long as the food supply held out and the necessary timber and grass were available the band could and often did remain in that location all winter.[44]

All authors single out shelter as a crucial factor in the selection of a wintering area. The historical record frequently mentions the hazards of remaining on the open plains during the winter. Edwin Denig, a 19th-century fur trader, wrote that

the winters are variable, mostly very cold, with deep snow. In the severest cold the mercury freezes and the degree cannot be determined in this way. It often remains frozen for several days and for weeks ranging between 30 and 40 degrees below zero. The snow storms in these times are terrible and certain death befalls those who are caught on the plains.[45]

Thompson, while crossing the open plains in winter from the Souris River to the Mandan villages on the Missouri River, documented the dangers of such an undertaking. A journey that required 33 days to complete would have taken only 10 days in good weather. Temperatures reaching −32°C and frequent severe storms led him to comment that

I am utterly at a loss to account for such violent winds on this part of the Plains, and this may account for the few Bison we have seen, and the smallness of the herds, which rarely exceed twenty; ... we have not seen the track of the Deer, and even a Wolf is a rare animal, as for Birds we have seen none.[46]

The Assiniboine with whom Alexander Henry (the Elder) was travelling during the winter of 1776 impressed on him the dangers of travelling on the plains during both summer and winter:

> The Chief informed me . . . that the intervening country was a tract destitute of the least appearance of wood. In the winter, as he asserted, this tract cannot be crossed at all; and in the summer, the traveller is in great danger of perishing for want of water; and the only fuel to be met with is the dung of the wild ox. It is intersected by a large river [Saskatchewan] which runs to the sun's rising, and which has its sources in the mountains.[47]

The ethnohistorical reports indicate a rather late occupancy of the winter camps (as late as November) for the historical equestrian tribes. I suggested a much earlier occupancy for the precontact pedestrian peoples because of the dangers of bison hunting during the rut and the predicted behaviour of bison (altered during the rut) essential for the successful manipulation of herds during a drive.[48] Acquisition of the horse significantly reduced the dangers of hunting herds engaged in rutting activities. The "chase," a technique that evolved with acquisition of the horse, was the preferred method of hunting during spring and summer.[49] The chase, as described by Ewers, "was a straightaway rush by mounted men, each hunter singling out an animal from the herd, riding alongside it and killing it at close quarters."[50] As can be inferred, the chase required little more than the element of surprise for its successful operation. Therefore, prior to contact with Europeans, Indigenous communities would have moved into the winter bison range in a period from about mid-August to mid-September.

An equally crucial factor in the selection of a wintering area was the presence of sufficient surface water, not emphasized in the historical documentation but likely considered a given. Since water is intermittent in a small tributary, many sections become dry by fall. As a result, stream-edge vegetation (riparian species) would be associated primarily with beaver-occupied areas and mainly restricted to north-facing slopes, ravines/coulees, and the stream edge itself. In a large tributary, water is more abundant, and the flow continues well into October; the mean number of days of flow per year is 190.8.[51] In other words, water is more uniformly distributed and available. Accordingly, riparian species are of greater abundance and tend to be more continuous along the stream edge. Beaver can choose from a broader spectrum of suitable habitats and thus reach their highest densities on large tributaries. They can therefore create a more extensive and stable network of dams and ponds. These ecological conditions would have provided the ideal habitat for large winter camp sites.

Since tree/shrub species are also limited in Valley Complex systems, another factor that must be considered is whether the beaver's need for such species for building dams and lodges would have reduced the availability of adequate shelter materials for resident human populations. Different habitat requirements could have prevented direct competition between beaver and human for the same resources. Beaver are not only sedentary but also restricted to a narrow foraging range. There is general consensus that they use most trees within the first 30 m (100 ft) of the water; Joseph Hall specified that 90% of the cutting occurred within this range.[52] Estimates of the maximum foraging radius range from 91 m (300 ft) to 152 m (500 ft).[53] Thus, beaver-occupied areas would have been on sections of the waterway close to trees. Human populations, in contrast, needed a broad expanse of floodplain for a wintering area since groups at that time of the year were relatively large. Arthur concluded, on the basis of historical documentation, that the wintering patterns, or migration, of bison tended to include larger and more sedentary herds, offering an advantage for the formation of large Indigenous encampments within the vicinity of the winter bison range.[54] Therefore, the need for a larger area would have placed most wintering areas somewhat removed from where the waterway approaches the slope wall. In the fall, when the waterway became a focal point of surface water supply, weather conditions were still relatively moderate. A lack of shelter (open canopy) would not have presented any great hardship to the resident human populations. The removal of trees near the waterway by beaver could have been considered beneficial, initiating a succession to grasslands and attracting more herbivores.

With snow (in mid-November or later) removing the reliance on waterways for water, and the subsequent freeze-up of ponds, human groups would have moved to treed areas adjacent to north-facing slopes or ravines. Ewers described how seasonality affected the distribution of groups occupying wintering areas: "When the band arrived at the site chosen for winter camp they usually pitched their lodges in the open for a few weeks. As the weather grew colder, around the end of November or early December, the chief gave orders to move the lodges in among the thick timber of the valley."[55] Considering the beaver's narrow foraging range, most of the wooded areas (often aspen) along the slopes would have been inaccessible, especially along larger waterways. Merrill Hammond found that along the lower Souris River most aspen stands were usually several hundred metres from the river and generally not available for use by beaver.[56]

I have also stressed another factor influencing selection of the Valley Complex as a wintering area: the abundance of bison.[57] By fall, the availability of superior forage, as well as the presence of surface water, drew herds back to the winter range. Grasses were still green and nutritious, particularly in Valley Complexes. Herds tended to concentrate near waterways until late November, making conditions favourable for intensive bison drives. When the first snows provided alternative water sources, herds tended to move back onto exposed grassland areas, and during this time the encamped Indigenous groups would have drawn heavily on their dried provisions. Alternative sources of meat such as elk and deer also became important components of the diet. Mild winters allowed herds to remain on the exposed grasslands for prolonged periods, but adverse weather soon forced them back into sheltered areas. Once herds re-entered sheltered areas, they tended to remain in them for the rest of the winter.

The movement of bison into sheltered areas for the winter was recorded in the historical period by several authors. Hind noted that "the prairie buffalo . . . generally avoids the woods in summer and keeps to the open country; but in winter they are frequently found in the woods of the Little Souris, the Saskatchewan, the Touchwood Hills, and the aspen groves on the Qu'Appelle."[58] Mandelbaum generally concurred with Hind.[59] Alexander Mackenzie made similar observations for the North Saskatchewan River: "On the West and

North side of this great river, [the land] is broken by the lakes and rivers with small intervening plains, where the soil is good, and the grass grows to some length. To these the male buffaloes resort for the winter, and if it be very severe the females also are obliged to leave the plains."[60] While camped near a wooded lake in the Aspen Grove Region of Saskatchewan, Henry vividly documented the seeking of shelter by bison during winter storms:

> In the morning, we were alarmed by the approach of a herd of oxen, who came from the open ground to shelter themselves in the wood. Their numbers were so great, that we dreaded lest they should fairly trample down the camp. ... The Indians killed several, when close upon their tents; but, neither the fire of the Indians, nor the noise of the dogs, could soon drive them away. Whatever were the terrors which filled the wood, they had no other escape from the terrors of the storm.[61]

With herds close to wintering areas, communal hunting techniques resumed and were carried out for the duration of the winter. Traditional hunting techniques, those employed before acquisition of the horse, appear to have been identical to drives used on the Northern Plains during the late precontact period.[62] The success of these hunting techniques depended on the manipulation or enticement of bison herds to processing areas with a minimum disruption of their behavioural patterns. All animals captured during a specific drive were killed, for it was believed that if they escaped they would transmit knowledge of the drive to other animals, thus jeopardizing the success of future drives.[63] Such ecological knowledge—in this case, awareness of bison behaviour—led to the evolution of nondisruptive hunting techniques, "guaranteeing the presence of the herds in an area for subsequent hunting operations, an important survival factor for pedestrian peoples."[64]

Among the different waterways, surface water would be most abundant and therefore most stable in main waterways. Beaver occupying such waterways under normal conditions would not directly contribute to maintenance of the water level. The strong flow of the Qu'Appelle River generally acts against the construction of dams and lodges, but beaver populations that maintain surface water in tributaries would indirectly contribute to continued flows into the main waterway. However, tree/shrub species inaccessible because of expansive floodplains place a limit on food resources, which in turn restricts beaver populations.[65] Similarly, for human populations, too great a distance between surface water and nearby shelter and firewood would have prevented the main waterway from being a suitable wintering area. With the coming of spring, the cycle was complete. Melting snow and spring runoff created excess water, and the movement of herbivores to the open plains again led human populations away from Valley Complex systems. Human occupation of the bison winter range should have been from eight to nine months.

Drought Conditions

No evidence exists to suggest that a single year of drought on the plains would have greatly inconvenienced the human population or led to significant mortality among bison populations. Climatic fluctuations on a year-to-year basis are common, and bison populations stabilized to the point where drought conditions could be accommodated if they were the exception rather than the rule.[66] As noted in the previous chapter, the years 1986 to 1988 coincided with what was considered the worst drought cycle of the 20th century. Using climatic data recorded during this time as a reference point, I attempt to infer here how Indigenous populations on the Northern Plains, prior to contact with Europeans, would have coped with or adjusted to similar conditions.[67]

During the initial stage of a drought cycle, neither human nor bison movements to the summer range would have been significantly affected. Given spring runoff, surface water along migration corridors would not have been greatly reduced. However, reduced precipitation and/or higher temperature during the vegetative season would have brought about several environmental changes: (1) local water resources would have evaporated sooner, (2) grassland productivity would have been reduced, and (3) the grasslands would have reached the curing stage earlier. Reduced capacity and earlier curing of grasslands might have impelled bison to return earlier to their winter range, which might actually have been advantageous to human populations, reducing their length of dependency on dried provisions and alternative food supplies.[68]

Increased water loss would have resulted in contractions of beaver dams and ponds. Some would have become dry, whereas others would have separated into discrete pools, and some beaver populations would have been forced to re-establish themselves at lower levels, generally on the same waterway. Thomas Collins found that, in the Snake River in Wyoming, though some abandonment of dwellings occurred during high water in spring, the most pronounced movements occurred during low water in mid-September.[69] When side channels became dry, beaver moved to main channels. Colonies that re-established themselves in their own territories moved an average distance of 262 m (560 ft). Nevertheless, during periods of drought, beaver ponds, whatever their sizes, might have been the only source of water available, particularly on small tributaries. Larger waterways would not have been affected to as great an extent.

Going into fall and winter, critical variables of a drought cycle would have come into play: reduced fall rain and winter snow (and thus decreased runoff the next spring). In Cottonwood Creek, for instance, during the second year of drought in the 1980s (1987), the flow during spring runoff was reduced by 58%. So, in the second year of a drought cycle, on the summer range, water sources—dependent mainly on snowmelt—would have been markedly reduced. In addition, reduced precipitation coupled with high temperature, and therefore greater evaporation, would have further diminished remaining water resources, leading human populations to vacate the bison summer range at an earlier date. As they moved to the bison winter range, they would have noticed marked reductions of water resources along migration corridors/smaller tributaries as well. Given the human knowledge of ecological processes, these reductions would have been predictable, and the Indigenous groups of the Northern Plains would have relied on their awareness of the most stable beaver-occupied areas as crucial sources of water.

It was fortuitous that these groups returned to the winter range before the majority of the bison. Considering the immense sizes of the herds, by the time winter snows arrived, the bison would have depleted most of these ponds. David Dary, who documented several occasions when bison herds drank a waterway dry, noted that an old bison hunter recalled seeing a "herd of buffalo drink the Solomon River dry and the river was twenty-five feet wide and a foot deep before the buffalo came."[70]

Even abandoned beaver ponds could provide water. The resistance of ponds dammed by beaver to climatic perturbations was observed by Thompson: "Dams erected by the art of Man are frequently damaged ... or wholly carried away by violent freshets but no power of water has ever carried away a Beaver Dam."[71] Contemporary ecological studies also point out the durability of beaver dams. As beaver colonies mature, repairs to dams are made mainly with mud, and "such repair adds a degree of permanence because the dam eventually approaches an earth dike in composition."[72]

Remaining surface water resources, mainly discrete ponds of standing water, would have been highly stagnant, yet the historical record indicates that water quality did not seem to be a major problem. While travelling with a group of Mandan and Hidatsa on the open prairie in the summer of 1806, Henry observed that "we suffered much from want of good water; that in the pond was a mere poison to the taste and smell, though the Indians drank it with pleasure. These savage brutes can drink stinking, stagnate[d] water with as good a stomach as if it were spruce beer."[73]

As ecological conditions on the bison summer range worsened through the second year and into the third year of a drought cycle, diminished grassland and water resources would have jeopardized the survival of bison, forcing them to expend more energy in grazing and drinking and to migrate to their winter range much earlier. Herds would have entered their winter range physically weakened, resulting in high mortality. In areas where nomadic grazing is practised, drought conditions can be so widespread that half or more of the domestic animals might die. Reduced birth rates also contribute to population decreases. When forage supplies are inadequate, the birth rate of cows, for instance, drops the following season. Reduced overall bison populations would have been balanced by concentrations of remaining herds near diminished water resources.[74]

The climatic data from the winter of 1987–88 (the second winter of the drought in the 1980s) indicate just how critical water resources can become. During November and December, when freeze-up usually occurs, only 4.4 cm (1.7 in) of snow fell; the norm is 28.2 cm (11.1 in).[75] Therefore, frozen beaver ponds were likely a major source of surface water for Indigenous populations on the Northern Plains during similar times of drought. Beaver can also keep their primary ponds open for some time after freeze-up. Thompson observed a beaver lodge on a river in November with a few yards of open water around it, which the beaver kept from freezing.[76] This would have been an easily accessible source of water for nearby human populations.

Furthermore, the exceptionally dry winter of 1987–88 resulted in no spring runoff in Cottonwood Creek, while in the Moose Jaw River the discharge flow was negligible: only 0.001 cms. Grasses thus remained dormant until the first spring rains, and the absence of snowmelt meant no local water surplus. Extrapolating this situation to the Northern Plains in the time period under study, I infer that already weakened bison herds would have suspended migrations to their summer range.[77] Ecological studies by Linda Maddock on migratory herds in the Serengeti, a savanna region in East Africa, indicate parallels in terms of which factors alter, and in some cases suspend, migratory movements. Herds such as wildebeest, zebra, and Thompson's gazelle move to the plains in the rainy season and back to the woodlands in the dry season. Maddock observed that migrations are the means by which these populations use the plains, where forage is available only during the wet season. She concluded that "the main migratory patterns are thus determined by food supply, which is largely dependent upon rainfall. Yearly variations in the migrations are also related to rainfall. Animals use the plains only while there is sufficient rain to produce green grass. . . . This flexibility is essential in an environment with widely fluctuating rainfall."[78] Given that bison migrations to the summer range were likely suspended during times of drought on the plains, I also infer that major movements by associated human populations were likewise suspended (though more local movements within the Valley Complex were likely common).

So, during a drought cycle, migrations of faunal populations, especially beaver and large herbivores, to main waterways would have been likely. Dary hints at this type of migration.[79] During the summer of 1868, drought prevailed throughout Kansas and most of the states from Texas to the Dakotas. Water was limited, vegetation was sparse, and most of the small streams had dried up; only the largest rivers still contained water. Vast numbers of bison, stretching for nearly 50 km (30 mi), were seen converging on the Smoky Hill River, driven there by the lack of water. Normally, beaver contribute little directly to the maintenance and control of water in main waterways. However, during a prolonged drought, there would be a progressive drop in water level and flow, and such conditions, which generally stimulate beaver dam-pond construction on smaller waterways, would probably initiate similar behaviour on main waterways. The availability of surface water combined with vast floodplains providing superior forage, compared with that on the prairie uplands, would have resulted in huge concentrations of large herbivores along main waterways. Given these concentrations, human populations would also have been drawn to main waterways during spring, summer, and fall to hunt bison. And soon, inclement weather would have prompted them to seek shelter among larger tributaries, where firewood was more readily available. Likewise, many large herbivores would eventually have been drawn to these sheltered areas.

Beaver and Wood Resources

Like water, trees are a limited resource on the plains, and it might seem that beaver and human populations would have been in direct competition for them in the past to meet their needs for food and construction (beaver) and shelter and firewood (humans). The historical record suggests that the felling of trees by beaver provided firewood and construction material for associated human populations.

Historical and ethnographic documentation shows that the "collecting" of firewood was the work of women. More specifically, as Richard Dodge and Michael Kennedy each noted, it was the task of older women. Grinnell observed that girls, as soon as they were strong enough, also carried wood and water for their mothers. Among the Mandan and Hidatsa, driftwood was the primary source of firewood and construction material. Charles MacKenzie noted that "drift wood supplies the villages with fuel, which as well as the timbers for their houses, is dragged home always by the women." George Catlin, while among the Mandan, also observed that one of the principal occupations of the women of the village was procurement of wood and water.[80]

The historical record generally implies that dried wood—branches rather than trunks—was the primary source of firewood.[81] The most common method of procuring firewood, as in the case of driftwood, was simply to gather it. According to Wissler, in earlier times stone hammers were used to break dry branches.[82] Henry observed several methods of procuring wood among Piegan women, who

> have much difficulty in collecting firewood. Those who have no axes fasten together the ends of two poles, which two women then hook over dry limbs of large trees, and thus break them off. They also use lines for the same purpose; a woman throws a line seven or eight fathoms long over a dry limb, and jerks it until the limb breaks off. Others again set fire to the roots of large trees, which having burned down, the branches supply a good stock of fuel.[83]

Wissler suggested that after contact, commercial axes were used to obtain wood.[84] However, Henry noted that "the trunk is seldom attacked by those who have axes, as chopping blisters their hands."[85] Grinnell offered a comprehensive analysis of the methods of collecting firewood among Cheyenne women:

> During the morning parties of women and young girls started off to get wood. . . . When the place was reached where they were to get wood, some gathered the sticks lying on the ground; others climbed up into trees, breaking off and throwing down the dead branches, while those below trimmed and made them ready for the ropes. The wood was divided into even loads, and when all these were prepared, each woman took hers on her back, and, in single file, they set out for the camp.[86]

A significant amount of dried wood collected for fuel was likely felled by beaver.

According to Grinnell, timber was often used to construct pounds: "The Sik'-si-kau [Blackfoot] built their pis'kuns [pounds] like the Crees, on level ground and usually near timber. A large pen or corral was made of heavy logs about eight feet high."[87] Mandelbaum noted that among the Plains Cree "the shaman who directed the construction and operation of a pound, chose the site in a thicket; a circular area thirty to forty feet in diameter was cleared. The cut brush and felled logs were heaped up to make a wall ten to fifteen feet high. Loose boughs, interwoven between standing trees, furnished a foundation for the wall."[88] Henry, who claimed that the Assiniboine were the most expert of the Plains inhabitants in running drives, described their pound: "The common size is from 60 to 100 paces or yards in circumference, and about five feet in height. Trees are cut down, laid upon one another, and interwoven with branches and green twigs."[89] Most of the historical references suggest that Indigenous Peoples chopped or cut the trees used to make their pounds. With the advent of the fur trade, steel axes were a highly prized trade item, but it is unlikely that stone tools would have been as efficient or necessary in earlier times, for the trees were already felled and trimmed by beaver. In the pursuit of their habitat requirements, beaver populations provided human populations with useable sources of firewood and construction material.

Summary

Because surface water is limited on the plains, beaver activity (i.e., building dams and thus creating ponds) secures it in specific areas, which enhanced the potential for survival of early human populations. In fact, in an intense drought, without beaver colonies, human occupancy of the plains might not have been possible at all. Since pedestrian peoples had limited mobility, knowing where beaver-occupied areas were would have been a critical factor in their annual movement and settlement patterns. Traditional stories among Plains Peoples portrayed the beaver as a protector of humans and warned against harming, killing, or eating it. Indigenous religion reinforced the ecological basis of not hunting such a valuable resource.

Such environmental knowledge among hunter-gatherer societies is the underlying theme of this study. On the plains—subject to pronounced climatic fluctuation and uneven resource distribution—familiarity with certain areas was crucial for peoples to determine the levels of local resources. Awareness of the beaver's ability to stabilize surface water allowed for the repetitive use of an area. Ewers observed that "the Blackfoot had knowledge of the locations of all running streams, clear lakes, and springs in and near their hunting grounds that afforded clean drinking water for themselves and their dogs."[90] Treshow notes that "familiarity and predictability are vital to the maximum utilization of an environment" and that "hunting success . . . is predicated upon detailed knowledge of the area being hunted. It is likely that hunting success for both humans and animals is inversely proportional to the distance from the familiar range."[91]

Beaver not only conserved surface water but also, by felling trees and shrubs, provided firewood and construction material for early peoples on the Northern Plains. Beaver dam-pond systems—oases of water and greenery with the focal beaver lodge—also attracted a wide range of faunal forms, which served as alternative food sources for these peoples. Parallel needs thus placed human and beaver in close association, the former, for the most part, being the beneficiary. This kind of relationship is defined as "commensalism," "in which one population is benefited but the other is not affected."[92]

Environmental knowledge of these early peoples included intimate understanding of bison behaviour and the use of fire on grasslands to attract bison. By burning certain areas in fall and spring, early occupants were able to maintain herds near their wintering areas. They could also drive herds to pounds and kill sites with a minimum of disruption to their habits, and other herds would thus stay in the vicinity and be available for subsequent hunts, allowing for traditional hunting techniques during most of the year.

I estimated that, under normal climatic conditions, human occupancy of the bison summer range was up to three and a half months, whereas human occupancy of the bison winter range was up to nine months. During a drought cycle, however, there would have been greater dependence on the winter range for essential resources. Eventually, in a severe and prolonged drought, the human population might have been forced to remain in the Valley Complex system year-round. Because of diminished water and forage resources on the prairie, bison would also have congregated in Valley Complexes, likely suspending their normal migration to the summer range. There is no evidence that Plains communities occupying such systems experienced a scarcity of resources. In fact, given year-round residency in such systems (a marked increase in a sedentary lifestyle), less energy would have been necessary to procure essential resources.

THE WOODLANDS

Food Resources

In the woodlands, compared with the plains, food resources are more diversified and dispersed. Given the extent of the area involved, there are variations in the resource base, and corresponding differences existed among the various Woodlands communities in the basic foods used. In 1804, while a fur trader among the Saulteaux, Peter Grant observed that moose

> are seldom found in large droves like the elk or buffaloe, but are generally scattered in small bands, which frequent the thickest wood, and feed upon the tender branches of the willow, birch or poplar. . . . The size of the animal, its skin and meat, which is of the most excellent quality, make the hunting of it an object of the first consequence with the Natives; it may, indeed, be reckoned their staff of life, and a scarcity of moose in the winter season is sure to cause a very severe famine.[93]

Grant also noted that beaver and bear were considered important food sources; however, otters, cats, fishers, martens, muskrats, and so on were hunted only for their furs.[94] Alanson Skinner similarly found that among the Northern Saulteaux, the moose was the most important food source. He listed a range of other animals eaten, including caribou, white-tailed deer, bear, lynx, beaver, and muskrat.[95]

Thompson defined the forested area north of the Saskatchewan River as "Muskrat Country," the home of the Nahathaway Indians (Woodlands Cree). He also singled out moose as their most important food source: "The flesh of a Moose in good condition, contains more nourishment than that of any other Deer." Other animals Thompson listed as food sources included reindeer (caribou), bear, and beaver; however, he implied that prior to acquisition of trade metal goods, Indigenous people were unable to hunt beaver effectively.[96] Skinner suggested that rabbit or hare was the most important source of food for the Woodlands Cree.[97] Referring to the historical record, Edward Rogers noted that in earlier times the major occupation of the Mistassini Cree was the hunting of large mammals, particularly during autumn and winter. Fur-bearers, grouse, and waterfowl provided supplements to the diet. Beaver, which Rogers classed as big game along with bear, caribou, and moose, were an important part of the diet. Referring to Skinner, Rogers suggested that rabbits were taken during periods when large game was not available.[98]

Daniel Harmon, a fur trader, observed that the large game animals were hunted mainly for their meat, principally when they were fattest, during fall and winter.[99] Ray also noted that in the woodlands region only two large game species were found: caribou and moose.[100] Small game was abundant, however, and muskrat and beaver were considered significant sources of food; cub beaver was considered a delicacy. Fishing was considered important by all the groups noted above.[101]

Some of the animals were exploited more heavily during specific seasons. Large game, particularly moose, was hunted mainly in winter.[102] Beaver appeared to be hunted most frequently in spring and fall.[103] Ray suggested a seasonal use of different environmental zones by the Woodlands Cree and certain groups of the Assiniboine.[104] The bands spent March, April, and May in the forest fishing and hunting along the shores of lakes and rivers. In August, September, and October, they hunted in wooded areas adjacent to prairie areas, taking moose and trapping beaver. From November to March, they moved into parkland areas to hunt bison and trap wolves. Ray's subsistence pattern for the Woodlands Cree and Assiniboine can best be considered a manifestation of the historical period, when the Cree were advancing into the Saskatchewan Plains and exhibiting a mix of woodlands and plains traits, such as trapping beaver (a woodlands trait) and pounding bison (a plains trait).

Human-Beaver Relationships

The following analysis attempts to ascertain the importance of beaver in the hunting-gathering strategies of Woodlands Indigenous communities prior to contact with Europeans. Thompson provided a perspective on early human-beaver relationships:

> The Beaver, they were safe from every animal but Man, and the Wolverine. . . . Except the Great Lakes, . . . [they] occupied all the waters of the northern part of the Continent. Every River where the current was moderate and sufficiently deep, the banks at the water edge were occupied by their houses. To every small Lake, and all the Ponds they built Dams, and enlarged and deepened them to the height of the dams. Even to grounds occasionally overflowed, by heavy rains, they also made dams, and made them permanent Ponds, and as they heightened the dams [they] increased the extent and added to the depth of the water. . . . Small Streams were dammed across and Ponds formed; the dry land with the dominions of Man contracted, everywhere he was hemmed in by water without the power of preventing it: he could not diminish the numbers half so fast as they multiplied, and their houses were proof against his pointed stake, and his arrows could seldom pierce their skins.[105]

Thompson went on to state that the acquisition of metal trade goods allowed Indigenous people to hunt beaver more efficiently:

> For the furrs which the Natives traded, they procured from the French Axes, Chissels, Knives, Spears and other articles of iron. . . . Thus armed the houses of the Beavers were pierced through, the Dams cut through, and the water of

the Ponds lowered, or wholly run off, and the houses of the Beaver and their Borrows laid dry, by which means they became an easy prey to the Hunter.[106]

Thompson's statement that the beaver had few natural predators has generally not been disputed. William Rutherford similarly noted that the beaver had few natural predators, while Ernest Thompson Seton listed several animals capable of attacking the beaver—otter, wolverine, black bear, and so on—but admitted that these predators had little impact on beaver populations.[107]

No one would disagree that prior to the fur trade beaver were abundant in the woodlands, nor would anyone argue, particularly in contemporary times, about the beaver's ability to inundate large areas. Thompson, however, underestimated the ability of earlier peoples to hunt beaver effectively or, better put, to alter their environment significantly.

The following historical descriptions give hints on beaver-hunting techniques that might have been used prior to contact. Information from Nicolas Denys came from his association with the Mi'kmaq of the Eastern Woodlands. He noted that hunting techniques varied considerably during different seasons: "In summer the most common way to hunt beaver ... was to break their dam, and make them lose the water. Then the Beavers found themselves without water, and did not know any more where to go; their houses showed everywhere. The Indians took them with blows of arrows and of spears; and, having a sufficiency, they left all the rest."[108] Beaver were hunted with arrows when they took to the woods. In winter, according to Denys, beaver hunting was assisted by dogs, which located the houses containing beaver.

> The Indians made a hole in the ice in front of the house and another one up to 30 paces away. At the latter hole, an Indian stood with a bow and arrow tipped with a harpoon (a cord was attached at one end). At the other hole, an Indian reached through the opening into the Beaver House to find the Beaver. Stroking them gently he found the tail, and pulled the beaver onto the ice, and killed it. It was possible

to remove three to four in this manner before the rest took flight. Not being able to breathe, they attempted to surface through the other hole at which they were harpooned.[109]

Skinner also discussed winter hunting techniques of the Eastern Cree, noting that a creek would be closed off by rows of stakes driven through the ice to the bottom of the stream along the banks above and below the houses. The houses would be broken from above. Some beaver would be caught, and those that escaped would pass along the stakes until they reached an opening covered with a net. When the hunter felt one struggling, he drew the net tight, catching the beaver. When beaver holes (burrows) were found in the bank, they were blocked up and the beaver dug out.[110]

Thompson gave a clearer picture of some of the problems of beaver hunting in winter, even when iron tools were available. He noted that the surest way was to stake up the doorway to the lodge; however, beaver might hear the approach of humans and escape to their burrows. Some hunters preferred to find the burrows first and close them up with stakes and then stake the lodge. Thompson also noted that dogs were used to locate beaver houses and burrows; then, with axe and ice chisel, hunters would break into the house or burrow and, using the same tools, kill the beaver.[111]

Father Louis Hennepin provided additional information on beaver hunting from his experiences among the Sioux in Minnesota in 1680. His description of beaver hunting in winter also indicates breaking apart the lodge and the ice around it. In this case, the net was placed directly over the entrance to the lodge in order to trap beaver. His description is important in that it stresses how labour intensive beaver hunting was in winter, "because there is often a foot of earth and wood to be broken and cut by blows of the axe, the whole being frozen as hard as stone. . . . They labor with the same force, often from morning to night, without taking anything. Sometimes they catch only three or four."[112] Henry, who described beaver hunting among the Chippewa, similarly noted that during winter the most frequent method of taking beaver was by breaking their lodges with trenching tools (chisels). He also observed that beaver could escape to their burrows but then be drawn out by hand, and this is the only reference besides Denys to this method of capturing beaver.[113] In 1804, Grant noted that among the Saulteaux, beaver were taken in fall with steel traps set under the water; he added that "the most simple method, however, is by destroying these houses, and draining the pond on which they are situated, so that the animals, being alarmed and deprived of the water so necessary to their existence, take immediately to flight and become an easy prey to the hunters."[114]

In earlier times, hunting beaver entailed taking the whole colony. Denys noted that in winter "few in a house are saved; they would take all. The disposition of the Indians is not to spare the little ones any more than the big ones."[115] Thompson also observed that "not one escapes, but all [are killed] with hard labor: Such was the manner of killing the Beaver until the introduction of Steel Traps, which baited with Castorum soon brought on the almost total destruction of these numerous and sagacious animals."[116] Taking the whole colony made practical sense. The tremendous effort expended in hunting beaver, particularly in winter, could only be compensated by the greatest return in food. Perhaps surprisingly, killing all beaver in a lodge also made ecological or at least humane sense: breaking apart lodges and burrows in winter would have exposed the remaining beaver to winter's inclement weather, and likely they would have died from exposure. In addition, with their lodges broken, they would have been highly susceptible to predation.

The previous descriptions suggest that, prior to the use of steel traps baited with castoreum—which had an addictive effect on beaver, according to Thompson—little evidence exists to show that traditional hunting techniques changed markedly during the historical period.[117] Hunting beaver in winter continued to be labour intensive. Acquisition of the chisel and hatchet to break apart lodges appears to have been the only major change. However, prior to contact, Indigenous hunters could draw beaver from their lodges without breaking the lodges apart. The most effective way to break the ice, even in historical times, continued to be with wooden tools such as axe handles and poles. The gun was ineffective at such close quarters. Harmon noted that when Indigenous hunters broke into lodges, they speared beaver. Hunting during the rest of the year also underwent no major changes. Breaking dams and draining ponds were still the most effective and productive methods of accessing beaver resources, though the gun was used more frequently.[118]

Although early European historical accounts tend to emphasize Indigenous beaver hunting in winter, the question to be asked is whether this was truly the case in earlier times. In this period, intensive hunting of the beaver was spurred by its value as a fur-bearing animal. Henry implied that winter hunting was tied to the fact that beaver fur was most valuable at that time of year.[119] Harmon noted that "from the month of June, until the latter end of September, all animals have but little fur; and therefore, at this season, the Indians do not hunt them much."[120] However, prior to the fur trade, the intensity of beaver hunting was determined by food needs, which exceeded fur needs: "They killed animals only in proportion as they had need of them.... They never made an accumulation of skins of Moose, Beaver, Otter, or others, but only so far as they needed them for personal use. They left the remainder where the animals had been killed, not taking the trouble to bring them to their camps."[121] The historical record also implies that large mammals such as moose were important sources of food in winter. Considering how labour intensive beaver hunting was at this time, the beaver was likely mainly a supplement to the diet, particularly when larger mammals were scarce. However, in the historical period, fur—as the medium through which trade goods were obtained—began to replace food as the priority. Beaver meat, rather than beaver pelts, was now the surplus.

Interestingly, using traditional hunting methods with only the addition of the chisel and hatchet and occasional use of the gun, beaver populations were markedly reduced. Steel traps were not introduced to the hunting of beaver until 1797.[122] Ray noted that, in 1795, Cumberland House journals indicated that the lands around the post had been trapped out for a number of years.[123] In territories to the east, fur-bearing species had been eliminated even earlier. In other words, traditional beaver-hunting techniques were highly effective and could have significantly affected beaver populations when employed intensively. This did not occur prior to contact because the demand for beaver as a food source never exceeded its supply. In fact, an overabundance of beaver might have been a major problem for subsistence strategies. The historical record strongly substantiates that beaver were abundant prior to contact. In 1729, La Vérendrye stated that

> the whole right bank of the great river [Winnipeg] as you go down from the Lake of the Woods as far as Lake Winnipeg is held by the Cree, and it is the country of the moose and marten, while beaver is so plentiful that the savages place little value on it and only collect the large skins which they send to the English. These people dress themselves in winter in beaver skins and in spring they throw them away, not being able to sell them.[124]

More contemporary times indicate the consequences (e.g., flooding) of an overabundance of beaver and their activities. In Elk Island National Park, for example, from the time beaver were introduced, there was exponential growth in their populations.[125] In the wood bison area of the park, because of beaver activities the area covered by water increased from 2% to 9%, and sedge cover was reduced by 3%.[126] These changes brought about a marked reduction in ungulate food sources. Knudson also noted that inundation of low-lying areas and floodplains brought about the destruction of species such as willow and alder, important browsing sources for many game animals. The anaerobic and/or toxic conditions associated with long-standing beaver ponds generally prevented riparian tree and shrub species from re-establishing themselves.[127]

On a larger scale, from 1940 to 1986, beaver increased their habitat use from 71 dams to 835 dams on the Kabetogama Peninsula in northern Minnesota. Less than 1% of the peninsula was impounded in 1940, compared with 13% in 1986.[128] Rapid increases in beaver populations were attributed to extensive fires and logging operations at the turn of the century, resulting in a large supply of aspen and a scarcity of predatory wolves. From a long-term perspective, large-scale forest fires would bring beaver back to the burned areas by increasing aspen growth.

More importantly, our contemporary perspective on the successional pathways associated with beaver activities must be reconsidered:

> We envisioned that beaver built dams on a stream and through time the ponds age, are abandoned, meadows form and mature, and eventually a stream is reformed as a new channel is cut. . . . In the boreal forests of northern Minnesota, Quebec, and Alaska, however, we see a complex pattern that may involve the formation of emergent marshes, bogs, and forested wetlands, which appear to persist in a somewhat stable condition for centuries.[129]

In other words, beaver dam-pond networks were highly resistant to environmental perturbations. I suggest that this successional pattern no longer appears to be operative because of two factors: the control of natural fires in contemporary times and the discontinuance of traditional burning practices by Indigenous Peoples.

The propensity for beaver to inundate large areas, markedly reducing food sources for large ungulates as a consequence, must have been highly problematic for early Indigenous groups. Yet, as I have stressed, their environmental awareness was the most important aspect of their hunting and gathering strategies. My focus here is on how Woodlands inhabitants applied their knowledge of fire ecology to manipulate and regulate their immediate environments and, more specifically, to control beaver populations and create habitats for a range of animals.

The ethnographic studies of Henry Lewis among the Indigenous groups of northern Alberta brought into focus the importance of fire technology in their hunting and gathering strategies. "Prescribed fires were once part of the Indian's own pattern of 'landscape management,'" Lewis wrote. "Their selective employment of fire for boreal forest adaptations indicated an understanding of both the general principles and the local specific environmental relationships that are the subject of modern fire ecology."[130] In addition, Indigenous burning patterns were diverse, including not only fire "yards" composed of meadows and small forest openings but also fire "corridors," which included traplines, trails, streams, and lakesides.[131] Lewis found that fire was used "to increase both the diversity and [the] productivity of plants and animals"; more specifically, he observed that the early growth of grasses on burned meadows attracted game such as moose, making hunting much easier.[132]

The creation of beaver meadows was a sophisticated expression of traditional environmental knowledge. The breaking of dams and the draining of ponds served a dual purpose: they comprised an effective beaver-hunting technique, and they provided the initial phase of the process of creating a beaver meadow. Beaver meadows have particular attributes that make them easy to maintain. Mature beaver ponds that become meadows are especially resistant to tree or shrub invasions because of the toxic quality of the soils caused by the previous impoundment. The inhibiting effect can persist for up to 10 years. The eventual reoccupation of the areas is usually by willow and alder, important sources of browse for ungulates. The question is how to prevent beaver from reoccupying the areas. The answer lies in the use of fire. One Woodlands Cree informant gave important clues about the effect of fire on beaver populations: "As for the beaver, it takes a while before they move into an area that was burned; about four years after the burn. The reasons why it takes that long for the beaver to come to those places is that the aspen don't grow as fast."[133] Therefore, to keep beaver out of a meadow area, Indigenous Peoples only had to burn the periphery, about once every three or four years, to keep new-growth aspen from maturing. Large-scale fires would also eliminate beaver from the affected area. It would take at least four years before beaver could begin to reoccupy the area. There would also be a significant lag before pre-fire conditions would be reached, allowing sufficient time for a beaver meadow to become established. Large fires would actually be detrimental to Indigenous Peoples in the vicinity. Whereas small-scale, prescribed fires would concentrate herbivores in specific areas, thus facilitating hunting of them, large-scale, uncontrolled fires would have the opposite effect. A large fire would bring vegetative uniformity to the affected area, with grassland and shrub areas being predominant. As a result, with a marked increase in suitable habitat, large ungulates (e.g., moose) would be more dispersed, making hunting more difficult.

In contemporary times, the control of natural fires and a marked reduction in prescribed burning by northern Indigenous groups have resulted in many of these open grassland areas reverting to forest. Lewis noted that his informants pointed out that meadows, if not burned, would periodically be taken over by forest. More specifically, one of his Cree informants from Fort Vermilion stated that the "country was a lot more open then and wasn't so hard to travel. Not like now. You can hardly travel in the bush and it's not so good for hunting. I haven't been on [the] trapline in a long time now. So much brush you can hardly get through."[134]

Beaver and Firewood

The chores of Indigenous women in the woodlands, like those on the plains, included collecting firewood. Among the Woodlands Cree, according to Mackenzie, women "dress the leather, make the clothes and shoes, weave the nets, collect wood, erect the tents, fetch water, and perform every culinary service."[135] Others similarly observed that among the Northern Cree the task of collecting firewood was done by women, while Denys noted that among the Mi'kmaq firewood was collected by women and girls and was of two types: "They [the women] went to the woods to fetch dry fuel, which did not smoke, for warming and for burning in the wigwam. Any other kind of wood was good for the kettle, since that was always outside the wigwam."[136]

Skinner noted that fire was carried about for days smouldering in birch punk, the underbark of a dead tree, kept dry to be used as kindling while travelling.[137] The need to carry fire and dry kindling, and the differentiation of dry wood and damp wood, pointed to a paradox peculiar to the woodlands: whereas tree and shrub species are abundant, dry firewood is not. Higher rainfall, lower temperature, and a heavy canopy result in a pervading dampness in the forest understorey. Consequently, the importance of beaver activity as a source of dry firewood is greatly reduced. Lewis observed that dry firewood was often obtained by deliberate burning: "Burning took place in spring. The trees preferred were aspen, though burnt willows were regularly used for kindling. If possible, enough wood was burned to last through the summer and winter months. Much wood was to be found at the edge of meadows where repeated spring burns would scar and subsequently kill a few trees."[138]

The trunks of beaver-cut trees were probably used to make wooden kettles. Denys noted that Woodlands people "took the butt of a huge tree which had fallen; not having tools fitted for that, nor had they the means to transport it; they had them ready made in nearly all the places to which they went."[139]

Summary

The Woodlands Indigenous communities occupied a vast area that provided a variety of game animals that, with the exception of caribou, were generally dispersed. Moose, the most important food source, was hunted mainly in winter. Through their knowledge of animal behaviour and fire ecology, Woodlands groups created browsing and grazing areas that not only provided additional food sources for large game animals but also concentrated them in specific areas, greatly facilitating hunting. Beaver also ranked high as both a significant part of the diet and a source for clothing.

Seasonal variations existed in beaver-hunting techniques. During fall and spring, when beaver were most frequently hunted, the simplest technique was to break their dams and drain their ponds; beaver were thus exposed and easily taken. Winter hunting techniques were highly labour intensive, with a good return not always predictable. In earlier times, hunting beaver in winter was probably carried out when large game animals were scarce. The emphasis on hunting beaver in winter during the historical period was related to the fact that its pelt was most valuable in that season.

The historical record clearly indicates that traditional hunting techniques significantly affected beaver populations. Long before introduction of the steel trap, beaver had been eliminated from many areas. This did not occur before the advent of the fur trade because the demand on beaver primarily as food did not exceed supply. It was during the historical period that fur needs, to procure trade goods, exceeded food demands and supplies, setting the stage for destruction of the beaver.

Prior to contact, Woodlands inhabitants might have been faced with an overabundance of beaver. With no important natural predators, unchecked beaver populations would have had a marked effect on the environment and consequently on the associated human populations. In contemporary times, mainly because of the control of natural fires, beaver are progressively inundating low-lying areas containing browse and graze species (willows, grasses, and sedges), important sources of food for game animals like moose. Prior to contact, such changes, resulting in the dispersal of large game animals, would have been problematic. For Indigenous Peoples, a scarcity of game in winter would have been particularly serious because mobility was reduced. Through their knowledge of animal behaviour and fire ecology, they came up with an effective solution. The creation of beaver meadows provided not only grassland areas that attracted game animals but also an effective means to control beaver populations. Thus, the destruction of dams and the draining of ponds served as both an effective technique for beaver hunting and a necessary phase in the creation of beaver meadows. These meadows also have special attributes that facilitate easy maintenance. Their soils are toxic to tree and shrub species, and the inhibiting effect lasts up to 10 years. The trees that first invade the meadows are important browse species such as willow and alder. To prevent beaver from reoccupying the areas, it was necessary only to fire their peripheries every three to four years to prevent new growth of aspen.

CONCLUSION

On the plains, then, beaver populations were low, and to Indigenous groups the beaver was important in maintaining surface water, a scarce resource, and thus had to be protected as much as possible. In contrast, in the woodlands, Indigenous groups were faced with an overabundance of beaver. In this environment, beaver maintenance of surface water had a detrimental effect: the flooding of browse and graze areas effectively dispersed the large game animals on which Woodlands communities depended for food.

In the next three chapters, I fine-tune this general proposition by examining a particular region of the Northern Plains, the Qu'Appelle River Valley Complex, for ecological, historical, and archaeological evidence, respectively. I consider past and present beaver populations, historical data prior to equestrian bison hunting, and archaeological records. I then present a more comprehensive model to explain the different responses of equestrian Northern Plains peoples to the changing dynamics of the historical period based upon their relationships with beaver prior to contact.

CHAPTER 3

THE ECOLOGICAL
EVIDENCE

The non-hunting of beaver by early Plains Indigenous groups was a sound decision ecologically. These groups realized the beaver's important role in maintaining and stabilizing surface water, the availability of which is limited on the plains. Given their low population and highly visible and stationary lifestyle, beaver were highly susceptible to hunting by humans—another reason for the prohibition on hunting them. Therefore, protecting beaver helped to maintain larger tributaries within Valley Complexes, the most favourable habitat for human and beaver populations. This chapter presents contemporary observations of beaver activities and effects in order to develop a more rigorous model of human-beaver relationships in the context of pedestrian bison hunters of the precontact Northern Plains.

I selected for analysis tributaries of different sizes in the Qu'Appelle River Valley Complex: the Qu'Appelle River itself (the main waterway), Moose Jaw River and Wascana Creek (large tributaries), and Cottonwood Creek (a medium tributary). My intention was to determine to what extent beaver, through the storehouse effect of their dam-pond systems, were able to maintain surface water, particularly during times of drought, in these different waterways. Furthermore, to pinpoint the contrasts and similarities between woodlands and plains ecosystems, and the resulting effects on human-beaver relationships, I undertook field research in Elk Island National Park. This area is categorized as part of the Parkland–Boreal Forest transitional zone.[1]

REVIEW OF THE LITERATURE

Since the study of beaver behaviour required a broad perspective, encompassing both plains and woodlands environs, I reviewed the available literature to supplement my field research. Prior to the arrival of Europeans in North America, beaver had an extensive geographic distribution, occupying aquatic habitats from the arctic tundra to the desert of northern Mexico, with an estimated population as high as 400 million.[2]

This distribution suggests that beaver populations could successfully adjust to a wide range of ecological conditions, including zonal macroclimatic variability. S. Charles Kendeigh cautioned, however, that it is not sufficient to consider only macroclimatic conditions in the study of animal behaviour, since animals also respond to the microclimatic conditions of their particular habitats.[3] This generalization is particularly true of beaver when one considers their highly sedentary nature and restricted foraging radius. As previously noted, there is general consensus that they utilize most trees within the first 30 m (100 ft) of the water, with estimates of a maximum foraging radius ranging from 91 m (300 ft) to 152 m (500 ft), although Hind found that beaver were able to forage somewhat greater distances, up to 137 m (450 ft), on fairly steep slopes.[4] In Colorado, Rutherford found that "the area suitable for beaver food production is limited to watered valleys and immediately adjacent slopes and seldom exceeds 2.5% of the total watershed area."[5] These foraging restrictions no doubt contributed strongly to observed opportunistic beaver behaviour. For instance, A.W. Allen referred to the beaver as a generalized herbivore, noting that it eats the leaves, twigs, and bark of woody plants as well as many species of aquatic and terrestrial herbaceous vegetation.[6] Glenn Bradt went further, noting that beaver use nearly every species of plant growing within their foraging ranges.[7]

Arlen Todd defined beaver habitats as basically either streams or lakes/potholes.[8] Since my focus is on the plains environment,

I concentrate on stream/river systems as the main beaver environments, which in turn are integral parts of the Valley Complex. Pronounced microclimatic variability is caused primarily by factors other than zonal climate. Degree of slope, depth of valley, and so on create habitat variability not only in the vertical plane (i.e., from the uplands to the stream/river edge) but also in the horizontal plane, most visibly in contrasts between northern-exposed and southern-exposed slopes. Thus, along any specific tributary, a wide range of habitats can be found, with marked differences occurring not only in species composition but also in species abundance. Correspondingly, at any point in time, resource utilization by beaver along a particular waterway can be variable. In research along the Rio Grande River in Texas, Paul Strong pointed out that the five beaver colonies monitored varied greatly in habitat structure, and consequently the use of food resources varied among the colonies.[9] Resource variability also occurs within a relatively limited space, and as one food species becomes depleted another becomes more intensively utilized. For example, aspen is often referred to as a sub-climax community because prolonged beaver use generally leads to depletion; if willows and sedges are present, they become the mainstays of the beaver diet.[10] Also, the depletion by beaver of one species can stimulate the development of another, altering the resource base. As aspen is depleted in the riparian zone, and the area becomes more open, shrubs such as alder and hazel become the dominant forms.[11]

Robert Naiman, Carol Johnston, and James Kelley stress the importance of beaver activity in structuring a stream ecosystem: "A beaver-impounded landscape is thus a mosaic of different vegetation types—due to the dynamic hydrology of beaver ponds, the diversity of preimpoundment vegetation, and the changes caused by beaver foraging in the riparian zone."[12] Therefore, beaver habitat requirements are related, through time and space, to a highly variable (often beaver-induced) resource base, on both a macroclimatic level and a microclimatic level. The opportunistic or flexible nature of beaver allows them to cope with or adjust to these varying complexities.

Several authors have attempted to establish models of suitable beaver habitat.[13] Admittedly, it would be difficult to accommodate microclimatic variability in a broad habitat model; however, regional or macroclimatic differences and their effects on beaver habitat requirements often were not recognized. These authors also drew their information from studies of beaver populations in more mesic or northern woodlands areas. Many of their assessments, particularly of limiting factors, have little applicability to more arid areas. For example, Brian Slough and R.M.F.S. Sadleir, who carried out their research in northern British Columbia, did not include water depth as one of the parameters in their land capability system for beaver, claiming that this factor was rarely limiting.[14] In more arid areas, such as Colorado and Wyoming, insufficient surface water was emphasized as one of the most important limiting factors, especially by fall.[15] Todd calculated that to ensure movements between lodge and food cache, water had to be from 91 cm (3 ft) to 152 cm (5 ft) deep.[16]

Another example relates to beaver food resources. Authors such as LeRoy Stegeman (who carried out research in Huntington Forest, New York) and Kenneth Hodgdon and John Hunt (whose research area was in Maine) not only stressed the preferential use of aspen by beaver but also claimed that the distribution of beaver is largely determined by the distribution of aspen.[17] However, in more arid areas, tree species are less abundant and exhibit a different spatial distribution. In North Dakota, for example, aspen was present but rarely accessible to beaver, being several hundred metres from the river.[18] Stephen Jenkins, aware of such problems, cautioned that studies of aspen and willow in northern areas, in which these tree species tend to be the predominant foods for beaver available in riparian habitats, should not be generalized too quickly to other regions in which riparian vegetation might be more diverse. Referring to the beaver's opportunistic use of food and the diversity of its habitat, Jenkins also criticized attempts by investigators to rank a list of preferred beaver foods.[19]

The same problem arises in determining the effects of beaver activity on the environment. Most studies have not been of sufficient geographic extent to incorporate macroclimatic variability; therefore, authors have had highly different perspectives on this aspect of beaver ecology. From their research in more northern regions (i.e., Quebec, Minnesota, and Alaska), Naiman, Johnston, and Kelley broadly documented environmental alterations caused by beaver, noting that the animal's activities reduced erosion, created wetlands (by flooding), modified riparian zones, and affected the composition and diversity of plant and animal communities.[20] However, they omitted one of the most significant environmental modifications attributed to beaver, particularly in more arid areas: the impounding of water, thereby conserving and maintaining surface water. This omission is understandable given that their research was conducted in more northern mesic environments, where water resources are more than abundant. Although the immediate effects on the environment are highly localized because of the beaver's sedentary nature, the repercussions can often be zonal in extent and beneficial.[21] Yet Jeffrey Foss offers a very different picture of beaver activity as "environmental harm or habitat destruction," noting that "millions of acres of land are flooded each year by beaver causing death of trees and other plants and destroying the habitat that they provide for birds, mammals, and insects."[22]

RESEARCH MODEL

The beaver habitat models noted above provided an initial framework for my own studies of beaver ecology. Woodlands and plains are different environments that have different effects on beaver populations, and to relate these ecological conditions to human needs— particularly patterns of settlement—requires a shift in focus to the microclimatic level. With the exception of some trade in lithic materials, the peoples associated with bison hunting prior to contact were dependent on their immediate environments for essential resources. To perceive these smaller ecological conditions, I carried out field research in specific areas of both plains and woodlands.

Below, I determine beaver habitat requirements and how environmental conditions in the particular study areas accommodate these requirements. I also determine which components act as restraints on beaver populations. I give special consideration to the availability of adequate surface water on the plains, assumed to be the main limiting factor for animal and human populations. I also assess the availability of trees and shrubs on the plains, likewise assumed to be a limiting factor. More specifically, I focus on whether beaver habitat requirements affect the abundance of tree/shrub species. My focus in the woodlands area is different because surface water and treed areas are not limited. Open areas, however, are restricted, and they provide the main sources of herbaceous foods (grasses/sedges) and many shrub species considered important components of the beaver's diet. I examine the beaver's response to this limitation.

In determining the effects of beaver activity on the environment, I focus exclusively on the availability of surface water. I test the nature and extent of beaver conservation of water from two perspectives:

1. I assess the effectiveness of beaver dam-pond systems in maintaining water resources (during the vegetative season) by measuring water levels from spring runoff to fall freeze-up. I consider several factors: runoff, precipitation, temperature, and evaporation.
2. I also determine structural aspects of water control such as dam porosity, dam size, pond depth, and ratio of dams/lodges per unit area.

I then compare the different tributaries to determine the effects of their specific habitats on beaver settlement patterns.

For the woodlands area, I examine several aspects of beaver activity and their corresponding short- and long-term effects on the environment. Perhaps the most deleterious effect is flooding, which destroys important browse and graze species. I also assess the effects of beaver tree cutting, which include changes in abundance and distribution of vegetative species.

THE PLAINS

Study Sites and Methods

Initially, I chose Wascana Creek for both ecological and archaeological analyses. However, problems arose almost immediately regarding its suitability as an ecological research area. Consultations with the Water Resources Branch of Environment Canada (since renamed Environment and Climate Change Canada) indicated that Wascana Creek is subject to marked discharge fluctuations that bear no relation to natural climatic perturbations. The primary source of these fluctuations is Regina; the city's treated sewage as well as its stormwater flow into Wascana Creek.

The Qu'Appelle River was also a poor prospect for ecological analyses. Its water levels are artificially maintained by a channel joining Buffalo Pound Lake with Lake Diefenbaker. Water is diverted from Lake Diefenbaker to the Qu'Appelle River Valley Dam.[23] It would therefore be difficult to determine the extent to which information on contemporary beaver activity would be representative of a "natural state."

Environment Canada recommended that the Moose Jaw River above Thunder Creek would be more suitable because its flows show closer approximations to natural conditions and it is comparable to Wascana Creek in drainage area. I decided to continue the archaeological survey of Wascana Creek but conduct the ecological research along the Moose Jaw River. Local perturbations also affected analyses of the Moose Jaw River, though general trends remained predictive and accurate.

One major disturbance was agriculture. Fields were often cultivated too close to the waterway, resulting in the destabilization and increased erosion of riverbanks. Thus, tree and shrub areas were also greatly reduced, diminishing the availability of both food resources and building materials for beaver populations. Overgrazing by cattle of both browse and grasslands in another portion of the research area no doubt contributed to the lack of beaver there. Another problem was the complete eradication of beaver from one area by the resident farmer, who claimed that they had destroyed farmyard trees. (This problem also occurred along Cottonwood Creek.) Human patterns of residence strongly influenced responses to beaver in a given area. Families who chose to live on floodplains, close to beaver, tended to perceive them as a nuisance. Problems associated with beaver included the destruction of ornamental trees and the flooding of basements by raised water tables. Generally, though, the presence of beaver was considered advantageous, particularly as a means of maintaining surface water for cattle and gardens.

Research conditions were more favourable in Cottonwood Creek since agriculture was not extensive along it; in fact, some areas still retained natural prairie. Many areas had also been allowed to revert back to grasslands and were used primarily as pastures. The waterway generally experienced fewer disruptions, with many of the original stream beds still retaining their viability. As a result, I carried out most of the ecological studies along Cottonwood Creek, beginning in early June 1986. I surveyed the area from the confluence with Wascana Creek to the Canadian Pacific Railway (CPR) dam near the town of Rufus (38.5 river km), mainly trying to locate archaeological sites. Ecological analyses concentrated on establishing the extent of beaver occupation in the tributary. Water levels were measured at two sites: Campbell I (see Figure 5) and Young. These measurements were discontinued at the end of August. In 1987, my field research was also restricted to Cottonwood Creek. Water levels were again measured at Campbell I and Young and discontinued at the end of August.

In 1988, I expanded the research area to allow for a comparative analysis, both archaeological and ecological, of waterways of different sizes: Qu'Appelle River, Moose Jaw River, Wascana Creek, and Cottonwood Creek (see Figure 2). Pronounced microclimatic variability also prompted consideration of two additional research sites along Cottonwood Creek: Campbell II and Thompson III. Each area exhibited a unique combination of physical and vegetative attributes and variations in surface water availability. My hope was that the study would determine the extent of common beaver behaviour as well as the opportunistic responses elicited by the habitat variations. In 1988, water measurements were discontinued at Young because most of the beaver ponds had become dry. Water measurements at Campbell I began on May 29, at Campbell II on June 5, at Thompson III (see Figure 6) on July 13, and on the Moose Jaw River (see figure 7) on August 17. All measurements were discontinued on October 30.

I also attempted in 1988 to quantify the availability of surface water in the different waterways. Water depth and width measurements were taken every 10 m (32.8 ft) in the different tributaries between August 15 and August 20. In Cottonwood Creek, three research sites were measured: Campbell I (0.60 river km); Campbell II (0.75 river km); and Thompson III (0.41 river km). Measurements from Campbell I and II were combined, totalling 1.35 river km, in the comparative analysis with the Moose Jaw River, in which 1.54 river km were measured. In the statistical analyses, water depths at lodges were generally based on an average of the two nearest measures (i.e., taken every 10 m) from the lodge. This calculation of water depth sought also to mitigate the effects of food caches (often 20 m/65.6 ft in extent) on water levels.

In addition, I attempted to quantify, though not extensively, beaver foraging and construction strategies at the Campbell I site. Because my focus was on determining the effects of beaver activity on treed areas, considered a limiting factor, I restricted my studies to the most abundant tree species: chokecherry and maple. For the chokecherry population, a random sample was taken from a 5 m (16.4 ft) by 30 m (98.4 ft) plot perpendicular to the water's edge. Since all maples were felled by beaver within the first 15 m (49.2 ft) and 10 m (32.8 ft) from the stream edge, at Campbell I and II, respectively, the measurements were restricted to a cut sample. At Campbell I, a random sample of 60 diameter measurements was taken from one lodge and one dam and compared with the cut species populations.

COTTONWOOD CREEK—At Campbell I, the dam-pond system consisted of six dams, four lodges, and one burrow (see Figure 5). Dams 3 and 5 were primary dams: the original dams built when the beaver colony first occupied the area and usually directly associated with the pond containing the lodge. Dams 1, 2, 4, 6, and 7 were secondary dams that regulated water flow. Dams at the site were built from stream sediment mixed with tree and shrub stems and branches. The upstream sides of the dams were composed primarily of mud, while the downstream sides were reinforced with large sticks.

At Campbell II, at initiation of the study (June 5, 1988), the dam-pond system consisted of four lodges, one burrow, and four dams, three primary and one secondary (see Figure 5).

At Thompson III, at initiation of the study (July 13, 1988), the dam-pond system consisted of three primary dam-pond units and eight lodges, of which two were active (see Figure 6). At this time, surface water was continuous throughout the research area, which appeared to have been occupied for some time considering the number of abandoned lodges. Most occupations appear to have occurred when water conditions were more favourable. For example, in pond 1, there were three lodges in close proximity, with the active one located at the lowest level. Dams 1 and 2—large, solid, and almost earth-like in composition—also attested to the maturity of beaver occupancy of the area and suggested long-term repair and reinforcement. These dams had also been reconstructed when water levels were substantially higher. On July 13, dam 1 measured 1.57 m (5.15 ft) in height from the water and 24.5 m (80.4 ft) in length, while stream height at the dam was only 8.5 m (27.9 ft). Dam 3 was 1.2 m (3.9 ft) in height and 22.7 m (74.5 ft) in length, while stream height at the dam was 7.7 m (25.3 ft).

MOOSE JAW RIVER—The Moose Jaw River has a low gradient (0.016%) and a valley width ranging from approximately 500 m (1,640 ft) to 600 m (1,969 ft) approaching confluence with the Qu'Appelle River.

At initiation of the study (height of the drought), the research area, which encompassed 4.1 river km (see Figure 7), contained 16 lodges (lodge 5 was a burrow). Five of the lodges (2, 10, 12, 13, and 16) were active. Old food caches were found in association with lodges 3, 5, and 16. Recognizable dams totalled eight, while possible dams and/or fans totalled six. Of the five active lodges, 2 and 12 were abandoned during the study. That might have reflected the new colonies established in late fall at A and B, which included burrows with food caches. Measurements were not taken from lodges 12 to 16 since they were in the vicinity of a spring, which would seriously have jeopardized the study. The positive effect of the spring was easily observed since most of the active lodges were close to it. In fall, along 5.8 river km, which included the research area, there were seven active lodges (A, B, C, D, 10, 13, and 16), of which four were concentrated in the area (1.3 river km) influenced by the spring. Overall lodge density was 1.2 lodges per river km.

All of the remaining lodges had been abandoned prior to the study. Since water depth measurements ranged from 47 cm (18.5 in) to 82 cm (32.3 in), insufficient depth was a plausible explanation. Because most of the lodges also showed deterioration, siltation after abandonment was another plausible explanation, since stream flow was continuous. Lodge 10 was the only one for which there were depth measurements.

At this active lodge, by October 30, the water level had dropped to 94 cm (37 in), still a sufficient depth for the resident colony to winter there successfully. Lodge 9 had exposed entrances, assumed to be the reason for abandonment. Lodge 16 was interesting in that an old food cache was still present in front of the lodge; however, a new food cache was added to it. Lodge 14 was situated high on the bank, suggesting use during times of much higher water.

Comparison of the Waterways

Given the marked annual variations in discharge volume, days of flow, and initiation and termination of flow exhibited by the different waterways studied, only broad generalities can be deduced. Because summer precipitation normally evaporates, spring runoff— primarily from snowmelt—is the major source of surface water. As a result, maximum discharge occurs during spring runoff, with reduced flow or no flow during the rest of the year, establishing a general pattern of high water levels in spring progressively dropping to low water levels in fall.

Among the tributaries studied, there were substantial variations in surface water availability and stability. Climatic fluctuations explain marked annual variations in discharge volumes and days of flow in the tributaries. The Qu'Appelle River was generally excluded from these analyses because its water levels were artificially maintained.

In the Moose Jaw River, the annual discharge flow ranged from 4.47 cms for a period of 223 days in 1983, to 0.002 cms for a period of 58 days in 1984, to 0.313 cms for a period of 91 days in 1985. In Cottonwood Creek, the annual discharge flow ranged from 0.098 cms for a period of 105 days in 1983, to 0.064 cms for a period of 64 days in 1984, to 0.147 cms for a period of 73 days in 1985. The average annual discharge flow in the Moose Jaw River (2.64 cms) was significantly greater ($df = 54$; $t = 5.098$; $p = < 0.000$) than that in Cottonwood Creek, which registered an average annual discharge flow of only 0.452 cms, or 17% of the Moose Jaw mean.[24] Clearly, water is more abundant in the Moose Jaw River than in Cottonwood Creek.

The chi-square test also indicated significant differences ($p = < 0.000$) in water depth and width between Cottonwood Creek and the Moose Jaw River (see Figures 8 and 9). The data indicated that water in a large tributary is more continuous—that is, more uniformly distributed. Only 9.3% of the depth readings from the Moose Jaw River fell within the 0–20 cm (0–8 in) depth category (see Figure 8), whereas 47.6% of the depth readings from Cottonwood Creek fell within the 0–20 cm category. In other words, water in the creek was mainly restricted to discrete beaver ponds, which showed significant differences in abundance of water (see Figures 19 and 20). If one were to accommodate the long stretches of dry beds in the creek outside the ponds, then the overall differences in water depth would be even greater.

During the drought from 1986 to 1988, the flow in the Moose Jaw River dropped to 0.500 cms, whereas in Cottonwood Creek it dropped to 0.041 cms, or only 8% of the Moose Jaw mean. Therefore, during a period of drought, the amount of discharge flow was reduced to a greater extent in Cottonwood Creek. At the height of the drought (1988), discharge flow in the Moose Jaw River almost ceased (0.001 cms), while at Cottonwood Creek no flow occurred.

This difference points to another important attribute of the Moose Jaw River: a greater ability to withstand macroclimatic perturbations. Although initiation and termination of flow at both tributaries can exhibit marked variability, the general trend is for flow to begin in March, with maximum flow occurring sometime in April. The significant difference is that in Cottonwood Creek flow tends to end by July, whereas in the Moose Jaw River flow continues well into October. This difference is reflected in the number of days of flow per year: for the period from 1974 to 1988, in Cottonwood Creek the mean was 73.9 days, whereas in the Moose Jaw River the mean was 150.5 days. This indicates that, under most climatic variations, Cottonwood Creek is an intermittent stream, whereas the Moose Jaw River has flow during most of the vegetative season. The greater resistance of the Moose Jaw River to macroclimatic fluctuations is again exhibited in the relationships between the amounts of flow and the days of flow. In the Moose Jaw River, the correlation was weak ($R^2 = .24$), whereas in Cottonwood Creek the correlation was much higher ($R^2 = .63$).

In terms of vegetation along the waterways, constant factors such as slope are more important than zonal climatic changes. Tree and shrub species are not abundant along the different tributaries, but they reach their highest densities on northern-facing slopes. Grasses are the dominant form of vegetation on southern-facing slopes and the floodplain. The same species are found along the different waterways, with some similarities in abundance and distribution. Aspen is located most often on middle and lower portions of northern-exposure slopes, on floodplains adjacent to slope edges, and in coulees. Maple is the most common tree species, found on northern-exposure slopes, in ravines, and on floodplains. A riparian species, it is also located along the edges of the waterways. Ash is found in the valleys, most frequently on northern-facing slopes, and near the water's edge. Elm, although present, is scarce, whereas chokecherry is ubiquitous. Saskatoon, hawthorn, and rose tend to be most abundant along northern-exposure slopes and can fringe the waterways. The most important and generally ubiquitous riparian species are willow and dogwood.

Important variations exist among the different waterways, however, in regard to the distribution and abundance of tree and shrub species, and these variations are related mainly to the availability of surface water. In a smaller tributary, water is restricted by fall mainly to where the waterway cuts a slope wall. Therefore, tree species tend to be found mainly on northern-facing slopes and ravines and can fringe the waterway when it approaches these areas. When the waterway is more centrally located, its water tends to evaporate by fall, and riparian species are absent or restricted to shrubs. Along a larger waterway, the water is more abundant and continuous during most of the vegetative season, providing a broader range of suitable habitats for tree and shrub species. Species such as maple and ash are not restricted to northern-exposure slopes and can flourish along the banks of the waterway under more open conditions. Ash, particularly, is more abundant along a larger tributary, replacing chokecherry, to some degree, in the various habitats. Riparian species such as dogwood also appear to be less common along large waterways, perhaps being more suited to the open canopy of smaller tributaries. Aspen is also more abundant along larger tributaries, where deeper valleys and coulees provide more suitable habitats.

Beaver Habitat

Along with the quantity of surface water, the distribution and abundance of vegetative species strongly influence beaver habitat and thus activity. Aspen and poplar are absent from many areas, but when present they tend to fringe valley slopes, which generally are outside the beaver's foraging range but are readily used when accessible. Accessibility is strongly affected by the width of the valley floor. The floodplains of large tributaries such as the Moose Jaw River are much broader (reaching up to 0.5 km/1,640.4 ft) compared with those of small tributaries such as Cottonwood Creek (whose valley widths rarely exceed 0.25 km/820.2 ft). Although aspen is more abundant along a large tributary, when the waterway is more centrally located, tree species like aspen tend to fringe the valley slopes and are generally inaccessible to beaver. A central waterway, having little canopy, is highly susceptible to evaporation. Even during normal climatic conditions, such a waterway can contain water only during the early vegetative season and thus become unsuitable for beaver occupancy. On the main waterway (the Qu'Appelle River), compared with its tributaries, the broad floodplains are the main factor acting against beaver occupancy. These floodplains range from 2 km (1 mi) to 3 km (2 mi). Although the Qu'Appelle River is highly sinuous, it rarely approaches the slope wall to within the beaver's foraging range, and many vegetative species are thus inaccessible (see Figure 15). Food sources tend to be limited to riparian species such as willow and dogwood.

Along a small tributary such as Cottonwood Creek, suitable beaver habitat is primarily restricted to the creek's proximity to treed northern-exposure slopes; when water is of sufficient quantity, beaver, through their dam-pond systems, can effectively maintain the depth and width necessary for their lodges and winter food caches. Given the beaver's narrow foraging range, the proximity of the waterway to treed slopes greatly enhances resource availability. Because erosion is greatest where the waterway approaches the slope wall, the stream is deeper in these areas. Higher banks, more suitable for lodges and dams, and a deeper waterway (greater volume of water) provide the initial attributes that beaver can then easily manipulate and control.

This habitat structure also optimizes spring runoff. Treed northern slopes increase snow capture, and shading by both trees and slopes reduces evaporation. Beaver dam-pond units near treed slopes capture significantly larger amounts of spring runoff than other areas of the system. If the slopes also have breaks, such as gullies or coulees, then these physical features are even more effective in capturing snow. In addition, these breaks act as basins for precipitation, which is then fed directly into associated ponds during the vegetative season. Therefore, not only do the ponds register higher water levels during spring runoff, but also water loss is retarded during summer.

Along the Moose Jaw River, suitable beaver habitats are not as restricted because the waterway is deeper and its water thus more continuous. Tree and shrub species are more abundant and continuous along the waterway, thus providing more resources for beaver and resulting in their greater distribution. Maple and ash are not restricted to northern-exposure slopes and can flourish along the banks of the river under more open conditions. However, beaver still tend to cluster in areas where the waterway cuts northern-facing slopes.

When beaver first occupy a suitable area of a smaller tributary, it is crucial that their activity be directed toward the capture and maintenance of water. They begin to build primary dams, which close the waterway so as to generate sufficient volume for beaver to manipulate. All dams have the downstream side reinforced with tree/shrub trunks and branches, while the upstream side is mainly made of soil. Rocks as well as pieces of lumber, telephone poles, and so on are occasionally incorporated into primary dams, but most of the dams in the study area were built with soil. They are triangular in cross-section. As the water level drops, the width of the associated dam increases, permeability decreases, and, consequently, water flow out of the pond diminishes. In primary dam-pond units, which are the deepest, this process continues to the point where the dam becomes impermeable—often the case during drought. The dam can also withstand other perturbations, such as trampling by cattle, and continue to contain water long after beaver have abandoned the area.

Under normal climatic conditions, as spring runoff subsides, beaver dams begin to emerge. As early as late April, beaver begin to store water so that sufficient amounts remain, by the end of the vegetative season, for wintering. Later in the season, intricate systems of secondary dam-pond units might be built to aid in this process of maintenance. Several features of secondary dams distinguish them from primary dams. The former are generally shallow, and their surfaces are permeable. Water continues to percolate through them until ponds eventually become dry. In other words, a secondary dam allows most of the water to continue downstream, so water losses are high. This indicates the major function of secondary dams: when located upstream, they regulate and prolong water inflow, thus replenishing primary ponds during the vegetative season; when located downstream, they back up water against primary ponds, which contain the lodges, reducing water outflow. Downstream secondary dams tend to be deeper, and water losses are thus lower.

During construction of the dam, beaver incorporate bank and bottom sediment removed as they deepen the pond to the depth (up to 1.5 m/4.9 ft) required for wintering. In other words, a simultaneous deepening and widening of the pond occurs. Tests in the small tributary showed that water near lodges was significantly deeper than water in the overall waterway (see Figure 18).[25] Deeper ponds are more resistant to evaporation, thus helping to conserve water in the primary dam-pond unit, which (whether occupied or abandoned) exhibits the most stable conditions: that is, the smallest drop in water resources during the vegetative season.

In a larger tributary, the greater annual discharge flow, continuing through most of the vegetative season, affects beaver behaviour. Because surface water is more abundant, there is no need for the intricate system of primary and secondary dam-pond units found in smaller tributaries. Containment of water does not usually begin till late in the season when the flow has subsided, with a corresponding drop in water level. It is probably not possible structurally for dams to contain water earlier in the season because stream flow is too strong. When dams first emerge, they are generally flat and fan-like, because strong stream flow has eroded their tops and deposited sediments along the closed ends. There is usually a channel (1 m to 2 m [3.28 ft to 6.56 ft] wide), cutting through the dam along one side of the waterway, allowing for the free movement of water and beaver. As late as August in the Moose Jaw River, the dam-pond systems were generally still open. Complete closure of the waterway, and resulting containment and regulation of surface water, did not occur till September, even at the height of the drought. These differences in beaver alterations of tributaries of different sizes are reflected in the correlation coefficient between water depth and stream width. In Cottonwood Creek, it was strong (R^2 = .770), reflecting the simultaneous widening and deepening of the waterway, whereas in the Moose Jaw River it was weak (R^2 = .209).

In a larger tributary, because of greater erosion, beaver must work harder to maintain the depth needed for movement in the winter between lodge and food cache. Tests in the Moose Jaw River did not indicate a significant difference between overall water depths and depths near lodges; however, to obtain a large enough sample, both abandoned and active lodges were included in the analyses. Water depths around abandoned lodges were often shallower than the overall mean. Abandoned food caches and lodges, acting as impediments, increased siltation near them. In a smaller tributary, because the stream is regulated almost from spring runoff, erosion is markedly decreased. The water depth needed to ensure movement between lodge and food cache is one of the few precisely defined beaver habitat requirements that must be met regardless of the regional setting. Todd calculated this depth to be 91 cm to 152 cm (3 to 5 ft).[26] Two active lodges in Cottonwood Creek at the end of 1988 conformed to this range, having water depths of 96 cm and 122 cm. The one active lodge in the Moose Jaw River for which a depth measurement was available registered 94 cm. The low readings attested to the severity of the drought.

In Cottonwood Creek, even under average climatic conditions, water is unevenly distributed, even in beaver-occupied areas (see Figures 19 and 20), and many areas of the creek become dry by fall. By the end of the drought cycle in the late 1980s, most of the tributary, including many areas previously occupied by beaver, had become dry. The remaining water was locked mainly into discrete beaver ponds (mostly abandoned) of various depths. In the Moose

Jaw River, the pattern was somewhat reversed. There were long stretches of continuous water separated by short, dry sections that often contained a few isolated pools, mostly influenced by beaver activity. In the Qu'Appelle River itself, beaver rely solely on bank dens; lodges are not built because of swift stream flow. One can assume that construction of dams would also be severely hampered by the flow. Yet, because of the greater abundance of water, dam-pond systems are not really required. The main waterway can also withstand the effects of drought more effectively. However, during a prolonged drought, as the stream flow is reduced and the water level drops, resident beaver might be forced to construct dams to maintain sufficient water levels.

Field research during what was considered the severest drought cycle of the 20th century (1986 to 1988) gave me the opportunity to study its effects on beaver movements. In both the Moose Jaw River and Cottonwood Creek, abandonment of lodges was initially caused by fluctuations in water level, exposing lodge entrances and necessitating movements, generally localized, to lower levels. In Cottonwood Creek, because water was more limited, several other factors came into play as the drought intensified. Some dam-pond systems began to disintegrate into a series of small ponds, some of which, despite having adequate depths, were abandoned because of insufficient extent to accommodate both lodge and food cache. However, insufficient water depth was the major factor in more permanent movements of beaver from the tributary. By the fall of 1988 (at the height of the drought cycle), approximately 13 areas that had exhibited evidence of beaver occupation had been abandoned. In the Moose Jaw River by fall, though two lodges had been abandoned, two new ones had been established in the vicinity. In other words, beaver movements were localized to areas where water was more abundant.

What happens to beaver colonies when they are forced to abandon an area for a prolonged period of time or permanently? Previous studies of beaver populations in the Qu'Appelle River indicated that, during a drought year, in late fall active colonies increased in some areas by 48%. That implies an inward movement of beaver populations from small and medium tributaries to larger waterways, initiated by the diminishing availability of surface water. Some of these colonies can re-establish themselves in larger tributaries, whereas others might be forced to move to the main waterway. Implicitly, when the drought cycle ends, there should be a gradual movement outward of these beaver colonies back to the smaller waterways. Beaver population densities should thus show the greatest fluctuations in the main waterway, increasing markedly in the fall. Nevertheless, because of limited food supplies, they would not be high. A previous survey calculated an overall density of 0.61 lodge per river km but also noted marked variations among more specific areas.

It has been suggested that, since large tributaries most frequently provide suitable beaver habitat, they should exhibit the highest densities of beaver colonies. As previously noted, the average density in Pheasant Creek, a large tributary of the Qu'Appelle River, was 1 lodge per river km.[27] An area including part of the Moose Jaw River and a small section of the Qu'Appelle River had the highest beaver density (1.61 colonies per river km) in the valley.[28] In the Moose Jaw River during the height of the drought, beaver density was 1.2 lodges per river km along 5.8 river km (including the research area). This density would be too high for the overall tributary, for a clustering of lodges occurred in an area affected by a spring, which contributed substantially to surface water amounts. During the height of the drought, beaver density in Cottonwood Creek was 0.13 lodge per river km.

Field research on beaver foraging strategies was restricted mainly to Cottonwood Creek, along which tree species are of limited abundance and distribution. Riparian species such as willow and dogwood are most frequently found in beaver food caches. Other species, such as chokecherry and saskatoon, are also used, though not as frequently. Aspen is not common along the tributary, but when present and accessible it is used as both food and construction material. In other words, availability is the major factor influencing resource selection. Along large tributaries, there is a shift to ash and maple in beaver food caches. Again, the greater abundance of these species is the determining factor in their selection. Chokecherry continues to be an important component of food caches, reflecting its ubiquitous distribution in the Qu'Appelle Valley. Aspen is also more abundant, but the floodplains of larger tributaries are broader, so this tree species remains mostly inaccessible to beaver. Along the main waterway, with its central positioning in the broad floodplain, riparian species—mostly willow—are the major components of beaver food caches. Herbaceous plants were no doubt important parts of the beaver's diet in earlier times. It was observed that in late fall, the use of woody materials increased substantially for both immediate food and cache construction, perhaps because of the curing of grassland species.

Along smaller tributaries such as Cottonwood Creek, choke-cherry—both abundant and accessible—was the major component of dams and lodges, replacing aspen and poplar (see Figure 17). Small amounts of maple were also used. Beaver preferred cutting choke-cherry trunks of larger diameters (2 cm to 4 cm) in greater proportion than was available (see Figure 16). This selection pattern was also observed for dogwood and willow. The preference for larger diameters is ecologically advantageous since it accelerates growth of smaller trees, making the species more resistant to heavy use by beaver. Along a larger tributary like the Moose Jaw River, ash was an important component of lodges and dams, also reflecting its abundance. In the main waterway, lodges and dams were not usually built.

The availability of dry wood and logs in the Qu'Appelle Valley can be attributed primarily to beaver activity. When large trees like maple, ranging from 12 cm (4.7 in) to 34.8 cm (13.7 in) in diameter, were felled, beaver debarked only the lower portions of the trunks and infrequently removed the branches. Branches removed from maples ranged from 1.5 cm (0.6 in) to 15.7 cm (6.2 in) in diameter. Some of these branches were incorporated into dams and lodges, while others were strewn around the sites. Several of the larger branches were sectioned by beaver into more manageable portions and then abandoned. The primary impetus for felling these trees appears to be a strong preference for open canopy. As a result, regardless of diameter, trees close to the stream edge and particularly those close to lodges were felled. This preference for open canopy explains the high wastage or non-use of many felled trees. This phenomenon is most prevalent during initial occupancy of an area. In subsequent years, the use of maple is minimal and generally seasonal. On aspen trunks, ranging from 8 cm (3.15 in) to 16.2 cm (6.4 in) in diameter, almost all of the branches were removed. Large trees such as ash, elm, and maple were often deeply chewed and debarked without being felled. These trees eventually died, becoming standing dry wood.

Fluctuations in the water level, particularly low water in fall, often leave lodges above the water line and expose good portions of the dams so that the wooden components are dry. In addition, flooding in spring removes appreciable amounts of materials from dams and lodges, which make up the driftwood found along the banks.

Along the different tributaries, there was some evidence that beaver requirements for food and construction material significantly affected distribution or abundance of the associated tree and shrub species. As noted above, the preference for open canopy led to the removal of large trees near the waterway and lodge. Along a small tributary, this behaviour stimulated the succession to grasslands and shrubby species such as chokecherry and saskatoon. Along a large tributary, the removal of trees also resulted in the succession to more shrubby species. Beaver conservation of surface water (e.g., raised water tables) also affects associated vegetation communities, stimulating growth and delaying curing.

THE WOODLANDS
Elk Island National Park
The research area selected to represent a woodlands environment was Elk Island National Park, east of Edmonton. The park is divided into two areas: the main area, north of Highway 16, and the wood bison area, south of Highway 16. The main park area (136 km²/52.5 sq mi) consists of two sections: the north area, around Astotlin Lake, and the south area, around Tawayik Lake. Two research sites (A and B) were established in the north area (see Figure 10).

The vegetation of the park is somewhat more complex than the term "woodlands" denotes. C.B. Blyth and R.J. Hudson define its vegetation as that of a transitional area between the prairie to the south and the boreal forest to the north, and they suggest that the most suitable classification is "Parkland–Boreal Forest Transition Zone."[29] Several factors have influenced the park's vegetation. The broader region within which Elk Island is situated features flat to gently rolling topography, whereas the park is located in a hummocky area known as the Beaver Hills. This rough terrain, plus poor soil and restricted drainage, have allowed the development of small areas of boreal forest. In earlier times, frequent fires and large herbivore populations served to maintain the parkland vegetation. However, human-made changes, such as the elimination of fire and natural levels of herbivores, have altered the vegetation "from open grasslands with small groves of aspen and spruce to today's aspen and spruce forests with grassland openings."[30] The vegetation consists of pure and mixed stands of aspen, balsam poplar, and white spruce. Tree species found in wetter areas include black spruce, tamarack, white birch, water birch, and speckled alder.[31] Shrubs and herbs include hazel, prickly rose, willow, sedges, and grasses.[32]

Climatic data have been drawn from Blyth and Hudson, who used weather records from Edmonton as their primary source. January is the coldest month, with a mean minimum temperature of –16.5°C. Mean temperatures of 0°C are experienced during spring (late March) and fall (late October). The mean maximum temperature occurs in July and is 23.4°C.[33] The total annual precipitation is about 480 mm (18.9 in), with approximately 345 mm (13.6 in) being rainfall and the remaining 135 mm (5.3 in) occurring as snowfall. Most of the rain occurs between April and October, whereas snowfall occurs between September and May, with December, January, and February receiving the largest amounts.[34]

Elk Island is located in the North Saskatchewan River system, which drains into Hudson Bay. Surface water flow and storage are constrained within five local drainage basins. They all drain away from the park because it is situated on high ground. The lakes in the park are shallow, and small fluctuations in water levels can cause flooding. Snowmelt is a significant source of surface water in spring. Water levels generally decline during summer but do increase after a large rainfall. In fall, because of lower temperatures, reduced evaporation causes lake levels to rise prior to winter. The three aquatic environments in the park are lake, slough, and intermittent stream. Blyth and Hudson note that the hummocky topography, with its many depressions in which small lakes can form, combined with abundant aspen provides the ideal habitat for beaver.[35] Indeed, the traditional name of the area, Beaver Hills, attests to its suitability as beaver habitat in earlier times. By the 1880s, however, the fur trade had eliminated beaver from the area. In 1907, two beaver were re-introduced. Since no natural increase occurred in 16 years, it was believed that both were male. In 1942, a productive population was established. From 1942 to the present, exponential growth of beaver has occurred in the park.[36]

Study Sites and Methods

The research carried out in Elk Island National Park was not as comprehensive as that carried out in the plains area. However, considerable previous research on beaver populations in the park provided a general framework for my analyses. The objectives of this study of the woodlands generally paralleled those of the study of the plains: determination of beaver habitat requirements and which ecological components limit beaver populations and effects of beaver activity on the environment. The focus of this study, however, was markedly different. Compared with the plains, surface water and trees in the woodlands are not limiting factors; therefore, it would be pointless to analyze them from that perspective. Open areas, major sources of terrestrial herbaceous food (e.g., grasses and sedges), are limited in the woodlands, so I examined the role of beaver in establishing and maintaining these areas.

I selected two beaver-occupied areas, both associated with sloughs, as research areas. Site A represented initial beaver occupancy of an area. Site A was occupied by beaver in the spring of 1989, and I began research in the area in July.[37] Site B represented an area occupied for some time—a minimum of 10 years.[38] This temporal difference allowed a broader developmental approach to the analysis of beaver behaviour and its consequences. I took some measurements of water depth in a stream leading from Goose Lake.

Site A was located west of a road following the west shore of Astotlin Lake and leading to the Administration Centre. I divided the research area into two sections: Section 1, the northwest-facing edge of the slough, which also has a bank lodge; and Section 2, the south-east-facing edge of the slough. In August, in each research section, 50 m (164 ft) was marked off at 10 m (32.8 ft) intervals along the slough edge. The research area extended 5 m perpendicular from the edge. The site parameters were generally dictated by the beaver's foraging range. In August, all beaver-felled trees were found within 5 m of the slough edge. The exception was on side A2, which in October was extended 10 m from the slough edge to include all the felled trees.

Analyses of the foraging behaviour of beaver were restricted to two species: alder and poplar. Most of the willow was inundated, so the extent of beaver use was generally not visible. Hazel was not analyzed mainly because use of it was negligible and diameters were too small. Skinner notes that when trees or shrubs less than 2 cm (0.8 in) in diameter are cut, it is difficult to distinguish beaver markings from those of snowshoe hare.[39]

Site B was located near the north shore of Astotlin Lake and crossed by a nature trail. In August, research was mainly limited to qualitative observations. However, diameters of poplar trees were measured in a single plot (5 m by 20 m) randomly chosen from a sample of five plots. Measurements were restricted to trees that appeared to have been recently cut. The plot (area 1) was located on the east side of an older section of the pond system. The slough contained two lodges: an abandoned older island lodge and what appeared to be a recently constructed island lodge, abandoned by October; no food cache was observed.

In mid-October, at site B, quantitative analyses were approached from a different perspective and carried out in different areas. A phenomenon observed at site A—trees felled by blocks—was also observed at this older beaver-occupied area. Area 2 was located by the bridge crossing the south side of the slough, which contained the active bank lodge. The research area was 15 m by 10 m, representing a general containment of the felled trees. Area 3 was east of the lodge and contained an isolated mature stand of trees approximately 15 m by 20 m. I made no attempt to analyze alder since its occurrence in the study areas was negligible. Likewise, willow was not present in any significant amount.

Beaver Habitat

R. Schwanke and Keith Baker estimated that during 1975 and 1976 in Elk Island National Park, the majority (143, or 69%) of the 206 active beaver lodges were found in sloughs, followed by lakes (22.3%) and then by intermittent streams. They also noted that the most common habitat types associated with active beaver lodges were marsh-sedge wetland bordered by aspen forest (34.5%) and marsh-sedge shrubby wetland bordered by aspen forest (25.2%), for a total of 59.7%. The next closest habitat type was marsh-sedge wetland, grassland, and aspen forest at 8.2%. The remaining 10 habitat types were occupied by 32.1% of the active lodges.[40]

The great abundance of surface water is perhaps the most obvious common feature of the whole research study. Studies in the park, and generally in most northern areas, note the adverse effects of beaver-induced flooding. Beaver appear to be particularly adept at stabilizing water in sloughs. Unless artificially drained, most ponds retain their water levels. Schwanke and Baker, while measuring water depths near beaver lodges, observed no differences between 1975 and 1976.[41] While water levels do fluctuate somewhat in lakes, beaver have no control over these fluctuations. In the newly occupied slough (site A), the initial damming process involved a slow rise in the water level during the vegetative season.

Several authors have discussed beaver foraging strategies in Elk Island National Park. Schwanke and Baker noted that aspen and balsam poplar were the species most commonly utilized by beaver; further, they stated that 61% of the above combined species were cut in the 0–6.4 cm (0–2.5 in) class, followed by 9% in the 6.4–8.9 cm (2.5–3.5 in) class.[42] For comparative analysis, Skinner grouped active beaver colonies into four age classes ranging from class 1 (one to three years of occupancy) to class 4 (nine years or more of occupancy). He made some broad conclusions, noting that, for aspen and poplar, there was no evidence that foraging patterns were influenced by colony age or distance from shore.[43]

I found variations in beaver foraging strategies strongly influenced by age of the colony (initial occupancy of an area in contrast to a mature colony) and seasonality. At site A, one of the initial beaver activities was felling of most of the poplars along the water's edge within the 50 m (164 ft) research area on both sides of the pond. This activity was intensified near the lodge. Because wastage was excessive, I concluded that an affinity for open canopy led to this behaviour, which makes good ecological sense. First, accessibility to trees of smaller diameter was contingent on removing the larger trees. Smaller-diameter trees tend to become lodged if the area is not cleared or open. William Longley and John Moyle similarly noted that wastage was a problem with smaller-diameter trees because when cut they were too light to crash to the ground in heavy forest.[44] By contrast, large trees when felled typically had the momentum to crash to the ground through most impediments.

During summer, woody species were not generally used as food. Extensive use of poplar was not visible at either site A or site B. Alder was extensively cut at site A; however, the evidence pointed to leaves, rather than bark, as the source of food. The importance of herbaceous plants in the beaver's diet during the summer has been strongly confirmed by Skinner's analysis of beaver stomach contents (between April 30 and August 10). Graminoids and leaves were the principal components, making up 74.4% of the stomach contents, followed by bark at 17.1%.[45]

Alder was a major source of materials used in lodge construction. Unpeeled willow and some peeled poplar made up the remaining construction materials, which together gave a mean diameter of 3.1 cm (1.2 in). Skinner similarly noted that recently constructed lodges were smaller than older lodges and consisted mainly of unpeeled woody material about 3 cm in diameter.[46] The importance of alder as a structural material cannot be denied, but alder leaves as a source of food might also be crucial to a young colony. Grasses and sedges would be in short supply during early occupancy. A certain time span is required after beaver clear-cut a sufficient number of trees to allow for a succession to grasses and sedges. In mature colonies, extensive sedge/grass areas would markedly reduce the need for alder as a food source. In Elk Island, in most mature colonies, beaver have created sedge/grass meadows of about 15 m to 20 m radius around slough edges. However, at site B and other mature sites, the flooded areas or ponds did not provide new willow or alder habitats. In fact, these species, with few exceptions, were not observed near mature beaver ponds. Therefore, reduced use of willow or alder at mature sites might also be related to unavailability.

There were also significant seasonal changes in the use of some species. At site A in fall (mid-October), use of alder was negligible, mainly because the lodge was built and alder bark was not a food source. At all sites, the use of tree species went up dramatically in fall. The most important reason was the need to construct winter food caches. Some repairs of dams and/or lodges were carried out; however, most visible was a marked increase in the use of woody materials (bark) for immediate consumption. At site B, bark was stripped from the upper third to half of large trees, a foraging pattern not common earlier in the season. This new pattern of behaviour might be related to the curing of herbaceous vegetation, a process that brings about marked changes in its chemical composition, perhaps rendering it unpalatable for consumption by beaver. S.E. Clarke and E.W. Tisdale found that the average chemical composition of five major grass species changed markedly during the growth stage. At the leaf stage, protein was 18.33%, dropping to 4.85% at the cured stage. Phosphorus dropped from 0.252% to 0.084%, while calcium decreased from 0.390% to 0.337%. Fibre, in contrast, increased from 25% to 34.5%.[47] This change might have shifted the food preference among beaver to woody species.

Skinner also focused on fibre content as an important factor in species selection by beaver: "At Elk Island National Park selection of tree species is strongest for poplars, which are characterized by low fibre content."[48] Citing previous literature, Skinner related this preference to the low ability of beaver (about 30%) to digest cellulose in their diet. Skinner also suggested that beaver avoid smaller aspen poplar because of the high toxic levels of phenols, induced by browsing.[49] There might be some validity to the inference that smaller aspen is not extensively used. In my study, at site A1 in August, 42.6% of the poplar was from 1 cm to 5 cm in diameter, but only one specimen was cut. However, though beaver cut large-diameter trees, the bark on the lower portions was rarely used.

In fall (mid-October), a significant type of foraging strategy was discerned that had little to do with diameter or nutrition: trees were mostly block-cut at all research areas. This feature was particularly evident at site A2, where control was maintained over an area 50 m by 10 m. Of the 19 trees felled, 86% were restricted to an area 10 m by 10 m, and the remaining ones were located at the periphery of this plot. At site B2, 40 (or 81.6%) of the trees were cut within a plot 10 m by 15 m. At site B3, a mature isolated stand, 9 of 10 trees were cut. Individual trees were still cut sporadically throughout the area, but the block-cutting pattern was prevalent. It is a highly efficient foraging strategy since it reduces wastage: that is, lodging is reduced. The ecological significance of block cutting is that it hastens the succession of treed areas to open areas. The succession to herbaceous vegetation, an essential source of food, is markedly accelerated.

Specific field research to determine which factors affect population movements and sizes was not carried out; however, previous research in the park provides many clues. Since 1942, as noted, beaver populations have been increasing in Elk Island, and the latest survey (1988) indicated a continuing increase in beaver populations in certain areas of the park. For the park as a whole, Dave Flato calculated that active lodges increased from 1.57/km² (0.61/mi²) in 1986 to 1.61/km² (0.62/mi²) in 1988.[50] In other words, it did not appear that the carrying capacity of the park had been reached. Research in Elk Island also provides some clues on the effects of burning. In particular, beaver did not appear to fell trees on which the lower trunks had been singed or charred.

Effects of Beaver Activity

In Elk Island National Park, according to Schwanke and Baker, "the greatest influence of beaver on their habitat is the result of tree cutting and flooding which kills terrestrial vegetation."[51] Blyth and Hudson stress that many water bodies in the park were the results of two factors: topography and beaver activity. More specifically, they note that, in the north park, surface water increased from 0.6% in 1924 to 8% in 1983, while in the south park surface water increased from 3.7% to 7.8% over the same period.[52] They attribute these changes to beaver dams and some human dams.

What are the initial effects of flooding? Beaver generally create many of the sloughs by impounding low-lying areas, which tend to be willow-dominated shrublands with a heavy layer of sedges and grasses between the willow shrubs.[53] Alder, though not as abundant, would also be a component of this habitat. Flooding results in the rapid death of the above species. Knudson observed that most tree and shrub species found on floodplains are intolerant of long-term flooding and begin to die after a few months; most are killed after a year of inundation.[54]

The felling of trees also has a profound effect on the environment. My study indicated that the initial clearing of treed areas can be rapid. When beaver first occupy an area, they chew down many trees, particularly those near the lodge, to create an open canopy and foster new growth of food resources and building materials; wastage of these trees is therefore extremely high. The block- or clear-cutting of treed areas also creates small open spaces, within a season, so that succession to herbaceous vegetation begins early during beaver occupancy. Many have observed this aspect of beaver activity—that is, initiating the succession from treed areas to sedge/grass meadows. Schwanke and Baker commented on the positive attributes of this activity, noting that browse and graze production increased when beaver cut down large areas of trees because the canopy opened up, allowing sunlight to penetrate to the ground, thus stimulating vegetative growth.[55]

That beaver activity creates grass/sedge meadows is not denied, but that it increases browse/grass production is debatable when one considers the area lost to flooding. Schwanke and Baker calculated that the average area of open water in a slough is 1.3 ha (0.013 km²), whereas the mean amount of area utilized by beaver is 0.4 ha (0.004 km²).[56] In other words, 1.3 ha of grass/sedge/shrub vegetation is lost to flooding, whereas only 0.4 ha of open area (grass/sedge vegetation) is created. In addition, though there is an appreciable replacement of the herbaceous vegetation lost to flooding, such is not the case with tree and shrub species. Throughout the park, willow and alder killed by flooding do not re-establish themselves either along the slough edge or higher up. As beaver ponds age, they can develop attributes that inhibit the re-establishment of these species. Knudson notes that "the pH rating of the soil is so low after drainage of the ponds that tree and shrub species cannot invade the basin until the soil is freshened by many years of percolating rain water and snow run-off."[57]

S.A. Wilde, C.T. Youngberg, and J.H. Hovind observed that toxic gases in the soils of active beaver ponds partially destroy the mycorrhizal fungi on the roots of shrubs and trees.[58] The growth of many trees and shrubs is dependent on the activity of these fungi. The toxicity of beaver pond water can permeate the soil near the pond, inhibiting the re-establishment of alder and willow in the area. Knudson also suggests that sedge and grass communities can be inhibiting: "The sedge-grass community with its fibrous root mat is often so thick that its physical presence alone offers severe competition to roots of tree and shrub seedlings."[59]

The above dynamics have affected the vegetation composition of the park. For example, as previously noted, Schwanke and Baker calculated in 1975–76 that marsh-sedge wetland bordered by aspen forest was occupied by 34.5% of active beaver colonies.[60] D.S. Leach found that 64% of active lodges were in the above habitat type; meanwhile, beaver colonies in the marsh-sedge "shrubby" wetland habitat had decreased from 25.2% to 13%.[61] These differences in frequency also strongly hint that alder and/or willow do not re-establish themselves in beaver habitats after initial destruction by flooding. These dynamics reveal a progressive maturing of beaver-occupied habitats.

Wes Olson's analysis from 1950 to 1983 of the effects of beaver activity specifically in the wood bison area correlates strongly with the above assessments. He notes that the area covered by carex (a sedge) had declined by 3%, whereas the area covered by water had increased from 2% to 9%. In addition, large areas of grassland and willow had been flooded. He calculated that because of beaver-induced flooding, ungulates had lost 450 hectares of food resources. He concluded that "in all areas of the park, grassland, shrubland and, in the Wood Bison area, sedge meadows are decreasing in area due to encroachment of forest and increased flooding by beaver."[62] Ecological conditions change dramatically, however, when beaver ponds are drained. Because of the toxicity of their impounded water, and the subsequent effect on pond soil, the invasion of beaver meadows by shrubs and trees is very slow. Knudson found that, in drained beaver ponds, with 100% initial killing of trees and shrubs, no woody recovery occurred in the first two to five years.[63] Beaver ponds drained for up to 10 years showed only slight recovery of woody plants, the most common being sparse stands of willow and tag alder. These beaver meadows or drained ponds play an important role in the woodland environment. Not only are they an important source of browsing and grazing for a wide range of animals, but they also affect the distribution of fauna, concentrating them near these areas.

CONCLUSION

In a small tributary on the plains, water is intermittent, even under average climatic conditions, with flow normally ending by July. By fall, only certain areas, primarily those manipulated by beaver, contain appreciable amounts of surface water. These areas are usually close to treed slopes facing north, preferably with gullies or coulees, and water is of sufficient quantity that beaver—through their dam-pond systems, created soon after spring runoff—can maintain the depth and width essential for lodges and food caches in winter. During a prolonged drought, however, many of these dam-pond systems disintegrate because of evaporation. Most beaver colonies are then forced to leave the waterway permanently. Those that remain are generally confined to a primary dam-pond unit. However, because erosion in a small tributary is not severe, the unit can continue to capture water after the beaver have left.

A large tributary, with a greater volume of water, is generally continuous and flows during most of the vegetative season. It is thus more resistant to macroclimatic perturbations such as drought. Because water is more abundant and continuous, tree and shrub species, particularly trees, are also more abundant and broadly distributed. These ecological conditions provide more suitable habitats for beaver populations, which reach their highest densities in large tributaries, especially those with treed slopes facing north. Given the water's availability, beaver expend considerably less energy in maintaining it. Dams, for instance, do not generally become operative until late fall. During a drought, the reduction of water might lead to local movements, but major movements are rare.

Water is the most stable in a main waterway. It is doubtful that beaver contribute significantly to controlling or maintaining it during average climatic conditions. First, the water level is probably adequate for wintering; second, the strong stream flow makes dam construction difficult and likely not necessary. However, during a prolonged drought, beaver might be forced to construct dams to maintain a sufficient amount of water. And, as water diminishes, there is a gradual movement of beaver from smaller tributaries to larger tributaries and especially the main waterway. Yet, because the main waterway is in a broad floodplain, most tree and shrub species associated with slopes are inaccessible, thus limiting beaver populations.

In a woodlands biome, treed areas and aquatic environments are abundant. Although beaver create grassland openings, the browsing areas lost to beaver-induced flooding exceed those created by beaver tree cutting, greatly reducing food resources for ungulates. Beaver populations in the woodlands have been increasing rapidly, mainly because beaver have few natural predators and because natural fires are controlled, aiding in the creation of beaver meadows.

CHAPTER 4

THE HISTORICAL
EVIDENCE

This chapter tests the theoretical model presented earlier from a historical perspective—that is, eyewitness observations and/or interpretations—and examines the assumption that the aversion to beaver hunting was most entrenched among Indigenous groups entering the Northern Plains as pedestrian peoples. The main groups discussed here include the Blackfoot Nation (Piegan, Blood, and Blackfoot), the Gros Ventre, the Plains Assiniboine, and the Plains Cree. My focus here is to establish the origins of the various groups, their times of entry onto the plains, and their territorial/political alignments.[1]

The time periods studied here are the protohistorical and early contact periods, which began in the early 17th century. Toward the latter part of this time period, "peddlers" (independent French and English fur traders) began to infiltrate the plains and initiate direct trading relationships with Indigenous Peoples. Faced with diminishing returns, the Hudson's Bay Company (HBC) decided to establish inland trading posts, the first being Cumberland House, in 1774 (see Figure 11). During this time, many changes began that would greatly intensify during the historical period, irrevocably altering pedestrian lifeways. Acquisition of the horse was perhaps the most important event, and its impact will be discussed more fully in chapter 6, which details these changes and explores their effects on traditional ecological and socioeconomic relationships.

According to Arthur Ray, prior to establishment of the HBC in 1670, the Assiniboine and Western Cree were linked to the Ottawa Indian–French trading network and considered the most important suppliers of furs.[2] He also observed that the construction of company posts on Hudson Bay resulted in northwesterly movement of the Assiniboine and Cree as they became middlemen in the fur trade oriented toward York Factory. On the basis of documentary evidence, Ray concluded that, in the late 17th century, the Assiniboine territory reached from the southeast side of Rainy Lake to central Saskatchewan in the northwest. He places the Cree along the northern border of the Assiniboine territory and the Gros Ventre along the Upper Qu'Appelle Valley and lower Saskatchewan River. These social alignments, particularly with regard to the Assiniboine, ignore the historically documented division into Woodlands and Plains Indigenous groups. Ray notes that these distinctions might have some validity, but he also points out that they have been used "to play down, and minimize, the interregional contacts which existed between these groups," a central focus of his research.[3] Intratribal divisions are central to my study since they form the basis underlying several important cultural distinctions, including the non-hunting of beaver.

Joseph La France, who travelled in the region beginning in 1739, provides the earliest documentation of the Assiniboine division and the broad geographic placements of several Northern Plains groups:

> Upon the West side of Lake Ouinipique [Winnipeg] are the Nation of the Assinibouels of the Meadows, and farther North a great Way, are the Assinibouels of the Woods. To the southward of these are the Nation of the Beaux Hommes [Gros Ventre], situated betwixt them and the Sieux Indians. The Indians on the East Side are the Christinaux [Cree], whose tribes go as far North on that side as the Assinibouels do on the other.[4]

Henry Kelsey's earlier travels, in 1690 and 1691, also hint at this division of the Assiniboine and more specifically at the extent of their western penetration. Travelling with Woodlands Assiniboine, who traded at York Factory, Kelsey encountered other Assiniboine groups in the vicinity of Carrot River and as far south as the Touchwood Hills; these latter groups, referred to as the "Mountain Poets," were most likely part of the Plains division of that group.[5] Ray claims that the Touchwood Hills represent the western limit of Assiniboine territory at this time (see Figure 11).[6] Morton, however, suggests that the "Eagles Brich Indians," whom Kelsey also met, were the Eagle Hills Creek Nation (also Assiniboine) from the elbow of the North Saskatchewan River.[7] If this identification can be accepted, then the western extent of Assiniboine territory was much greater.

Kelsey's travels also imply a more northerly placement for the Gros Ventre than that suggested by Ray. When Kelsey left the Touchwood Hills, he travelled north, according to Morton, 43.5 km (127 mi) in the direction of the Nipawi Falls to meet the Gros Ventre.[8] Supporting evidence of this geographical positioning comes from David Thompson, who states that the former residence of the Gros Ventre, whom he calls the "Fall Indians," was on the rapids of the Saskatchewan, about 160 km (100 mi) above Cumberland House (see Figure 11).[9] Kelsey's narrative also indicates that the Gros Ventre appear to have been under constant threat from the Cree to the north and the Assiniboine to the east.[10] This might be indicative of a northwest displacement of the Gros Ventre by the Assiniboine.

Interestingly, no mention is made of the Blackfoot at this time. As early as about 1723 to 1728, Thompson's informant noted that the Piegan resided in the vicinity of the North Saskatchewan and Eagle Hills, the region where the Eagle Hills Assiniboine supposedly were located.[11] I will discuss this territorial positioning of the Blackfoot later in association with the Shoshone intrusion into the area, but I assume here that in Kelsey's time the Blackfoot were in a more southerly location than the Assiniboine.

Morton accepts La France's division of the Assiniboine, noting that, prior to the coming of the whites, the Woodlands Assiniboine were north of the Plains Assiniboine. However, when addressing migrations, most authors, including Morton, deal with the two divisions as one. He states that when the Assiniboine split from the parent group, the Sioux, they first occupied the valleys of the Red and

Assiniboine Rivers.[12] Robert H. Lowie's assessment of Assiniboine migrations stems from a longer temporal perspective: "In the middle of the seventeenth century the Assiniboine seem to have inhabited the neighborhood of the Lake of the Woods and Lake Nipigon. Thence they moved northwest towards Lake Winnipeg, where they came in contact with the Cree, and continued their westward migration as far as the Assiniboine and Saskatchewan rivers."[13]

If we accept the Plains/Woodlands distinction within the Assiniboine, then the following questions arise: When did it occur? And could it have evolved from the groups having different migration routes? In part, the answer lies in establishing the date of separation from the parent group, the Sioux, a date that has been highly debated. Ray observes that the early contact record implies a date ranging from prior to 1640 to as late as 1757.[14] Lowie notes that the argument presented for separation of the Assiniboine from the Dakota for only a short period just prior to contact is based upon the similarity of Assiniboine to other Dakota languages.[15] He argues, however, that the Assiniboine developed at least two language varieties after their secession from the Sioux, a fact that indicates a greater length of time than has been suggested.[16] The two groups compared were the Stoneys of Alberta at Morley and the Montana Assiniboine at the Fort Belknap reserve. More specifically, Morton refers to the Assiniboine at the Morley reserve as Mountain Stoney because they lived and hunted in the Rockies, thus placing them in the Woodlands Assiniboine division.[17] The Montana Assiniboine were part of the Plains division.

With regard to movement patterns, Stephen Return Riggs hints that Assiniboine migrations might have occurred in more than one direction: "They [the Assiniboine] appear to have been occupying the country of the Red River of the North, probably both on the eastern and western side. Their migrations have been northward and westward."[18]

Thus, it is argued, one group of Assiniboine, the Woodlands division, continued to be involved with the fur trade. In conjunction with the Cree, northern movements continued along the eastern side of Lake Winnipeg as this group was drawn to the English posts at Hudson Bay. The Assiniboine who would become the Plains division moved west to the Red River, and then along the Assiniboine River, eventually becoming established along the lower Qu'Appelle and Souris Rivers.

It is also assumed that the Plains/Woodlands distinction represents more than just geographic positioning. The movements of the groups through different environmental zones would have led to the development of some cultural characteristics oriented to these zones, in this case the increasing orientation of the Assiniboine toward the plains environment. One of the earliest distinctions was related to use of the canoe. In the woodlands, the canoe was essential for transportation and, with the advent of the fur trade, the only means of contact with fur trade forts on Hudson Bay. For the Plains Assiniboine, moving along the Assiniboine and Qu'Appelle Rivers, the canoe would have been an impediment. As previously noted, the extreme sinuosity of these waterways negated the value of the canoe, and distance could be covered more quickly on foot. Non-use of the canoe as a distinct Plains division characteristic was first noted by Kelsey when he was informed by the Assiniboine that the Gros Ventre did not know how to use a canoe.[19]

Over a number of generations, the loss of canoe use, and the corresponding knowledge of its manufacture, would have severely impeded the movements of all plains-oriented groups into the woodlands and generally acted against direct contact with the fur trade at Hudson Bay. These travel limitations would also have increased the isolation and separation (at least seasonally) of the two Assiniboine groups and stimulated the development of distinct dialects. Ray similarly pointed to abandonment of the canoe as a consequence of the developing grassland orientation of many groups. Ray also observed that the Sarcee and Blackfoot travelled to the posts on occasion but always in the company of the Assiniboine and Cree.[20] He suggests that they were not permitted by the HBC to travel to the posts without the escort of the latter groups; just as plausible an explanation, however, is that they did not have the means to do so without the help of these groups.

Perhaps the most important distinction between the two divisions of Assiniboine, at least with regard to my study, was brought to the attention of La Vérendrye. While travelling through the parklands in 1738, he was informed by a group of Cree that he would meet Assiniboine (Plains) who did not know how to kill beaver and whose clothing was made from buffalo skins.[21] Kennedy provides additional information on the cultural distinctions between the two Assiniboine groups:

> Sometime after the seventeenth century there was a noticeable division, probably consisting of a more vigorous western group of buffalo hunters who ranged more and were more warlike, and a more sedentary eastern group who chose to restrict themselves to the lakes and woods regions, living on moose and deer, cooking their wild rice, generally neighborly with the Chippewas and Crees, and eager to trap and trade with the French and English.[22]

The earliest information on the Blackfoot is derived mainly from Thompson's informant, a Piegan Chief named Saukamappee (a Cree by birth), whom Thompson met in the winter of 1787–88.[23] According to Saukamappee (who was 75 to 80 years old at the time), when he was about 16 (the mid-1720s) the Cree, including him and his father, were asked to aid the Piegan in a battle against the Snakes (Plains or Eastern Shoshone) that occurred on the Plains of Eagle Hill, which probably corresponds to the contemporary Eagle Hills (see Figure 11). Although the Cree possessed a few guns, they did not use them in the battle, the outcome of which was indecisive. A second battle occurred around 1734. During the interval between the two skirmishes, the Snakes used horses in their battles against the Piegan. As Saukamappee noted, "Our enemies the Snake Indians and their allies had Misstutim (Big Dogs, that is, Horses) on which they rode, swift as the Deer on which they dashed at the Piegans, and with their stone Pukamoggan [club] knocked them on the head, and they had thus lost several of their best men."[24] In the ensuing battle, the Cree and Assiniboine, who had again come to the aid of the Piegan, were armed with 10 guns. Terrified by this new weapon, the Snakes fled.

Referring to Saukamappee's narrative, Morton suggests that at this time the Piegan were on the plains around the North Saskatchewan River and Eagle Hills and that the Blood and Blackfoot proper were probably near them.[25] This interpretation places the Blackfoot tribes from about 1723 to 1734 in the Eagle Hills area. This territorial alignment was undoubtedly of short duration. Francis Haines estimates that the Shoshone of Idaho acquired horses between 1690 and 1700.[26] Early acquisition of the horse allowed the Northern Shoshone to penetrate as far as the Saskatchewan River Valley early in the eighteenth century.[27] It is suggested that their intrusion brought about the northern displacement of the Blackfoot tribes to the areas referred to by Saukamappee. Therefore, Blackfoot occupancy of the plains around the North Saskatchewan River would have occurred between 1700 and 1734.

The notion of a short-term northern displacement of the Blackfoot groups by the Shoshone stems from the debate over Blackfoot origins. There is general consensus that the Blackfoot were among the earliest occupants of the Northern Plains. Ewers notes that Blackfoot, of all the Algonkian languages, differs the most in its word formation from proto-Algonkian and the languages spoken by tribes in the Great Lakes region. He suggests that the Blackfoot were the earliest of the Algonkian tribes to move, in precontact times, from the woodlands to the plains.[28] Alice Kehoe proposes, more specifically, that Blackfoot ancestors "may have migrated along the northwestward-trending parkland bordering the Plains, through eastern North Dakota and southern Manitoba to western Saskatchewan."[29] She estimates that the Blackfoot lived on both sides of the Alberta-Saskatchewan border from at least 1400. Grinnell, however, has proposed a migration for the Blackfoot from the north, around Lesser Slave Lake.[30] Wissler disagrees with Grinnell, noting that no traces exist of a woodlands orientation in their traditional culture.[31]

Perhaps the most conflicting reference to Blackfoot origins comes from Thompson's informants:

> They [the Piegan] have no tradition that they ever made use of canoes, yet their old men always point out the North East as the place they came from, and their progress has always been to the south west. Since the Traders came to the Saskatchewan River, this has been their course and progress for the distance of four hundred miles from the Eagle

Hills to the Mountains near the Missouri but this rapid advance may be mostly attributed to their being armed with guns and iron weapons.[32]

Like Wissler, Thompson noted the lack of evidence of a woodlands tradition. However, from a short-term historical perspective, the northern origin could be correct; recently abandoned northern areas might have been the Blackfoot homeland for some 30 years. The ethnohistorical record generally points to an eastern woodlands origin for the Blackfoot in precontact times. Kehoe suggests that the Gros Ventre occupied south-central Saskatchewan and northwestern North Dakota in the late precontact period after separating from the Arapaho.[33]

The northern displacement of the Blackfoot by the Shoshone would have resulted in at least a partial encroachment on Assiniboine and possibly Cree lands if the territorial alignments suggested for Kelsey's time are correct. The Shoshone intrusion no doubt also forced a northern displacement of the Plains Assiniboine, who in their recent migrations had brought about a similar northern displacement of the Gros Ventre. It appears that the Shoshone posed a greater immediate threat than the territorial realignments occurring among the Northern Plains groups themselves; as Secoy notes, the threat of the Shoshone was sufficiently grave to bring about the establishment of a loose coalition among the Blackfoot, Sarcee, Atsina (Gros Ventre), Assiniboine, and Plains Cree that he calls the "Allied tribes."[34] The defeat suffered by the Shoshone at the hands of the combined Cree, Assiniboine, and Piegan forces signalled the beginning of Blackfoot movements in a southwesterly direction, driving the Shoshone before them.

These events brought about marked changes in territorial alignments in the Saskatchewan River Valley. For the beginning of the historical period, Morton places the Piegan on the Bow River and along the Rockies (see Figure 12).[35] The Blood were on the Red Deer River, and the Blackfoot proper were on the upper waters of the Battle River, south of what is now Edmonton. Their allies, the Sarcee, migrants from the Peace River, moved to the left bank of the North Saskatchewan, while the Gros Ventre occupied the plains to the south. The Assiniboine claimed the North Saskatchewan, the lower Battle River, and the Eagle Hills. The Cree took possession of the north bank of the Saskatchewan and the wooded country north of it. Ray's tribal distribution map for 1765 shows the Assiniboine also occupying the lower waters of the Qu'Appelle and Assiniboine Rivers.[36] This geographical positioning probably represents reoccupation by the Plains Assiniboine of their southern territories following the retreat of the Shoshone. The Gros Ventre, as allies of the Blackfoot, were also able to relocate southward, sharing the Touchwood Hills with the Assiniboine and re-establishing themselves on the upper Qu'Appelle and lower South Saskatchewan Rivers.

The locations of the various historical Northern Plains groups strongly reflect the resource/territorial rights among these groups, and these placements can be inferred on a smaller scale for the pre-contact period. These alignments suggest that access to bison herds was secured by claiming lands along the major river/stream systems in the bison winter range (see Figure 12). It was there that bison herds and human populations, prior to contact, were able to remain for up to nine months of the year. Dodge notes that "the winter camp is regarded by the Indian himself as his true home."[37] In addition, he observes that the Indians regarded the bison in their territory as their property, with the result that, "each year, the country occupied by the buffalo became a vast battle-ground, the proper owners attacking the interlopers at every favorable opportunity."[38] On the Northern Plains, Morton noted, the limits of the hunting grounds of the various Indigenous groups were understood, and any trespass was regarded as an act of war. Exceptions were made for friendly groups, allowed to hunt for their subsistence needs.[39] Trapping for the sake of furs was forbidden. While travelling in Blackfoot country, Anthony Henday noted that, though beaver were plentiful, the Indians in his company killed only enough to provide food and clothing.[40] After he made several attempts to persuade them to trap more wolves and beaver, they replied "that the Archithinue Natives would kill them, if they trapped in their country."[41] "Archithinue" is a general term for the Blackfoot tribes and their allies, the Sarcee and Gros Ventre.[42]

The bison summer range remained unclaimed and/or shared by all Indigenous groups for several reasons: (1) the convergence of bison herds from all wintering areas to this range; (2) the greater mobility of the herds during this time of year; and (3) the relatively short time that the summer range was used, up to three and a half months.[43] This sharing of the summer range was also pointed out by Thompson: "The Stone Indians [Assiniboine], a numerous tribe of the Sieux Nation possess the country southward and westward of this River [Assiniboine], to the Missisourie [Missouri] River, but this latter in common with several other Tribes."[44]

Whereas the French were probably the first white men encountered by the Blackfoot, the first HBC man to journey to their territory, in 1754, was Henday. By this time, the Blackfoot had acquired both horses and guns and driven the Shoshone back to the Missouri River and the Kutenai back across the Rocky Mountains.[45] During Henday's visit, the area appeared to be relatively peaceful: the Assiniboine were seen in the company of the Blackfoot groups, and intergroup trade was flourishing. Such trade during Henday's time provides hints (though they are confusing) about the non-involvement of the Blackfoot and their allies in the beaver trade. The Indigenous groups told Henday not to be too concerned about trapping, "for they would get more Wolves, Beaver &c from the Archithinue Natives in the spring, than they can carry."[46] Although this statement implies beaver trapping by the Blackfoot, later in the spring Henday noted that "our Indians bought a great many Wolves from them [Archithinue] for old axes &c." Several days later, Henday again confused the issue by stating that "I bought 30 Wolves' skins from them [the Archithinue], and the Indians purchased great numbers of Wolves, Beaver and Foxes etc."[47] The question is, if the Blackfoot groups had beaver pelts for sale, why did Henday purchase inferior skins such as those of wolves, which just a short time later would be rejected by the French trading post?[48] The answer is that the Blackfoot were not beaver hunters; they simply obtained beaver pelts from the other groups. Henday identified the Assiniboine as a major supplier of furs.[49] Morton states that Henday, on his route along the North Saskatchewan, was joined by many Woodlands Cree and Assiniboine, expert trappers, canoe builders, and traders.[50] Henday observed that the Assiniboine not going to Hudson Bay gave their heavy furs, for which the French would not trade, to the Indigenous Peoples accompanying him with instructions on what to trade them for.[51] Therefore, the Woodlands Cree and Assiniboine middlemen normally obtained beaver pelts and other valuable furs from other Woodlands Indigenous groups in addition to what they themselves managed to trap during the winter.

Henday's attempts to convince the Archithinue to trade at Hudson Bay were met with strong refusals.[52] Henday was informed that they did not know how to use a canoe, did not eat fish, could not live without bison meat, and would not leave their horses. To his suggestion that they would obtain guns at the fort, they replied that they killed their bison with bows and arrows. Ray observes that traditional hunting favoured continued use of the bow and arrow.[53] A gun could not be fired rapidly, and it could prematurely stampede the herds. Arthur, referring to the historical record, also notes that when herds were pounded, they were killed with arrows, knives, and lances and that firearms might have been prohibited.[54] Ray concludes that, during Henday's time, European metal goods were the main trade items for the Plains communities, whereas furs, and some horses, were the main trade items for the Assiniboine and Cree middlemen.[55]

Other HBC men, such as Joseph Smith and Isaac Batt, also travelled into the interior and brought back Indigenous people to trade with at York Factory. However, competition from the peddlers was increasing. These independent French and English fur traders from Montreal went farther inland and established posts there.[56] The English policy of waiting for the Indigenous people to come to the forts was in serious jeopardy. As Morton notes, Andrew Graham, the acting chief of York Factory, considered that the only way to increase the fur trade was to establish inland trading posts.[57] Matthew Cocking was dispatched to the interior in 1772 to report on the situation. Travelling with Woodlands Cree, he covered much of the same area that Henday had explored. He too hoped to find the Archithinue and persuade them to come to York Factory to trade. Cocking's journey provides concrete evidence of Plains Assiniboine who could not make a canoe or paddle one. These Plains Assiniboine also confirmed the use of middlemen (Woodlands kin) to barter their furs at the fort. Cocking also encountered Cree who were becoming plains oriented: trapping wolves and pounding bison.[58]

While in Archithinue lands, Cocking's Indigenous companions attempted to repair and operate one of their pounds; however, they were inexperienced and could not drive the herds to the corral. Pounding was obviously a hunting technique that required time and skill to be successful. They also informed Cocking that the trade items obtained from the Archithinue in exchange for European goods included horses, bison-skin garments, and wolf and other furs.[59] There was no mention of beaver pelts as a trade item.

When the Archithinue (Cocking identifies them as Gros Ventre) arrived at the pound, they successfully carried out a drive, leading him to note that "indeed not only at this Game . . . but in all their actions they far excel the other Natives. They are well mounted on light, Sprightly Animals; Their Weapons, Bows & Arrows: Several have on Jackets of Moose Leather six fold, quilted, & without sleeves."[60] At this time, the gun-poor Shoshone were the main enemy of the Blackfoot. Warriors were still armed with bows and arrows, so the leather armour still fulfilled an important function.[61] The Archithinue again refused to travel to the fort, claiming, like the Plains Assiniboine, the non-use of canoes as the main reason, plus the possibility that they would starve on the voyage.[62]

In summary, the early contact period was still relatively peaceful. The Cree and Assiniboine were still on friendly terms with the Blackfoot and their allies, the Gros Ventre and Sarcee, for two main reasons: the continued threat from their mutual enemy, the Shoshone; and the establishment of trading relations between the Plains Blackfoot alliance and the Woodlands Cree.

During this period, observations by HBC traders such as Henday and Cocking gave important insights into the lifeways of the Indigenous inhabitants of the plains and implied their non-hunting of beaver. The Blackfoot tribes and Gros Ventre traded furs such as wolves and foxes, some horses, and bison-skin garments for metal goods and guns. The Woodlands Cree and Assiniboine who acted as middlemen obtained the more valuable furs, such as beaver pelts, from their kin or trapped them themselves. There were also some Cree on the plains at this time, and they exhibited plains traits such as pounding bison and hunting wolves. At still an earlier period, in 1738, the Plains Assiniboine were already identified as not being beaver hunters.

Interactions between fur traders and Indigenous Peoples provided clues about some of the plains-oriented traits that had developed: (1) abandonment of the canoe; (2) non-hunting of beaver; (3) primary reliance on bison for subsistence; and (4) development of communal bison hunting (jumps and pounds). The aversion to beaver hunting was exhibited by groups who had entered the plains as pedestrian peoples: the Blackfoot Nations (Blood, Piegan, and Blackfoot proper), Gros Ventre, Plains Assiniboine, and small groups of Woodlands Cree.

CHAPTER 5

THE ARCHAEOLOGICAL
EVIDENCE

I n previous chapters, the theoretical framework for traditional beaver-human relationships was supported by ecological data and historical documentation, with important inferences on early human settlement patterns in Valley Complex systems. The regional archaeological analysis presented in this chapter is the final test of the primary hypothesis and its corollaries. Although the definition and location of winter camp sites are my primary focus here, an accurate understanding of the archaeological record requires a more comprehensive analysis. Within any particular area, in this case the Valley Complex in the bison winter range, a variety of site types can occur. In addition, variability within and between sites can be expected from a single cultural system, influenced by a range of factors, such as seasonality, variation in activity, duration of stay, and so on. As Lewis Binford states, "sites are not equal and can be expected to vary in relation to their organizational roles within a system."[1]

As I have noted, the Plains communities were overwhelmingly dependent on one resource: migrating bison herds.[2] They chose to follow the herds on their annual migrations between summer and winter ranges, thus reducing their dependency on stored food. They occupied the summer range in late spring and early summer and the winter range during late summer, fall, winter, and early spring. The shift from winter range to summer range was fairly local, from winter areas on valley bottoms to summer areas at higher elevations. People of the plains were not only "collectors" but also "manipulators" of resources. Their knowledge of bison behaviour allowed them to manipulate herds to move to strategic areas near their camps, where they could carry out communal hunting techniques. They used fire to concentrate herds in certain areas for continued resource utilization. Such manipulative techniques enabled bison hunters on the plains to remain for longer periods in or near Valley Complexes, which, as previously discussed, provided the optimum conditions for survival, particularly during adverse climatic conditions such as droughts, when beaver aided in conserving and maintaining surface water in dam-pond systems.

Studies of hunter-gatherer settlement patterns have been attempted by other researchers, including Sally Thompson Greiser, who compiled an overview of subsistence and settlement strategies on the high plains.[3] Her time frame, however, is much earlier than that for my study, and her analyses are much broader. J. Michael Quigg undertook a more specific study of settlement patterns in southwestern Alberta, in the Belly River Valley, which presents some parallels to ecological conditions in the Qu'Appelle River Valley. Quigg concluded that from 1000 BCE to 1850 CE the Belly River Valley was primarily occupied in winter by nomadic hunting groups.[4] He pointed out ecological conditions I have stressed in my study that made the Valley Complex the ideal winter habitat:

> The geographic setting of the Belly River valley would make it a prime location for winter camps. It is well sheltered from the winter winds and provides an abundance of water and wood for fuel and shelter. Game congregated in the valley areas in the winter thereby affording readily available food sources. Bison, in particular, tended to winter near the foothills.[5]

Given that the Valley Complex was the major source of resources such as wood, water, and shelter, it was a focal point in subsistence strategies and settlement patterns of early Plains inhabitants, influencing not only the types of archaeological site but also their patterns of distribution.

In this chapter, I rely on archaeological evidence to confirm the following hypotheses:

1. Since the most favourable environmental conditions for winter habitation (e.g., adequate surface water, shelter, and wood) were most frequently found along large tributaries, large winter camps and kill sites should reach their greatest frequencies in these areas.
2. Along small or medium-sized tributaries, limited surface water, particularly during times of drought, would prevent most areas from being used for any length of time by human populations. Temporary camp sites should therefore be the most common type in these areas.
3. In the main valley, inaccessibility to treed areas (with wood and shelter), because of the considerable extent of the floodplain, would generally act against its suitability as a wintering area for human populations. Therefore, temporary camp sites should be the major type in this area. Special-purpose seasonal sites (e.g., for fishing) should also occur.

STUDY SITES AND FIELD METHODS

As indicated in earlier chapters, the waterways that I chose for archaeological analysis were the Qu'Appelle River (the main waterway), Wascana Creek (a large tributary), and Cottonwood Creek (a medium sized tributary). The survey of Cottonwood Creek was carried out in the summer of 1986 and included the area from the CPR dam to the confluence with Wascana Creek (see Figure 13), for a total of 38.5 river km. The survey of Wascana Creek was carried out during the summer of 1988 and included the area from near the sewage plant to the bridge just past the Gilmore site, for a total of 37.6 river km. I did not survey the Qu'Appelle River since other researchers had carried out a survey of the main waterway, upon which I base my analysis.[6]

My field research faced many constraints—such as limited funding, time, and personnel—that prevented the survey from being as thorough as I desired. Also, little previous archaeological research had been undertaken in the designated areas, and information from most of the recorded sites was sketchy at best. As a result, most of the sites had to be resurveyed; moreover, because the geographic descriptions of some of the recorded sites were extremely vague, I could not locate the sites.

My focus was on the floodplains and associated terraces, where it has been postulated that winter camp sites are most likely to be found. I surveyed some of the uplands but did not do so extensively, since many of the previously recorded sites were located on exposed prairie. These sites were highly visible because of erosion.

Available cultural materials from the research areas were restricted almost entirely to surface collections held by the Saskatchewan Museum of Natural History and the University of Regina. Previous excavations were limited to the Gilmore site and a kill site partially excavated by researchers from the University of Regina. The importance of surface artifacts in finding sites and determining excavation strategies has long been acknowledged; however, surface collections are increasingly being used as sources of primary data for confirming important research questions.[7] More specifically, Dennis Lewarch and Michael O'Brien state that intensive surface collection is important in solving site-specific problems.[8]

Many of the sites in my research areas, particularly along Wascana Creek, were on land that had been under cultivation for over 50 years. Much of the land was in crop, which normally would have made analysis difficult if not impossible; however, because of the drought at the time of my research, growth was minimal, and erosion was intense, which exposed many artifacts between crop rows. Using the site as the research unit, I carefully walked along several rows for the extent of the site to ascertain artifact samples and raw materials. Most of the sites were highly disturbed because of yearly cultivation, so displacement—both lateral and vertical—was significant. Most of the sites in the valley bottoms were also multi-component sites, and several cultural traditions could be distinguished in the surface collections, verifying that vertical displacement caused by tillage was pronounced.

Along Wascana Creek, there were site disturbances more destructive than agriculture, and most artifact collections would be considered salvage operations at best. For example, one site was discovered because of massive earth displacements during the construction of a picnic area. Another site was an eroding green on a golf course, while several other sites were located in a park topographically altered for dirt bike trails. One sample was fallout from an eroding stream bank.

Along Cottonwood Creek, site discovery was hampered by the lack of disturbance. Many areas still maintained natural prairie, and site potential was thus often indeterminate. The extent and nature of several of the sites were assessed by evidence exposed by rodent holes. Also, many previously cultivated areas had been converted to pasture. However, because of the drought, growth was minimal and erosion was extensive; as a result, combined with the effects of overgrazing, many artifact clusters became partially exposed. These clusters, distributed over a large area, indicated a specific site type, for instance, Thompson II, possibly a wintering area. Generally, artifact materials were left in situ.

Several authors have attempted to distinguish site types for hunter-gatherer societies, deriving evidence from a wide range of sources.[9] Greiser defines four major site types for the hunter-gatherers of the high plains. Her camp site category is analogous to Binford's residential base, and like Binford she stresses that the focus of activities was on maintenance rather than extraction. She also states that "campsites are generally located near water, and depending on the climate, sometimes near a fuel source and shelter."[10] Her kill site category, compared with Binford's location site, is more restricted, referring mainly to mass kills of large animals (e.g., mammoths, ungulates). Her kill sites are also more area specific, being associated with a "natural" or contrived trap. Kill sites are also exclusively extractive, the main activities including killing and primary butchering of animals. She introduces a new site category: processing sites, locations to which packages of meat were transferred from nearby kill sites. She also considers these sites extractive, their activities including secondary processing of large amounts of meat. The fourth category is the quarry site, located at the sources of lithic raw materials.[11] The entire band as well as a specific task group could relocate to a quarry site. Main site activities included extraction of materials from the matrix and initial tool manufacturing. Binford, however, states that the procurement of raw materials was often embedded within some other strategy.[12] Greiser does caution that site categories are not mutually exclusive, that butchering in kill sites could overlap in processing sites, which in turn could overlap in camp sites.[13] She cites topography, number of animals involved, and environmental factors as affecting the degree of site overlap.

Quigg distinguishes four site types in the settlement patterns of the Belly River Valley of southwestern Alberta prior to European contact.[14] However, he does not elaborate on site type attributes. Again, kill sites and camp sites are important types, but Quigg lists two additional categories commonly recognized in plains archaeology: tipi rings and cairns. The importance of Quigg's research lies in his recognition of seasonality in site patterning and, more specifically, the definition of a winter camp site, from both an environmental perspective and an archaeological perspective.

In my study, I use these site types within the annual cycle of the Northern Plains bison hunters. Many factors, some highly specific, affected settlement patterns, generating some site types that correspond to the above classification and some that do not. For example, bison migrations, which in turn influenced major human movements, generated site types distinguished not only by season but also by region. Cultural factors, such as the ability to manipulate bison, also strongly affected site variability. The degree of specificity of my study has also resulted in substantial subdivisions of the above categories as well as omissions and new categories.

The categories of residential base/camp site and location/kill site are acceptable only in a general sense. Major human movements between summer range and winter range resulted in two distinct residential phases, and the resulting subdivisions are winter/summer camp sites and winter/summer kill sites. Tipi ring sites have been considered problematic, and the usual paucity of cultural materials has led to highly speculative analyses. There is general consensus that a major function of the rocks was to anchor tipis.[15] Because I focused my analyses on the bison winter range, I excluded processing sites since they would not be easily discerned, for during the winter they were not operative as separate sites. I concluded that, because of frequently inclement weather, some primary and most secondary butchering was undertaken at the residential base or winter camp site. A new category, generated by major movements between bison winter and summer ranges, is a temporary camp site used repeatedly. Binford's concept of special-purpose sites can be used here with minor adjustments and some omissions.[16] On the plains, the site category station would be restricted to one type, the observation post, used for monitoring herbivore movements. The other station types (i.e., ambush location and hunting stand) are less applicable. The field camp is a legitimate site type among bison hunters on the plains. Caches would be somewhat synonymous with cairns, being storage facilities.

In the Cannon Reservoir region of Missouri, O'Brien and McDaniel, using surface collections to determine site artifact densities and frequencies of artifact classes, made predictions about site functions.[17] They identified two site types, residential and procurement-processing, on which I draw in the following analyses. These analyses of site types draw on a range of sources: ethnohistorical research, ecological conditions, and previous archaeological literature. The model for a winter camp site is the Garratt site, which I have analyzed extensively.[18]

CAMP SITE TYPES

Temporary Camp Site

The use of such a site was temporary, generally an overnight stay, resulting in only a few activities. Therefore, artifact densities are low and the range of artifact types is limited. This category can be subdivided into frequent- and/or infrequent-use camps. Frequent use would be distinguished by low artifact densities over a larger area, whereas infrequent use would be characterized by low artifact densities over a smaller area.

Frequent-use camp sites had specific attributes that allowed habitual use. Such sites, found in valley bottoms, functioned mainly as temporary stopovers during fall movements from the summer range to the winter range along the larger tributaries. These sites consistently provided water (particularly limited in fall) and wood, and beaver occupation guaranteed these resources. Such sites were often in an open area on the floodplain, suggesting that shelter was not a primary prerequisite. Artifact densities tend to increase toward the stream edge.

Infrequent-use camp sites tended to be in random locations: that is, movements were not planned in anticipation of using the sites. These sites were most often used by smaller groups such as hunting parties that made short trips from the residential base to collect alternative food sources such as deer, elk, and waterfowl. In wintering areas, these sites would be found along valley bottoms close to stream edges. The length of stay could have been even shorter than overnight, and artifact remains would thus be scant. This type of site correlates strongly with Binford's category of field camp, defined as a temporary centre where a hunting group slept, ate, and generally maintained itself while away from the residential base.[19]

Another camp in this category would be found on the uplands, resulting from the manipulation of herds toward the kill site. Peter Fidler noted on December 28, 1792, that "the Young Men sleep out all night in general—when they bring the Buffalo to the pound—and sometimes they will bring whole herds above 40 miles [about 64 km] off and sleep two or three night[s] according as they drive them in a direct manner or not towards the Pound."[20] Joe Ben Wheat's description of a short-term camp site, at the Jurgens site in Colorado, provides some parallels.[21] Wheat also notes that artifact and bone densities are low and that the number of lithic artifact types is restricted, with scrapers and projectile points being the most common. He also observes that quartzite is the most abundant raw material in the lithic debitage (fragments from the making of stone tools). However, some flakes made of better-quality materials are also present.

Winter Camp Site

As discussed in previous chapters, certain ecological conditions, including beaver activities, pointed to the Valley Complex (particularly the larger tributaries) as providing the most favourable conditions for human winter habitation, especially during adverse climatic conditions. Habitat along larger tributaries most consistently provides the essential resources of water, shelter, and wood. This configuration occurs when the waterway approaches a treed northern-facing slope and when water is of sufficient quantity that beaver can maintain their dam-pond systems, guaranteeing not only the availability of surface water but also other essential resources during adverse climatic conditions.

Ethnographic studies give information, albeit conflicting, about the possible size of a winter camp and the duration of stay in it. Earlier studies of lifeways on the plains stress a dispersal of the bison herds in winter, with a corresponding scattering of the Indigenous groups.[22] In his studies on the Blackfoot, Ewers also claims that these groups wintered separately, yet he makes the somewhat contradictory statement that "many of them tended to select the same river valley, the individual bands strung out along the course of that river for many miles at intervals of a few miles or less."[23] Arthur's comprehensive research on the historical record strongly contradicts the above observations: "In early fall, after the rutting season, the bison moved onto their winter range where they tended to form larger, more sedentary herds and aggregate herds, thereby permitting the formation of large Indian encampments in the vicinity of these herds which were exploited by the use of traditional bison drive methods throughout the fall and winter."[24] Arthur also attempts to determine the actual sizes of these camps, noting that Fidler, in January 1793, reported that a large camp of 220 tents consisting of Piegan, Blackfoot, Sarcee, and Cree was pounding bison. Using the estimate of eight persons per tent, Arthur calculated that 1,760 people were camped together.[25]

Historical documentation consistently provides evidence that backs up Arthur's observations. Henry indicated in mid-February 1776 that the Assiniboine, pounding bison, had a village of about 200 tents.[26] Fidler's journal entry of January 15, 1802, for Chesterfield House, while commenting on the Fall Indians (Gros Ventre), noted that "the whole nation is at three pounds."[27] Dodge not only stresses the existence of large winter camps but also suggests that several tribes might have shared a wintering area. He notes that in December 1868, Custer attacked one end of a camp of Cheyennes, Arapahoes,

Kiowas, and Comanches, which extended for more than 32 km (20 mi) along the Washita River.[28] More specifically, Dodge indicates that environmental factors such as the nature of the stream or the level of the valley affected the residential patterning of the winter camp site, the result being that "one winter a camp of one hundred and fifty lodges will occupy scarce a mile, another winter it may be extended four, five or even six miles along the stream."[29]

The ethnohistorical record also provides valuable insights into the length of occupancy of a winter camp site. Dodge suggests that occupancy ranged from three to five months.[30] According to Ewers, "generally the Indians spent between five and six months in their winter camps, from late October or early November to late March or early April."[31] A major difference exists between precontact and historical Indigenous groups regarding occupation of winter camps. In the historical period, the horse provided the means to exploit the bison concentrated during the rut; in the precontact period, the rut made hunting techniques of any nature extremely dangerous for a pedestrian people. It has been estimated that sometime around mid-August the summer range would have been vacated by the pre-contact human populations.

Thomas Kehoe's informants provided more specific information on winter camp locations and spring evacuations of them. One informant noted that "when you see these tipi rings along the creeks and in the valley bottoms, they are the winter camps. In the spring when it floods they move up on the benches and high ground." Another informant stated that "our people camped in the brush of the sheltered valleys near the buffalo drives in the winter."[32]

Spring runoff in the Moose Jaw River (a larger tributary) often begins in mid-March and peaks in April. Therefore, on the basis of the above ecological and ethnohistorical information, occupation of winter camp sites prior to contact should generally have occurred from mid-August to mid-March, a period of approximately seven months. Arriving at the winter range by the end of August at the latest relates to the crucial need for dependable surface water. As previously noted, snow, the alternative source of water, does not occur in sufficient quantities until mid-November. There is also some evidence that human groups tended to return to the same wintering areas. In his studies of the Blackfoot, Grinnell notes that, "in the early autumn, all the pis'kuns [pounds] were repaired and strengthened, so as to be in good order for winter."[33] Arthur also stated that "annual herd movements into specific localities over long periods of time occurred with regularity when we consider that many bison pounds and jumps became deeply stratified sites through repeated use."[34] As well as attesting to the regularity of bison movements, the ethnohistorical record indicates—more importantly—that early human populations were aware of these regularities, allowing them to return to the same areas, an important factor for the survival of pedestrian peoples.

Because slope walls constrained winter camp sites in Valley Complexes, archaeological remains would be spread along the valley bottom parallel to the stream edge. However, since floodplains are often subject to flooding, cultural debris from earlier years might be buried by silt. In such cases, new occupation levels can be established over old ones.

On the basis of the above ecological and ethnohistorical data, it can be inferred that winter camp sites occupied large areas. Since the annual occupation of such sites was approximately seven months long, and the activities performed at them various, artifact types and densities should be high compared with other types of camp site.[35] Artifacts that should be found frequently at a winter camp site include tools in different stages of manufacture and pressure flakes, the debitage resulting from both manufacture and maintenance of tools. Many unnotched projectile points should also be found at a winter camp site, along with Knife River flint, a trade item from quarries in North Dakota, highly valued in making small chipped stone tools. At the Garratt site, 32.2% of tools were constructed primarily from Knife River flint.[36] Bone tools were also important components of a winter tool kit. Because only surface collections were available for my analyses, these artifacts, because of susceptibility to weathering when exposed, were not present (with one exception: a flesher, used to strip meat from skins).

Large butchering tools would be particularly definitive of a winter camp site since most secondary butchering, and possibly some primary butchering, would be carried out at the residential base because of inclement weather. Such weather forced bison herds to abandon the plains and seek shelter in wooded areas and/or valley bottoms, where winter camp sites were also located. At Buckingham House along the North Saskatchewan River, on December 20, 1796, Fidler observed that "we are but middlingly off for provisions, having only three weeks stock before hand, but hope the buffalo will be soon nearer us than before by reason of the severe weather that has of late prevailed."[37]

The winter of 1799–1800 was particularly difficult for both traders and Indigenous Peoples because the mild weather that continued for some time allowed the bison to remain on the plains for longer. Food scarcities became acute. James Bird, at Edmonton House, observed on February 24, 1800, that "the two parties [Blackfoot] brought us 494 made beaver [a unit of evaluation standardized by the HBC] in wolves and small foxes but no provisions of any kind; indeed they complain of not being able to procure sufficient provision for their own families, there being a scarcity of buffalo everywhere owing principally to the amazing warmness of the winter."[38]

Henry's observations at the Red River on January 1–2, 1801, corroborate the correlation between severe cold and abundant bison but also the difficulties of butchering them under such conditions:

> I soon came near the buffaloes, and found an Indian who had killed a cow, and was cutting her up. But the cold was so intense that it obliged him to give it up and return to his tent. I fired many shots, but killed only three; it was impossible to cut them up. I contented myself with raising the fat and tongues, and returned at dusk with a heavy load on my back.[39]

More specifically, McGillivray's observations during a visit (November 24, 1794) to a Piegan winter camp site to witness the operation of a pound provide evidence not only that meat processing was done at the camp but also that the kill site was located close by. There also appeared to be a high tolerance of the odour generated by the kill site: "It proceeded from the Carcases in the Pound and the mangled limbs of Buffaloes scattered among the Lodges, but another substance which shall be nameless contributed the most considerable part of this diabolical odour."[40]

During the fall, under more temperate conditions, butchering would have been more extensive at the kill site, but in the winter, given the harsh weather, butchering at the kill site would have been minimal. The major objective would have been to partition the carcass into portions small enough to be portable to the residential base. This basically entailed quartering the animal and separating the meat from the skeleton, as described by one informant: "In butchering the bison, the *mano* was sliced off, alongside the boss ribs. *Mano* is a 'roast.' Then the carcass was quartered, the front legs taken off with the shoulder blade and the hind legs cut at the femur—pelvis joint."[41] Remains from the Garratt site and the winter camp sites in the Belly River Valley reflect the above butchering process.[42]

Spring Camp Site

This type of camp site was most often located on the adjacent uplands of Valley Complexes, sometimes on an elevated area with an unobstructed view not only of the valley but also of the surrounding plains. Although spring runoff in the valley bottoms initiated movements onto the uplands, elevated areas were equally important for monitoring bison herd movements.[43] By this time, the herds had also abandoned the sheltered areas, lured by the emergence of spring grasses on the uplands and upper southern-facing slopes.[44] The herds were beginning to move to the summer range. Less frequent locations for this type of camp site were on upper slopes or across several elevations, including uplands and upper slopes. The associated wintering area and kill site would have been nearby in the Valley Complex.

Evacuation of the winter camp sites corresponded to the start of spring runoff, which occurs most frequently about mid-March. This in turn signalled the beginning of occupancy of the spring residential base. Movements of bison herds to the summer range peaked sometime in early May and would have initiated human movements shortly thereafter.[45] Therefore, the maximum length of stay on a spring residential base would have been from around mid-March to around mid-May, or approximately two months. Repeated use implies that this camp site would have occupied a large area.

Most spring camp sites are also tipi ring sites. Holding down tipis with rocks would have been essential during this time of year: not

only were spring camp sites in more exposed locales, but wind velocities are greater then. Longley notes that on the prairies "well-orga-
nized storms with deep low pressures are more frequent during the
spring and fall so that the mean winds have maxima in April or May
and again in October."[46] Unfortunately, in my study area, all upland
areas were cultivated, so it was impossible to determine if the spring
camp sites were associated with tipi rings. Because these were spring
camp sites, and the weather was more temperate, a large percentage
of activities should have occurred outside tipi rings. However, inclement weather also occurs sporadically, so evidence of hearths and
cooking should also occur within tipi rings.

Some of the Alkali Creek tipi ring sites in Alberta exhibit several
attributes that would place them in the spring camp site category
and support the above assumptions.[47] An eight-ring site is located
on a narrow bluff overlooking the valley of Alkali Creek, a tributary of the Red Deer River. Historically, this was a wintering area.
Fidler, who established Chesterfield House at the junction of the Red
Deer and South Saskatchewan Rivers, observed several groups (Gros
Ventre [Fall Indians], Blackfoot, and Blood) wintering in the area. He
noted on January 4, 1801, that the Fall Indians were coming to trade
from a pound 20 mi (about 32 km) away. On November 27, he also
observed that the Blackfoot were making a pound not 6 mi (nearly 10
km) from the trading house. Then, as early as April 3, 1802, he noted
that he had seen the last of the Blackfoot; finally, on April 16, he concluded that the bison were scarce and that "no more Indians are now
expected here by the lateness of the season."[48]

Gary Adams infers that the eight-ring site, because of its exposed
location, was a summer camp.[49] The ethnohistorical record indicates,
however, that by mid-spring the area had been abandoned as the
various Indigenous groups followed the bison herds onto the summer range. Archaeological remains also support the inference of both
favourable and unfavourable weather during occupancy of the site.
The presence of interior hearths in the four excavated rings suggests
the need for warmth as well as cooking during inclement conditions.
However, the presence of two hearths outside the rings, as well as
higher frequencies of both lithic tools and debitage outside the rings,
signal more temperate conditions.[50]

During these two months, activities would have focused on preparations for movements to the summer range and back again. There would have been a heavy reliance on dried provisions, so provisioning would have been a major activity at the spring camp site. The use of fire would have concentrated herds in specific areas in order to continue communal hunting practices and ensure adequate provisioning.[51]

There is another possibility. During winter, because of mostly below-zero temperatures, waste of bison resources was negligible. Stockpiling after primary butchering could easily have been accomplished. Milder spring weather would have necessitated an intense period of conversion of these resources into dry provisions essential for spring migrations. Little evidence in the archaeological record supports this assumption, yet Frison suggests that an arrangement of stone piles with a post mould in one pile at a tipi ring site might be the remains of a scaffold structure. Such a structure could have been used for drying meat.[52] Other important activities would have included preparing and cooking food. In addition, maintaining and recycling personal gear would have been important. Manufacturing new tools would have been minimal since major movements entailed abandoning many tools rather than making more of them.

Because the length of stay was significantly shorter in the spring camp site, overall artifact densities should be significantly lower than at winter camp sites. Given the short duration and the prospect of a major movement to the summer range, lithic debitage should mainly reflect maintenance and/or repair of tools rather than manufacture of new ones. The type and number of tools should also be high given the need to abandon many bulkier tools (to facilitate major movements) and discard worn-out tools, many of which remained from the winter tool kit. Because of this carry-over, it can be difficult to identify positively which tools reflect site function. Mauls, anvils, ceramics, and pestles, indicative of winter camp sites, should be absent or nearly so from spring camp sites. However, if provisions were being prepared, then some large tools used to pound and dry meat might be present. Tools used to construct hide bags for pemmican should also appear, along with small amounts of ceramics, carry-overs from nearby winter camp sites. Large tools, such as those used in primary butchering, should be mainly absent.[53]

I have described here the primary spring camp site on the winter range. As the group moved toward the summer range and stopped at water sources (e.g., tributaries, lakes, depressions), secondary spring camp sites were established. They would have been occupied for shorter periods, and therefore relatively few archaeological remains would be present.

Summer Camp Site

This type of camp site is beyond the scope of my study, so I will only briefly provide some broad attributes. Through the use of fire and non-disruptive hunting techniques, bison herds could be maintained on the summer range in selected areas, specifically those suited for pounding and associated with adequate water resources.[54] As a result, human populations could lead relatively sedentary lifestyles during the summer months. I estimated occupancy of the summer range at about three and a half months.[55] Site locations would have been near Valley Complex systems. High humidity, insect pests, and treed areas that reduced cooling winds would have acted against occupation of floodplains. Relocating to middle or upper slopes would have allowed summer breezes to mitigate most of these adverse conditions, while access to water resources would still have been within reasonable distances. Killing and butchering areas would have been appreciable distances from the residential base because of the effects of spoilage.

KILL SITES

Drives

Two hunting techniques are found within this category: jumps and pounds. Jumps are found most frequently along the Rocky Mountains, whereas pounds are more common on the level prairies.[56] Richard Forbis describes the differences between a pound and a jump. A pound was an enclosure into which bison were driven. It was bounded on one side by an escarpment, frequently along a creek, and on the other three sides by a wooden fence. A jump was a cliff or steep slope over which bison were driven.[57] Forbis also notes that artificial fences were often built to guide bison to the kill site. These fences were constructed from various materials: turf, stone, dung, or brush.[58]

In my study area, the drives were mainly into pounds. A winter pound tended to be close to the winter camp site. Frequent inclement weather made easy accessibility an important consideration. The same climatic conditions made it possible to remain close to the kill site without malodorous consequences.

Drives were generally carried out all winter. Compared with a summer kill site, a winter kill site should show a greater accumulation of cultural remains. The area occupied by the winter kill site should also be larger. Skinner notes that, for the Plains Cree, "sometimes when the people were camping by a pound all winter, they found it too small for their needs, and were obliged to enlarge it by piling up the buffalo meat already dried or frozen to make new pounds."[59]

Surrounds

Historical documentation by Arthur indicates that this hunting method could be carried out by a wide range of techniques: setting up lodges around herds, women setting up travois in a semicircle, using fire to surround herds, and having mounted hunters surround herds.[60] In my study area, the serpentine waterways form cul-de-sacs (natural surrounds) into which bison herds could be driven and killed. These areas have high frequencies of bone and some fire-cracked rock. Lithic materials are scarce, consisting primarily of large flakes and shatter.

OBSERVATION POSTS

This type of site was used basically for collecting information on the presence or movement of game animals.[61] Although hunting stands per se would not have been built by bison hunters on the plains, some of their attributes would be applicable to observation posts. Binford notes that the site was chosen to provide "maximum visual coverage for a large area."[62] He also stated that activities at these sites were mostly related to reducing boredom. In other words, watching game did not itself generate archaeological evidence. More specifically, he observed that at the Mask site (a Nunamiut hunting stand), archaeo-logical remains primarily reflected eating, playing games, and doing crafts. He also noted that these sites were rarely occupied overnight.[63]

In the Valley Complex systems, some of these sites would have been on the uplands close to the valley rim to provide a good view of the valley and occasionally the surrounding prairie. They would also have been located near the main residential base in the valley bottom. These sites would have been used mainly in fall and early winter after the Indigenous groups returned from the summer range and settled in the winter range. The main function of this site type was to monitor the movements and behaviours of a range of herbivores, such as bison, deer, and elk. Treed areas in the valleys are not abundant but instead are concentrated in specific areas such as northern-facing slopes and associated floodplains. Deer and elk (alternative food sources) would be attracted to these areas, and their movements could easily have been monitored from observation posts. Likewise, the movements of bison herds in and out of the valley system could easily have been monitored. Observations of herds in areas suitable for surrounds could quickly have been turned to the observers' advantage.

Observation posts from which to monitor herds to be manip-ulated by drives would have been located on elevated parts of the uplands. From this elevated point, which would look away from the valley, herds would be monitored and runners sent out to bring them closer. Runners could go as far as 80 km (50 mi) to bring in animals, which might have taken three to four days.[64] These elevated areas might also have been used to observe when runners were returning with herds, to put the camp on alert for a drive. Henry noted that "there is always a sentinel on some elevated spot to notify the camp when the buffalo appear."[65]

Use of observation posts in late fall/early winter implies some in-clement weather, so campfires might have been lit. The site should have a hearth or at least some fire-cracked rock if the area was dis-turbed. Food might have been prepared at the main camp site and brought to the observation post, or cooked there, so faunal remains might be present. To combat boredom, games were probably played. There might also be a lot of lithic debris, for this would have been a good opportunity to stockpile lithic blanks or preforms for later tool construction.

ARCHAEOLOGICAL RESULTS
Cottonwood Creek
Fifteen sites along Cottonwood Creek (see Figure 13) were surveyed.[66] Ten temporary camp sites represent 66.6% of the sites, followed by two spring camp sites (13.3%). Two winter camp sites (13.3%) and one surround (6.6%) complete the pattern.

INFERRED TEMPORARY CAMP SITES—The temporary camp sites tended to be located in open areas, and artifact concentrations were generally observed near the stream edge. The exception was Volke I, with artifact clusterings along a northwest-facing slope (i.e., under sheltered conditions). In the artifact assemblages, several broad patterns were discerned for both frequent types and infrequent types. In the General Debitage category, flakes and shatter were found at all sites; however, pressure/retouch flakes were absent from all sites. In the Chipped Stone tool category, no representative tools were recovered in the infrequently used sites; in the frequently used sites, the number of tool types ranged from zero to two and were mostly unifaces. In the Cobble Stone Industry category, spalls were the most common tool. For all sites, there was a basic artifact assemblage consisting of bone, fire-cracked rock, several flakes and/or shatter (mostly chert [fine-grained sedimentary rock]), and at least one cobble spall.

The minor differences between the two site types represent temporal variations. At frequently used sites, accumulations would occur. As a result, General Debitage would have higher frequencies. Over time, several Chipped Stone tool types would also have been deposited because of occasional use. The Cobble Stone Industry in particular would have more representation since spalls would have been necessary each time the site was occupied, for lithic reduction and/or food preparation, activities specifically associated with the temporary camp site. In fact, the Cobble Stone Industry was the most important industry in this site type.

INFERRED WINTER CAMP SITES—The site designation of winter camp relied heavily on ecological characteristics because artifact materials, particularly at the Campbell site, were too few for many diagnostic features to be discerned. Both the Campbell site and the Thompson II site (see Figure 13) exhibited the ecological conditions ideal for winter habitation. Both sites are associated with treed, northeast-facing slopes and nearby waterways. A supportive characteristic was the proximity of two large spring camp sites on the uplands. Spring camp site EdNf-3 was a short distance upstream from the Thompson II winter camp site and directly above the Thompson III beaver-occupied area. Spring camp site EdNf-2, 5 was directly above the Campbell site.

At Thompson II, artifact concentrations were greatest on the first terrace along the slope edge, where shelter would have been available. In the artifact assemblages, three point types were identified: the Plains/Prairie, Avonlea, and Besant. These types are associated with the late Plains Indian period, dating from 2000 BP to 170 BP.[67] The General Debitage category had a sufficient amount of initial lithic reduction debitage, such as shatter and core fragments, to suggest that tool manufacture was an important activity. Chert was the most common lithic raw material. Several characteristics indicative of winter occupation were noted. The number of Chipped Stone tool types (seven) was much greater than that demonstrated at the temporary camp sites. The presence of a tubular uniface (incisor) hints at winter camp site activities. The absence of ceramics, however, is a negative attribute in terms of a winter camp site designation. A positive attribute is the possible presence of a kill site in the vicinity.

At the Campbell site, artifact materials extended from a disturbed homestead yard across the creek to an undisturbed native grassland area that ended at another loop in the stream, a distance of about 0.6 km (0.37 mi) (an extent expected for a wintering area). In the undisturbed area, rodent activities indicated that densities of cultural materials—mostly bone, fire-cracked rock, and General Debitage—were substantial and continual. The one artifact diagnostic of a winter camp site, a pestle, was found in the undisturbed area. The pestle was part of the winter tool kit designated as "site furniture": artifacts that remained on site when a group moved to other areas.

INFERRED SPRING CAMP SITES—Two sites were distinguished as spring camp sites (see Figure 13). The most definitive attribute was their location on the exposed uplands of Cottonwood Creek. The locations gave a strategic view of the tributary and, in the case of EdNf-2, 5 (slightly elevated), a reasonably good view of the surrounding prairie. Another distinguishing factor was their large size, up to 0.8 km² (0.3 sq mi), indicating repeated use over an extended period of time.

Particularly significant is that both spring camp sites were close to the only sites designated as wintering areas along the tributary. Both winter sites were located on the west side of the tributary in association with treed, northeast-facing slopes. The locations of the spring camp sites on the west side of the creek would have enabled the Indigenous groups to move directly to the summer range without the hardship of crossing the tributary during high water.

Supporting archaeological evidence, however, was elusive. It was inferred that spring camp sites were usually tipi ring sites with associated diagnostic features. Unfortunately, these sites have been completely disturbed by cultivation and subsequently reseeded to pasture. Most evidence is therefore obscured. Inferences are restricted to several surface artifact collections with no spatial control. However, both EdNf-3 and 5 were large collections, so some characteristics can be discerned to support their designation as spring camp sites.

The diagnostics suggest a long span of occupation, from the early Plains Indian period to the historical period (10,500 BP to 100 BP).[68] The point types with the greatest representation were the Plains/ Prairie and Besant, both from the late Plains Indian period (2000 BP to 170 BP).

Debitage components such as cores and shatter should be limited because maintenance of old tools, rather than construction of new tools, would have been the primary function of a spring camp site. At all sites, flakes and fragments generally dominated the General Debitage category. A large sample of cores was found only in the EdNf-5 artifact assemblage. Some other suggested site attributes were more easily discerned. Site furniture recognized for a winter camp site—anvils, mauls, and pestles—was absent. Small amounts of ceramics were recovered from the sites, implying carry-over from a nearby winter camp site. Large cobble core tools, associated with primary butchering, were absent; this might reflect the bias of private collectors, since such tools were considered inferior collectors' items.

Almost the complete range of tool types in the Chipped Stone tool category was represented at these sites. At a site type with occupancy suggested to be two months at most, this variety implies carry-over of a winter tool kit from a nearby wintering area. Many of these tools were either broken or incomplete and mainly showed pronounced patterns of wear, thus indicating the discarding of exhausted tools.

INFERRED SURROUNDS—One site was found on the floodplain at a point where the waterway formed a cul-de-sac. Fire-cracked rock and bone were the most abundant cultural materials. Lithic materials were restricted to shatter.

Wascana Creek

Twenty-seven sites were surveyed along Wascana Creek (see Figure 14). Overall artifact densities were significantly greater along Wascana Creek than along Cottonwood Creek. Underlying the specific site concentrations of artifacts was a level of low-density cultural materials, ubiquitous along the valley bottom, consisting primarily of bone and, to a lesser extent, lithic debris such as shatter flakes and blocks. It was difficult to discern the low visibility, infrequently used, temporary camp site. Site type classification along Wascana Creek was restricted to the broader category of temporary camp site.

INFERRED TEMPORARY CAMP SITES—The five sites in this category had more varied positions along Wascana Creek than was found for the sites along Cottonwood Creek. Only two sites (EcNe-10, EdNf-35) were located on the floodplain. One site (EdNf-44) was found along a sheltered slope wall; another (Grant III) was on a terrace; and the remaining one (EdNf-27) extended midway up a slope. Four of these sites were associated with open conditions.

The artifacts exhibited much the same patterns as those of the frequently used temporary camp sites along Cottonwood Creek. The Chipped Stone tool category was again poorly represented. Only four of five sites had tools, and the number of tool types found was from one to three. The Cobble Stone Industry category was again important, being associated with four of five sites. Spalls were the most common tool type.

INFERRED OBSERVATION POSTS—All sites were located on the uplands. More specifically, three sites (EdNf-37, EdNf-43, and EdNf-46) were located on valley spurs, which give an unobstructed view of the valley. Three of the sites were also close to designated wintering areas.

Both the Chipped Stone and the Cobble Stone Industries were poorly represented. Chipped stone tools were found at only two sites (one and two tool types, respectively). The General Debitage category was strongly featured at all sites. It was inferred that, during monitoring of game animals, lithic reduction activities might have been carried out to reduce boredom.

INFERRED WINTER CAMP SITES—Eight of the 13 sites designated as wintering areas were associated with dry stream beds, while another site was being eroded away by the waterway, thus strongly indicating that the position of Wascana Creek was of recent origin (see Figure 14).

Ten of the sites (77%) were located on the floodplain, while the remaining sites (23%) were located on higher levels (terraces). All sites were associated with treed, northern-facing slopes: five with northeast-facing slopes, five with northwest-facing slopes, and one with a north-facing slope. One large site (Sherwood Forest I) covered the entire floodplain on both sides of the tributary. At all sites, the waterway either cut the associated slope wall or was close to it.

The sites were large, and artifact densities were high. Bone was generally ubiquitous at all sites. In the General Debitage category, pressure retouch flakes were identified at nine sites, suggesting the construction and maintenance of chipped stone tools. The most diagnostic features were the abundance and variety of tool types in the Chipped Stone Industry. With the exception of one site, the number of tool types ranged from five to 13. The exception, Baker I, demonstrated only two tool types. It was designated a winter camp site because of its proximity to the Baker III winter camp site directly across the tributary; it was inferred that the former site might be an extension of the latter one. Recovery of artifacts from the site was poor because it was a pasture, and artifacts were thus difficult to discern. Ceramics were recovered, however—an important indication of a wintering area. Ceramics were also present at eight other sites. It was inferred that winter camps should exhibit high frequencies of ceramics, but this was not the case along Wascana Creek. The Besant point type was the most abundant diagnostic, and it is not usually associated with high numbers of ceramics.[69] At the Gilmore I site, mainly related to a Plains/Prairie side-notched point type, ceramics were abundant.

Unnotched projectile points were identified at four sites, suggesting staged manufacturing of personal gear. Site furniture (mauls and pestles) were recovered from five sites. The Cobble Stone Industry was strongly represented, implying that butchering was an important function at the winter camp sites.

INFERRED SPRING CAMP SITE—Only one spring camp site (Baker II) was identified, and it was located on the uplands directly above the Baker I winter camp site. Another previously identified site (EdNf-13) was close by and considered to be part of the same site. The site was extremely large, and artifacts were concentrated along the valley rim. Artifact densities were also high. The Chipped Stone Industry was strongly represented at the Baker II site. The number of tool types was 10. This large representation was consistent with the assumption that, prior to major movements to the summer range, a high percentage of the winter tool kit would be abandoned to facilitate the movements.

Ceramics were not recovered from the Baker II site, but they were found at EdNf-13. It was postulated that small amounts of ceramics would occur at a spring camp as carry-overs from the wintering area.

The Besant point type had the highest frequency. It was identified at seven sites, followed by the Plains/Prairie side-notched type (six) and then Pelican Lake (two).

Qu'Appelle River

The following data set was derived from an unpublished report on the Qu'Appelle Basin Archaeological Project.[70] The research area began at the town of Craven, at the confluence of the Qu'Appelle River and Last Mountain Creek, and extended to the Piapot Indian Reservation (see Figure 15).

All sites were defined by type: camp site, tipi ring site, cairn, and kill site. Detailed descriptions—provided for only 29 of 74 sites—included physical features, cultural features such as the number and size of tipi rings, and artifact assemblages. The environmental descriptions allowed for inferences on additional sites near those described.

The 74 sites included 36 tipi ring sites (49%), 26 camp sites (35%), seven kill sites (9%), and five cairn sites (7%). Of these sites, only two (3%) were located on the floodplain of the Qu'Appelle River. One was a large camp site (EeNe-1) situated at the confluence of the Qu'Appelle River and Last Mountain Creek; the other (EeNe-16) was a small camp site close to the slope wall. Thirty of the tipi ring sites (83%) were located on the uplands along the valley rim. Four of the remaining sites were in the main valley on lower slope areas, while two were located on terraces in a coulee entering the main valley from the north.

Of the 26 designated camp sites, 17 (65%) were on the uplands. The remaining sites had various locations: two were associated with confluences, three were on mid-slope areas in the main valley, three were associated with coulees, and one was located on the floodplain. This site designation was problematic since many of these upland sites were located on cultivated areas and probably were tipi ring sites originally.

Understandably, the kill sites were all on lower slopes or bottom slope locations. Two were directly associated with coulees. Five cairn sites, with the exception of one (EeNd-37), were associated with other site types and will be discussed within that context.

The overall picture in the survey area was a clustering of site types around a specific physical feature. The determination of settlement patterns was best served by focusing on these site type configurations as the unit of analysis rather than on specific site types.

A major feature of the Qu'Appelle Valley is the width of the floodplain, which ranges from 1.3 km to 2 km (0.8 mi to 1.2 mi). The river tends to meander centrally on the floodplain and only infrequently approaches the valley wall, so the distance between shelter and water generally acted against the suitability of the main waterway as a wintering area. The archaeological record strongly supports this assumption: only two sites were recorded on the floodplain of the main valley.

Associated with the main valley were three site type combinations that might have been wintering areas, with related types such as spring camp sites, kill sites, and cairn sites. Only one of these wintering areas was found in the main valley (see Figure 15). The specific wintering area (EeNe-1) was found at the confluence of the Qu'Appelle River and Last Mountain Creek. The site's suitability was greatly enhanced by the fact that the confluence occurs at the slope edge rather than more centrally, where exposure to inclement weather would have been greater. The two other wintering areas were not directly associated with the main waterway. One of these areas (EeNe-12) was found on the floodplain of a large tributary just prior to its confluence with the main waterway; the other sites (EeNe-30, 32, 33) were located in a large coulee entering the main waterway. These areas provided sheltered conditions and accessible water resources.

Most of the sites were tipi rings clusterings along the rim of the valley uplands, not associated with any wintering areas. The most important configuration included tipi ring sites, cairn sites, and kill sites. These sites were often located around a coulee with natural springs, or an intermittent stream, which provided local sources of water. The kill site was usually near the coulee bottom. According to informants, a suitable location for a pound was a natural drop such as a ravine.[71] Tipi ring clusterings could also occur along the valley rim where the main waterway cut the slope edge directly below. The main waterway, in this instance, became an accessible source of water. Many of these site clusterings contained large numbers of tipi rings and covered large areas, suggesting repeated use. The main advantage would have been the availability of surface water such as springs. The exposed nature of these sites suggests use during temperate conditions, most likely in spring, when tipi stones were particularly necessary because of high winds.

The main waterway of my research area would have been occupied during normal climatic conditions primarily in spring. Lakes in the Qu'Appelle Valley would have been a major source of alternative food such as fish, and spring fishing camp sites could be found, as the Lebret site demonstrated. The floodplain of the valley was generally unoccupied, but wintering areas occurred at confluences or in large adjacent coulees. The valley uplands were the main areas of occupation, serving as temporary stopover points during movements to the bison summer range. These areas were usually found near water sources and land forms (e.g., coulees and ravines) suitable for bison drives. In prolonged times of drought, the main waterway might have been an important area of occupation during the vegetative season.

CONCLUSION

In earlier chapters, I relied on ecological and ethnographic studies, along with the historical record, to test my primary hypothesis that beaver played an important part in the conservation and maintenance of surface water on the Northern Plains, especially during dry conditions. In addition, I suggested that the large tributaries of the Qu'Appelle River provided the most suitable wintering areas for early occupants. In this chapter, I have tested these assumptions from an archaeological perspective.

If large tributaries provided the most favourable conditions for wintering, then large winter camp sites and kill sites should appear most frequently along such tributaries. Along Wascana Creek (a large tributary) and Cottonwood Creek (a small/medium-sized tributary), the survey areas were of comparable extent: 37.6 river km and 38.5 river km, respectively. Fifteen sites were designated as winter camps along the combined tributaries, of which 13 (87%) were found along the larger tributary. The evidence of kill sites was not as definitive; however, along Wascana Creek, one kill site was conclusively identified and two other areas were inferred as possible kill areas.

I also proposed that on a small tributary limited surface water prevented most areas from being used for any length of time, particularly during a period of drought; therefore, temporary camp sites should be the most common type. Along Cottonwood Creek, 15 sites were identified, of which 10 (66.6%) were temporary.

Cottonwood Creek was the ideal area for carrying out studies to determine if any relationship could be inferred between site formation and available water. Modern agriculture was not extensive, and many areas on the valley bottom still retained natural prairie. Perhaps most important, the waterway has generally experienced few disruptions, so many of the original stream beds retained their viability. At the height of the drought in the mid-1980s, appreciable amounts of surface water were found at only six beaver-occupied areas and at one abandoned dam-pond system. Three of these beaver-occupied areas were directly associated with archaeological sites: Volke I, a frequently used temporary camp site; EdNe-3, a spring camp site; and Campbell I, a winter camp site (see Figure 13). An abandoned beaver pond system was associated with Thompson I, also a winter camp site.

I did not carry out research along the main waterway of the Qu'Appelle Valley, but a previous survey provided information on site types and possible settlement patterns. Seventy-four sites were identified, of which only two (3%) were found on the floodplain, strongly supporting the assumption that the main valley was not suitable for human occupants. One of these sites was a winter camp at a confluence. Two other wintering areas were identified close to the main valley: one in a coulee entering the main valley and the other on a tributary near its confluence with the main waterway. Tipi ring sites were the most common type (49%) on the uplands. Spring fishing camps, such as at Lebret, were found near lakes in the main valley.

Along the tributaries, some broad characteristics were discerned for the individual site types, which had distinct locations within the Valley Complex. Temporary camp sites occurred on the floodplain, generally in open areas. Observation posts were found on the uplands, often on spurs that provided unobstructed views of the valley. Winter camp sites were located on the floodplain close to where the waterway approaches and/or cuts a northern-facing slope. Kill sites were found on the floodplain near treed ravines and coulees. Spring camp sites, which commonly consisted of tipi rings, were found on the prairie along the valley rim.

Although not conclusive, a pattern of intersite positioning was observed. This pattern was most fully developed at the Baker sites along Wascana Creek (see Figure 14). Located on the east side of the tributary, on the floodplain, was a large wintering area (Baker III, a and b). Due north of this site, near a ravine, was a kill site (Baker III, c). Directly above the wintering area was an observation post (Baker IV).

Directly across the tributary from Baker III was another wintering area (Baker I), which might have been an extension of the former. Just above Baker I was a spring camp site (Baker II).

Some broad attributes, specific to site type, were also exhibited in the artifacts. Activities inferred for temporary camp sites included initial lithic reduction and food preparation (butchering) and cooking. These activities were generally associated with the Cobble Stone Industry, which had a strong representation in this site type, especially in frequently used sites. Cobble spall tools were the most common tool type, highly suited to both chopping and cutting. The main activity proposed for observation posts was monitoring animal movements. The General Debitage category consistently dominated the lithic assemblage, the Chipped Stone and Cobble Stone Industries being poorly represented. Its prominence tends to confirm the assumption that lithic reduction was carried out to reduce boredom.

Broad characteristics of the winter camp site included high artifact densities, with bone generally ubiquitous throughout the site area and a high representation of the Chipped Stone Industry. Chipped stone tools were not only abundant but also varied. Since the wintering area was occupied for a prolonged period, a wide range of activities would have been undertaken. More specific attributes included pressure/retouch flakes, reflecting the manufacture and maintenance of chipped stone tools; site furniture such as ceramics, mauls, and pestles; and many unnotched projectile points, indicating the staged manufacture of personal gear. The Cobble Stone Industry was strongly represented, and it was inferred that butchering was an important activity during winter.

Specific characteristics of artifacts associated with the spring camp site were more difficult to discern. The Chipped Stone Industry was strongly represented, reflecting the assumption that, prior to major movements to the bison summer range, parts of the winter tool kit were abandoned to facilitate these movements. Small amounts of ceramics were also found, reflecting carry-over from the winter camp site. However, there were variations of the spring camp site. As the Indigenous groups moved to the summer range, they would have had frequent stopovers, and the artifacts would exhibit characteristics of a temporary camp site.

Along the main waterway, one site configuration inferred for the tributaries was also present. One of the winter camps was associated with a kill site, and tipi rings and cairns were present on the uplands directly above it. Another intersite configuration consisted of tipi rings and cairns on the uplands and a kill site in a nearby ravine.

Briefly, using the sites in the research areas as focal points, we can reconstruct the annual cycle of the early occupants of the Northern Plains. The Qu'Appelle River Valley Complex lies at the southern periphery of the bison winter range (see Figure 4). Indigenous groups would occupy wintering areas (e.g., Baker III) on the floodplain of Wascana Creek (see Figure 14). Just prior to ice breakup, they would cross the tributary and take up spring residence on the uplands (e.g., Baker II). They would then move directly to the summer range. In the fall, they would return, via the smaller tributaries, to their wintering areas. Cottonwood Creek would be one of those migration corridors. During normal climatic conditions, areas suitable for wintering (e.g., Thompson II, Campbell) would be occupied (see Figure 13). During a prolonged drought, wintering areas along Cottonwood Creek would be abandoned, and movements to the summer range would be suspended for both human and bison populations. Large herbivores (bison, elk, deer) would be drawn to the main waterway (Qu'Appelle River), where appreciable amounts of water and forage would still be found. As a result, the tipi ring, cairn, and kill site clusterings on the uplands of the main valley (see Figure 15) could represent two different functions. During normal climatic conditions, they would be temporary spring stopovers during major moves to the summer range. During times of drought, they could be occupied for much longer. The human populations would also be drawn to the main waterway to pound the bison herds that had gathered there. Site occupancy could extend from spring to late fall. As winter approached, the people would move to the sheltered areas along the large tributaries.

CHAPTER 6

CHANGING LIFEWAYS ON THE NORTHERN PLAINS

In previous chapters, using ecological, historical, and archaeological evidence, I developed the model of human-animal relationships that evolved on the Northern Plains prior to contact with Europeans and acquisition of the horse. The model posits that, because surface water and treed areas on the Northern Plains are limited and variable, restricted mainly to Valley Complex systems, these systems aided the movement and settlement patterns of Plains communities as they followed the bison in their yearly cycle to summer and winter ranges. Crucially, in fall, beaver maintain water levels in small and medium-sized tributaries (e.g., Cottonwood Creek) through their dam-pond systems—often the only sources of water, especially during times of drought (stronger stream flow in a main waterway such as the Qu'Appelle River acts against dam and lodge construction). Primary dam-pond units, which contain lodges, are significantly deeper and wider to provide access to food caches in winter. Regulated by secondary units, these primary units are highly resistant to evaporation, and they raise water tables to the benefit of nearby trees, shrubs, and grasslands, which (along with the available water) attract elk and deer, on which early occupants relied for additional sources of food. By felling trees, beaver also supplied dry firewood and construction materials.

As the archaeological record indicates, Plains Indigenous groups were drawn to these areas along smaller tributaries for more temporary camp sites (e.g., in fall beside Cottonwood Creek) and along larger tributaries for more permanent camp sites (e.g., in winter beside Wascana Creek). Without beaver, most Valley Complex systems would have been uninhabitable, certainly during periods of drought, and understandably many Plains groups developed an aversion to, and even a taboo against, hunting beaver. Their very lives depended on sharing habitat with beaver. Early Europeans, especially those involved in the fur trade, could not comprehend this reluctance to kill beaver for their pelts and acquire trade goods in exchange. They were exasperated by this aversion and simply did not realize its sound ecological basis.

Beginning in the protohistorical period and culminating in the historical period, however, changing lifeways on the Northern Plains significantly altered traditional human-animal relationships. The historical period has two parts. The first part generally includes dynamics between 1763 and 1821, where 1763 signifies signing of the Treaty of Paris, which decreed the cession of Canada by France to Great Britain, and 1821 refers to the merger of the Hudson's Bay Company and North West Company. The second part continues from 1821 to the end of the bison-hunting tradition, marked by destruction of the herds in the late 19th century. My focus in this chapter is on how acquisition of the horse affected bison-hunting techniques and pedestrian lifeways among Plains communities and how the changing fur trade and provisions market and diminishing bison herds, along with intergroup warfare and the introduction of alcohol, forced some Plains Peoples to abandon their aversion to beaver hunting and begin to kill beaver for their pelts.

THE IMPACT OF THE HORSE

During the historical period, when the horse was introduced, Plains communities had variable responses to and roles in the fur trade. Chad Oliver noted "important differences among the sociocultural systems of people who live in different ecological situations, and it does offer a reasonable explanation for the similarities among the

Plains tribes, as well as the differences which persisted between them to the end."[1] Some of the cultural diversity exhibited during contact, which persisted well into the historical period, can be related directly to how long Indigenous groups had been on the Northern Plains and hence reliant on beaver to maintain surface water. Oliver also stressed introduction of the horse as a "prime mover" in cultural change on the Northern Plains:

> This basic technological change [the horse] triggered a whole series of cultural modifications. However, it is not technology alone that is so important—it is rather the role played by technology in the total ecological system. The complex interrelationships between the technological systems and the environment of other men, other animals, and other societies were certainly key factors in the developing Plains situation.[2]

I also see the horse as having played a pivotal role in irrevocable changes that affected traditional human-animal relationships on the Northern Plains in the historical period. From near Santa Fe, New Mexico, horses were distributed north along two lines: the Great Plains, and west of the continental divide. The latter route went to the Snake River, along which the Navaho, Apache, Ute, and Shoshone took horses to the Pacific Northwest. Haines suggests that the Blackfoot obtained horses from the Shoshone, but Ewers disagrees, stating that horses were more likely obtained from the Flathead, Kutenai, Nez Perce, or Gros Ventre.[3] Ewers broadly places acquisition of the horse by the Blackfoot in the second quarter of the 18th century and suggests that the horse might have spread to the Assiniboine and Plains Cree from the Blackfoot and Gros Ventre.[4]

Research on the impact of the horse on Indigenous populations has resulted in widely divergent opinions. Diamond Jenness claimed that the ease with which bison could be hunted on horseback attracted communities from the forest to the prairie.[5] Both Wissler and Roe disagreed with the view that the horse affected migrations.[6] Wissler perceived the horse as simply intensifying original patterns on the Northern Plains.[7] Other authors claim that the horse had a profound impact on many aspects of Indigenous life. For example, Ewers states "that the influence of the horse permeated and modified to a greater or lesser degree every major aspect of Plains Indian life."[8]

I agree with the interpretation that the horse strongly affected the lives of Indigenous populations of the plains. Acquisition of the horse was highly disruptive of the earlier pedestrian way of life, and the changes it brought were not always beneficial. As discussed in previous chapters, Plains populations used ecological knowledge as a major component of their subsistence strategies. A thorough understanding of their environment allowed them to predict natural events, some of which they manipulated and enhanced. By not hunting beaver, they maximized water resources; by using fire, they controlled bison movements. Knowledge of bison behaviour also helped them to develop traditional communal hunting techniques that did not disrupt predictable patterns. Early Plains Peoples were able to occupy the bison winter range for up to nine months and return to the same areas in subsequent years. Prolonged and repetitive use of an area was an important survival strategy for a pedestrian people. Arrival of the horse, and its use, would disrupt these predictive patterns.

Initially, Morton points out, the horse gave Plains communities greater mobility and thus greater accessibility and strongly altered territorial alignments: "Before the horses reached them the range of the tribe was limited by the mobility of the foot passenger. With the horse, the expansive prairie ceased to separate tribe from tribe."[9] Greater mobility immediately fostered new concern for territorial boundaries. More importantly, it provided the impetus for territorial expansion, with those acquiring the horse first having a tactical advantage over those who did not yet have it. Because expansion was not limited to occupation of unclaimed areas, population dislocations became common.

The Southern Plains witnessed the most spectacular territorial changes and increased animosities as a result of acquiring the horse. The Comanche were relative latecomers to the area, arriving about 1700. They had acquired horses as early as or before the Shoshone and they began rapid expansion, claiming a vast part of the Southern Plains as their own by 1836.[10] Earlier acquisition of the horse had allowed the Shoshone to penetrate as far north as the Saskatchewan River in the early 18th century. This invasion resulted in a northward displacement of the Blackfoot and possibly also the Plains Assiniboine.

The new hunting technique of chasing bison on horseback greatly disrupted their movements during the historical period. Ewers claims, however, that "this new hunting technique was more efficient and adaptable than any method previously employed. Not only did it require a fraction of the time and energy but it was less dangerous and more certain of success than other methods."[11] He implies specifically that bison drives by pedestrian peoples must have been very dangerous and time consuming and sometimes resulted in failure.[12] He further states that the migratory habits of bison and the limited mobility of pedestrian groups must have caused periods of food scarcity, particularly in winter. He believes that drives did not extend past November and December, leading him to conclude that "the greatest advantage horse users enjoyed over their pedestrian ancestors lay in their ability to transport quantities of dried provisions to their winter camps in the fall of the year as insurance against hunger and starvation during the most inclement winter months."[13]

Arthur concludes, on the basis of extensive historical documentation, that bison drives (jumps and pounds) were used effectively throughout the winter and that the production of large amounts of dried provisions in fall was neither undertaken nor necessary. He further notes that it was the presence of large bison herds, and not the horse, that was a factor in the existence of large encampments, given that the horse-poor Plains Cree and Assiniboine always wintered in large camps.[14]

As for drives being dangerous, that would have been the exception rather than the rule. A drive was a hunting technique whose success depended on manipulation and stealth, and those taking part in it were only infrequently placed in direct confrontations with herds. The chase, though, with its straightforward rush into stampeding herds, was fraught with danger. In describing a chase on horseback, Martin Garretson noted that "the dangers, of course, were many and accidents occurred on almost every hunt of any size, some of which were fatal. Occasionally in the excitement of the chase and careless handling of weapons, the hunter shot and killed his own horse."[15] The historical record shows little evidence suggesting that the horse made an essential contribution to a successful drive; in fact, it was often considered disruptive. Arthur states that horses were seldom used to bring herds to drive sites; however, if a herd had been enticed to the mouth of a drive line, then horses could be used to stampede it into the pound.[16] According to Henry,

> horses are sometimes used to collect and bring in buffalo, but this method is less effectual than the other; besides, it frightens the herds and soon causes them to withdraw to a great distance. When horses are used, the buffalo are absolutely driven into the pound, but when the other method is pursued they are in a manner enticed to their destruction.[17]

The suggestion that the chase was a superior hunting technique, compared with a traditional drive, is also debatable. Traditional drives continued to fulfill the same functions in the era of the horse as they had in the era of pedestrian culture. As previously noted, the success of this hunting technique lay in enticing herds to kill sites with a minimum of disruption so that herds would remain in an area for subsequent hunting. Continued occupancy of wintering areas, particularly during adverse conditions, would have facilitated survival during the horse era as well as prior to contact. The nature of the traditional hunting technique enhanced this possibility. Ewers admits that the horse was generally not suitable for winter hunting, especially during inclement weather.[18] Given the consequences of a chase (disruption and dispersal of herds), frequent use of this technique would have seriously jeopardized the possibility of winter hunting areas being maintained for extended periods.

Admittedly, from a short-term perspective, the horse made it easier to follow and hunt herds during their dispersal to the summer range. There was also one time during the annual cycle that the chase would have been effective without causing serious herd disruption, and that was during the rut. As I have noted, "the resulting dispersal of the herds, one of the detrimental effects of the chase, is temporary—the attractions of the rut favoring a resumption of the large groups."[19] From a long-term perspective, however, continuing to pursue herds on horseback severely disrupted bison movements, considerably diminishing the possibility of their return to specific wintering areas. Moodie and Ray agree that hunting mobilized herds and scattered them over large areas. As supportive evidence, they quote the remarks of the post journalist at Fort Edmonton in January 1822: "We are anxious . . . to have a number of these animals killed as quick as possible, fearing . . . that the different tribes of Indians, who are daily in search of them, and chasing them from one part of the Country to [the] other, will drive them out of our reach."[20] Since the Indigenous Peoples of the plains could no longer depend on herds to appear at their former wintering areas, the horse was now needed more frequently to search for them, further exacerbating the situation. Consequently, these groups would have been forced to make increasingly frequent moves during winter, and opportunities for traditional drives would have been considerably reduced. Arthur also suggests that the reduced use of drives in the horse period resulted from the increasing unpredictability of herd movements.[21] Continued harassment of herds made them more wary and skittish, and such changes in behaviour would have seriously affected drives (if not chases on horseback).

In general, bison hunting in the historical period involved drives from fall through winter, whereas the chase on horseback was the preferred technique during spring and summer.[22] Drives were discontinued because chases on horseback disrupted the predictable patterns on which successful drives depended. Although use of the horse created the uncertainty, its mobility also provided the solution, intensifying the dilemma. The chase on horseback was an important factor in the increasing nomadism that pervaded the historical period. The implication that in this period the drive fell into disuse because of its replacement by superior hunting techniques (the chase) is untenable. The traditional drive (to a pound or jump) was one of the most successful developments in the subsistence strategies of the early bison-hunting tradition. As Forbis notes, "with the horse, which first appeared between AD 1700 and 1750, methods of hunting changed; and though the practice of driving the buffalo was then largely forsaken, it is by no means certain that this practice produced a less abundant livelihood."[23] Jumps and pounds continued to fulfill the same functions in the early historical period.

During the era of the horse, increased warfare also contributed significantly to the disruption of bison herds. Moodie and Ray observe that in 1813 "the failure of the buffalo to approach the parklands along the North Saskatchewan in early winter was attributed to the Blackfeet massing for an attack on the Assiniboine."[24] Most researchers agree that increased intergroup animosities were related directly to the horse. Ewers noted that "it was the continuing economic need for horses, periodically heightened by serious losses of horses from enemy raids, destruction by plagues or severe winter storms, that made horse raiding the most common form of Blackfoot warfare and tended to perpetuate this type of warfare."[25] Secoy claimed that because the Blackfoot captured more horses than the Cree and Assiniboine, with whom they were originally allied, tensions led to their separation into hostile camps.[26] Concurring with this interpretation, Mandelbaum observed "that the unceasing hostility between the Plains Cree and their enemies was not due to any dispute over territory or struggle for trade advantages, but was largely the result of the continual raiding and counter-raiding for horses."[27] According to Henry, "the Crees have always been the aggressors in their disturbances with the Slaves [Blackfoot]."[28] The Cree and Assiniboine threatened from the east, with the Gros Ventre (an ally of the Blackfoot) absorbing most of the impact of the hostilities. In the southwest, the Crow, Flathead, and Kutenai were on the offensive, with the Piegan bearing the brunt of the attacks.

The mobility of horses greatly facilitated increasing warfare, which in turn was stimulated by the need for horses. As Morton states, with the horse the prairie "became a highway by which a whole tribe could strike a distant foe as swiftly and suddenly as a bolt from the blue."[29] With every group accessible and vulnerable, increased mobility became an essential factor in survival: "The endemic raiding warfare of the Plains area put a premium on flexibility and mobility, for both offense and defense. A group that was tied down in one place was a sitting duck; what was needed was a reasonably large group that could move in a hurry and react quickly."[30] The habitat requirements of the horse also contributed to increasing nomadism among Plains Peoples in the historical period; bands with large numbers of horses were often forced to move their winter camps several times in order to secure sufficient pasturage.[31]

In summary, acquisition of the horse brought about both the development of a new hunting technique (the chase), which disrupted bison herds, and increased intergroup conflict (mostly horse raiding); in the end, it placed a premium on mobility for survival. These developments seriously disrupted the pedestrian bison-hunting tradition. The historical period was thus a time of intensified nomadism and intergroup animosities directly related to use of the horse. Black similarly noted that "the horse made nomads of many tribes which there is abundant evidence to show were formerly almost sedentary in character."[32] In a slightly more philosophical vein, Hubert Howe Bancroft reflected on the situation: "It is by no means certain that the possession of the horse has materially bettered their condition. Indeed ... the horse may have contributed somewhat to their present spirit of improvidence."[33]

THE FUR TRADE AND PROVISIONS MARKET, 1763–1821

Following the Treaty of Paris in 1763, trading posts held by the French were abandoned in what are now Manitoba and Saskatchewan. However, peddlers from Montreal began to expand into the interior along the Saskatchewan River. In 1768, the trade restrictions imposed by the treaty were rescinded, opening up the West to all traders. The influx of rival groups forced the Hudson's Bay Company to construct inland posts. During this period, and until the 1821 amalgamation, its major competitor was the North West Company and its many successors, referred to collectively as the Nor'Westers.[34] The fur trade also expanded into the basins of the Athabasca and Mackenzie Rivers, which posed serious problems for both companies. The boreal forest could not provide sufficient food for the men. The parkland and prairie areas became the sources of provisions for the western fur trade. To collect provisions, the two companies built posts along the North Saskatchewan, Red, and Assiniboine Rivers between 1770 and 1881. In 1779, the HBC built Hudson House on the North Saskatchewan River to obtain provisions (see Figure 11). The foods supplied were primarily dried or pounded bison meat, grease, and pemmican. Butchering and processing were done by Indigenous women.[35] These two events—the establishment of direct trading and the development of the provisions market—would profoundly affect the relationships among the various Indigenous groups and between the fur trade companies.

According to Ray, increased conflict between the Blackfoot and other groups, such as the Assiniboine and Western Cree, occurred because the fur trade undermined the economic basis for cooperation among them.[36] The latter groups, no longer able to operate as middlemen, were forced to compete with other groups to obtain the same goods for trade at the posts. Secoy also stresses the replacement of Indigenous groups by Europeans in collecting furs as a major change, but he does not perceive it as a cause of increased animosities. He suggests that the Indigenous people acting as middlemen were actually relieved to relinquish this activity because at best it was only a part-time occupation.[37] My investigations of the historical record support Secoy's claims. As previously noted, the Woodlands Cree and Assiniboine acted as middlemen for the Plains communities, which included their own plains-oriented groups. These latter groups, however, did not trap beaver for their valuable fur, which was the main trade item at the posts. The Woodlands Cree and Assiniboine themselves trapped fur-bearers and acted as middlemen for kin who chose not to make long journeys to posts.

In the northern forest, this changed situation had a much different result. The Cree had been middlemen by conquest, driving many Athabascans out of their territories and pillaging them of their furs. Direct trade allowed these deposed groups to obtain guns and ammunition, thereby putting a stop to the advance of the Cree and in many areas forcing them to retreat.[38] However, as Mackenzie noted in 1789, the Cree continued to invade the Saskatchewan River Valley from the east.[39]

Woodlands communities were beaver hunters and Plains communities were not, but this distinction is complicated because the Assiniboine and Cree were found in both regions. The historical record provides more specific information on the geographical positioning of the various divisions. Mackenzie observed that the Indigenous groups hunting beaver were located at the source and on the northwest side of the North Saskatchewan River.[40] The "strong woods" of the Beaver River and the upper valley of the Battle River were considered prime fur country. The (Woodlands) Cree, the most important beaver hunters, were located near the Beaver River, whereas the Strong Wood Assiniboine, also beaver hunters, were found near the Battle River.[41] The Plains Assiniboine were along the Assiniboine and upper Qu'Appelle Rivers. Harmon, a fur trader at Fort Alexandria on the upper waters of the Assiniboine River, distinguished the Assiniboine in the area as non–beaver hunters: "The Indians who come to this Establishment are Crees & Assiniboins. . . . The former generally remain in the strong or thick Woods and hunt the Beaver, Moose & Red Deer &c. but most of the latter live out in the spacious Plains and hunt the Wolves (of different species) Foxes, Bears & Buffaloe &c."[42] McDonnell similarly observed that the Assiniboine along the Assiniboine River were not beaver hunters.[43] In addition, Glover notes that Fort Esperance was established on the Qu'Appelle River in 1787 mainly to obtain bison meat from the Assiniboine (see Figure 11).[44]

Information on the Cree is less conclusive. As early as Cocking's time (1772), there were some plains-oriented Cree on the Saskatchewan Plains.[45] However, as late as 1789 to 1793, Mackenzie noted that the (Woodlands) Cree were still advancing onto the Northern Plains from the east.[46] Conditions were different then: the Cree possessed guns and were acquiring horses. They still exhibited woodlands traits (beaver hunting) but were acquiring plains traits (pounding bison). However, the plains-oriented Cree were a sufficiently visible and distinct group for Henry to imply (after 1808) a distinction between Woodlands and Plains Cree, the latter of which were reluctant to trap animals for their furs. Henry noted that the Cree who lived in the strong wood country were able to purchase trade goods, whereas the Cree on the prairie would not procure furs to purchase the same items.[47] Morton also refers to the Cree as one of the great equestrian tribes that roamed the plains and traded only bison and wolf skins.[48] Also complicating analysis is that the fur trade record of Indigenous trade items did not always distinguish these intratribal divisions, and both divisions often traded at the same post. John McDonald, while wintering at Fort George in the 1790s, observed that "the tribes of

Indians who visited us during the winter were the Strong Wood and Prairie Crees: the Strong Wood and Prairie Assiniboils, the savage Blackfeet, the Piegan and Blood Indians."[49]

The groups on the Northern Plains during the early part of this period were relatively independent of the trading posts. As noted by McGillivray, a fur trader at Fort George on the North Saskatchewan River (see Figure 11),

> the Inhabitants of the Plains are so advantageously situated that they could live very happily independent of our assistance. They are surrounded with innumerable herds of various kinds of animals, whose flesh affords them excellent nourishment and whose Skins defend them from the inclemency of the weather, and they have invented so many methods for the destruction of Animals, that they stand in no need of ammunition to provide a sufficiency for these purposes. It is then our luxuries that attract them to the Fort.[50]

These luxuries included rum, tobacco, and ammunition. McGillivray pointed out that ammunition "is rendered valuable by the great advantage it gives them over their enemies in their expeditions to the Rocky Mountains against the defenceless Slave Indians, who are destitute of this destructive improvement of War."[51] The increased need for guns and ammunition was the Achilles' heel of the Plains communities, with disastrous consequences for their relationships with their enemies. Accessibility to guns and ammunition was largely determined by whether or not the group hunted beaver. Beaver hunters were given preferential treatment by traders. McGillivray detailed the privileges bestowed on beaver hunters when they arrived at the post, noting that

> before their departure they are equipt with Ammunition, Tobacco and many other articles as exigencies may require, and this is renewed as often as they come to the Fort. This with little difference is ye manner in which the Beaver Hunters are treated, but the Gens du large consisting of

Blackfeet, Gros Ventres, Blood Indians, Piedgans &c., are
treated with less liberality, their commodities being chiefly
Horses, Wolves, Fat & Pounded meat which are not sought
after with such eagerness as the Beaver.[52]

Plains groups thus lacked the commodities with which to procure sufficient arms. The advantage of the gun lay in its ability to kill, for arrows could be deflected by leather armour. According to Thompson,
"a war party reckons its chance of victory to depend more on the
number of guns they have than on the number of men."[53]

The crisis came to a head in 1793 when a group of Gros Ventre
were exterminated by the Cree near the South Branch Houses on
the South Saskatchewan River. Johnson and Morton concur that the
arms the Cree could purchase, because of their trade in beaver and
other prized furs, was the deciding factor in the defeat of the Gros
Ventre.[54] Morton notes that "the Fall Indians continued the prey of
their well-armed foes."[55] The Gros Ventre thus perceived the fur traders as allies of their enemies and, in the winter of 1793–94, attacked
the posts of both trading companies. This event later led to the
southwesterly retreat of the Gros Ventre from the Upper Qu'Appelle
Valley and lower South Saskatchewan Valley.[56]

Conditions worsened in 1809 when the London committee of
the HBC ordered that as few wolf furs as possible were to be traded
and dropped the standard for these furs from one to half a beaver.[57]
Since the concept of money was unknown to Indigneous groups at
the time, the HBC created a standard unit of evaluation termed the
"made beaver," equivalent to the value of a beaver pelt, and the prices
of all other trade goods were expressed in terms of it.[58] The policy of
not accepting wolf fur as a trade item had already been in place for
some time at the North West Company.[59] On hearing about these
new policies while at Fort Vermilion (an NWC post), Henry was led to
comment that "this will be a fatal blow to the natives; it will deprive
them of their usual supplies and probably make them troublesome."[60]
His concerns were prophetic, for two divisions of the Blackfoot (the
Blood and Blackfoot proper) became highly incensed and threatened to attack the forts.[61]

A similar situation was developing on the southern Blackfoot frontier. Earlier in the century, and with only a few guns, the Blackfoot tribes, allied with the Cree and Assiniboine, were able to drive the Shoshone back to the Missouri River and the Kutenai back across the Rocky Mountains. With the establishment of trading posts in the Rocky Mountains, the Flathead and Kutenai, not being averse to trapping beaver, were able to acquire guns and ammunition. In the summer of 1810, Thompson observed that the newly armed Flathead had decided to march to the plains to hunt bison. In an ensuing battle, the Piegan were forced to retreat. Thompson commented that "this was the first time the Piegans were in a manner defeated, and they determined to wreak their vengeance on the white men who crossed the mountains to the west side; and furnished arms and ammunition to their Enemies."[62] Henry's version of the above battle reveals more cautionary behaviour by the Piegan as well as their dilemma: "They fain would wreak their vengeance upon us, but dread the consequences, as it would deprive them in future of arms and ammunition, tobacco, and above all, their favorite liquor, high wine, to which they are now nearly as much addicted as those miserable tribes eastward."[63] The majority of the Piegan were not beaver hunters. Henry observed that only about 30 to 40 tents, in the wooded country, hunted beaver.[64]

The Piegan was faced with the same problem as the Gros Ventre: finding a commodity with which to purchase sufficient guns and ammunition. One alternative, particularly among the Blackfoot, was to seize beaver pelts from their enemies, most commonly white trappers. At Fort Vermilion in 1809, Henry, while complaining about the poor quality of furs that the Blackfoot brought to the fort, observed that "last year, it is true, we got some beaver from them; but this was the spoils of war, they having fallen upon a party of Americans on the Missouri, stripped them of everything, and brought off a quantity of skins."[65] Although the Blackfoot did not trap beaver, apparently it was acceptable to trade the pelts of those trapped by others.

The Gros Ventre, because of their inferiority in arms, continued to be casualties of war. In 1811, while Henry was at Rocky Mountain House, he reported that the Gros Ventre, just defeated by the Crow, had been unable to obtain guns and ammunition because their furs had been rejected. As a result, they threatened to attack the post. Henry mentioned that the Piegan managed to dissuade the Gros Ventre by providing them with

> all the dried provisions they needed, and represented to them the fatal consequences of such an affair; for surely never more would they see any traders in their lands, and where then could they get arms, ammunition, tobacco, and liquor? They would then be miserable indeed. The Piegans advised them to make buffalo robes with which to purchase ammunition to defend themselves.[66]

The Piegan thus cautioned the Gros Ventre about the repercussions of attacking the forts. According to Morton, the Blackfoot decided that "the Company was there for trade; not for war, therefore 'hands off the company' was the policy generally followed."[67]

The Plains Assiniboine did not have the same degree of difficulty as the Blackfoot and Gros Ventre in procuring guns and ammunition. They were able to obtain arms by trading with their allies, the Cree. Henry noted that "if they [the Cree] procure a gun, it is instantly exchanged with an Assiniboine for a horse."[68]

In many cases, fur traders were willing participants in escalating tribal animosities. Guns and ammunition were traded for the purpose of warfare. While Thompson was at Rocky Mountain House, he was informed by the Flathead Chief that the Flathead were preparing for war with the Piegan and their allies and required ammunition. As Thompson noted, "all this I knew to be true and reasonable, and reserving only a few loads of ammunition I gave him the rest."[69] Undoubtedly, the fact that the Flathead were beaver hunters influenced the preferential treatment shown to them compared with the Piegan.

The Blackfoot tried to prevent others from trapping beaver in their territories and did not allow trading posts to be established there. Morton notes that "although willing to live at peace with the company the Blackfeet were not willing to allow trading posts to be maintained in their country," and Bow Fort near Calgary and Chesterfield House at the confluence of the Red Deer and South

Saskatchewan Rivers were abandoned because of pressure from the Blackfoot (see Figure 11).[70] Trappers caught in Blackfoot territories often met with dire consequences. In 1802, near Chesterfield House, the Gros Ventre killed 14 Iroquois and 2 Canadians who had come to trap beaver.[71] Thompson alludes to 350 hunters (mostly of French origin) killed by the Piegan or Blackfoot during his acquaintance with the tribe.[72]

During the early 19th century, the Blackfoot remained successful in keeping fur trade companies out of their American territories. According to Ewers, the Missouri Fur Company built a fort on the forks of the Missouri River in 1810. Attacks by the Blackfoot were so constant that little trapping was done, and more than 20 trappers were killed. After only a year, the area was abandoned. It was not until 1831 that the American Fur Company was successful in establishing operations in Blackfoot country.[73]

Although the prohibition against beaver hunting eventually eroded, there is little evidence from this time period that the Plains groups were a major contributor to the destruction of beaver in the plains and parklands of the western interior. As Ray points out, until the merger in 1821, the intense rivalries between the HBC and NWC led to intense exploitation of fur and game animals in the region. In forested areas, beaver had long been exhausted, and most pelts taken were of the less valuable marten and muskrat. Large game animals such as moose and caribou had also been severely reduced in the eastern forest. In the parklands, the destruction of animals occurred at an even more rapid rate. Fur-bearers such as beaver, muskrat, marten, and fisher were concentrated in a few areas, leaving them highly susceptible to discovery and destruction. In the Assiniboine River valley, these animals were virtually exterminated. In the country adjacent to the North Saskatchewan River between the forks and Edmonton House, beaver were also severely reduced, though low-value furs such as wolves and foxes were still abundant. Game conditions in the parklands were still favourable, with bison present in large numbers.[74]

Trading returns at posts confirmed that Plains people did not participate in the beaver pelt trade. In 1794, at Fort George (NWC post) on the North Saskatchewan River, McGillivray stated, the Blackfoot and Blood had "traded 16 Bales of 50 Wolves each, 800 lbs. Pounded meat, with a sufficient quantity of Fat to employ twice as much, 20 Buffalo robes and 12 Bear Skins."[75] In 1809 at Fort Vermilion, also an NWC post on the North Saskatchewan River (see Figure 11), Henry complained that "trade with the Slaves [Blackfoot] is of very little consequence to us. They kill scarcely any good furs; a beaver of their own hunt is seldom found among them; their principal trade is wolves, of which of late years we take none, while our H.B. neighbors continue to pay well for them."[76] The situation was similar at HBC posts on the Saskatchewan River. As reported in the Edmonton House journals between 1795 and 1800, whenever furs were traded by the Blackfoot, Blood, and Gros Ventre, they consisted primarily of wolves and foxes. For example, in 1798, George Sutherland, stationed at Buckingham House, estimated that "a tribe of Blackfoot Indians came in who brought upwards of 500 [made] beaver in wolves and foxes."[77] At Chesterfield House, Peter Fidler's trade in 1801 among the Blackfoot, Gros Ventre, and Blood was the largest (12,000 made beaver) sent to London from York Factory and, according to his accounting, consisted of foxes, wolves, and cats (likely bobcat and lynx) but no beaver.[78]

Aside from non-human factors, then, which groups were responsible for the destruction of beaver populations? William Tomison, chief of the Saskatchewan trade for the HBC, placed the blame firmly on eastern Woodlands Indigenous groups:

> In the summer of 1801 the North West and XY Companies had brought in more than three hundred "Eroquees" or Mohawk Indians on three-year contracts. These Indians, who left "nothing wherever they Come," had swarmed over the Saskatchewan District to complete the destruction of the beaver which had already been started several years back by the "many Bungee Tawau Mischelemacana [and] Eroquee Indians" who had followed in the wake of the Canadians.[79]

From a broader perspective, Thompson similarly observed that in the great western forest the Natives had thus an anual supply of furrs to trade all they required, and had the furr trade been placed in the hands of one company under the control of govern[ment] might have continued to do so to this time; but from Canada the trade was open to every adventurer, and some of these brought in a great number of Iroquois, Nepissings and Algonquins who with their steel traps had destroyed the Beaver on their own lands in Canada and New Brunswick.[80]

McGillivray's journal at Fort George gave insights into local Indigenous groups who actively participated in beaver hunting:

The Country around Fort George is now entirely ruined. The Natives have already killed all the Beavers, to such a distance that they lose much time in coming to the House, during the Hunting Season. The Lower Fort will only therefore serve in future for the Gens du Large, whilst the Crees Assiniboines, and Circees, being the Principal Beaver Hunters will resort to the Forks.[81]

White trappers also appear to have been major contributors to the destruction of beaver populations. These trappers were generally of two categories: free Canadians and company servants.[82] With regard to the latter, McGillivray noted in 1795 that "all the men are now returned from the Meadows [plains]; they have Killed in all about 2,000 Beavers most of which are of the first quality."[83]

As for non-human factors, Ray suggests that disease, fire, and drought might have contributed to the reduction in numbers of fur-bearing animals. He goes on to state that, "in the case of beaver, it may have been the combination of a particularly fatal epidemic at the beginning of the nineteenth century and the continued intensive trapping of the animal which led to its near extermination in many districts of the west."[84]

The developing provisions market, especially after 1812, eventually provided Plains communities with an abundance of trade items with which to purchase guns and ammunition and other goods. Increased

European travel over the Northern Plains also provided a market for horses.[85] Plains Peoples had finally gained a high degree of independence and could often dictate the terms of their relationships with fur trade posts. By 1823, the governor of the HBC had become aware of the problem:

> The Plains Tribes . . . continue as insolent and independent if not more so than ever; they conceive that we are dependent on them for the means of subsistence and consequently assume a high tone, but the most effectual way of bringing them to their senses would be to withdraw the Establishments/ particularly those of the Saskatchewan/ for two or three years which . . . would enable us to deal with them on fair and reasonable terms. . . . This however cannot be [e]ffected until [the] Red River settlement has the means of furnishing us with a considerable stock of Provisions for our Transport business.[86]

According to Ray, the increasing provisions market allowed the Western Cree and Assiniboine to shift their focus from furs to provisions.[87] This observation is no doubt true for the Western Cree, but since at least La Vérendrye's time (1738) the Plains Assiniboine had been a distinct group and non-hunters of beaver. A major problem with Ray's study is its omission of the Blackfoot and Gros Ventre. As the earliest inhabitants of the Northern Plains, they had been major participants in the provisions market since the establishment of inland posts.

As Ewers observed, the Blackfoot were not beaver hunters but "loved to hunt buffalo. . . . They offered quantities of fresh meat, dried meat, and pemmican to the traders. Consequently, the Blackfoot trade became primarily a source of provisions for the fur traders who could use this food while they were engaged in their more lucrative quest for beaver among the Indians north of the Saskatchewan."[88] The Edmonton House Journals from 1795 to 1800 indicate that dried provisions comprised an important component of the trade goods that the Blackfoot, Gros Ventre, and Blood brought to the post.[89] Accounts of goods brought by these groups to Fort George at this time also emphasized the importance of provisions as trade items.

THE END OF TRADITIONAL WAYS, 1821–80S

With amalgamation of the two fur trade companies, George Simpson was installed as the new governor, and he instituted a series of reforms to ensure a continued supply of pelts. To achieve this goal, he attempted to end the practices of taking summer fur and cub beaver and using steel traps. His most important policy, one that would strongly affect the lives of Woodlands communities, was the attempt to settle families permanently in well-defined territories. Faced with declining resources and growing dependency on the company, Woodlands groups were forced to accept most of the economic reforms. Initially, Parklands groups were able to resist most of the changes because the company continued to depend on them for food. However, this advantage was short-lived. One of Simpson's economic measures was to cut the fur trade labour force by about two-thirds. Most of the men released were of Indigenous-European ancestry and became known as Métis or freemen. They soon became serious competitors with Plains communities for the provisions market. By the 1840s, the Métis were bringing in more meat and pemmican than the HBC required.[90]

By this time, the increased market for bison robes compensated for the reduced provisions market for Plains groups. This demand resulted from expansion of the American fur trade up the Missouri River during the early 19th century. The HBC was never able to compete with American fur traders for the robe and hide trade of these groups because of transportation costs. The Americans had a cheap transportation route via the Missouri and Mississippi Rivers, whereas the HBC had to rely on an expensive overland route.[91] The growing market for bison robes was particularly a boon to the Blackfoot groups and Gros Ventre, who had used this commodity whenever possible as a trade item since contact. Ewers observed that the American traders "knew the Blackfeet were indifferent beaver hunters but would provide large numbers of buffalo robes. As the demand for beaver declined markedly after the invention of the silk hat in the early thirties, trade in buffalo robes increased, and the buffalo robe became the standard of value in the Blackfoot trade with the Big Knives [Americans]."[92] In 1867, Isaac Cowie made a similar observation at Fort Qu'Appelle: "Among the Blackfeet a buffalo robe took the place of the beaver skin."[93]

To the south, the rich beaver preserve of the Blackfoot country on the upper waters of the Missouri River was again penetrated by American fur traders. However, as before, these lands were fiercely protected by the Indigenous inhabitants. In 1821, a reorganized Missouri Fur Company sent an expedition up the Yellowstone River that was attacked by the Blackfoot, resulting in the deaths of seven whites and the loss of their property. In 1822, the Rocky Mountain Fur Company met similar resistance and abandoned the area.[94] The Blackfoot were particularly hostile to white trappers in the mountain regions. According to Ewers, "through the remaining years of the twenties and the thirties war parties of Blackfeet and Gros Ventres ranged far and wide on both sides of the Rockies south of the Three Forks. Repeatedly, they attacked the mountain men in their isolated camps or on the trail."[95] A foothold was finally gained in Blackfoot country in 1831. Kenneth McKenzie of the American Fur Company, with the help of an old trapper named Berger, established contacts with the Piegan, who agreed to let him build a fort in their territories. These negotiations were successful because the agreement stipulated that the Piegan themselves would collect furs and bring them to the fort. As the Blackfoot chiefs told Sanford, an Indian agent, "if you will send Traders into our Country we will protect them & treat them well; but for your Trappers—Never."[96]

In the fall of 1831, Fort Piegan was built in the angle between the Missouri and Marias Rivers (see Figure 11). During the first 10 days after the fort was built, 2,400 beaver skins were traded.[97] The Piegan capitulation was a major break in the long-standing policy against the presence of traders in Blackfoot territories. Apparently, not all members of the confederacy were in accord with this agreement. That winter a large force of Blood people besieged the fort, intent on destroying it and taking the furs traded by the Piegan. They eventually withdrew. Shortly after this event, the Blood again appeared at the fort, implicating the HBC as the instigator of the attack. This time they brought 3,000 bison robes for trade since the Canadian traders would not accept them, the robes being too heavy for transport.[98] If the attack had been for economic gain, as implied, then it was a rather futile effort.

The Blood were not beaver trappers and thus were dependent on the American posts for the sale of their main trade item, bison robes.

This event marked the beginning of intratribal dissension within the Blackfoot Nation. While at Fort McKenzie, Maximilian of Wied, a German explorer and naturalist, observed the Piegan firing on the Blood. In addition, he "saw in the fort the wife of the chief of the Blood Indians, . . . who much regretted the misunderstanding that had arisen between the Piekanns [Piegan] and her tribe."[99] By treating the Piegan preferentially, the trading companies, both American and British, also encouraged dissension among the three groups.[100]

When the traders abandoned Fort Piegan in the summer of 1832, it was burned down. Later that summer a new post, Fort McKenzie, was established in the vicinity (see Figure 11). Its completion marked a permanent foothold in Blackfoot country.[101] Attacks on beaver hunters continued; however, it appears that the Blood and Blackfoot proper were now the main antagonists. At Fort McKenzie in 1833, Maximilian noted that

> they are always dangerous to white men who are hunting singly in the mountains, especially to the beaver hunters, and kill them whenever they fall into their hands; hence the armed troops of the traders keep up a continual war with them. It was said that in the year 1832 they shot fifty-eight Whites. . . . In the neighbourhood of the forts they keep the peace, and the Piekanns, in particular, behave well and amicably to the Whites, whereas the Blood Indians and the Siksekai [Blackfoot proper] can never be trusted.[102]

According to Ewers, "in 1837, Alfred Jacob Miller reckoned the beaver trappers' losses averaged forty or fifty men a season, [and] Blackfoot losses may have been even greater."[103] Later in 1834, Maximilian was dissuaded from going farther up the Missouri River for the same reason: the Blood and Blackfoot proper were dangerous. Maximilian's narrative indicates that animosities also developed between the Blackfoot proper and the Piegan.[104]

After the 1840s, the provisions market changed again. In forested regions, game animals continued to decline such that the pemmican needs of the HBC increased. The departments of the Saskatchewan territory were unable to meet these demands because of the southerly and southwesterly contraction of the bison range.[105] The contraction was such that the remaining herds were gradually shifting into Blackfoot territories and abandoning areas inhabited by other groups. The Blackfoot had always occupied choice bison country. As a result, according to Morton, there was constant encroachment from other tribes, and the Blackfoot were virtually always at war.[106]

Establishment of the American trading posts, southern contraction of the bison range, and increasing importance of the bison robe and hide trade strongly influenced movements of the Plains communities during this period. The Assiniboine, in the middle Assiniboine and Qu'Appelle River Valleys, began moving toward the international boundary. The Cree moved into areas vacated by the Assiniboine.[107] Ewers also found that establishment of trading relationships with the American posts on the Missouri River strongly influenced a southern shift of the Blackfoot Nations, especially the Piegan. The Blood and Northern Blackfoot now wintered north of the international line along the Belly River and summered along the Saskatchewan River.[108]

After 1870, the bison trade shifted from robes to hides. This new alternative continued to provide a market for Plains communities, but it meant that the Indigenous hunters faced severe competition from white hunters since it required little skill, compared with preparing a robe, to make a hide ready for trade. Increased hunting pressure played a major role in bringing about the destruction of northern bison herds. Sometime before final disappearance of the herds (in the 1880s), the main bison range had contracted to territories southwest of the Cypress Hills.[109] Therefore, what remained of the former vast herds was in the heart of Blackfoot territory. This area also largely coincided with the former bison summer range, which at contact had been commonly shared by all Indigenous groups. By the end of the historical period, this would be the most fiercely protected and fought-over area in the western interior. Pierre-Jean DeSmet, while stationed with the Oregon Missions from 1845 to 1846, prophetically noted that it is highly probable that the Black-Feet plains, from the Sascatshawin to the Yellow-Stone, will be the last resort of the wild animals twelve years hence. Will these be sufficient to feed and clothe the hundred thousand inhabitants of these western wilds? The Crees, Black-Feet, Assiniboins, Crows, Snakes, Rickaries, and Sioux, will then come together and fight their bloody battles on these plains, and become themselves extinct over the last buffalo-steak.[110]

It took somewhat longer than 12 years, but by 1868 Cowie observed at Fort Qu'Appelle that the scarcity of bison was forcing some Indigenous groups to encroach on Blackfoot territories. Groups usually at odds with each other were uniting to have sufficient numbers "to penetrate farther into the enemies' country." Cowie identified the groups gathering to go to war against the Blackfoot as follows:

So it had come about that the allied Crees and Saulteaux, the semi-Stony and Cree "Young Dogs," of Qu'Appelle and Touchwood Hills, a few English and French Metis belonging to these places and Fort Pelly, also some Assiniboines from Wood Mountain and a few from the North Saskatchewan, were all gathered together in a camp...containing a mixed population of probably two thousand five hundred or three thousand people, of whom about five hundred were men and lads capable of waging war.[111]

By the early 1870s, many Indigenous groups in what are now southern Saskatchewan and Alberta had come to realize that their traditional ways of life were coming to an end. Between 1871 and 1876, all Indigenous territorial claims were extinguished by Treaties 1 through 7.[112] The bison-hunting tradition, which prior to contact with white men had persisted for thousands of years, was gone.

THE PROHIBITION AGAINST BEAVER HUNTING

Direct trading between Plains communities and fur traders brought into focus the fact that the former were not normally beaver hunters.

Within the fur trade, a system of relative status among these groups was developed based upon beaver hunting versus non–beaver hunting, and beaver hunters were given preferential treatment.

As noted above, early in the 19th century there was a break in the Blackfoot's long-standing policy of not allowing fur traders in their country. The Piegan exhibited the most pronounced breakdown of the prohibition, allowing a trading post to be built in their country on the stipulation that they themselves would collect furs. As late as 1834, Maximilian noted that "the proper Blackfeet (Siksekai) and the Blood Indians catch but few beavers, being engaged in war parties, and especially selling meat to the Hudson's Bay Company. The Piekanns, on the other hand, catch the most beaver. Beaver traps (which are lent them) were distributed among them to-day, and many Indians went away to hunt beavers."[113] The historical record indicates, however, that by 1810 individual infractions of the prohibition were occurring among the Blood too. At Rocky Mountain House, for instance, Henry made several references to the Blood bringing beaver pelts to the fort for trade.[114] There does not appear to be any evidence that the Northern Blackfoot ever participated in the trade. First, they were involved in trading less valuable furs, such as wolves and foxes, as well as horses; then, they were major participants in the provisions market; and finally, when the trade in bison robes replaced the provisions market, they became important suppliers of this commodity.

The Gros Ventre also were not beaver hunters throughout the historical period. In 1810, at Rocky Mountain House, where both Blood and Piegan were trading beaver pelts, Henry noted that Gros Ventre traded only horses and wolves.[115] Chardon's journal indicates that even at this later date (1834 to 1839) the main item of trade for the Gros Ventre was the bison robe. The journal occasionally mentions the Gros Ventre bringing a few beaver pelts to the fort for trade; however, the Gros Ventre were infamous for attacking beaver trappers and using their furs as trade items.[116] As Hiram Martin Chittenden noted, "the Grosventres of the Prairies . . . were the most relentlessly hostile tribe ever encountered by the whites in any part of the West, if not in any part of America, and the trapper always understood that to meet with one of these Indians . . . meant instant and deadly hostility."[117] Apparently, these attacks on white trappers continued, as Chardon noted: "Traded a few Beaver skins from the Gros Ventres. . . . No doubt they have Kill'd and pillaged Old Carriere, who was hunting on Powder river."[118] Unfortunately, Chardon did not often distinguish how the beaver pelts brought to the fort had been procured, so the extent of beaver trapping by the Gros Ventre is indeterminate.

The historical record does not appear to suggest that, during the fur trade era, the Plains Assiniboine ever hunted beaver. Lewis and Clark, while travelling on the Missouri River in 1805, noted that "the principal inducement with the British fur companies, for continuing their establishments on the Assiniboine River, is the Buffaloe meat, and grease they procure from the Assiniboins, and Christanoes [Cree]."[119] Mackenzie even suggested that the non-hunting of beaver might have affected Assiniboine settlement patterns. He stated that the Assiniboine and Fall Peoples occupied the central part of the Assiniboine River, whereas the Algonquin and Cree occupied its source and the area near Lake Winnipeg: "They [Assiniboine] are not beaver hunters, which accounts for their allowing the division just mentioned, as the lower and upper parts of this river have those animals, which are not found in the intermediate district."[120]

The evidence regarding the Cree is not conclusive. Some Cree were on the Northern Plains at contact and probably were not beaver hunters. The main body moved onto the prairie at a later date, after acquisition of the horse, and seemed to be in an intermediate phase, exhibiting both woodlands and plains traits. By the time most of the Cree became permanent inhabitants of the prairie, most of the beaver had been trapped out. With regard to the Sarcee, Henry implied that, once in contact with the Blackfoot tribes, they appeared to develop an aversion to beaver hunting.[121] Perhaps this reflected an adherence to Blackfoot policy: friendly groups could trap in Blackfoot territories to the extent that doing so covered their subsistence needs. The Sarcee never settled on the Northern Plains, remaining in wooded areas such as the Beaver Hills and near the mountains. At Rocky Mountain House, the Sarcee were major suppliers of beaver pelts.[122]

CONCLUSION

What brought about erosion of the aversion to beaver hunting among some of the original inhabitants of the plains? Economic pressures—the need for guns and ammunition—were significant, particularly for frontier nations such as the Piegan and Gros Ventre. It is understandable that the Piegan showed the most pronounced breakdown of the prohibition. First, their aversion to beaver hunting was not as strong as that among other Blackfoot tribes, and a small group of Woodlands Piegan in the Rockies had always hunted beaver. The arming of their enemies (the Kutenai, Flathead, and Nez Perce) along the southwestern border, plus the increasing violations of their American territories in the early 19th century by white trappers and American fur companies, made the need for arms crucial. The American fur companies also applied economic pressures on the Piegan. The provisions market was in decline, and the bison robe, which only the American companies would accept, was the main trade item of the Piegan. Faced with these problems, the Piegan allowed the American Fur Company to establish a post in their territories, apparently deciding that if beaver were to be trapped, they themselves might as well be the trappers and reap the benefits.

Interestingly, the Gros Ventre were also a frontier tribe, bearing the brunt of Assiniboine and Cree advances onto the Northern Plains during the early fur trade. Their defeats were attributed to their inferiority in arms, generally accepted as the result of having no market for their less valuable furs. However, they mostly resisted direct beaver trapping, gaining many of their pelts through pillage. Economic pressures also contributed to the breakdown of the prohibition among the Blood. At Rocky Mountain House, Henry observed that "two Blood and their families brought in 14 fresh beavers—the meat, but no skins; these they preserve to enhance the value of the wolves they may kill this winter."[123]

Alcohol was also used to compel Plains communities to hunt fur-bearing animals. As McGillivray noted, "the love of Rum is their first inducement to industry; they undergo every hardship and fatigue to procure a Skinful of this delicious beverage, and when a Nation becomes addicted to drinking, it affords a strong presumption that they will soon become excellent hunters."[124] Commenting on the attack on Fort Piegan by the Blood that was repulsed by Kipp, the fur trader in charge, Chittenden also stressed the use of alcohol to force the Indigenous groups into submission: "Kipp then turned his own weapons of war—the war of the traders—upon the Indians, and poured into them incessant charges of alcohol until the whole band was utterly vanquished and surrendered body and soul to the incomparable trader."[125]

Of equal significance was the fact that the ecological basis of the non-use of beaver resources was weakened. It can be inferred that, prior to contact, the pedestrian peoples of the Northern Plains drew on their ecological knowledge to secure water resources by not hunting beaver. They also learned to manipulate bison herds directly or indirectly through the use of fire.[126] Knowledge of bison behaviour also led to the development of non-disruptive hunting techniques. These strategies allowed for prolonged and repeated use of their residential bases, the most important being wintering areas in Valley Complex systems. Early occupants of the Northern Plains thus became familiar with these areas and their resources. This information was particularly important in the Valley Complex, characterized by pronounced microclimatic variation. During droughts, this knowledge was critical. Familiarity with an area, especially when moving along a migration corridor, gave Plains communities knowledge of which beaver ponds still retained water.

Acquisition of the horse significantly altered previous pedestrian lifeways. First, the horse's mobility allowed for a wider range of resource exploitation and thus lessened dependence on a specific area. Dodge's observations confirm that this mobility provided choices in selecting a wintering area: "Experienced warriors have been sent to all the streams, most loved by the tribe, and to make a thorough examination of all the country. When all have returned a council is held. . . . They are closely questioned as to shelter, wood, water, and grass or cottonwood for the ponies."[127] Second, the chase on horseback, and horse-raiding parties, seriously disrupted bison movements, and there was no guarantee that herds would return to specific areas or remain in them. Third, the horse placed Indigenous groups within striking distance of each other and, with intensifying warfare, placed a premium on mobility. Frequent changes in the residential base might have been necessary for safety.

Although the horse was a major cause of marked changes in the historical period, its mobility in turn provided a solution to some of them. The destruction of beaver populations must have severely reduced the amount of surface water available and limited it to larger waterways, so the horse became vital in searching for pockets of water. Perhaps more important, destruction of the beaver removed it from the ecological dynamics of the Northern Plains ecosystem. It was no longer central to the ecological knowledge of the inhabitants of the plains and remained important only in the ideological dimension.

CONCLUSION

The advent of the fur trade in North America brought into focus the fact that Indigenous communities of the plains were not beaver hunters. Neither the enticement of trade goods nor pressure from fur traders could induce them to begin trapping the beaver for its highly valued pelt. Their aversion had a sound ecological basis that early explorers and fur traders did not comprehend: among Plains groups, the aversion to hunting beaver was based upon recognition of its role in maintaining surface water—a precious resource on the arid plains—in the tributaries of main waterways. Because beaver have a limited distribution and a highly visible and stationary lifestyle, they are susceptible to human overkill, and Plains groups therefore had taboos against hunting them. To kill beaver was to jeopardize water supplies that sustained not only these groups but also the plants and animals on which they relied for their very lives.

In my study area of the Northern Plains, surface water and treed areas are restricted mainly to the valleys of the Qu'Appelle and Saskatchewan Rivers and shallow saline sloughs. Within the Qu'Appelle River Valley Complex of southern Saskatchewan, I selected research sites for ecological and archaeological study along Cottonwood Creek (a small/medium-sized tributary), Moose Jaw River and Wascana Creek (large tributaries), and Qu'Appelle River (the main waterway). I also undertook ecological studies in Elk

Island National Park east of Edmonton to specify the differences and similarities between woodlands and plains ecosystems in the context of human-animal relationships. My model stressed the importance of bison in the subsistence strategies of early Plains Peoples, whose movements were strongly tied to migrations of herds to summer and winter ranges.

Within this annual cycle, local movements and residential bases of Plains communities were regulated by the availability of surface water and treed areas. Beaver and humans shared this habitat. For beaver, trees were necessary for food and construction material for dams and lodges; for humans, trees provided shelter, and those felled by beaver provided dry firewood. Beaver dam-pond systems also attracted a range of animals that became alternative sources of food for the Indigenous inhabitants. Parallel needs thus placed humans and beaver in close association, and conservation rather than exploitation of beaver thus greatly benefited early occupants of the Northern Plains.

Ethnographic studies and the historical record suggest that larger tributaries provided the most favourable wintering areas for these occupants, and ecological studies imply that suitable beaver habitat was most frequently found along such tributaries. During the drought of the mid-1980s in my research area, beaver populations in Cottonwood Creek (a small tributary) were reduced to 0.13 colony per river km. Plains groups became familiar with the various tributaries and their water levels, which fluctuated seasonally and yearly, and this ecological knowledge allowed them to use certain areas repeatedly. Once a suitable wintering area was selected, they were able to remain relatively sedentary for about seven months.

Among the Indigenous Peoples of the plains, an understanding of bison behaviour aided prolonged occupation of wintering areas. Herds remained near winter settlements and could be hunted using techniques (pounds and jumps) that permitted the Indigenous hunters to drive them toward kill sites with a minimum of disruption, an important advantage for pedestrian people during severe winter conditions. In spring, bison herds left sheltered areas and scattered over the prairie, lured by the emergence of new grasses on the uplands. Again, an understanding of environmental conditions allowed early occupants of the Northern Plains to deal with herd dispersal. The prescribed burning of grasslands concentrated herds in preselected areas near spring camps. The Indigenous occupants were thus able to continue communal hunting until most of the bison moved to the summer range. Herds on the summer range would have been dispersed and mobile. Once more, through the prescribed use of fire, Plains communities maintained herds in strategic areas, such as close to water and trees. Similarly, burned areas continued to attract herds in fall, greatly facilitating their hunting at that time of year. These areas would have been fired just prior to the return to the winter range.

By fall, surface water was restricted mainly to river/stream systems, and smaller tributaries served as migration corridors as groups moved through valley systems to their wintering areas beside larger tributaries. The importance of beaver in maintaining surface water became especially evident in fall. In a small tributary, water would have been mostly restricted to beaver-occupied areas, which not only provided crucial water but also attracted elk and deer because of the availability of superior forage.

During a drought cycle, marked changes occur in the Northern Plains environment. The initial stage (the first two years) sees progressive declines in surface water, most pronounced in small tributaries. As Indigenous groups moved along migration corridors to the bison winter range, knowledge of areas that still contained surface water would have been vital. At the height of a drought, winters are usually dry, so spring runoff becomes negligible. Most small tributaries become dry stream beds dotted by isolated beaver ponds. By this time, bison populations would have experienced high mortality. Because of the unavailability of surface water, both human and bison populations would have suspended movements to the summer range. Some areas of large tributaries would also become dry, but evidence points to most beaver-occupied areas being able to withstand a drought. As a result, most wintering sites would not have been affected, and Plains communities would have been able to occupy the most suitable sites. During a drought, many animals, including beaver and large ungulates, are drawn to the main waterway because essential resources (water and forage) are concentrated there. There is a marked drop in the water level and thus reduced stream flow. Beaver are forced to begin constructing dam-pond systems to maintain a sufficient amount of water, again contributing to the maintenance of a scarce resource. Plains groups would have been drawn to these areas, from late spring to late fall, to pound bison off the valley slopes. With winter freeze-up, they would have returned to their winter camps along the larger tributaries.

So, using environmental knowledge as an important part of hunting and gathering strategies, early occupants of the Northern Plains were able to remain relatively sedentary during most of the annual cycle—an important survival factor for peoples with limited mobility. Without beaver, the region would have been inhospitable, particularly during droughts, and beaver dam-pond systems with their focal lodges—oases of water and greenery in a parched landscape—must have had a strong impact on these peoples. Even limited hunting of beaver could affect the availability of surface water and associated resources, so beaver had to be protected. Supernatural control was invoked through traditional stories, ritual, and ceremony. Their stories implied adverse repercussions if beaver were harmed or, conversely, supernatural benefits if they were protected. The above dynamics underpinned the aversion to beaver hunting that the advent of the fur trade brought strongly into focus.

Woodlands Peoples had different relationships with animals. Compared with Plains Peoples, those in the woodlands used a greater variety of animals for food. The moose was the most important, but unlike the bison it was dispersed and hunted only seasonally, in winter. Through the prescribed use of fire, Woodlands communities created browse and graze areas, which attracted and concentrated large game animals, in order to facilitate hunting. The beaver was also an important source of food and, prior to contact, probably hunted mostly in spring and fall. The simplest way to hunt beaver during more temperate conditions was by breaking dams and draining ponds. Because beaver hunting in winter was highly labour intensive, and a good return was not often predictable, it was carried out mainly when large game was scarce. During the historical period, beaver hunting was undertaken in winter mostly because the pelt was most valuable then.

Traditional hunting techniques continued to be used with little modification well into the historical period and, as the historical record clearly shows, had significant impacts on beaver populations. Long before introduction of the steel trap, beaver populations in many northern areas had been destroyed or significantly reduced. This did not occur in earlier times because the demand for beaver, mainly as food (fur was always a surplus), did not exceed supply. It was during the historical period that the need for fur to trade for items becoming essential exceeded food needs and supplies, setting the stage for destruction of the beaver. The historical record also indicates that beaver populations were high prior to the fur trade. In fact, the Woodlands communities might have been faced with an overabundance of beaver and the effects of their activities, such as inundation of browse/grass areas that were important food sources for large game animals, consequently resulting in their dispersal. My research in Elk Island National Park confirmed that the inundation of such areas in a woodlands biome, in which beaver populations are high, markedly exceeded the areas opened up by beaver activity. In other words, beaver-induced flooding appreciably reduces the food resources of ungulates.

With their knowledge of animal behaviour and fire ecology, Woodlands Peoples came up with a solution. They created beaver meadows that not only provided grassy areas for large herbivores but also controlled beaver. Breaking dams and draining ponds served a dual purpose: they were both an effective technique for beaver hunting and the initial phase in creating a beaver meadow. Such a meadow has special attributes that facilitate its maintenance. The soils are toxic to tree and shrub species for up to 10 years, and the first species to invade the meadow are important browse species such as willow and alder. To prevent beaver from reoccupying a meadow, the people burned its peripheries every three or four years to stop new growth of aspen.

Several parallels can be drawn between Plains and Woodlands groups. For both, environmental knowledge was vital in hunting and gathering practices. Since both groups tended to return to specific areas during their annual life cycles, they used their knowledge of fire ecology and animal behaviour to steer large game animals toward their residential areas, thus facilitating hunting and prolonging occupancy. Intentional burning was more important among the

Woodlands communities since it created new habitats (open grassland/shrub areas) for game animals. For the Plains communities, beaver-occupied areas served much the same purpose, attracting game animals because of water and superior forage.

It was in their relationships with beaver that we find major differences related to environmental conditions. On the plains, beaver dam-pond systems maintained surface water, mainly within the parameters of waterways, and flooding was not common. Beaver were not abundant; Plains Peoples thus refrained from hunting them. In the woodlands, beaver were abundant and an important source of food, and their activities generally resulted in the flooding of important browse/graze areas and the subsequent dispersal of large game animals. Woodlands Peoples were thus not averse to hunting beaver for either their flesh or their fur.

During the early contact period, observations by fur traders such as Henday and Cocking confirmed the non-use of beaver by Indigenous groups that had entered the Northern Plains as pedestrian peoples before acquisition of the horse. The Blackfoot and Gros Ventre exchanged less valuable furs (wolves and foxes), horses, and bison-skin garments for metal goods, guns, and ammunition. Some Cree exhibited plains traits such as pounding bison and hunting wolves. As early as the beginning of the 18th century, the Plains Assiniboine were already identified as not being beaver hunters. Some plains-oriented traits that had developed by this time included abandonment of the canoe, non-hunting of beaver, primary reliance on bison for subsistence, and development of communal hunting techniques such as jumps and pounds.

The archaeological survey that I undertook along Wascana and Cottonwood Creeks was intended to test my hypotheses related to settlement patterns of early occupants of the Northern Plains. If a large tributary provided the most suitable wintering area, then evidence of large winter camp sites should be found along such tributaries. Of the 15 sites designated as winter camp sites along the tributaries surveyed, whose survey areas were of comparable extent, 13 (87%) were located along Wascana Creek. I also proposed that the limited water of a small tributary would have made camp sites along it more temporary, and I found that 10 (66%) of the 15 sites were temporary based upon the archaeological evidence. I also predicted that along the main waterway (the Qu'Appelle River), inaccessibility to treed areas (shelter) because of the considerable extent of the floodplain would have acted against its suitability as a wintering area. Only 2 (3%) of 74 recognized sites in the area were found along the main waterway.

In the historical period, direct trading between Indigenous groups and fur traders favoured groups who trapped beaver for their pelts, putting Plains communities at a disadvantage. Beaver hunters such as Woodlands Cree and Assiniboine were given preferential treatment. Increasing animosities among groups made possession of guns and ammunition crucial, and because most Plains groups traded in less valuable furs they were unable to buy a sufficient supply of arms. The defeat of the Gros Ventre by the Cree was attributed to this factor and led to their abandonment of the upper Qu'Appelle and lower Saskatchewan Valleys. Similarly, the newly armed Salish went on the offensive, and the Piegan were forced to retreat, giving up part of the bison range. Because they did not hunt beaver, the Piegan and Gros Ventre suffered both military defeats and detrimental territorial realignments. Conditions became even more precarious when the HBC not only devalued by half the wolf pelt (a major trade item) but also ordered that as few as possible be purchased. The Plains Assiniboine worked around this problem by trading horses for guns from their allies, the Cree. The Blackfoot and Gros Ventre circumvented the prohibition against beaver hunting to some extent by confiscating pelts from trappers and trading them at posts. Although Plains communities continued to adhere to their policy of not hunting beaver, by the end of the 18th century beaver had been trapped out in many areas. Blame can be placed on several groups: the Woodlands Assiniboine and Cree and the Sarcee; the Eastern Woodlands groups, particularly the Iroquois; free Canadians; and company servants.

The early 19th century witnessed the first break in the long-standing policy of the Blackfoot tribes not to allow traders in their country. The Piegan, who had also begun to trap beaver, allowed a fort to be built in their country on the stipulation that they themselves would collect the furs. This event also signalled the beginning of animosities between the Piegan and other members of the Blackfoot

Nation (Blood and Blackfoot proper). By this time, some infractions of the prohibition against beaver hunting were beginning to occur among the Blood. The historical record contains no evidence that the Blackfoot proper, Gros Ventre, or Plains Assiniboine ever actively participated in the trapping of beaver. The greatest aversion to beaver hunting was witnessed among the Blackfoot nations, who are generally acknowledged to be the earliest inhabitants of the Northern Plains. The evidence for the Cree is more equivocal. Some Cree were on the prairie at contact and showed signs of being non–beaver hunters. The main body moved onto the plains at a later date, after acquisition of the horse, and appear to have been in an intermediate phase, exhibiting both woodlands and plains traits of trapping beaver and pounding bison, respectively.

The developing provisions market eventually provided Plains communities with the means to obtain sufficient trade goods, including arms, and gave them some independence from fur traders. However, with amalgamation of the two fur trade companies, many men were released from service and became serious competitors with Plains people in the provisions market. By this time, however, a reduced provisions market was counterbalanced by an increased market for bison robes.

The prohibition against beaver hunting eroded for several reasons: economic pressures, intensifying animosities, and dependence on alcohol, which increasingly made Indigenous Peoples more susceptible to the persuasions of traders. More specifically, several events led to the decision of the Piegan to allow traders in their country: the arming of their enemies, the Kutenai and Salish; the increasing encroachment on their territories by white trappers and fur trade companies; and the need to appease the American Fur Company, which provided the only market for their bison robes. Also important was the fact that the environmental basis for the non-use of beaver was weakened with acquisition of the horse, the consequences of which significantly altered pedestrian lifeways. Whereas the presence of beaver had been important for securing and maintaining surface water, allowing early plains occupants to return to specific areas, the mobility of the horse allowed for a wider range of resource exploitation. Dependency on a specific geographic area was no longer crucial. In fact, the mobility provided by the horse placed groups within striking distance of each other and made mobility crucial, with frequent changes in the residential base necessary for safety.

In addition, chasing bison on horseback, engaging in horse raiding, and using fire as an economic weapon seriously disrupted bison movements. It was no longer possible to predict when bison would come near or which areas they would frequent. Bison drives were discontinued because the chase disrupted the predictable patterns upon which they were based: movements of herds to specific areas and specific herd behaviour that could be manipulated to bring the animals to kill sites. Paradoxically, while acquisition of the horse and development of new hunting techniques using it created such uncertainties, mobility provided by the horse increasingly offered solutions but further intensified conditions. The advent of the horse was a major factor in the nomadism that pervaded the historical period.

An important question raised by my research along the Qu'Appelle River and its tributaries is whether, considering the pronounced microclimatic variability associated with the Valley Complex, it is applicable to other areas of the Northern Plains. The broad assumptions presented here should be relevant within a wider geographical framework. Perhaps the most important assumption is that, because surface water is limited on the prairie, beaver activity is important in stabilizing and maintaining this crucial resource. Parallel needs placed beaver and early occupants of the Northern Plains in close association along larger tributaries of main waterways and allowed these occupants to remain settled in winter camp sites for many months. Smaller tributaries, because of their limited surface water, only infrequently provided the conditions necessary for winter occupation, and along any specific tributary local microclimatic conditions would affect such occupation. A natural spring might enhance surface water and thus increase the frequency, whereas a cobblestone substratum would act against beaver occupation and thus decrease the frequency.

On the Northern Plains, ecological differences are pronounced when the Qu'Appelle River and Saskatchewan River Valley Complexes are compared. The former is a prior glacial spillway, explaining its distinct geological features: an underfed stream in an extremely broad floodplain. The latter is of preglacial origin[1] and was thus formed by different geological processes. Its distinctive features are the results of erosion from water originating in the Rocky Mountains. As a consequence, it is deeply incised with extremely narrow floodplains. Both features—the broad and treeless floodplains of the Qu'Appelle River and the general absence of suitable floodplains of the Saskatchewan River—limited these waterways as wintering areas for early Plains Peoples. Hence, their contrasting ecological features do not contradict the general patterns of human settlement predicted by my model.

The ethnohistorical record also strongly implies that the aversion to beaver hunting has broader geographic applicability to the Central and Southern Plains. The Hidatsa, village tribes along the Missouri River, were reluctant to hunt beaver. As fur trader Charles MacKenzie observed, "beaver were plentiful, but the Indians will not take the trouble of attending them."[2] Prior to contact, the Cheyenne were not beaver hunters.[3] Citing ethnographic references, Alice Marriott noted that the Osage considered beaver their ancestors and did not kill them.[4] Likewise, the Shoshone were not fur trappers, and free trappers took most of the furs from their lands.[5] Among the Comanche, the Beaver Ceremony was the most powerful of all curing ceremonies. During the ritual, beaver ponds and effigies were reconstructed.[6]

The evidence thus strongly suggests that the aversion to beaver hunting occurred within a larger framework, the North American Plains. At the advent of the fur trade, this aversion came to the fore, and, if European explorers and fur traders did not understand the sound ecological reasoning behind it, Plains Peoples certainly did. Their very lives depended on a close association with beaver in Valley Complex systems to secure water, shelter, and firewood, especially during their occupancy of winter camp sites and during times of drought. Without beaver activity, the Great Plains would have been an inhospitable place.

AFTERWORD

CULTURAL KEYSTONE SPECIES AND TRADITIONAL ECOLOGICAL KNOWLEDGE ON THE NORTHERN PLAINS AND BEYOND

Cristina Eisenberg

Since 2006, I have studied food-web relationships and Indigenous knowledge, focusing on bison, fire, and wolves in the Fescue Prairie of southwest Alberta. I partner in this work with
the Canadian federal government in Waterton Lakes National
Park, Alberta; with the Kainai (Blood) First Nation, a member of the
Blackfoot Confederacy, on the Blood Timber Limit and the Blood
Ranch; and, since 2014, with Earthwatch Institute, the non-profit organization that funds my research. As a Western-trained scientist of
mixed Indigenous descent, I have learned that parsing the ecology of
this landscape using Indigenous knowledge about the ancient ecological relationships here provides the most effective path to restoring a
prairie degraded by 19th-century Euro-American colonialism.[1] Killing all the beavers, bison, and wolves, and eliminating fire to advance
capitalism, including modern agriculture, industrial forestry, mining,
and energy extraction, profoundly degraded a once healthy, productive landscape.[2] Climate change is exacerbating these impacts.
In working to understand the ecological damage done by colonialism and help heal it, I have found much inspiration and wisdom in

Dr. Grace Morgan's visionary work, in which she identifies the relationships between people, beaver, and bison essential to restoring ecological well-being to this land.

Two personal experiences within the past week highlight the relevance and need for more widespread knowledge of Dr. Morgan's work. First, in a collaboration on a policy document with a colleague who is a Western scientist, this individual sent back my draft document about Indigenous knowledge of relationships in the natural world with a comment that I should temper my words, because, after all, Indigenous people were responsible for the last megafaunal extinction ca. 10,000 BCE. As the Western science story goes, early humans arrived in North America via the Bering Land Bridge ca. 12,000 BCE and most large-bodied mammals became extinct shortly thereafter, primarily due to overhunting by humans. Second, a graduate student who interned on my research project in southwest Alberta wrote an essay based on his time afield with me in which he explains that "primitive man" arrived in North America only very recently via the Bering Land Bridge, although there are speculative hypotheses about human movement into the Americas earlier by boat across the ocean and then up the Pacific Coast. The colonialist bias in the statements of these two well-intentioned, educated individuals illustrates the importance of publishing Dr. Morgan's book, *Beaver, Bison, Horse: The Traditional Knowledge and Ecology of the Northern Great Plains.*

In responding to these colleagues, I explained that abundant data clearly demonstrate that the Late Pleistocene megafaunal extinctions had multivariate causes, including climate change, with humans but one contributing factor; that early human presence in North America went back far before those extinctions; and that these Indigenous Peoples had sophisticated ways of stewarding the land.[3] While Indigenous settlement of North America and Pleistocene megafaunal extinction are not the primary focus of *Beaver, Bison, Horse*, Dr. Morgan capably addresses both. In response to questions about these topics and others, I look forward to soon being able to simply hand copies of her book to colleagues and say, "Read this." I am deeply honoured to have been invited to contextualize her brilliant work within the challenging socio-ecological landscape we are navigating today in our rapidly warming world.

OF KEYSTONES AND TRADITIONAL ECOLOGICAL KNOWLEDGE

Dr. Morgan's research was based on the knowledge held by Indigenous people worldwide that while all life-forms touch humans, some species are more important to human survival than others, so much so that they have the capacity to shape the cultural identity of the people who rely on them. These species become ingrained in people's songs, ceremonies, dances, stories, and ethos.[4] Awareness that some species are more powerful than others and are necessary for the health and well-being of whole human and non-human communities inspired the Western science concept of *keystone species*.

In 1969, ecologist Robert Paine introduced the term "keystone species," originally intending it to apply to food-web relationships in which a dominant predator consumes and controls the abundance of a particular prey species, a herbivore, which in turn competes against and dominates other herbivore species. He envisioned this metaphorical ecological concept functioning similarly to a Roman arch: when you remove the keystone, arches and ecosystems collapse.[5] Since then, scientists have broadened the concept to include non-carnivorous species that exert strong influence on whole food webs, such as beaver and bison. These species can be thought of as *ecosystem engineers*, whose absence can potentially intensively alter and diminish ecosystem function.[6] By their very presence, they benefit myriad others, increasing biodiversity and resiliency to climate change.[7] These effects are called *trophic cascades* ("trophic" means related to food).[8]

Rooted in Western science, Paine's insights about keystone species were based on the multifactorial replicated experiments he conducted in the intertidal community in Washington State, working with sea stars (*Pisaster* spp.). Going far beyond Western science, Dr. Morgan's work demonstrates that the concept of a particular species shaping whole ecosystems is ancient and indeed is foundational to the Indigenous view of the earth.[9] More recently, ecologists and Indigenous scholars Ann Garibaldi and Nancy Turner linked the traditional way of seeing relationships in the natural world that Dr. Morgan depicts in her work to Western science by creating the term "cultural keystone species," defined as "culturally salient species that shape in a major way the cultural identity of a people. Their importance is reflected in the fundamental roles these species play in diet, materials, medicine, and/or spiritual practices."[10]

As is the case with ecological keystone species, cultural keystone species are context dependent. This means a species may not have the same function or value for all Indigenous groups or members of a group. Dr. Morgan discussed such nuances when she contrasted the relationships between the Woodlands communities and the Plains communities and the beaver, with the first group killing beaver for their pelts for trade purposes and the second group having strong taboos that prohibited use of beaver as food or for their fur. Beaver trapping was a key part of colonizing Canada, so much so that the nation can almost be said to have been founded on the pelts of dead beavers. However, the Plains communities were not involved in this slaughter.[11] Why? This difference can be explained by the different relationship the Woodlands groups had with water (mesic environment, abundant water) compared with the Plains groups (arid environment, scarce water). Dr. Morgan illustrated the complex contextual nature of these relationships with the Cree, who had groups living on the plains and others living in woodlands. She showed how even within one community, based on where people lived, relationships with beaver were different. As Garibaldi and Turner explain it,

> The cultural value of a cultural keystone depends on the community's ability to use it for food, material, or technology or in narratives or spiritual practices. Cultural keystone species are expressed along temporal, spatial, and social axes, varying from one culture to another and from one region to another. Some may play key social roles within a restricted time, space, or social context, whereas others may be more widely recognized for a longer period and in a broader social context.[12]

Ecosystems are not just assemblages of organisms; they are expressions of human, floral, and faunal co-evolution in response to past environmental conditions. They are shaped by Traditional Ecological Knowledge (TEK): knowledge and practices passed as stories and songs from generation to generation informed by strong cultural practices and rituals, such as traditional dances. TEK includes sensitivity to change and *reciprocity*, that is, a give-and-take relationship with nature that acknowledges a responsibility to care for and respect the rights of all living beings.[13]

Tewa anthropologist Gregory Cajete coined the term "ecosophy," also known as Native science, to describe TEK and sees it as an epistemological way of living in the world.[14] Unlike Western science, TEK observations are qualitative and long term and are about context and relationships.[15] Observers tend to be people engaged in subsistence practices, such as hunting, fishing, and gathering. Their survival is linked to the health of the land. Most importantly, TEK is inseparable from a culture's spiritual and social fabric. In the Indigenous worldview, according to Anishinaabe ecologist Robin Wall Kimmerer, it takes all of what it means to be human—body, mind, heart, and spirit—to understand something ecologically.[16] This means that TEK offers not only important ecological insights but also a cultural framework that includes values that can help solve environmental problems. In the process, Cajete suggests, Native science creates an *ensoulment* of nature, a spiritual ecology, and an Indigenous map of the world.[17] Moreover, TEK and Native science do not see nature and "sustainability" through a Western materialistic, command-and-control Pinchovian lens. Instead, according to O'odham ecologist Dennis Martinez, TEK redefines sustainability as a *kincentric* view of nature: "an ancient way of being with nature, not only with plants and animals, but with the primal natural forces of fire, water, wind, and earth—a way of relating respectfully to all life as kin and the earth as a nurturing mother."[18]

TEK practices increase biodiversity and ecological resiliency by creating fine-grained, patchy landscape mosaics. Used by Indigenous people for millennia to increase natural production of food and medicine, these practices include setting fires to modify vegetation and coexisting with and honouring beavers as the cultural keystone species that they are.[19] TEK includes selectively gathering certain plants and letting others rest, and for precontact agricultural people, such as the Algonquian tribes in what is today called New England or the Masai in Kenya, planting crops and grazing cattle in rotational cycles so as to not deplete the soil and grasslands, instead leaving the land enriched by these practices. Along these lines, Dr. Morgan considered the beaver the "sacred cow" of the plains, as described in chapter 2 of this book. Her ideas were influenced by *cultural materialism*: the concept that ethics and values drive a culture's relations to the environment, including how they sustain themselves.[20] Northern Plains communities knew something else about the relationship between themselves, the beaver, and water. Dr. Morgan demonstrated with her research that these tribes knew that water was life. They learned through observation that beavers helped create an ecological oasis within a dry and arid landscape. They discovered that protecting beavers would enable human access to water and food, thereby ensuring human survival and well-being.

Ecological restoration is the process of assisting the recovery of an ecosystem that has been degraded, damaged, or destroyed. The science of repairing the damage done to ecosystems is called restoration ecology.[21] Today Western science is learning what Indigenous people have always known: that sustaining cultural keystone species and using TEK practices, such as prescribed fire, can be one of the most effective ways to restore ecosystems and that saving nature means saving ourselves.[22] Dr. Morgan's 1990s work on fire and bison in Elk Island National Park, Alberta—in which she found that fire and bison interacted to create healthier, more vigorous grasslands, in keeping with Northern Plains TEK about using fire to improve bison habitat and bison carrying capacity—provides a compelling example of how TEK can inform ecological restoration efforts today.[23]

As Dr. Morgan so effectively demonstrated, oral histories and cultural artifacts such as the Beaver Medicine Bundle can inform restoration efforts directly, from planning through implementation and monitoring, by providing a baseline and guidelines—a reference system for ecological restoration. However, oral histories have only recently been allowed to inform restoration. The colonial epistemologies and methodologies and their ideological and rhetorical validity for Western science so prevalent when Dr. Morgan did her research on bison and beavers created an academic environment in which TEK oral histories were not respected or fully acknowledged. However, this is changing thanks to her persevering work and the work of many other Indigenous scholars, such as Leroy Little Bear and Robin Wall Kimmerer, as well as Dr. Morgan's own former student, settler-scholar James Daschuk. This change is due in part to her legacy and her enduring vision.

* * *

The story of the Beaver Medicine Bundle, as Dr. Morgan explains early in her text, is considered one of the oldest and most sacred, and it warrants inclusion here, but with care and respect I have chosen only to point to it, for the message is powerful and the strong influence it had and continues to have on the Blackfoot and other Northern Plains communities is vital and significant. A version of it is found in *The Old North Trail* by Walter McClintock.[24] In 1886 McClintock journeyed to northwest Montana as a member of a US Forest Service expedition. Chief Mad Dog, the high priest of the Sun Dance, adopted him as a son, and McClintock spent the next four years with the Blackfoot. He tells the story he learned about the Beaver Medicine Bundle from the Chief and that story—its spirit and the Beaver Medicine Bundle and all it signifies as I understand it as an Indigenous woman—is what I believe lies at the core of Dr. Morgan's work. As an anthropologist and ecologist, Dr. Morgan dug deeply to show the powerful connections between oral tradition and cultural artifacts and to explore why such oral histories are as relevant and critical to today as they have always been. Today, Northern Plains communities continue to keep the Beaver Medicine Bundle. Indeed, one of the field technicians on my fire and bison ecology project is a keeper of this bundle. He is working on his Bachelor of Science degree in natural resources management, incorporating trophic cascades and Western science into Native science, inspired by his sacred stories, but also by visionary work like that of Dr. Morgan's.

* * *

The late Blackfoot Elder Narcisse Blood—who was an Oxford University scholar, University of Lethbridge professor, and one of the leaders of the Blackfoot Confederacy effort to repatriate their cultural artifacts and traditions and restore species such as bison, beavers, and wolves—understood these relationships well.[25] According to Narcisse, from a Native science perspective, trophic cascades and keystone species concepts made perfect sense, because they align closely with Blackfoot traditional ways of viewing relationships in the natural world. "All that trophic cascades science is really a no-brainer," Narcisse said one night when he and his wife, Alvine Mountainhorse, visited me at the fieldhouse in Waterton Lakes National Park, where I was working. He laughed and said, "It just explains how the world works—or should work, if modern humans didn't keep mucking things up. We Blackfoot always have known about the 'web of life,' as you call it. Everything is connected. You touch one species, and all the others feel it. Bison, beavers, wolves, fire—they created our world and held it together."[26]

Narcisse and I talked about how if we let bison return, they also will keep elk moving, in the process creating more varied, rich vegetation—a mosaic of native grasses interspersed with smaller patches of shrubs. This improves habitat for many other species. And if we allow the return of fire, which was present in this community for thousands of years until Euro-American settlers suppressed it, energy begins to move through this ecosystem more rapidly and plants begin to grow more vigorously. These linked relationships keep the whole community—pollinators, birds, beavers, bison, elk, wolves, and people—healthy and thriving.

The Beaver Medicine Bundle has particular significance to me as an ecologist doing research in Waterton Lakes National Park because, according to oral history, *Ksisskstaki* (Beaver) gave the bundle to *Niisitapi* (the Blackfoot) at a lake that is in my study site. This oral history is so important to the Blackfoot that in the mid-1990s, Narcisse was involved in repatriating the Beaver Medicine Bundle. The bundle had been acquired by Euro-Americans, as were many cultural artifacts between the 1800s and early 1900s. Narcisse and his colleagues obtained it from the Peabody Museum, near Boston, and brought it home to their community in Alberta, where he was among those who then kept it and honoured it.[27] That bundle exemplifies so many things—among them, Native science and how it can save nature today.

The night he came over for dinner to the Waterton research house was the last time I would see Narcisse, although this great man became my mentor and friend. Over the years we often exchanged humour and hope, in equal measure. In February 2015, Narcisse had been advising me about deepening and expanding my research, in which I was investigating how two primal forces of nature, wolves and fire, work together to shape ecosystems. He had asked me to think about bison—the "what if" of their return here. He'd also asked me to consider extending our research onto Indigenous land. To further explore these ideas, he and Alvine had made plans to join me and my crew afield. Days later I learned that Narcisse had died in a three-car collision, which had taken several other lives as well, outside of Regina. And today I am working on Kainai land as he had suggested, with the support and collaboration of the community.

TROPHIC MEDICINE BUNDLES

How do beaver and bison function as cultural keystone species? Dr. Morgan found that in a drought-prone ecoregion, such as the Northern Plains, beavers, because of their ability to alter streamflow and impound water through their dam building, create oases of water in an otherwise dry environment. This in turn sustained bison, people, and other beings through the long winter season, even in drought years. Accordingly, in winter, Plains communities would move their camps to riparian areas, which had beaver-created reliable water sources. Here the population found the many things they needed to sustain them, because beavers, by impounding water, created habitat for plants such as berry-producing shrubs, willows, and trees, as well as habitat for animals such as deer and bison. Since the Northern Plains winter lasts roughly from early November until late April, beaver communities were critical to human survival throughout the year.

Recently, scientists from the University of Alberta measured the role beavers play in creating and maintaining wetlands. They found that beavers increase the volume-to-surface area ratio of wetlands by 50% and wetland perimeters by more than 575%. Beavers also increase stream-channel length and width, thereby creating a more complex, heterogeneous landscape. These scientists concluded that removal of this ecosystem engineer can reduce ecological resiliency, and conversely, restoring beavers can create healthier landscapes, particularly in drought-prone areas.[28] Additionally, in a world where humanity is struggling to retain carbon stores, scientists are finding that beavers can help significantly with this. Ecologist Ellen Wohl found that beaver ponds and beaver-created wetlands store 23% of the carbon in a landscape and that these benefits apply in North and South America, and in Europe and Asia, wherever this broadly distributed species historically existed.[29] Collectively, this recent research confirms Dr. Morgan's earlier work but also expands its influence and relevance with regard to our current awareness of the importance of healthy grasslands and riparian areas as carbon sinks in this era of rapid climate change.

In North America, prior to contact with Euro-American settlers, beaver communities drew human communities and bison. These relationships were ancient, as the Beaver Medicine Bundle attests. A recent large wildfire in my study site in Waterton Lakes National Park revealed the depth of this beaver medicine.[30] In September 2017, the lightning-caused Kenow wildfire burned most of the park with extreme severity, including every tree and shrub to the point that few survived. In spring 2018, I went into the park to survey the damage. The snow had recently melted, revealing a landscape powerfully transformed by wildfire. I was there with my field crew, which consisted of my field technicians as well as ten students and four teachers from Kainai High School, there as Earthwatch Community Conservation Fellows to learn field methods and teach me about their oral history and TEK. Generous grants from the Kainai Board of Education, the AGL Foundation, and the Davin Family Fund supported this program, then in its third year, and these fellows. As part of the process of reconciliation, students were learning ecological restoration within a research project rooted in their traditional ways. Our objective was to empower these young people to heal the damage that colonialism has done to their land. Elliot Fox led my mostly Kainai field staff, who functioned as role models for the students and as mentors for me in helping increase my awareness of prairie ecology from a TEK perspective. A member of the Kainai First Nation, Elliot had worked for the Blood Tribe Lands Department for years, leading his community's natural resources conservation program. We were very fortunate to have him working on our project as a field technician.

The conflagration had been so extreme that it had incinerated the ground, removing as much as two feet of topsoil in some places. I knew so because years earlier I had placed rebar stakes in the ground to permanently mark plots in which I'd been measuring biodiversity by counting songbirds. To make these metal markers unobtrusive, I'd set them so that only one foot was exposed. Now three feet of rebar were exposed above the soil surface. In many places, the wildfire had effectively removed the earth's "skin," revealing amazing things. Exposed roots lay everywhere: aspen roots, pale grey, and also the distinctive russet, tangled roots of kinnikinnick—roots normally buried under two feet of soil. Fascinated, I explored an erstwhile aspen stand with the students. Astonished and enthralled by the revelations of the wildfire, we began to find things besides roots. One young woman picked up the jawbone of what turned out to be a wolf—an ancient bone from the weathered, yellowed looks of it. Another student picked up the skull of a beaver. Nearby were some stone tools that looked human-made. Given that it takes a thousand years for an inch and a half of soil to form in this part of the West, those bones could've been as much as 10,000 years old. Kainai technician Alex Shade found an intact bison skull on the ground. Judging from its jutting horns, which were far straighter than those of a modern bison, it was likely the skull of a *Bison antiquus*, a Pleistocene species that had become extinct 10,000 years ago.

Kainai Elder and anthropology PhD student Mike Bruised Head said it was probably a young buffalo that had been trampled in a stampede to a nearby cliff. He shared stories about how his Blackfoot ancestors had used this landscape to run these animals over cliffs, called buffalo jumps. The animals would plummet to their deaths, to be harvested by the community for food. A Blackfoot tradition, burning made the grasses sprout more vigorously, in effect "calling in" the bison. Dr. Morgan had examined these relationships in Elk Island National Park, where managers treated the prairie with fire to improve habitat for bison.[31] As Mike Bruised Head explained it, Native science was inseparable from Blackfoot spirituality, which incorporated their deep connections to the beaver, and to the bison and wolves that roamed that land, whom they saw as teachers. That day, we stood there in reverie, bearing witness to the antiquity of the relationships we were studying. Mike made a tobacco offering. We left the buffalo skull and the other discoveries where we found them, as they had lain for millennia.

* * *

Indigenous Peoples frequently set fires to improve wildlife habitat. These light fires created early-seral plant communities, increased berry-producing shrub yield for deer and elk, and kept grasslands open for bison, in this manner improving subsistence resources for humans.[32] On the Northern Plains, Indigenous Peoples set fires in the late-spring dormant growing season but in other regions (e.g., the midwestern United States) set them later in the year. Dormant-season fires occur when there is less above-ground annual growth of perennial grasses and shrubs to burn, resulting in lower fire severity and improved forage.[33] Late growing-season fires occur when grasses and shrubs are tall and dry. Because the biomass of above-ground fuels at that time is greater, these fires can be higher in severity than dormant-season fires and do more damage to plant communities.[34] In my southwest Alberta study site, Waterton's prescribed fire program is an attempt to return the foothills-parkland ecoregion within the park to historic conditions (e.g., more open grassland; smaller, more structurally complex aspen stands), based in part on Indigenous fire regimes in this landscape. The Kenow wildfire was the first wildfire that had burned in my study site in over 100 years.

Native grasslands have been declining in North America in general and in the Waterton foothills-parkland ecoregion since the 1880s.[35] Ecologists attribute this to several factors: elimination of bison and wildfire, introduction of non-native agronomic grass species, and suppression of the prescribed fires set by Indigenous people.[36] Today parks like Elk Island and Waterton are reinstating these relationships by reintroducing prescribed fire and a full suite of native wildlife, from beavers to wolves. And communities like the Kainai First Nation are working to rekindle prescribed burning on their rangelands. However, as Dr. Morgan pointed out, there's still something missing from the Northern Plains, and that missing piece is the bison.[37]

The Iinnii Initiative (the Blackfoot term *Iinnii* means buffalo), a partnership between the Wildlife Conservation Society, the Blackfoot Confederacy, and several Canadian and US government agencies, aims to restore bison to Blackfoot lands that span the US-Canadian border. Other conservation organizations, such as the World Wildlife Fund and the American Prairie Reserve, are collaborating in this effort. Accordingly, the Iinnii Initiative has been making strong progress toward establishing the policy and partnerships that would enable bison reintroduction on the Northern Plains (e.g., on the Blackfeet Reservation in Montana, where a currently captive herd of what were originally 88 animals sourced from Elk Island is being held, and in the Chief Mountain area, which would include Waterton and the Blood Timber Limit). This initiative is encouraging a shift in the management status of this species at provincial and state levels in Canada and the United States from "livestock" to "wildlife." Currently, this North American species has "Near Threatened" status on the International Union for the Conservation of Nature (IUCN) Red List of Threatened Species.[38]

Dr. Morgan and others have found that the presence of bison, a primarily grass-eating species, increases prairie biodiversity and resiliency to climate change.[39] This ecosystem engineer's grazing patterns include several-hundred-kilometre seasonal migrations, which intensively alter the biophysical environment. Bison fertilize the soil with their urine; they horn up saplings and shrubs, keeping grasslands open. Like a domino effect, a bison's presence in an ecosystem improves soil resources available to other species, changes plant and animal composition, and increases biodiversity and energy cycling, creating communities more resilient to climate change, although these effects are quite complex.[40]

However, in order to be ecologically effective, ideally bison must be wild and free-ranging. Captive bison (those confined within fences) can have similar ecological impacts as introduced, non-native domestic cattle and can produce overgrazed, ecologically degraded pasture conditions, if not managed properly.[41] Since less than 3% of historic fescue grasslands remain in North America—attributed to the elimination of bison and fire—restoring a keystone species linked to grassland resiliency is a conservation priority.[42]

While Indigenous people have long seen bison as central to their world, Euro-Americans only very recently acknowledged this species' full importance. In May 2016, US president Barack Obama signed the National Bison Legacy Act, adopting the bison as the national mammal. Subsequent legislative actions that may facilitate recovering wild, free-ranging bison (e.g., retirement of gas leases in the Badger–Two Medicine region of northwest Montana) demonstrate how broader political geographies and biophysical changes, such as Indigenous Peoples' repatriation and climate change, affect conservation at national and local levels. In North America, much progress is being made in bison restoration. However, the question remains: Are we moving rapidly enough with these efforts to enable bison to mitigate the impacts of climate change?[43]

A FOOD WEB UNRAVELLED BY COLONIALISM

The arrival of the horse portended the end of the harmonious eco-cultural relationships I described earlier, which had been in place for millennia.[44] The horse was ostensibly a gift that enabled rapid motion across the plains and more efficient hunting, yet Dr. Morgan presents an incisive analysis of the havoc this cultural keystone from another world created on the Northern Plains. Environmental historians concur. According to Flores, Native Americans on horseback were "out of balance" with trophic relationships on the plains that had been finely calibrated since the Late Pleistocene epoch.[45] Dr. Morgan elaborated on this, demonstrating that by moving the bison out of their traditional migration corridors, Indigenous hunters on horseback ended up disturbing the lifeways of the Plains communities. Horses also competed with bison for forage. During drought years, as horse numbers increased, this reduced the carrying capacity of the landscape for bison, contributing to a death spiral toward rapid extinction for this species.[46] Additionally, horses became vectors for diseases that killed both bison and humans.[47] When combined with extreme exploitation of the beaver for fur, to the point of extinction, this unravelled the ecology of the Northern Plains and, with it, the lifeways of the Plains communities.

RESTORING THE NORTHERN PLAINS AND BEYOND

In 2016, I spent time in Kenya with doctoral student Caroline Ng'weno, on a project funded by Earthwatch Institute, where I work as chief scientist. There, just north of Mount Kenya, in a semi-arid shrub-steppe grassland, the Masai people were reclaiming their traditional ways, and Caroline was using Western science to study the effects of this on food-web ecology.[48] Agriculture and cattle ranching had been part of Masai culture for several thousand years. Indeed, as in many other parts of Africa, their cattle were native to that landscape, never introduced from Europe as in so many places today.[49]

On Masai land, trophic relationships and TEK entailed using *bomas*—small, portable temporary corrals constructed of interlaced logs and branches—to confine cattle at high density at a particular site so they could graze intensively for short periods. After a week or two, the Masai would remove the boma and move the cattle to another location. This conveyed huge ecological benefits to the whole food web, because these cattle ate certain species of grasses selectively and left others alone. In the process, the cattle also deposited as much as one foot of fresh dung, fixing nitrogen within the boma with this powerful fertilizer. This caused grasses to sprout more vigorously than they would without this intensive grazing and resulted in increased pollinator and arthropod diversity.

Dr. Morgan found similar relationships in Elk Island National Park. Specifically, working with a captive bison population, she found that bison feces and urine increased nutrient availability for other species; bison grazing stimulated higher foliar crude protein levels in grasses, which benefited other grazing animals; and spring burning of secondary habitat shifted grazing pressure and improved grassland health and vigour. She recommended to the park that fire and grazing by bison were both essential to maintain grassland health and that without these "natural stimuli," grasslands would become degraded. Bison expert Wes Olson, the Elk Island warden who assisted Dr. Morgan logistically and accompanied her in the field in the 1990s, today is one of the key individuals involved in bison repatriation and conservation in Canada. Of her bison, fire, and herbivory work, he said, "I don't think I've seen a better description of the role of bison dung pats in a burned landscape. The well-described complexities associated with the time of year when the dung was deposited, within-dung moisture and below-dung moisture, fire severity and the effects on soil bacteria, and plant protein levels, all make this remarkable work." According to Olson, Dr. Morgan's work significantly predated much research on bison, fire, and herbivory.[50] In many ways, Dr. Morgan's Elk Island research foresaw the trophic cascades research done by scientists like Dr. Ng'weno today.

In Kenya, building on TEK and using modern technology such as trail cameras and GPS collars on lions and zebras, Dr. Ng'weno found that after boma removal, cattle would be moved to another site and zebras would arrive very shortly and would preferentially eat the grass species the cattle had not eaten. These two herbivores' diets differ, because their mouths and rumens are shaped differently. But beyond herbivores and their food, these relationships cascade to benefit lions. Zebras are lions' preferred prey. As zebras would congregate where the boma had been, to eat the grasses, lions would show up, to prey on the zebras. In this manner, lions would leave the cattle alone and focus on eating zebras. The people would have plenty of food in the form of beef, a traditional primary source of Masai sustenance, and the whole system would function in a healthy, dynamic equilibrium. After researching these food-web dynamics for her doctoral studies, Dr. Ng'weno is now reinstating these practices on other Masai lands to improve human coexistence with lions and increase grassland resiliency to climate change.

The above case studies from Kenya and Dr. Morgan's work demonstrate that, in sum, what we need today to solve global environmental conservation problems and live more sustainably on earth is a synthesis of Western science and Native science. Dr. Morgan's insightful work, which was far ahead of its time, did much to highlight how these two ecosophies can be used together to create an integrated ecology. In her view of the world, Western and Indigenous epistemologies can work synergistically to envision a vibrantly healthy Northern Plains where beaver and bison and other cultural keystones are able to serve their ecological roles, humans and other members of the ecosphere benefit, and the land and its inhabitants are more resilient to climate change.

These concepts regarding deep connections between species apply globally in most places where Indigenous people have had a presence. Exceptions exist, such as Easter Island, where, according to pollen records and archaeological evidence, Indigenous people removed all the trees ca. 1200 BCE, causing environmental degradation to the point of ecological collapse.[51] However, in general, most Indigenous people learned how to use the synergies within their native ecosystems to improve their ability to survive.

I recently spent some time in the Canadian High Arctic, studying the impacts of climate change on imperiled wildlife species such as polar bears and caribou. While there I explored Devon Island, the largest currently uninhabited island in the world, with Inuit Elder Peter Alareak, a soft-spoken bald man with a greying walrus moustache. Far north of the Arctic Circle, at 75° N, Devon was not always uninhabited. This mountainous island has a flat plain along the shore. There, Peter showed me the ghosts of more than a dozen houses— circular depressions in the ground rimmed by lichen-splattered boulders. Several had whalebone frames. Bowhead skulls and jawbones planted upright and perpendicular to the earth pointed boldly skyward, marking key structures in the houses. Ice-scoured caribou bones lay here and there. I wondered about the people who had lived here. On this day the site felt benign, warm, sheltered from the wind, but I knew this was misleading. When I looked to the northwest, I saw a massive snowstorm far in the distance, headed our way. Peter explained that Baffin Island Inuit had settled here in the early 1900s. However, high winds, a much colder climate, and the collapse of the Hudson's Bay fur trade had caused them to abandon the island in 1936.

Peter and I ended up walking about two miles on the tundra and beach that day. As we walked, I saw more caribou signs than I had seen anywhere in the Arctic thus far and many other houses, some more subtly marked by rocks. Caribou seasonal presence had drawn humans to this particular part of Devon over a hundred years ago, leaving an indelible, palimpsest-like ecological imprint on the tundra, by introducing nutrients into the soil. Caribou, a cultural keystone species, altered the soil with their dung and urine. They provided food for humans, creating a rich feedback loop. By slaughtering animals and doing what animals do—defecating and disturbing the ground—humans fertilized the soil, in this manner enriching this system and its plant communities, enabling it to support greater vegetation and higher densities of caribou than sites without humans. When caribou were not present, the people subsisted on marine mammals and trapped fur-bearing species for trade purposes. Humans respected the caribou and their lifeways, along with the whale and the seal; these species benefited mutually from one another's presence. However, in the end, colonialism in the form of the fur trade—and its eventual collapse—made survival here untenable for the Inuit.

CONCLUSION

Dr. Morgan hypothesized that the Northern Plains Indigenous groups were not beaver hunters, because to kill beaver meant jeopardizing water supplies that sustained communities and the plants and animals on which they relied. To test this hypothesis, she collected data within the Qu'Appelle River Valley Complex of southern Saskatchewan. There she examined Cottonwood Creek (a small to medium-sized tributary), the Moose Jaw River and Wascana Creek (large tributaries), and the Qu'Appelle River (the main waterway). In these reaches she surveyed beaver activity, plant communities, and archaeological sites that were the camps of the Plains communities. She compared this to a northern Alberta site, Elk Island National Park, the domain of the Woodlands communities, who lived in a moister, forested environment and who killed beavers for subsistence as needed. While she found complex dynamics, influenced by channel width and waterway size, in all the Saskatchewan sites she found that beaver functioned as a cultural keystone species.

Dr. Morgan took a holistic approach to her study, looking at how bison, a primary food source for the Plains Peoples, had benefited from beaver conservation, the prescribed burning of grasslands by these groups, and human migration patterns from summer camps on the prairie to winter camps near streams. She looked at historical records from the fur trade and found that the beaver pelts presented for trade came from Woodlands groups. In examining these relationships, her data demonstrated that Plains community aversion to hunting and trapping beaver could be applied to the larger landscape of North American Great Plains ecology.

Recent science shows that Dr. Morgan's findings can be contextualized on a far larger scale: a global one. The case studies I present here demonstrate that while species and landscapes of interest may have differed, the *relationships* between Indigenous people and the species on which they subsisted were the same. These relationships were based on reciprocity, caring, and respect. They were based on intimate knowledge and deep love for the landscapes in which these communities dwelled—what today we call *biophilia*. Kudos to Dr. Morgan for illuminating these relationships, their importance, and their capacity to help us find a way forward to heal the damage done by colonialism.

FIGURES

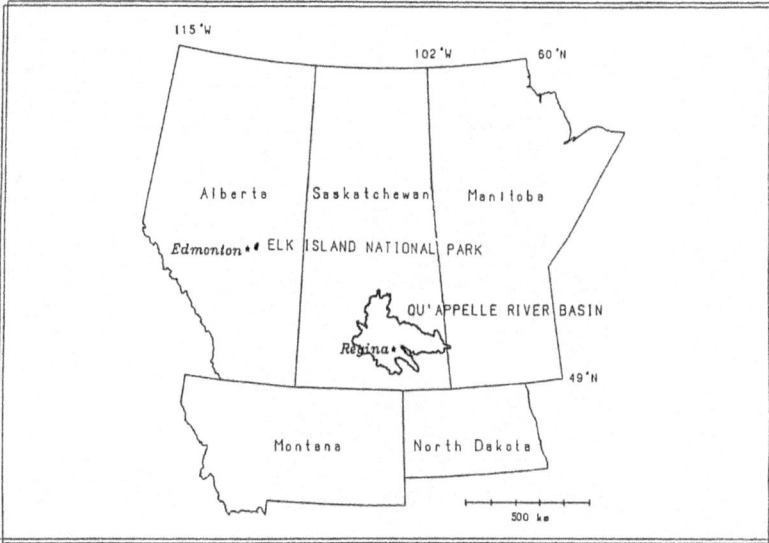

FIGURE I: Major Research Areas

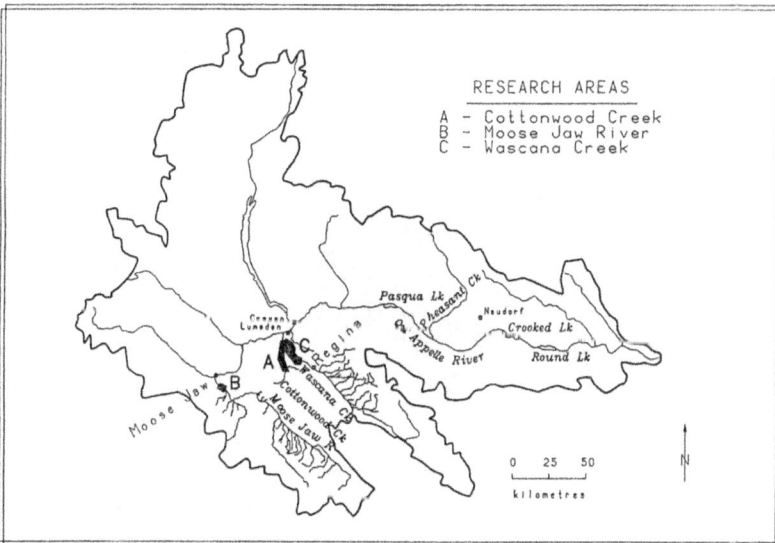

FIGURE 2: Qu'Appelle River Basin

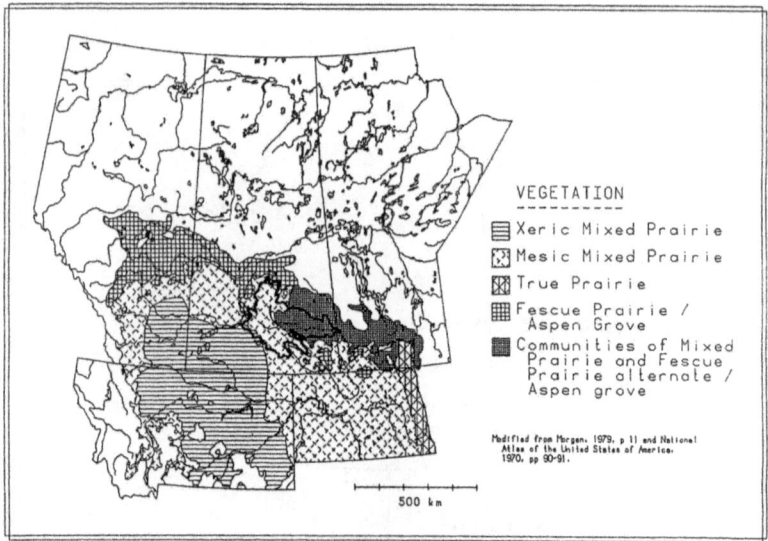

FIGURE 3: Vegetation Zones of the Northern Plains

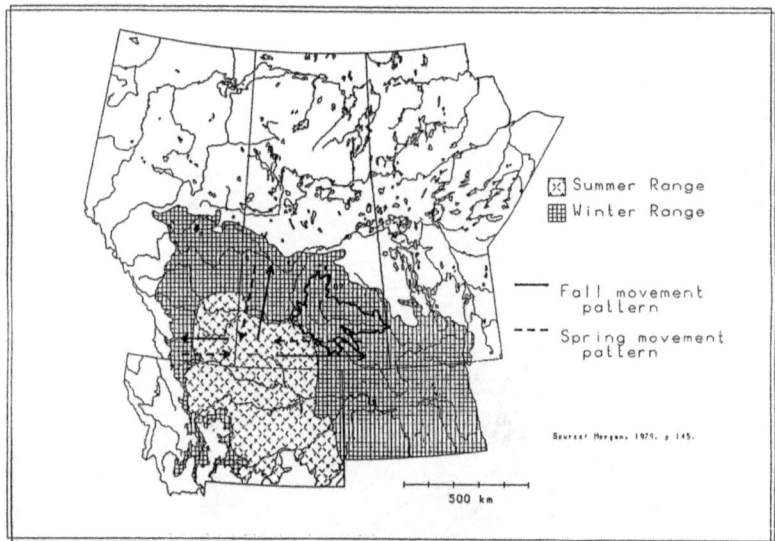

FIGURE 4: Precontact Bison Movement Patterns on the Canadian Prairies

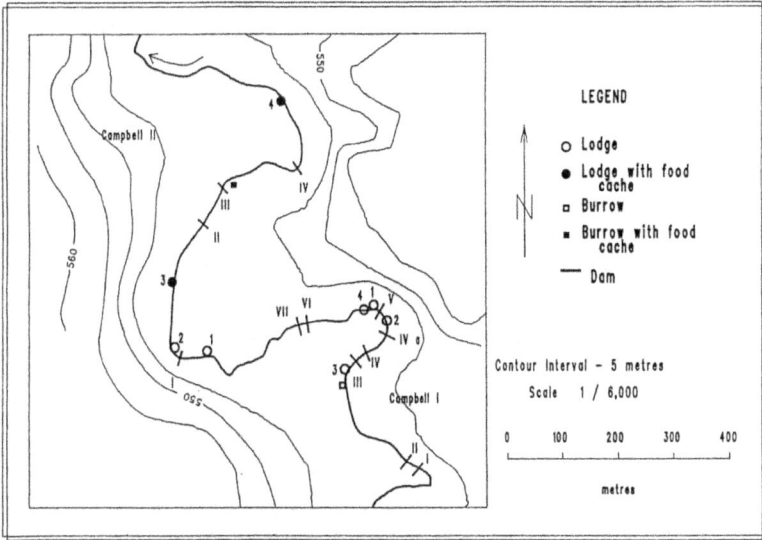

FIGURE 5: Campbell I and II Research Areas (Cottonwood Creek)

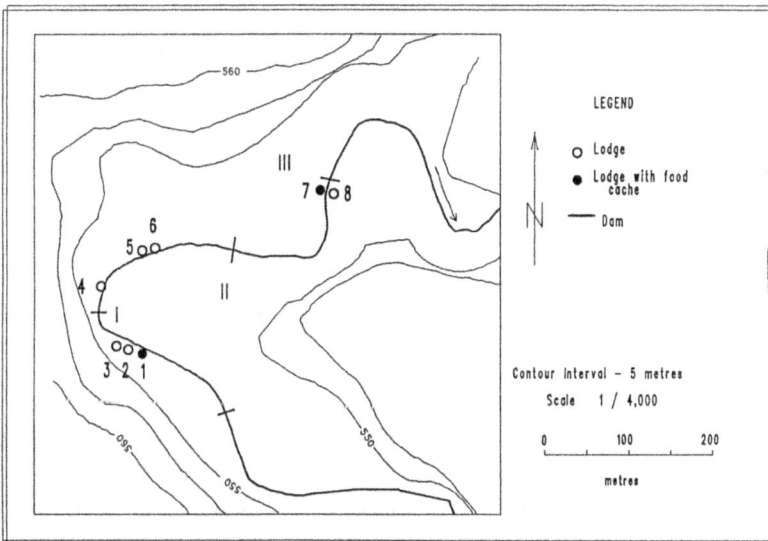

FIGURE 6: Thompson III Research Area (Cottonwood Creek)

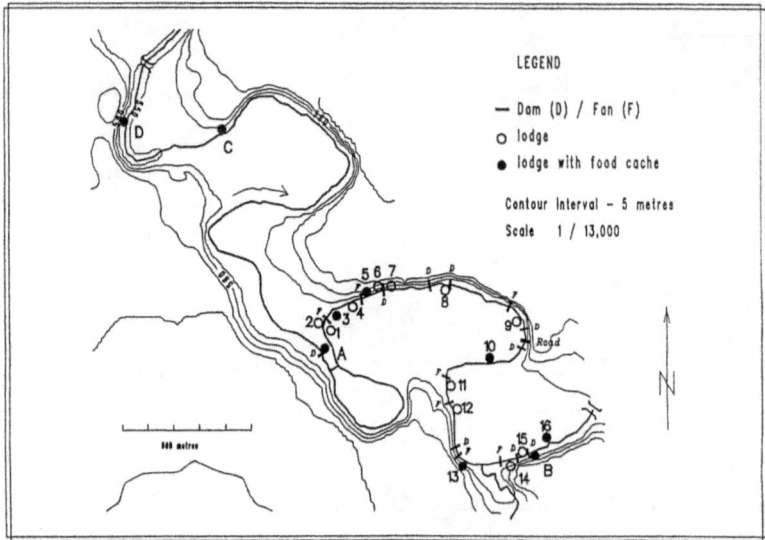

FIGURE 7: Moose Jaw River Research Area

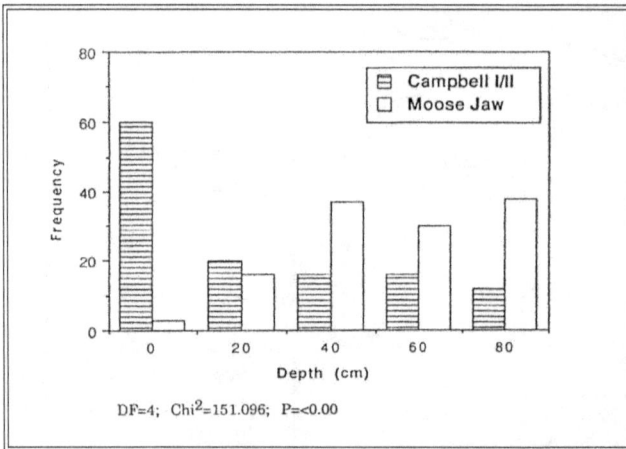

DF=4; Chi^2=151.096; P=<0.00

FIGURE 8: Comparison of Water Depths between a Large and Small Tributary

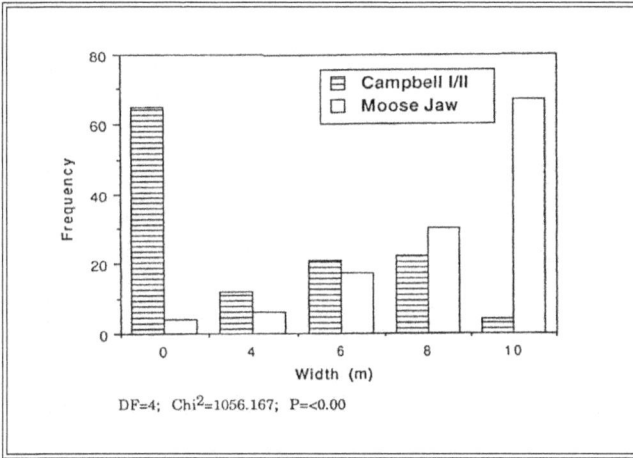

FIGURE 9: Comparison of Stream Widths between a Large and Small Tributary

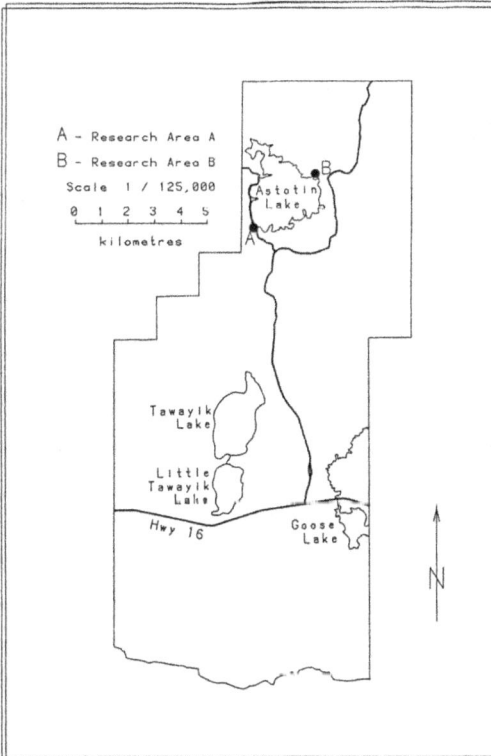

FIGURE 10: Elk Island National Park Research Areas

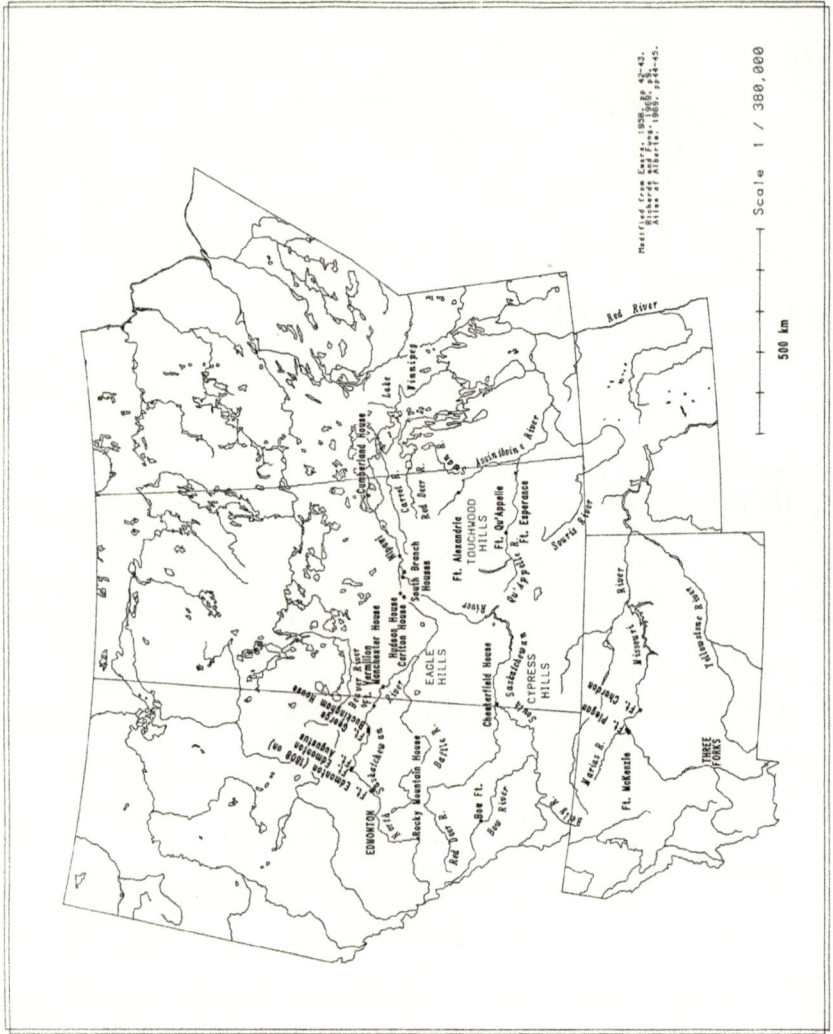

FIGURE II: Physiography and Fur-Trading Posts to 1858

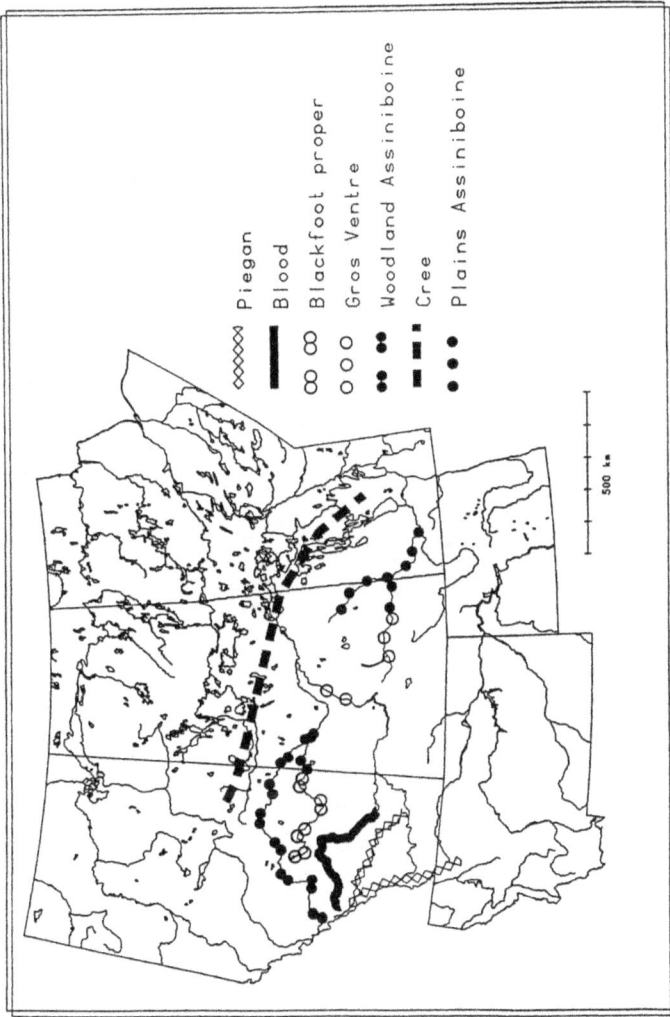

FIGURE 12: Distribution of Indigenous Peoples at Contact

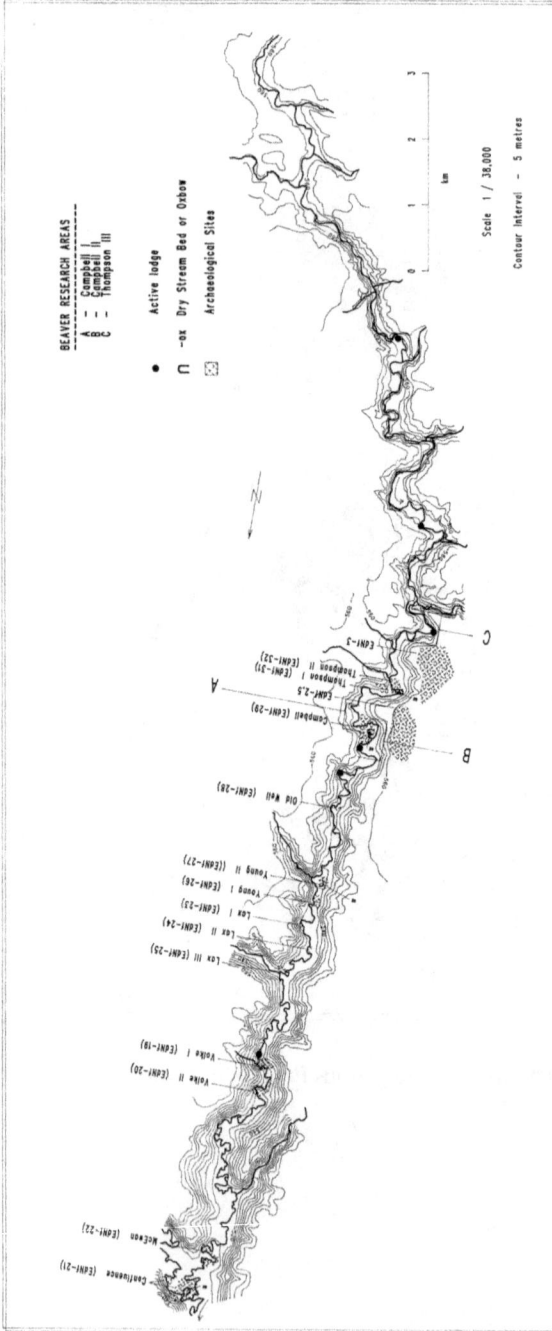

FIGURE 13: Cottonwood Creek Archaeological Sites and Beaver Research Areas

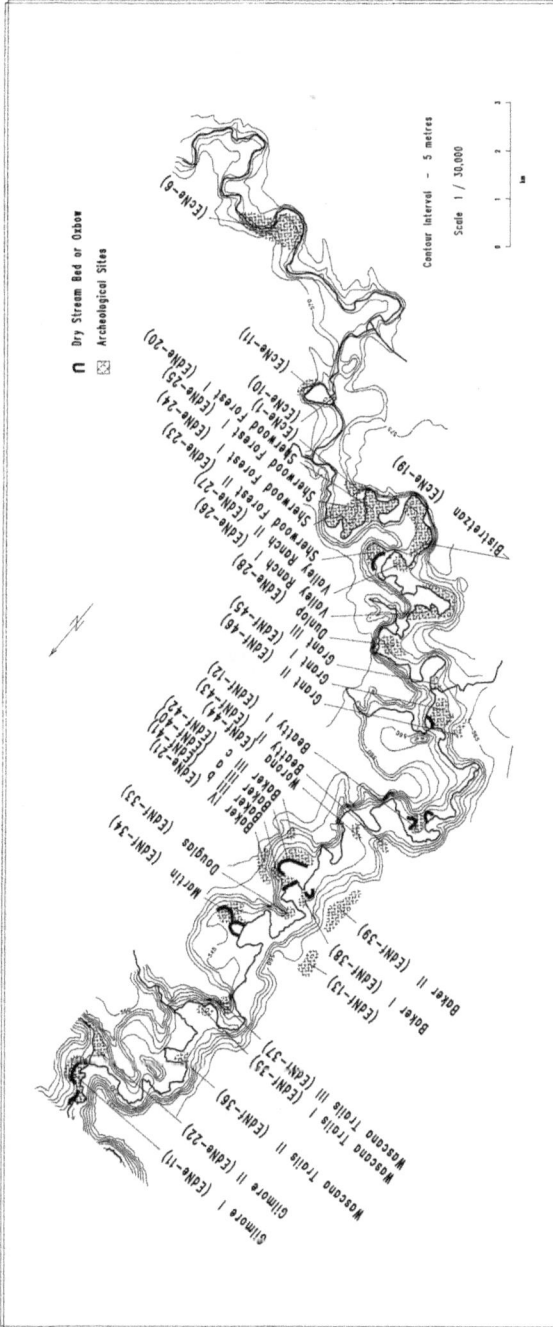

FIGURE 14: Wascana Creek Archaeological Sites

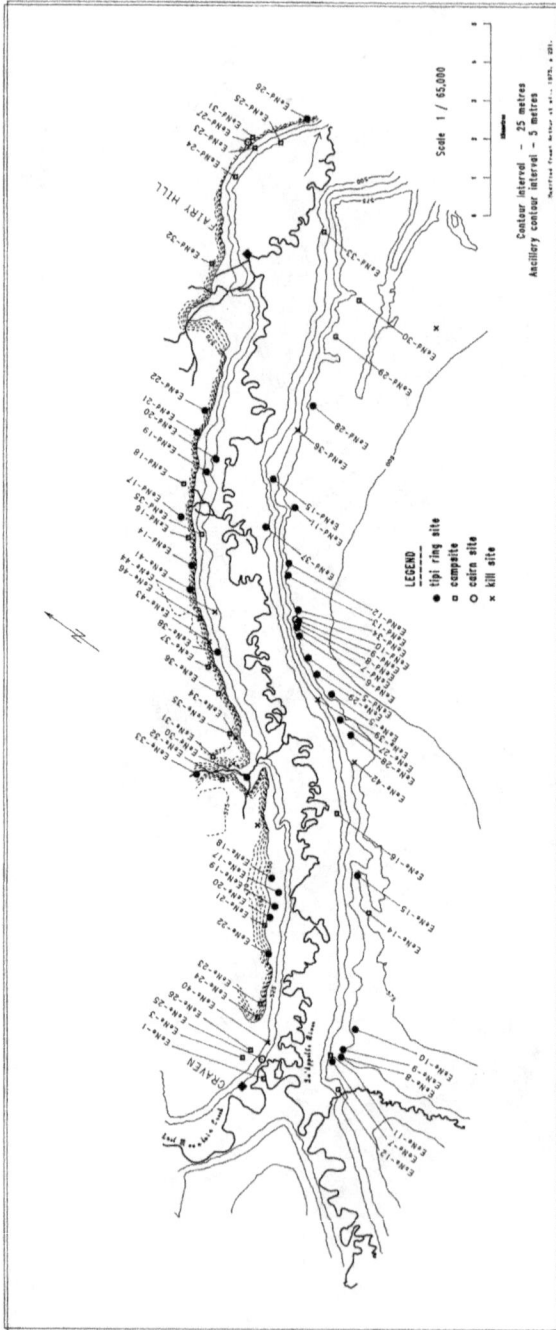

FIGURE 15: Qu'Appelle River Archaeological Sites

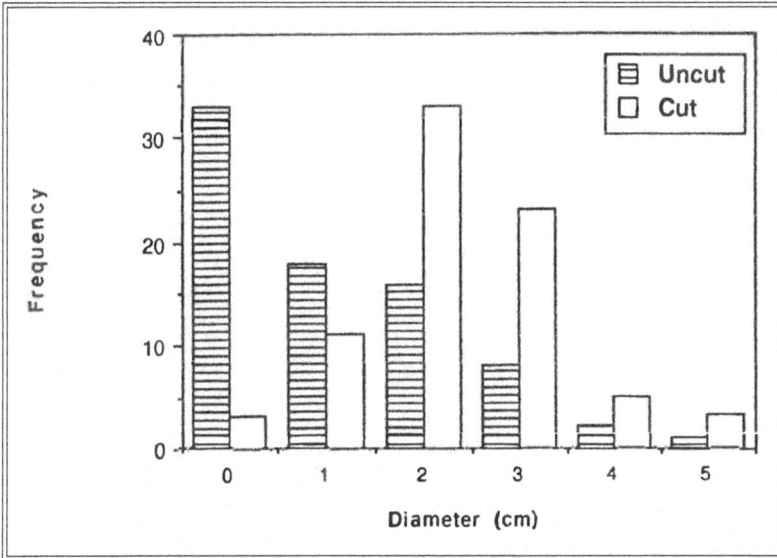

FIGURE 16: Beaver Selection of Chokecherry by Diameter Size

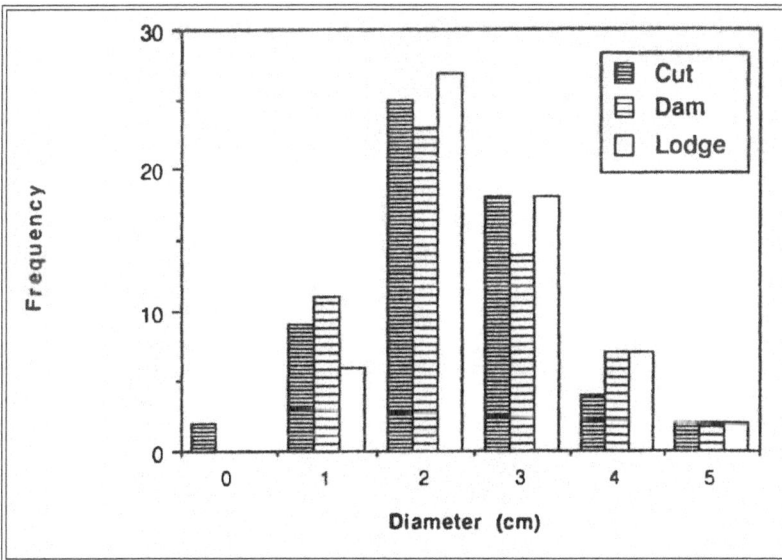

FIGURE 17: Beaver Selection of Lodge and Dam Materials as Compared to Cut Chokecherry Populations

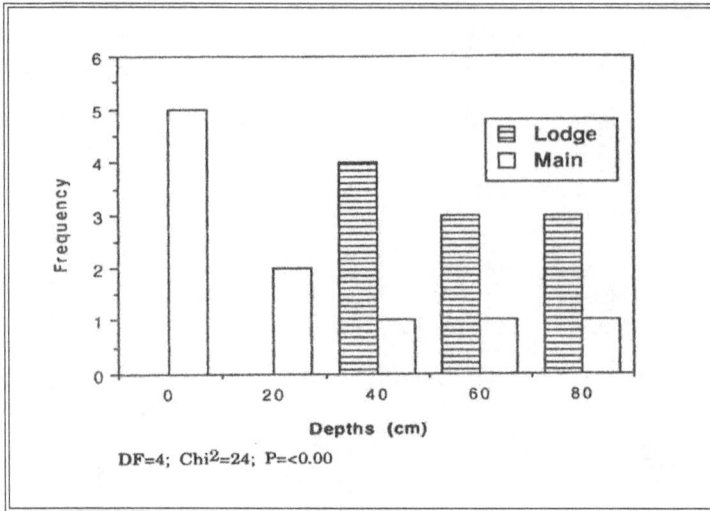

FIGURE 18: Campbell I/II: Water Depth Comparisons between Lodges and Overall Waterway

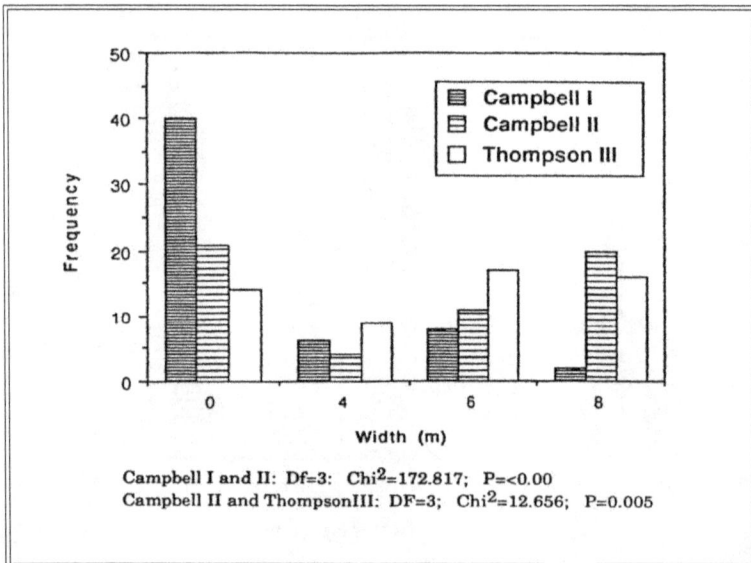

FIGURE 19: Cottonwood Creek: Comparison of Stream Widths at Different Beaver Dam-Pond Systems

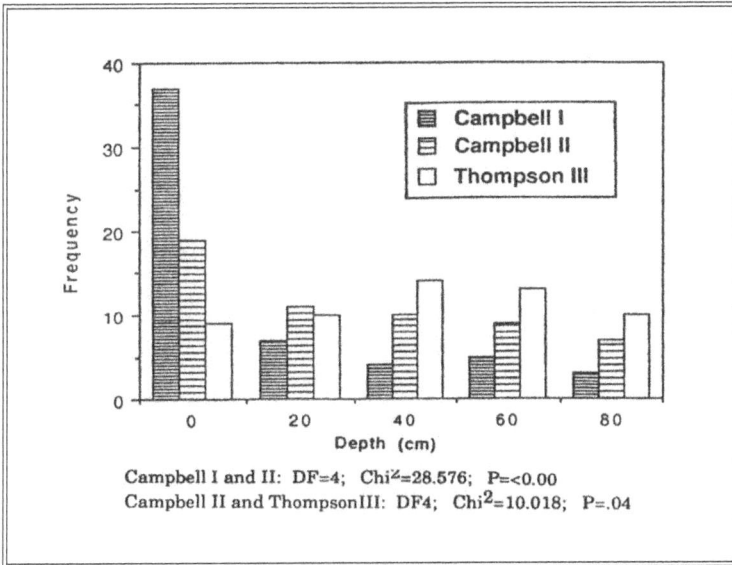

FIGURE 20: Cottonwood Creek: Comparison of Water Depths at Different Beaver Dam-Pond Systems

APPENDIX

DYNAMICS OF FIRE AND GRAZING BY BISON ON GRASSLANDS IN CENTRAL ALBERTA

R. Grace Morgan and R.J. Hudson

NOTE: This article was presented at the International Symposium on Bison Ecology and Management in North America, held in Bozeman, Montana, on June 4–7, 1997, and is previously unpublished. All references to the tables and illustrations presented at the conference have been removed for publication.

ABSTRACT

"Fire" of natural origins or ignited by man has had a profound effect on vegetative structure and dynamics of many environmental zones.[1] Burning patterns have modified the behaviour of many associated faunal forms, particularly herbivores. On the Northern Plains, the historical record clearly indicates that previously burned areas attracted bison and that Indigenous Peoples made use of this knowledge to manipulate and concentrate herds.[2] The historical record also suggests that Aboriginal groups on the plains were aware of the ecological (cause-effect) relationships between grasslands, fire, and bison. Trobriand noted that Indigenous Peoples claimed that cinders act as a fertilizer that stimulates the growth of grass, while Lewis commented that burning initiated an earlier growth.[3] Studies of contemporary bison herds confirm a selection for previously burned grasslands.[4]

Different ecological zones exhibit marked differences in grassland responses to burning. Raison cautioned that effects of fire can alter and/or change with the nature of the fire and the particular ecological state.[5] In more mesic areas where standing dry matter/litter accumulations can be considerable, the shading and/or inhibiting effect of litter may delay initiation of spring growth and reduce productivity.[6] Removal of litter by burning brings about microclimatic changes (higher soil temperatures and increased light intensities) that initiate earlier growth and increase productivity. In addition, higher temperatures stimulate microbial activity, the consequence being higher soil and foliar nutrients.[7] Hobbs and Schimel have also attributed higher total mineralized soil-N in burned grasslands to increased soil temperatures.[8]

In more arid areas (Mixed Prairie regions), litter accumulations are not sufficient to retard plant growth, burning does not appear to affect the initiation of growth, and productivity on burned grasslands is reduced.[9] On the Canadian Plains the historical record confirms this pattern.[10]

Grazing creates a patchy distribution of fuel loads and consequently marked microsite variability in grassland responses to burning. A grasslands grazing system is also characterized by a ubiquitous distribution of dung and urine deposits, which contribute to system complexity through small-scale nutritional patchiness and also significantly modify burning responses.[11]

Of critical significance in the current study is a specific behaviour pattern exhibited by bison: the immediate avoidance of vegetation close to dung deposits. This spatial configuration ("dung patch") allows for significant localized buildups of litter and standing dry matter. In earlier times, burning (i.e., natural or controlled fires) of native grassland areas converted these localized buildups of fuel into substantial burn residues (ash/charred matter), contributing to nutritional patchiness. The prolonged and intense heat generated by the burning of dung and associated dry matter may also contribute to microsite changes.[12] By removing dung patches, not only is rangeland capacity increased, but forage is of superior and/or increased nutritive quality.

Grazing or defoliation may maintain the selectivity initiated by burning. Palatability has been related to chemical constituents such as crude protein, which are enhanced.[13] However, foliar nitrogen differences between burned and non-burned areas tend to subside by summer.[14] Grazing stimulates nitrogen uptake by plants and maintains grasses in an immature (actively growing) form, which has higher nutritive values than the mature form.[15]

The general objective of the current study is to identify in a grasslands system the microsite changes initiated by burning that consequently lead to selective range use by bison. The main components of a grazing system chosen for analysis are grazed and non-grazed areas; urine and dung deposits; and bison grazing behaviour. The following step is to determine the impact of fire on these variables. The study is particularly concerned with the effect of burning on dung patches, often the only significant variable (in terms of fuel load) in heavily grazed areas. Chemical composition—more specifically, foliar crude protein content—is used as a proxy of palatability and nutritive value. Since plant productivity and nutrient content share an intimate and/or close relationship in their responses to burning, analyses of crude protein values will be closely correlated with plant growth. Finally, the study examines bison behaviour (grazing preferences) from the perspectives of burning and of grazing.

STUDY AREA

The study was carried out in Elk Island National Park, located east of Edmonton, Alberta. The general ecological region within which the park lies is the aspen parkland, more specifically, a hummocky area named the Beaver Hills, which contrasts strongly to the gently rolling topography surrounding the area. The rough terrain has strongly influenced the development of pockets of boreal forest.[16] Elk Island's parkland vegetation has been defined as a transitional phase between the prairies to the south and the boreal forest to the north.[17] The dominant forest overstory consists of balsam poplar (*Populus balsamifera*), trembling aspen (*Populus tremuloides*), and, in wetter sites, small groupings of spruce (*Picea* spp.). Important shrubs include hazel (*Corylus cornuta*), prickly rose (*Rosa acicularis*), and willow (*Salix* spp.). Lower wetter meadows are dominated by sedges (*Carex* spp.), while upland grassland areas are dominated by grasses.

The research paddock is located in the south area adjacent to the main park road and is approximately 50 ha (0.5 km²) in area. Aspen groves with grassland openings mainly occupy the northeast part of the paddock; grassland areas predominate in the remaining portion of the site. Dominant grasses are brome (*Bromus inermis*) and Kentucky bluegrass (*Poa pratensis*). A small stream fringed with sedge meadows enters the paddock from the west and feeds a small beaver pond.

Grazing intensities (percent utilization of forage biomass) in the paddock were high during the previous two years: 91% in 1989–90 and 87% in 1990–91.[18] In a grasslands area with a grazing history, the most visible features are grazed and non-grazed areas, containing a ubiquitous distribution of dung and urine deposits. On grazed areas, standing dry matter/litter accumulations are negligible. In preferred sites, non-grazed vegetation is mainly restricted to dung patches. In less preferred sites, ungrazed areas are more common, with small pockets of heavily grazed areas (highly variable in size and shape). In these less preferred areas, dung patches were infrequently clearly defined.

EXPERIMENTAL GRASSLANDS SITES
Burned Category

1. AREA C: This site mainly occupies a low-lying area that is naturally separated from area D by a small stream fringed with sedge meadows. Treatments and/or controls reflect mainly the burning of well-defined dung patches.

2. AREA D: This site includes a north-facing slope that declines toward the stream and a more elevated area extending away from the stream. Controls reflect the burning of non-grazed areas (i.e., not grazed the previous season) including dung deposits.

3. AREA H: This site is located in an alleyway adjacent to the paddock that generally has not been grazed for several years. The treatment thus reflects the burning of a non-grazed area with minimal and/or negligible grazing history.

Non-burned Category

1. AREA F: This site lies adjacent to area D and generally reflects similar ecological conditions. The controls reflect areas that were grazed the previous season and do not contain dung deposits.
2. AREA G: This site is also located in the alleyway adjacent to the paddock. The treatment reflects a non-grazed area with minimal grazing history.
3. AREA E: This area contains several aspen groves as well as open grasslands areas. It was generally a less preferred area, and non-grazed areas were common, some of which were heavily polluted. Analyses were restricted to grazed areas.

SPECIES COMPOSITION

Species composition was determined by Alberta Forestry Lands and Wildlife vegetation inventory system (MF5). In the paddock area the distribution of the major grass species was highly uneven: Kentucky bluegrass often occurred in pure stands, while timothy (*Phleum pratense*) was restricted to area E. More specifically, the abundance of the two major grasses, Kentucky bluegrass and brome, was especially variable and in the non-grazed controls tended to be inversely proportional (i.e., a decrease in one species generates an increase in the other). For example, in area C, the frequency distribution of Kentucky bluegrass and brome in one control cage was 77.3% and 1.6%, respectively, while in another control cage the frequencies were 38.9% and 45.9%, respectively. Both burned and non-burned areas exhibited this marked variability in species composition.

Variations in grazing intensities and the corresponding impact on species composition are were tabulated. In category A (pooled samples from G and H), which reflects grasslands with a minimal grazing history, species composition is as follows: Kentucky bluegrass, 59.25%; brome, 20.5%; dandelion (*Taraxacum officinale*), 4%; and white clover (*Trifolium repens*) is absent. Species diversity (14) and frequency representation, comparatively speaking, of "other" species is high (16.25%), with the most abundant being thistle (*Cirsium arvense*), followed by

American vetch (*Vicia americana*), yarrow (*Achillea millefolium*), agrimony (*Agrimonia striata*), and aster (*Aster* spp.). In category B (pooled samples from non-grazed controls C, D, and F), which represents grasslands with a previous grazing history, frequency representation of the two dominant grasses has not altered markedly, but invaders such as dandelion (7.42%) and white clover (1.9%) have increased. Diversity of other species is still high (16), but frequency representation has dropped to 8.2%. In currently grazed (22%) and non-grazed areas (category C), frequency representation of Kentucky bluegrass has not altered markedly, but brome dropped to 9.78%. Dandelion (17.2%) and white clover (5.68%) continue to increase, while frequency representation of the remaining species (13) has again declined (4.36%). In category D, which represents a 100% currently grazed area, Kentucky bluegrass (56.8%) retained its representation, but brome (0.2%) was almost eliminated. Dandelion (29%) and clover (12.3%) continue to increase, while frequency representation of the remaining species (reduced to 4) has again declined (1.7%).

METHODOLOGY
Grazing and Burning Treatments
Prescribed burning in the paddock was last conducted in the southeastern portion (F1) in 1987. On April 24, 1991, weather conditions at the time of burn (approximately 1:00 p.m.) were as follows: temperature 17.6°C; precipitation 0 mm; humidity 33.9%. Given that there was no precipitation during the prior 15 days and that temperatures during those days were unseasonably high, ecological conditions were ideal for a successful burn.

Area A represents a burned aspen grove; the unburned aspen groves were generally designated as area B. The wide range of microsite modifications associated with grasslands with a grazing history necessitated the definition of several experimental areas.

On May 3, 1991, six bison (four cows, one calf, and a yearling bull) were introduced to the paddock, and on June 3, three mature bulls were added to the group. Three additional calves were born later. The bison were allowed to move freely throughout the paddock, establishing their own grazing and selection patterns.

Structural/Chemical Changes

After the fire, burn residues were collected from both grass and dung deposits. The burned dung sample reflected the combined residues of three specimens. Chemical analyses were carried out to determine the nutrient quality of ash/charred matter residues. To determine the extent of sterilization (i.e., the area under a dung deposit that exhibited no vegetative growth during the season), diameter measurements were taken in August from a random sample (N=30) of burned dung areas.

Range Biomass and Forage Crude Protein Analyses

After the burn, control cages (three per area) were placed in subdivisions C, D, and F to provide non-grazed controls during the vegetative season. In area E, only grazed samples were collected for analyses. Mean diameter of cages was 1.91 m (6.27 ft), or 2.85 m² (30.68 sq ft) in area. Control cages were not required in areas H and G, as they were not accessible to the herds.

For the biomass and crude protein analyses, samples were collected once a month, between the end of May and the end of September. Hand-clipped samples were taken from the non-grazed controls and associated grazed areas using, at the beginning of a season, a 0.5 m² plot and, as biomass subsequently increased, a 0.10 m² plot. Species were not separated because the purpose of the study was to determine the total amount of biomass available for bison consumption. Furthermore, bison generally did not select for any specific species during grazing. At the beginning of the study, last season's dry matter was separated from the new growth. Specimens were oven dried and weighed.

During July, the effect of dung deposition on foliar crude protein levels was evaluated. Grass samples were taken from the avoidance area surrounding a dung deposit. Two types of dung were distinguished: old (that is, dung deposited prior to the current vegetative season) and new (that is dung deposited early enough in the current vegetative season to allow for an avoidance area to develop). In August and September, the effect of urine deposits on foliar crude protein values was similarly investigated. Given the attraction of bison to urine patches, these areas were generally heavily grazed.

Structural and Spatial Model

To better understand the structural and/or spatial patterning of a grazing system, a 20 by 25 m grid (1 m^2) was laid out in fall in area E (non-burned) after grazing patterns stabilized. We distinguished grazed and non-grazed areas, old and fresh dung deposits, and rodent disturbances. During the analyses, the grid was subdivided into 1,920 cells (0.5 m^2) to facilitate quantification of data. To determine the extent of utilization, cells were distinguished by two criteria: predominantly grazed or non-grazed.

To determine the spatial dimensions (size) of a dung patch, measurements were taken of dung deposits with the avoidance area completely defined. A random sample (N=33) was collected from area C (heavily grazed site). Because dung patches are more commonly oval than circular, two diameter measurements were taken and the mean used in the analyses. Diameter measurements include the dimensions of the dung deposit.

In late fall, transects (10 m apart) were carried out across areas C and D (burned) and area F (non-burned) to determine if bison showed preferential selection for burned areas. The categories were restricted to grazed and non-grazed, and measurements were taken every ten steps for a total of 1,697 observations.

RESULTS

Physical Effects of Burning

On areas with a previous grazing history (C and D) the combustion of herbaceous materials was patchy, as grazed areas generally had little standing dry matter/litter accumulation and thus many of these areas were completely passed over by the fire or, at best, the remaining standing dry matter, which rarely exceeded 3 cm in height, was partly singed. On grazed areas, effective combustion was generally restricted to dung patches. The burning of non-grazed areas (those that had not been grazed the previous season) involved not only dung deposits but substantial amounts of standing dry matter/litter. The burning of area H (which had not been grazed recently) was relatively uniform: the greater fuel load resulted in a more intense burn, and as a result the litter was more completely consumed.

Non-grazed stands of Kentucky bluegrass did not burn well. This species as it matures tends to flatten against the soil surface; consequently, it retains moisture more effectively and thus may be quite damp when burned. Brome, which cures erect, was more often completely consumed.

Dung combustion exhibits several unique characteristics. First, dung does not flame but smoulders, often for several hours after ignition. During combustion, the burn residues tend to retain the original form and/or shape of the dung deposit. Heat radiation is contained and is focused downward into the soil, amplifying its effect, so there was no vegetative recovery during the first growing season. The mean area of sterilization under a burned dung deposit was 0.05 ± 0.003 m^2. The degree of combustion of dung deposits exhibited a high degree of variability, ranging from completely consumed to only partly charred.

RANGE BIOMASS

Non-grazed

In May, biomass recovery on non-burned controls (areas G and F) was significantly greater (37.5%; paired t-test; P=.03; 1 tail) than in burned controls (H, C, and D). In June, because the growth rate in the burned controls (342%; P=<0.00) was more rapid than in non-burned areas (133%; P=.0042), biomass differences are no longer significant (P=.104). In the non-burned category, the growth rate in area F (176%; P=.015), which has a previous grazing history, was double the growth rate in area G (83%; P=.047), which experienced little grazing in previous years. In the burned category, the most rapid growth rate occurred in area H (389%), which reflects only the combustion of standing dry matter/litter accumulations, resulting in biomass estimates markedly higher than in areas C (P=.037) and D (P=.016), which represent the combustion of both dry matter and dung deposits.

In July, the growth rate continued to be more rapid in the burned controls (40.5%) than the non-burned controls (20%), so biomass differences widened: 53% higher (P=<0.00) in the burned controls. In the non-burned category, biomass in control G increased by 64% (P=.0064), while it declined slightly in area F (4%). Within the burned category, all controls continued to exhibit biomass increases with the greatest increase occurring in control D (61%; P=.0012); controls H and C increased only 38% (P=.0553) and 23% (P=.0683), respectively.

In August, biomass declines occurred in both burned (2.6%; P=.416) and non-burned (6.9%: P=.26) categories, but the greater decline in the non-burned controls resulted in widening biomass differences (60%; P=<0.00). Growth rates appear to have stabilized in the non-burned category, but in the burned category growth and/or decline rates are still highly variable with significant growth occurring in control C (52%; P=.01), while controls H and D both exhibited declines.

By the end of September all non-grazed controls had declined in biomass; however, the continuing more rapid decline in the non-burned controls (23%; P=.07) than the burned controls (16.2%; P=.03) caused a further widening in biomass differences (74%; P=.0048).

Currently Grazed

At the initiation of the study, biomass recovery on both burned and non-burned grazed areas was already markedly lower than on comparable non-grazed controls. Since grazing pressures rather than other variables, such as burning, were the dominant influence, samples were often pooled to reflect mainly grazed areas versus non-grazed controls. On May 3, grazing was first initiated on areas C and E. By the end of May, herbage on non-grazed controls (G, F, H, D, and C) was already significantly higher (99%; P=.01) than on grazed areas (E/G and C/G). These differences continued to widen during most of the vegetative season, peaking in August (1,394%; P=<0.00) and declining slightly in September (801%). These dynamics reflect the persistent attraction of bison herds to grazed patches on which grazing was first initiated.

There also were seasonal variations in total biomass recovery from currently grazed areas. In June, as compared with May, biomass recovery from grazed areas increased markedly (60.5%; P=.0012) and then dropped sharply in July (33.4%; P=.0018). The decline continued in August (47%; P=<0.00), but the figure increased in September (38.5%; P=.38).

FORAGE CRUDE PROTEIN

Non-grazed

By the end of May, foliar nutritive values (crude protein) were significantly higher (32%; P=.01) on burned than non-burned controls. Within the burned category, differences in crude protein values between the various burn areas (H, D, and C) were not significant, but it can be pointed out that the lowest crude protein levels were associated with area H where only standing dry matter/litter (however, the greatest accumulations) were ignited by the fire. Crude protein levels in area C and D, in contrast to area H, were 8% and 16% higher, respectively, and reflected the combustion of dung deposits as well as standing dry matter/litter accumulations.

In June, significant drops in foliar crude protein levels occurred in both burned (P=< 0.00) and non-burned (P= .005) controls. Because the decline was much greater in the burned controls (46.3%) than in the non-burned controls (30.5%), foliar crude protein differences are no longer significant (P=.4509).

In July, crude protein levels once more dropped significantly in both burned (P=<0.00) and non-burned (P=<0.00) controls. The decline continued to be greater in the burned controls (36.4%) than the non-burned controls (29.8%), resulting in slightly lower crude protein levels (8.7%) in the burned controls; however, the difference is not significant (P=.096).

In August, the drop in crude protein levels was minimal: 3.6% in the burned controls and 7.6% in the non-burned controls. However, the greater drop in the burned controls results in crude protein levels now being significantly lower in the burned controls (12.4%; P=.0012).

In September, significant declines in crude protein levels again occurred in both burned (P=.0023) and non-burned controls (P=<0.00). Since the drop in crude protein levels in the burned and non-burned categories has been of similar magnitude (26% and 26.5%, respectively), crude protein levels in the burned category continue to be significantly lower (13.2%; P=.0276).

Currently Grazed

By the end of May, crude protein levels in non-grazed burned controls were markedly higher than in the non-burned controls. This phenomenon was not exhibited in the currently grazed areas. Protein levels in grazed burned area C/G were only 6.5% (P=.14) higher than in non-burned area E/G.

The fact that crude protein levels were lower on the currently grazed burned area (C/G) than on the burned controls (H, D, and C) particularly highlights the nutritive patchiness occurring on a grazed field. As previously noted, dung patches are a localized manifestation; consequently, burning (controls C and D) results in areas and/or patches of high nutrient concentrations. Currently grazed grass specimens, being collected outside the control cages, were somewhat removed from the areas of highest nutritive concentrations. Also, many grazed areas, owing to low fuel loads, were not appreciably affected by the fire. As a result, some of the currently grazed grass samples may reflect the stimulatory effects of grazing rather than burning.

Since the stimulatory effect of grazing on foliar crude protein values was the dominant variable, samples (burned and non-burned) were pooled to reflect mainly grazed areas versus non-grazed controls. Protein declines in grazed areas were generally less rapid than in the non-grazed controls, and the differences progressively widened as a consequence. Beginning in May, crude protein levels in currently grazed areas (C/G and E/G) were only 4% higher than in the non-grazed controls. By June, crude protein values were 26% (P=.06) higher on currently grazed areas (C/G, E/G, and D/G), with the trend continuing into July (51%; P=<0.00) and peaking in August (54%: P=<.0.00), but in September a more rapid decline in the currently grazed areas narrowed the difference (40%; P=.01).

Crude protein levels generally declined throughout the vegetative season, but there were some variations in the rate. In June and July declines were significant: 28% (P=.02) and 23% (P=.01), respectively. In August the decline was negligible (4%; P=.08) but in September was again significant (33.7%; P=<0.00).

Within the currently grazed category, differences in grazing history may have affected crude protein values. In June, although differences were not significant, crude protein levels in area C/G and area E/G were 35% and 25% higher, respectively, than in area D/G. In area D/G, grazing pressures were initiated at a later date. In July, crude protein levels continued to be higher (P=.04) in areas (C/G and E/G) where grazing was first initiated compared with areas (F/G and D/G) on which grazing was initiated at a later date. These phenomena were generally not expressed during August and September.

IMPACT OF URINE AND DUNG

Dung

In July, dung patches containing older deposits had significantly lower crude protein levels (21.8%; unpaired t-test: P=.01) than vegetation associated with new dung (current season) deposits. When compared to the non-grazed controls, the avoidance areas associated with the old and young dung deposits both exhibited significantly higher crude protein levels: 33% (P=<0.00) and 70% (P=<0.00), respectively. However, there was no significant difference in crude protein values when the avoidance areas (both old and new) were compared to grazed areas. Seasonal differences also exist in nitrogen levels in dung deposits that would affect the amount available for leaching and consequently the amount available for plant uptake.

Urine

In August, crude protein levels on grazed urine patches were significantly greater than on grazed areas and non-grazed controls: 59.5% (P=<0.00) and 146% (P=<0.00), respectively. Although in September crude protein levels on urine patches were 23% (P=.08) lower than in August, they continued to be significantly greater than in grazed areas (85%; P=<0 00) and non-grazed controls (159%; P=<0.00).

STRUCTURAL/SPATIAL MODEL OF A BISON GRAZING SYSTEM

Spatial Distribution of Elements

A grid pattern was laid out in area E to define more precisely the key elements of a grazing system. There were several large non-grazed areas, some of which were highly polluted and were thus generally avoided by the bison, and several small persistently grazed areas whose parameters were generally defined by the placement of the dung deposits. Well-defined avoidance areas were not common.

The less preferred nature of the experimental area is expressed in the degree of utilization. The grid (25 m by 20 m) encompassed an area of 500 m², or 1,920 cells (0.5 m by 0.5 m), of which 75.8% was non-grazed and 24.2% was grazed. The number of dung deposits identified was 310, of which 43 were fresh (that is, insufficient time had passed for a visible avoidance area to have developed). The development of an avoidance area around a dung deposit, given sufficient time, is one of the few demonstrable absolutes (100% frequency).

Dung Patches
In area C, the number of dung deposits per avoidance factor generally ranged from 1 to 4, with a single deposit situation representing 57% (19) of the sample. The area of avoidance including the dung deposit (N=1 to 4) ranged from 0.2 m² to 3.5 m² (mean=1.01 m²; std. dev. =.866). The average area of a dung patch containing one dung deposit was .487 m². The size of the avoidance area in relation to number of deposits also exhibited a high degree of uniformity (r^2=.727).

Bison Behaviour
Transects carried out on burned (C and D) and non-burned (F) areas indicate that 46.7% of the burned area was grazed, while only 18.7% of the non-burned area was grazed; this indicates a significant preference (P=.0001) for grasslands on burned areas.

DISCUSSION
Physical Effects of Burning
Patchy burning on grasslands has been related to differences in fuel load, time of ignition, and thus fire intensity.[19] In the research area, patchy burning mainly reflected a mosaic of grazed and non-grazed areas, which was directly related to differences in fuel load (i.e., quantity of fuel per unit area). Even by the end of May 1991, biomass recovery from non-grazed controls was significantly higher (99%) than on the currently grazed areas, with differences in fuel load peaking in August (1.344%).

Raison and Daubenmire also argue that burn residues from grass burning may be too scant to affect any appreciable or beneficial differences in nutrient availability.[20] In the current study, these observations would only be applicable to grazed grassland areas where burn residues were scant; however, most non-grazed grass-lands areas in the research sites carried a substantial fuel load of standing dry matter/litter accumulations resulting in burn residues (some ash, mostly charred remains) of sufficient amounts to mark-edly darken the soil.

However, if we speak of ash as a potential fertilizer, then quality as well as quantity should be an important consideration because the percent or weight of residues after burning is not necessarily indica-tive of nutrient or alkali content.[21] A critical factor influencing the quality or nutrient content of burn residues is the degree of combus-tion. If combustion of plant material is almost complete, evidenced by burn residues of white ash, most of the C, H, O, N, and organic S and P are transferred to the air.[22] In the study area, ignition of grassland species (mainly Kentucky bluegrass) resulted in burn residues con-sisting primarily of black ash/charred remains, which are indicative of inhibited combustion and the presence of residual organic mate-rial and/or organic nitrogen.[23] Chemical analyses of charred grass re-mains from the research area confirm a high organic matter content (58.6 %) as well as small amounts of mineral (ammonium and nitrate) nitrogen. High nutrient ash residues (38% organic matter; total nitro-gen content of 7,100 ug/g) from the burning of chaparral (*Adenostoma fasciculatum*) led Christensen to comment that ash provides not only mineral nitrogen but a reservoir of organic nitrogen to the associated soils.[24] Also, regarding nutrient values of various types of ash residues, a survey of the literature found that the highest nitrogen content in ash (1.77%) was derived from the burning of herbaceous grasslands as compared with the burning of eucalypt branchwood (0.04%), euca-lypt wood (0.1–0.15%), and wood in Rhodesia (0.03%).[25]

The burning of dung patches must be considered as a different ecological manifestation, which in several ways simulates fire dy-namics more closely related to a forest ecosystem. Two factors con-tribute greatly to localized buildups of fuel: the avoidance by bison of vegetation proximate to dung deposits, and the durability of dung deposits. The historical record strongly implies that the lifespan of a bison chip can be considerable.[26] However, in the study area, durability was variable to some degree, influenced mainly by the season of deposition. Late spring/summer dung (consisting mainly of new green growth) is generally more liquid, less compact, and thus more susceptible to climatic degradation. Late fall/winter/early spring dung deposits are larger and more compact with reduced moisture content and thus have a greater resilience to climatic perturbations. This latter form also is the most common, reflecting up to 8 out of 12 months of deposition.

Although measurements were not carried out during the fire, information from several sources indicated that dung combustion generally occurred at high temperatures. From a historical perspective, Allen observed that dung burns like peat, making little flame but yielding a very intense heat.[27] In reconstructions of primitive pottery-firing techniques, Riegger found that a single layer of dung cakes is sufficient to fire pots properly: that is, to raise the heat to between 760°C (1400°F) and 871°C (1600°F).[28] Wright carried out a more comprehensive study on the thermodynamics of bison dung combustion. In his experiments, chips were loosely packed to form a mound and temperatures were measured by a thermocouple probe. The average fuel temperature attained after 20 minutes of combustion ranged from 313°C to 650°C (595.4°F to 1202°F). Under optimal conditions, the temperature of the chip pile peaked at 1003°C (1837.4°F). Wright related the large discrepancy in average temperatures to differences in moisture content, or the material quality of the chips.[29]

In the research area, the burning of dung also exhibited marked variability in the degree of combustion, ranging from complete conversion to ash to a partial charring of the deposits. Uneven moisture content acted against uniform burning. Dung surfaces, those next to soil, were often damp, so that upper portions usually burned first; then, there was an inward and downward process of combustion. When partial burning of dung occurred, the lower portions were those most commonly remaining. As to the effects of age, the older the deposit the more complete the combustion because it is beginning to deteriorate and the surrounding litter buildup is substantial, supplying additional fuel to facilitate combustion. Fresh dung deposits rarely burn because there has not been sufficient time for the avoidance area to develop. A unique attribute of dung combustion is heat containment, which can be largely related to the physical structuring of the deposits. After deposition, dung begins to develop an outer crust, a process that during the vegetative season is accelerated by winds and relatively high temperatures. The crust acts as a heat containment mechanism focusing heat radiation downward into the soil. This structural attribute combined with the compactness of a deposit explains the retention of the initial form or structure of the dung deposit (ash replica) during combustion, a phenomenon similarly observed by Wright.[30]

Retention of the structural integrity of the dung deposit during combustion also facilitates anaerobic conditions within the inner portions of the deposit. Combustion is thus rarely complete; if complete (white and/or grey ash), it is restricted to the exposed outer layers of the deposit, while the interior is black ash. Since black ash is the predominant component, burn residues from dung deposits are also high in nutrient content. Chemical analysis of ash recovered from completely consumed dung deposits contained 7.7% organic matter, including 0.34% organic nitrogen as well as mineral nitrogen. Burn residues containing 0.01% to 0.76% nitrogen can materially increase the total nitrogen content of the surface soil.[31] Since many dung deposits were only partially consumed, it can be assumed that organic matter and nitrogen components in the burn residues were even higher. The burning of dung patches resulted in substantial, but localized, deposits of high-quality burn residues contributing to the nutritive patchiness of a natural grazing system.

Heat containment magnifies the impact of dung combustion (intense soil heating) on a grasslands environment, whereas during slash and forest fires 80% of the fire dissipates upward.[32] Wright pointed out the uniqueness of dung combustion, noting that wood fuel constantly sheds combusted materials, while chips retain a mantel of ash and continue to burn to their interiors.[33]

RANGE BIOMASS

Non-grazed

At the end of May, greater productivity on non-burned controls generally reflects more favourable soil moisture conditions than those associated with burned controls. Hamilton and Scifres report that when soil moisture is adequate, biomass production on burned areas exceeds that on non-burned areas; however, when precipitation is scant, unburned plots produce significantly more biomass.[34] Thus, climatic conditions are an important consideration as they not only have a pronounced effect on grassland productivity but also strongly affect the grasslands' response to burning.

In Elk Island National Park, forage biomass production (1984 to 1991) generally shows a positive correlation with seasonal rainfall; 1991 was a year of reduced precipitation, or arid conditions.[35] However, in early spring, temperature is the critical factor initiating growth, with cool-season grasses beginning growth when the mean daily temperature averages 4.4°C (40°F).[36] Temperatures suitable for initiation of growth occurred much earlier (first week in April) than normal; generally, growing temperatures in the Aspen Grove Region are delayed until late April.[37] Except for a cool period in the second week of April 1991, temperatures until the date of burn (April 24) were ideal for rapid growth. Substantial snowfall in March (29.8 mm), slightly above the decade mean (21.1 mm), and some precipitation during the early part of April suggest favourable soil moisture conditions during initiation of growth. However, given the relatively high temperatures and the absence of precipitation since April 10, soil moisture would have experienced marked depletion by the time of burning. Nevertheless, by the date of burn, new spring grass was visible on many parts of the research area, reaching its highest growth on formerly grazed areas, mainly because of the absence of the inhibiting effect of litter and standing dry matter.[38]

Rainfall during the rest of April was limited and precipitation during most of May was highly sporadic; 90.6 mm (3.57 in) of rainfall was registered, almost double the decade mean (49.8 mm/1.96 in), but the effectiveness of this precipitation was reduced as more than half (52.4 mm/2.06 in) fell during a two-day period (May 13 and 14). Much of this precipitation would have been ineffectual, because showers in excess of 19 mm (0.75 in) result in loss by runoff.[39] Temperature conditions in May (monthly mean: 11.9°C/53.4°F) did not vary significantly from the decade mean (11.1°C/52°F).

It is suggested that the generally unfavourable (arid) climatic conditions combined with the effects of burning, which has also been related to decreased soil moisture conditions, would explain the appreciably lower productivity exhibited by the burned controls. There appears to be a general acceptance that burning reduces soil moisture levels.[40]

Investigators have identified several microsite changes relating to burning that can lead to soil moisture depletion. First, burning removes mulch which retards soil moisture depletion.[41] The conversion of standing dry matter/litter to ash/charred matter residues would also contribute to reduced soil moisture conditions. Although distribution is uneven, burn residues were substantial and, because of incomplete combustion, generally black. The blackened surface of a burned area would effectively absorb solar radiation; consequently, the surface layers would have been warmer during the growth period, increasing evaporation rates.[42] Also, ash inhibits the penetration of water, and runoff increases on burned areas.[43]

What has generally not been addressed is the immediate effect of the burn: that is, the heat generated during combustion as an important factor in reducing soil moisture conditions. Controls C and D, which were directly associated with the combustion of dung deposits, exhibited the lowest biomass production. During combustion of dung (which involves prolonged burning at high temperature) heat radiation is focused downward into the soil, which would particularly contribute to the drying of the underlying soils.

Another factor that may merit consideration is the fact that soil under a dung deposit is often damp. The substantial buildup of litter relating to the avoidance factor suggests that soils underlying this accumulation may also have a high moisture content. Since heat transfer in soils is mainly by thermal conduction, and conductivity increases with moisture content, the drying effect may have been more penetrating and/or widespread.[44]

Lower productivity on burned areas has also been attributed to new shoots being damaged or retarded by spring burning.[45] In regards to the latter, White and Currie found that productivity on a field burned in spring was much lower than on a fall-burned field, although soil moisture conditions were similar, but this effect did not persist; by mid-May both spring- and fall-burned fields had similar yields.[46] In the current study, if burning was an inhibiting effect, the effect did not persist; by the end of June, productivity on burned areas was substantially greater than on non-burned areas.

By the end of May, biomass recovery from non-grazed controls as compared with the currently grazed areas (both burned and non-burned) was already significantly greater. The continued return of bison herds to areas (both burned and non-burned) on which grazing was first initiated explains the differential in biomass recovery between grazed and non-grazed areas.

The selection of areas for grazing, however, was not random. At the initiation of the grazing season, bison chose areas that had previously been heavily grazed because, unencumbered by dry matter/litter accumulations, they were the first to exhibit new spring growth and thus the greatest availability of green matter. In a similar vein, several authors have identified higher live-to-dead biomass ratio and greater accessibility to green matter as some of the factors attracting bison to a prairie dog–altered (grazed) grasslands environment.[47] Burning generally had little effect on heavily grazed areas, owing to a light fuel load, and thus played no role in this early preference. Although slightly delayed, as new spring growth began to emerge on burned areas (i.e., those areas that had not previously been grazed or were associated with avoidance areas), those areas were grazed preferentially.

In June, substantial biomass increases in both burned and non-burned controls can be generally attributed to more favourable climatic conditions. Less precipitation was recorded in June (70.4 mm) than in May, but it was more effective, being more uniformly distributed over the month. Monthly mean temperatures (14.5°C) were normal (decade mean: 14.6°C).

The more rapid growth rate in the burned category (H, D, and C) suggests that more favourable climatic conditions may have triggered several ecological responses to burning that could positively affect productivity, including the following:

1. When soil moisture conditions are adequate, the effects of fire (higher soil/foliar nutrients levels) would increase productivity. As previously noted, accelerated growth on burned areas occurs only with sufficient moisture.
2. When climatic conditions (i.e., soils having been sufficiently wetted) set into motion the leaching of ash deposits, soil pH and available nutrients are increased.[48]

In the research study, the fuel load on most grazed areas was light; consequently, ash deposits were scant. On non-grazed grassland areas, incomplete combustion of litter and standing dry matter resulted in substantial and high-quality burn residues. Burn residues remaining after the burning of dung patches were even more substantial but in localized concentrations. Burning dynamics peculiar to dung deposits also resulted in incomplete combustion and therefore burn residues of high nutritive content. In addition to nitrogen, ash residues contain mineral salts such as magnesium, calcium, phosphorus, and potassium. Many of these minerals have been associated with increased productivity.[49]

Within the burned category, there were marked differences in the degree of biomass production, with area H exhibiting a substantially greater increase than areas C and D. The significantly lower productivity in areas C and D could be related to the greater severity of the burn associated with dung combustion. Area H reflects only the burning of standing dry matter/litter accumulations, and thus heat damage would have been less severe.

In the non-burned category, lower biomass production in area G than in area F reflects the continuing inhibiting effects of heavy litter accumulations: (a) retarding the absorption of precipitation by the underlying soil and (b) lowering soil temperatures.

In the currently grazed areas, as compared with the non-grazed controls, biomass differences widen, again reflecting the continued return of the bison herds to areas (both burned and non-burned) on which grazing was first initiated. Vinton and Hartnett similarly found that bison graze patches early in the season and then, during the rest of the season, they regraze these patches rather than creating new grazed patches.[50]

In July, climatic conditions can generally be described as highly arid: only 24 mm (0.94 in) of rainfall was recorded during the month (decade mean: 136.4 mm/5.37 in), with most occurring during the first 10 days of the month. Mean monthly temperatures were 17.8°C (64°F), slightly higher than the decade mean (16.6°C/61.9°F). The climatic data suggests that by the end of the month soil moisture stress would have been strongly operative. However, the increasingly higher productivity on the burned controls suggests that soil moisture conditions, at least during the early part of the month, were sufficiently adequate not to depress the stimulatory effect of fire. In the non-burned category, significant biomass increases in control G (minimal grazing history) again could be attributed to the effectiveness of litter accumulations in retarding soil moisture depletion and consequently increasing productivity. In the burned category, the significant biomass increase in area D may reflect a delayed response to more favourable climatic conditions. However, in area C, which also reflects the burning of dung deposits, recovery seems to be even slower.

In August, 60.4 mm (2.38 in) of precipitation was recorded—slightly above the decade mean (57.6 mm/2.27 in), but most (50.2 mm/1.98 in) fell during the first half of the month. A general decline in biomass in the non-grazed controls could be attributed to both arid climatic conditions (during the latter part of the month) and approaching maturation (the curing stage). In the burned category, the exception is area C (a low-lying area), where significant growth occurred. Marked biomass increases in control C also can be perceived as a delayed response to the effects of fire. Differences in biomass recovery between currently grazed areas and non-grazed controls continued to progressively widen, peaking in August, when biomass recovery from non-grazed controls was 15 times greater than that in currently grazed areas.

September signalled a return to highly arid climatic conditions, with only 11.2 mm (0.44 in) of precipitation recorded, well below the decade mean (49.7 mm/1.96 in). Climatic conditions thus suggest a marked depletion in soil moisture conditions by the end of the month. These changes are expressed in the marked biomass declines that generally occurred in all non-grazed controls.

In September, biomass recovery from currently grazed areas increased, reflecting changes in grazing behaviour rather than growth rates. Forage selection shifted dramatically, with bison beginning to feed more frequently and/or consistently on sedge meadows. This late-season preference may relate to changes in plant digestibility. Renecker and Hudson found that as the season progressed, fibre content of forages (including grasses) increased while cell solubles decreased—the exception being sedges, where there was an increase in cell contents.[51] In addition, a new grazing pattern became operative: top grazing. Bison are beginning to show a distinct preference for grazing seed heads (especially on brome) in non-grazed areas. Bison also continue to select for urine patches, given their higher crude protein levels and postponement of senescence (maturation). Day and Detling found that urine patches are a major source of forage and nitrogen for herbivores during the early and late periods of the growing season.[52]

In summary, by the end of July grazing preferences had stabilized, that is, new grazing patches were generally not being created. Preferred sites were identified as those having the largest grazed patches. On burned areas, the grazing of larger and/or more uniform areas was facilitated by the removal of dung patches (avoidance areas). Grazing pressures were generally uniform during most of the grazing season; that is, biomass recovery from grazed areas (burned and non-burned) was not markedly different.

FORAGE CRUDE PROTEIN

In May, higher foliar crude protein values on burned controls confirmed that when soil moisture conditions are inadequate, increased nutrient availability does not stimulate plant growth. This observation concurs with studies done in Texas and in Oklahoma.[53] In Texas, Sharrow and Wright concluded that during dry years, soil moisture, and not soil temperature, limits plant growth such that burning has no beneficial effects.[54]

The removal of litter by burning has been suggested as a primary determinant of post-burn changes, initiating microclimatic changes (i.e., higher soil temperatures) that increase microbial activity, leading to higher levels of available nitrogen in the soil and consequently increased foliar nitrogen levels.[55] There is no doubt that burning sets into motion changes, such as removal of standing dry matter and blackening of soil surfaces, that would stimulate higher temperatures on burned grassland areas. However, one of the other changes occurring simultaneously with increased temperatures is reduced soil moisture conditions, and evidence points to soil moisture as having a more critical effect than soil temperature on microbial respiration.[56]

Perhaps more important is the immediate but negative effect of burning (the heat component) on microbial populations. Burning studies indicate that reductions in bacterial populations are most frequently associated with dry northern temperate areas, while studies in humid tropical areas find that microbial populations rise immediately after fire.[57] Several investigators have observed an immediate reduction of bacterial populations relating to heat intensities, with decreases being greater on a severe burn than on a moderate burn.[58] More specifically, Aref'yeva and Kolesnikov found that burning kills a large number of micro-organisms (ammonifying bacteria were absent from burned litter) and that recovery does not occur for some time.[59]

Heat intensities generated by burning may be the initial factor that increases soil mineral nitrogen content and, consequently, foliar nitrogen levels. Controlled laboratory experiments confirm a positive relationship between ammonia production and increasing soil temperatures.[60] Specifically, temperatures of 65°C (149°F) were sufficient to cause a multiple increase in the amount of soil ammonia nitrogen, whereas this did not affect the amount of nitrate nitrogen.[61] During grass fires, temperatures ranging from less than 50°C (122°F) to 80°C (176°F) in the top 3 cm to 4 cm (1.18 in to 1.57 in) (but of only a few minutes duration) have been recorded, the latter temperature being more than sufficient for ammonia release.[62]

Burning studies under field conditions have also observed an immediate increase in soil NH_4-N (ammonium nitrogen).[63] Sharrow and Wright specifically note that after a burn in early April (at the Post site, Texas), burned plots had almost twice as much exchangeable soil ammonium in the 0–8 cm (0–3.15 in) depth as did unburned plots on April 21.[64] Aref'yeva and Kolesnikov concluded that the immediate release of soil ammonium after a burn could not be attributed solely to the activities of micro-organisms.[65]

Uptake of released NH_4-N by living plants is also generally rapid. Following pulse fertilization, when ammonia nitrogen is absorbed, it is rapidly built into amino acids that move in part into newly forming roots and in part to crowns and green herbage.[66] Field studies by Old found that grassland areas burned on April 27 had, by late May, a 65% higher foliar nitrogen content than the non-burned areas.[67] It has also been suggested that the concentration of nitrogen in foliage is proportional to the amount found in the soil.[68] Similarly, in the current study, higher foliar crude protein levels were observed in late May on grasslands areas burned on April 24.

In the study area, grazed areas generally were not appreciably affected by burning because of insufficient fuel load. At the same time, area H, prior to burning, had experienced little grazing over several years, so the fuel load was considerable. Crude protein levels being higher in area H than in a comparable non-burned grassland area (area G) suggests that ecological conditions (e.g., fuel load, soil moisture content) were such that combustion resulted in soil heating of sufficient intensity and/or duration to bring about an immediate release and/or increase of ammonia in the upper soil levels and correspondingly higher foliar nitrogen levels. However, in the burn category the highest crude protein levels were associated with controls C (mainly dung patches) and D, which strongly suggests that ecological dynamics particular to the combustion of dung may contribute to higher crude protein levels. As previously discussed, dung is a highly concentrated fuel source that burns at high temperatures for a prolonged period of time. Because of the formation of an outer crust, most heat generated by the combustion of dung radiates downward into the soil, amplifying its effect. It has been noted that the higher the temperatures, the greater the production of soil NH_4-N content.[69] The high heat intensities generated during the burning of forest habitats are also reflected in the amount of soil ammonia content. Approximately fivefold increases in soil ammonia content were noted after a burn in the forest areas of "Fenno-Scandia," in the

California Chaparral, and in the forested areas of the Transurals.[70] Hobbs and Schimel concluded that the larger increases in NH_4 in mountain shrub than in grasslands may be related to the more even nature of the burn and greater intensity of the burn.[71]

In the currently grazed areas, even at this early date, the stimulatory effect of grazing on crude protein levels has masked and/ or nullified the initial positive effects of burning (as demonstrated by the non-grazed controls) on crude protein values. Studies in the Serengeti by Seagle, McNaughton, and Ruess found that for control shortgrass and tallgrass simulations, grazing stimulated nitrogen uptake by both plants and microbes and maintained grasses in an actively growing and nutritious state.[72]

As previously noted, spring grazing was first initiated on grazed grassland areas. Nevertheless, although slightly delayed, when spring growth first appeared on burned areas, these areas were also preferentially grazed by the herds. Higher foliar crude protein levels (as expressed by the burned controls) were the critical palatability factor. The general absence of dry matter accumulations on burned areas may have contributed, in a minor sense, to selection. McGinty, Smeins, and Merrill pointed specifically to higher crude protein content as well as higher percent live biomass as factors attracting cattle to burned grasslands.[73] Willms, Bailey, and McLean attributed the selection for burned areas by cattle and deer to greater accessibility to green growth and chemical composition.[74] Vinton et al. stated that preferential grazing of burned areas by bison was probably the result of increased graminoid production and live/dead tissue ratios.[75]

Beginning in June, foliar crude protein levels declined more rapidly in the burned controls, dropping below those on non-burned controls by August; these dynamics concur with other studies.[76] More specifically, Knapp found that after a spring burn (late April) leaf nitrogen was initially much greater in the burned plot but by the end of June had dropped below the nitrogen values in the non-burned plot and continued for the rest of the growing season to be either slightly lower than or equal to levels in the unburned plot.[77]

Several factors may have been operative in the above dynamics. During the vegetative season, crude protein is highest during the leaf stage, decreases as the plants mature, and drops dramatically at the curing stage.[78] These dynamics are closely linked to the mechanism of translocation (i.e., the internal transport and/or recycling of nitrogen from above-ground to below-ground crowns and roots), whereby as much as one-third of the nitrogen present in green herbage at the height of the growing season undergoes internal translocation to below-ground parts by the latter part of the growing season.[79]

Burning appears to accelerate the above seasonal growth cycle, an event that may be related to differences in soil moisture conditions.[80] On the Canadian Mixed Prairie, lack of moisture in summer reduces the length of the growing season, while more favourable soil moisture conditions in the Aspen Park Region may postpone the dormant stage.[81] As noted earlier, moisture conditions are generally less favourable on burned areas. In addition, reduced soil moisture on burned areas has been attributed to increased transpiration by rapidly growing plants.[82] In the study area, by the end of June, biomass production on burned controls was substantially greater than on non-burned controls.

Microbial activity may also be a contributing factor to decreased foliar nitrogen levels. Seagle, McNaughton, and Ruess found that in simulations where microbial biomass was decreased by 50%, plant nitrogen uptake was reduced and net nitrogen mineralization by the microbial biomass declined, leading them to suggest that nitrogen sequestering by microbial populations returning toward control levels may have limited nitrogen availability for plant growth.[83]

In the currently grazed areas, beginning in June, grazing markedly inhibited the decline of crude protein levels. The inhibiting effect of grazing reached its strongest expression during August: crude protein values were double those found on non-grazed controls. In September, in both burned and non-burned controls, declines in crude protein levels were of similar magnitude, suggesting an adjustment or levelling process as the curing stage is approached and/or reached.

In the currently grazed areas, September marked the first time in the growing season that crude protein declines were greater than in the non-grazed controls; however, they continued to remain significantly higher. Grazed areas, with an absence of litter accumulations, little standing matter, and accelerated growth under the stimulus of defoliation are particularly susceptible to soil moisture stress under arid climatic conditions. The above events clearly explain the continued attraction during the growing season of the bison herds to areas (both burned and non-burned) on which grazing was first initiated. Vesey-Fitzgerald, referring to grazed areas as compared with non-grazed mature stands, concluded that the stage of growth is a more important characteristic of palatability than the species of grass.[84]

Within the currently grazed category, some internal variations in crude protein values may reflect differences in grazing histories. Crude protein levels generally were higher on areas where grazing was first initiated (both burned and non-burned), reflecting that the normal decline of crude protein levels was inhibited at an earlier date; however, this phenomenon generally did not persist for the duration of the growing season.

IMPACT OF URINE AND DUNG DEPOSITS ON HERBAGE CRUDE PROTEIN

Seagle, McNaughton, and Ruess link small-scale nutritional patchiness of grasslands to the deposition of dung and urine, noting that grazers concentrate nitrogen at urine deposition sites and small amounts of nitrogen and decomposable carbon at defecation sites.[85] In a natural grazing system, the age of dung deposits also influences the availability of nitrogen for plant uptake. The avoidance area (non-grazed vegetation) associated with older dung patches had significantly lower crude protein levels than vegetation associated with new dung, indicating a longer period of leaching and consequently less nutrients available for plant uptake. At the same time, the significantly higher crude protein levels exhibited by vegetation associated with older dung patches, when compared with the non-grazed controls, strongly suggest that leaching of nutrients from dung deposits continues well beyond a single vegetative season. However, no significant difference in nutritive values between the avoidance areas (old and new dung deposits) and the grazed areas were exhibited, again emphasizing the positive effect of grazing on plant nitrogen uptake.

Dung deposits also exhibit seasonal differences in crude protein levels that could affect the amount of nitrogen available for plant uptake. Fresh dung samples collected in June had a higher crude protein value than those collected in August. The decline reflects gradual maturation of diet grasses and a corresponding decrease in crude protein levels.

Urine deposits have an immediate and striking effect on the availability of nitrogen. Seagle, McNaughton, and Ruess observed that simulations of urine deposition resulted in marked increases in plant nitrogen uptake in both short and tall grass species.[86] Day and Detling also found that urine patches have 112g/m^2 more above-ground biomass and 2.53g/m^2 more plant nitrogen than controls.[87] Our studies concur with the above observations: in both August and September, crude protein levels on grazed urine patches were significantly higher than on both grazed areas and non-grazed controls. Interestingly, one of the important plant species in Day and Detling's study was *Poa pratensis*, or Kentucky bluegrass, which is the dominant grass form in the current study. They specifically point out that the large increase in *Poa* biomass on urine patches was a response to both increased soil nitrogen availability and its rhizomatous nature.

Crude protein levels on urine patches decreased between August and September. Seagle, McNaughton, and Ruess also observed decreases in plant nitrogen uptake in response to late, as compared with early, urine deposition.[88] However, crude protein levels in September are still appreciably higher than those associated with both grazed areas and non-grazed controls, explaining the continued preference by bison for urine patches long after most other grazed areas have been abandoned.

THE STRUCTURAL ATTRIBUTES OF THE BISON GRAZING SYSTEM

Given that the overall research area during the 1991 growing season was understocked (bison herd size was three bulls, four cows, one immature bull, and four calves), the attraction of bison to burned areas was clearly expressed and concurred with similar studies relating to grazing preferences by herbivores such as cattle, in one study, and both cattle and deer, in another.[89] Studies of contemporary bison herds also indicate a selection for burned areas.[90] More specifically, Vinton et al. found that bison preferentially grazed burned watersheds in spring and summer and that this preference was expressed by grazed patches being larger on frequently grazed burned areas than on non-burned areas.[91] A study of bison herds by Coppock and Detling discerned a sexual distinction in selection for burned areas.[92] Cow-calf bison groups exhibited a general preference for burned areas during the months of June, July, and August; in contrast, bulls selected for burned areas only in June, while use was low in July and August. Explanations for low use include better wallowing and forage conditions in adjacent areas. Observations in our study offer an alternative explanation. July and August signal the height of the rut. Although our herd was small, the dominant bull monopolized the cows, tolerated the immature bull, but successfully drove the other mature bulls away. Consequently, the sub-dominant bulls rarely fed in the same area as the cow-calf group.

The area (area E) chosen for the grid layout had no previous burning history and it exhibited most of the structural aspects and components of a grasslands grazing system. There were several small grazed areas whose parameters were delineated by the placement of the dung deposits and larger grazed areas that contained several well-defined avoidance areas. From a general perspective, the grid section could be defined as a less preferred area as only 24% was grazed. Heavy pollution was a major contributor to the low use, considering that within a 500 m² (5,382 sq ft) area there were 310 visible dung deposits, with substantially more deposits hidden by litter accumulations.

Area C, because of heavy utilization, represented an area where a random sample of well-defined avoidance areas could be obtained. The size of an avoidance area compared with the number of dung deposits found within it was highly uniform. Given this uniformity of size, we can broadly estimate the minimum impact of the avoidance behaviour on forage availability in the grid area. The average area of an avoidance area containing one dung deposit was 0.487 m² (5.24 sq ft) and the number of observable deposits was 310. It is calculated that the potential area taken out of forage production in the 500 m² area could be approximately 151 m² (1,625.4 sq ft), or 30% of the area.

SPECIES COMPOSITION

No variations in species composition were discerned relating to the effects of the fire. But, it must again be noted that the highly uneven distribution of the major species would have acted against changes being observed unless they were markedly significant. Previous studies on the effects of spring burning on species composition are varied. Knapp found that after a spring burn, the composition of a tall grass prairie was not greatly altered; however, Old found that after a spring burn *Poa pratensis* was all but eliminated from burned areas.[93] Moreover, several authors concluded that a single fire did not generally alter the overall species composition of a stand.[94]

The marked impact of grazing on species composition was clearly evident and can be related directly to bison grazing practices. As field results have shown, grazing maintains grasslands vegetation at high nutritive values—an important palatability factor. Therefore, bison tend to return to, or regraze, patches that were utilized early in the season. These areas thus undergo continuous grazing pressures during most of the vegetative season and often into subsequent years. As a result, brome was almost completely eliminated from many grazed areas. Walton, Martinez, and Bailey also found that brome under rotational grazing shows a steady decline during the vegetative season.[95] In the research area, Kentucky bluegrass appeared not to be markedly affected by grazing pressures, retaining similar frequencies under both grazed and non-grazed conditions. However, Moss and Campbell indicated that Kentucky bluegrass tends to become more frequent under grazing.[96] This may be true when competition does not occur from other species. In the study area, as brome progressively decreased, correspondingly invader species such as dandelion and white clover increased.

Although bison tended to uniformly graze most patches, there was some species-specific avoidance behaviour: goldenrod (*Solidago* spp.) was avoided during the entire vegetative season, while thistle was grazed during the early part of the season but generally avoided during the rest of the season.

CONCLUSIONS AND IMPLICATIONS

The historical record strongly emphasizes the attraction of bison to burned areas and implies that Indigenous Peoples often used this behaviour trait to manipulate the herds, thus enhancing resource procurement. In contemporary environmental studies, the attraction to burned areas has often been related to higher concentrations of chemical constituents, such as protein and phosphorous, or greater availability of green matter. However, regional differences in grassland responses to burning have complicated the determination of the specific and/or concrete microsite changes responsible for these dynamics. In more mesic areas where soil moisture is not a limiting factor, burning stimulates earlier growth and productivity is increased. In arid areas (Mixed Prairie regions) burning generally does not affect the initiation of growth and grassland productivity is reduced. There is general consensus that when soil moisture is limiting, burning does not increase productivity.

Another problem is that most studies have been carried out on non-grazed grasslands, which reflect a relatively homogeneous ecological state, bearing little reality to a natural grazing system. Grazing dynamics introduce a wide range of variables that in turn elicit a wide range of burning responses. Drawing on the information provided by the current study, as well as previous documentation, a tentative and/or preliminary herbivore grazing model was reconstructed to provide the broader framework needed to accommodate the in-site diversity initiated by grazing dynamics.

Also of importance in terms of model building is the awareness that methodological requirements and theory must accommodate a historical perspective (i.e., change through time) in relation to natural systems.[97] Change is a fundamental and/or intrinsic factor in ecological systems, whether seasonal or from a deeper temporal perspective. Therefore, determining the previous grazing history of the research area—that is, the herbivore grazing patterns that affected the physical structuring and the relational dynamics of the components in a parkland/grassland system—was of critical importance to the study.

In a grasslands ecosystem one of the most visible and/or structural modifications relating to a grazing history is the mosaic of grazed and non-grazed areas. Several variables that are integral parts of grazing events strongly modify this basic mosaic model: urine patches, dung deposits, and selective grazing patterns. Because selection processes act upon herbivore behaviour, grazing pressures are not uniform. In our studies, grazing was initiated on and preferences were shown for areas that had been grazed the previous season. Because bison consistently select for the same grazed patches during most of the vegetative season, little standing dry matter or litter accumulations remain—factors that generally inhibit the emergence of spring growth. The absence of these factors means not only an earlier initiation of growth but consequently greater availability and accessibility to green matter, which is an added attraction.

Another peculiar grazing behaviour that modifies the above features is related to the deposition of dung, which results in the immediate avoidance of the vegetative species in proximity to the deposit. In preferred areas, this configuration (dung patch) is a distinct feature made structurally visible by being completely grazed around its circumference. In preferred sites, grazed areas predominate, dotted by small islands of dung deposits fringed by non-grazed vegetation (the avoidance area). Urine deposits or patches do not illicit avoidance behaviour; on the contrary, they are strongly selected for and thus heavily grazed. In less preferred sites, non-grazed areas predominate but still exhibit the constituent urine and dung deposits. Understandably, the avoidance factor is often not clearly defined.

One of the most essential attributes of grazing is that most plant matter consumed by herbivores is returned in forms easily utilized by plants and micro-organisms.[98] More specifically, 80% to 85% of forage nitrogen ingested by grazers is excreted, 85% of it in urine.[99] Seagle, McNaughton, and Ruess linked urine and dung deposition to small-scale nutritional patchiness.[100] Our estimates of foliar crude protein levels on urine patches and non-grazed grassland species composing the avoidance area (i.e., proximate to dung deposits) strongly support Seagle, McNaughton, and Ruess's correlation of nutritional patchiness with grazing events. However, the nutritional patchiness associated with dung, as compared with urine, plays a different role in a grasslands grazing system. Urine nitrogen enters the soil ammonium pool directly, providing an immediate concentrated source of nitrogen for both plants and soil microbes. The higher foliar nitrogen values that urine provides immediately benefit herbivore populations and explain the attraction of bison to these areas. Day and Detling estimate that although urine patches covered only 2% of the experimental area, they provided 7% of the biomass and 14% of the nitrogen that herbivores consume during the growing season (June to August).[101]

Dung deposits mainly provide decomposable carbon and small amounts of nitrogen as well as other nutrients; however, it should be cautioned that pronounced seasonal variability exists in some of the nutrient constituents, especially nitrogen. Dung nutrients become available for plants and microbes at a slower rate, first through leaching (requiring favourable climatic conditions) and then later through decomposition. The deposition of dung provides little benefit to the herbivore populations, since grasslands species proximate to dung deposits are avoided—that is, not grazed. The benefits are mainly to the grasslands species, as deposition frequently occurs on areas that have experienced heavy grazing (and, consequently, nutrient depletion) given the continued selection for grazed areas during the growing season and into subsequent years. The persistent grazing of select areas also has a detrimental effect on species composition. Our studies found that species diversity was markedly reduced, brome was almost eliminated, and invaders such as dandelion and white clover had increased markedly. The removal of the vegetation in proximity to a dung deposit from grazing pressures allows regeneration and/or renewal (although patchy) with the added benefit of the nutrients provided by a dung deposit.

Grasslands with a grazing history exhibit highly variable and unique responses to burning. Burning responses are mainly affected by differences in the type of fuel and the amount (fuel load/unit area). There are basically two types and/or sources of fuel: herbaceous materials and dung patches (i.e., dung deposits with their associated non-grazed standing dry matter/litter accumulations). Grazing also complicates the grasslands responses to burning by generating a wide range of fuel loads. Burning has little impact on heavily grazed areas because of insufficient fuel load. The combustion of vegetation on most non-grazed areas would reflect what is generally accepted as a typical grasslands response to burning. But, in a grazing system there is also a ubiquitous distribution of urine and dung deposits (in both grazed and non-grazed areas), which have a profound effect (especially dung deposits) on burning responses and consequently microsite alterations. The burning of dung patches is particularly significant as they are often the only fuel source in heavily grazed areas. Urine patches rarely burn, being continually kept in an immature form through high nutrient content and persistent heavy grazing.

The peculiarities of dung combustion (i.e., those that enhance nutrient recycling) can be attributed mainly to the physical structuring of the dung deposit: specifically, the formation of a hard outer crust. Thus, dung does not flame but smoulders under mainly anaerobic conditions at high heat intensities for prolonged duration. Another critical attribute is heat containment, which focuses heat radiation downward into the soil (a major differential from forest fires)

High and prolonged soil heat intensities bring about an immediate release of soil nutrients (conversion of organic nitrogen to ammonia) suitable for plant uptake and, as a result, higher foliar nitrogen content. The burning of ungrazed herbaceous material can often lead to a change in soil chemistry that is similar, but generally of lesser extent and/or intensity. In our studies, high-quality burn residues (another important source of soil nutrients) reflect the burning of dung under anaerobic conditions so that combustion is incomplete. The burning of herbaceous vegetation also generally reflected incomplete combustion and consequently high-quality residues. The burning of dung patches, particularly on heavily grazed areas, also creates small-scale nutritional patchiness within the grasslands grazing system.

However, several burning studies have concluded that the removal of litter by burning was the critical factor in stimulating higher foliar nitrogen levels in the earlier part of the growing season. This explanation was highly influenced by the observation that higher foliar nitrogen values were also recorded on clipped vegetation, leading to the assumption that clear-cutting of an area simulates burning processes.[102] In contrast, White and Currie pointed out that the grasslands' response to burning showed little relationship to the clipped treatment response. They concluded that clipping is an unproductive technique for simulating burning conditions.[103]

However, clipping does simulate the effects of grazing and/or defoliation, which sets into motion microsite changes unrelated to the effects of burning. Grazing and/or clipping stimulates nitrogen uptake by both plants and microbes and maintains grasses in an actively growing immature form, thus in a highly nutritious condition.[104] Burning, on the other hand, increases the availability of soil nutrients for plant uptake: first, through heat conversion of soil organic nitrogen to ammonia, and second, through the formation of high-quality burn residues (ash/charred matter) that provide additional sources of nutrients through leaching.

After a spring burn the earliest and most rapid growth continues to occur on previously heavily grazed areas, under both burned and non-burned conditions, because ecological conditions on both areas are similar. Fire has little impact on heavily grazed areas because of insufficient fuel load. It was on these areas that the herds first initiated grazing, the selection factor again being the greatest availability of new spring growth. Most affected by burning were the avoidance areas and non-grazed grasslands, which carried a heavier fuel load. Spring growth on these areas was slightly delayed and/or reduced. Prior to burning, spring growth was delayed because of the inhibiting effect of dry matter/litter accumulations. After the burn, heat damage (retardation of growth rather than death of plants), as well as drying of soils, continued to inhibit the growth rate. As a result, in early spring, biomass production on non-grazed burned areas was significantly lower than on non-burned areas. However, when appreciable amounts of new spring growth occurred on these areas they were selected by the herds. The higher foliar crude protein levels found on burned areas—the highest being associated with the combustion of dung—was probably the significant palatability factor. As previously noted, higher crude protein values in the early part of the growing season were attributed to the heat conversion of soil organic nitrogen to ammonia. Accelerated growth on the burned controls resulted in biomass differences between burned and non-burned controls becoming negligible by early summer, progressively widening to become significantly greater on burned areas by late summer, continuing for the rest of the growing season. Greater productivity was generally related to more favourable climatic conditions combined with the effects of burning, such as the leaching of nutrients from burn residues.

The stimulatory effect of burning on foliar crude protein levels is a short-term event. Crude protein differences between burned and non-burned controls have disappeared by early summer and are significantly lower on burned areas by fall. Lower crude protein levels in burned controls were attributed to an acceleration of the growth or development cycle with a corresponding drop in crude protein levels. The acceleration of the growth cycle was related to soil moisture depletion because of increased water use by more rapidly growing plants.

The most important phenomenon is the stimulatory effect of grazing on crude protein levels, the consequence being that the decline in foliar crude protein levels on grazed areas (both burned and non-burned) is much slower than on non-grazed areas. Less than a month after grazing was initiated, differences in crude protein levels between grazed areas (burned and non-burned) were no longer significant. Differences in crude protein levels then progressively widened, becoming significantly higher on currently grazed areas by late summer and remaining so for the rest of the growing season. The above dynamics explain the continued selection by bison for areas on which spring grazing was first initiated: areas that were grazed the previous season (both burned and non-burned areas), which exhibit the earliest growth and consequently the greatest availability of green matter; and burned grasslands that initially exhibited significantly higher foliar crude protein levels (i.e., those that carried a heavy fuel load). Thus, continuous grazing pressures were the single most important factor stimulating higher foliar crude protein levels for most of the vegetative season.

Areas not grazed by early summer generally remain untouched for the remainder of the growing season. However, most grazed grassland areas are abandoned by late fall (with the exception of urine patches) and grazing shifts to sedge meadows and/or the grazing of seed heads (top grazing) on non-grazed grasslands.

The above provides a general picture of the bison/fire/grasslands model. However, within any growing season the responses of the various components to climatic variability as well as microsite variations can be highly diverse, providing a complexity of interplays attesting to the highly volatile and/or dynamic nature of living systems.

There appears to be a developing perception that grasslands in the absence of burning and fire are to some degree in a state of stasis, or at least less dynamic. Seagle, McNaughton, and Ruess note that in grasslands with a grazing history the rate of nutrient recycling is increased compared with litterfall.[105] The act of grazing can, by stimulating plant uptake of nutrients, also be perceived as a mechanism involved in accelerating the nutrient cycle. In turn, increased foliar nutritive values act as a selection and/or palatability factor, thus perpetuating the process by maintaining continuous grazing pressures. The review by Seagle, McNaughton, and Ruess concludes that defoliation stimulates grass nutrient uptake, resulting in high forage quality, which further increases the attractiveness of these areas to grazing animals.[106]

Burning also accelerates the nutrient cycle. Viro points out that burning releases large numbers of nutrients that through natural decomposition would take a very long time. Thus, the bulk of the matter would never decompose and can only be perceived as a potential nutrient reserve.[107] More specifically, Aref'yeva and Kolesnikov point out that burning intensifies "the physiochemical processes, manifested both in decomposition of the nitrogen-containing organic matter and in release of fixed ammonia from the soil minerals."[108]

However, dung deposits are highly impervious to climatic degradation, and so decomposition is a prolonged event. Given the progressive buildup of dung deposits, combined with the avoidance behaviour of the bison herds, a corresponding increase in the amount of biomass unavailable for forage could become a critical factor in the dynamics of a grazing system. Fire then becomes a key factor in grasslands restoration. The burning of dung patches and grasslands vegetation with a sufficient fuel load accelerates the nutrient cycle by an immediate release of soil nutrients (by heat conversion) suitable for plant uptake and also by the formation of high-quality burn residues, also a reservoir for soil nutrients. Of critical importance is the fact that the burning of dung deposits nullifies the avoidance behaviour, opening up new areas of high-quality forage for grazing. As a result, grazing on a burned area is more uniform and grazing pressures have partly shifted to areas that were previously not grazed.

In conclusion, climate, grazing, and fire are the most important factors in the character of a grasslands ecosystem. The influence of climate is encompassing and continuous, impacting on all aspects of a grasslands ecosystem. The latter two variables also markedly modify the grasslands biome, structurally and, more importantly, by accelerating the rate of nutrient recycling.

The above grazing/fire model has important implications for range management. Given the selection and subsequent continuous utilization of grazed grasslands patches during the season and into following years (regardless of the carrying capacity of the area), overgrazing (although patchy) is an inevitable consequence. Where grazed areas predominate, overgrazing can detrimentally affect the overall species composition/diversity and general viability of the grasslands biome. Spring burning of adjacent (less preferred) areas can shift grazing pressures, allowing for regeneration and/or restoration of overgrazed areas. An added benefit is that on burned areas, additional forage areas are now accessible that generally are more productive, given favourable climatic conditions. In addition, after a winter diet of low-quality (cured) forage, a deficiency in the maintenance or energy requirements of the associated herbivore populations could be a critical consideration. Spring burning provides high-quality forage during this critical period. McGinty, Smeins, and Merrill found that across a 155-day grazing period (beginning in June), the rate of heifer gains was significantly higher on the burned areas than on the controls.[109] A rotational burning program would bring about greater uniformity of grazing, as well as increased grasslands' productivity and forage quality, with negligible monetary output.

In regard to natural conservation and/or ecological restoration policies, a mental template must evolve that accommodates grazing/fire dynamics as integral or intrinsic factors in the viability of any grasslands system. Without these natural stimuli, grasslands systems degenerate or simulate climax (stasis) conditions markedly at variance with their systemic integrity.

ACKNOWLEDGEMENTS

My appreciation to the following agencies, which provided financial support: the Social Sciences and Humanities Research Council, Norwest Laboratories (Edmonton), and the University of Alberta Central Research Fund. The project would not have been possible without the logistical support and cooperation of the Warden's Service at Elk Island National Park; a special thanks to warden Wes Olson. Morgan Stromsmoe (warden service) carried out analyses of the species composition of the grasslands communities.

NOTES

Foreword

1 David G. Mandelbaum, *The Plains Cree*, Anthropological Papers of the AMNH, vol. 37, pt. 2 (New York: American Museum of Natural History, 1940), reprinted and revised as *The Plains Cree: An Ethnographic, Historical, and Comparative Study*, Canadian Plains Studies 9 (Regina: Canadian Plains Research Center, 1979). Page numbers refer to the 1979 rev. ed.

2 David Thompson, "The Natives of North America," n.d., 4, David Thompson Papers, MS 21, box 6, Thomas Fisher Rare Book Library, University of Toronto.

3 Arthur J. Ray, *Indians in the Fur Trade: Their Role as Trappers, Hunters, and Middlemen in the Lands Southwest of Hudson Bay, 1660–1870* (Toronto: University of Toronto Press, 1974).

4 James G.E. Smith, "The Western Woods Cree: Anthropological Myth and Historical Reality," *American Ethnologist* 14, no. 3 (1987): 434–48. See also Dale Russell, *Eighteenth-Century Western Cree and Their Neighbours* (Ottawa: Canadian Museum of Civilization, 1991); and David Smyth, "Missed Opportunity: John Milloy's *The Plains Cree*," *Prairie Forum* 17 (1992): 338.

5 Ray, *Indians in the Fur Trade*, xxi.

6 Christy Climenhaga, "Regina Experiences Driest July in 130 Years," CBC News, last updated August 1, 2017, http://www.cbc.ca/news/canada/saskatchewan/regina-experiences-driest-july-in-130-years-1.4230893.

7 See James Daschuk, "A Dry Oasis: The Canadian Plains in Late Prehistory," *Prairie Forum* 34, no. 1 (2009): 1–29; and Daschuk, "Who Killed the Prairie Beaver? An Environmental Case for Eighteenth Century Migration in Western Canada," *Prairie Forum* 37 (Fall 2012): 151–72.

Introduction

1 Alexander Henry, "Henry's Journal," pt. 2, "The Saskatchewan," in *New Light on the Early History of the Greater Northwest: The Manuscript Journals of Alexander Henry and of David Thompson, 1799–1814*, vol. 2, ed. Elliott Coues (1897; Minneapolis: Ross and Haines, 1965), 529–30.

2 John McDonnell, "The Red River" (c. 1797), in *Les Bourgeois de la Compagnie du Nord-Ouest*, vol. 1, ed. L.R. Masson (New York: Antiquarian Press, 1960), 281.

3 Alexander Mackenzie, *Voyages from Montreal on the River St. Laurence through the Continent of North America, to the Frozen and Pacific Oceans . . .* (New York: G.F. Hopkins, 1802), 45.

4 Edward Umfreville, *The Present State of Hudson's Bay: Containing a Full Description of That Settlement and the Adjacent Country . . .*, ed. W. Stewart Wallace (1790; Toronto: Ryerson Press, 1954), 103.

5   Duncan McGillivray, *The Journal of Duncan M'Gillivray of the Northwest Company at Fort George on the Saskatchewan, 1794–1795,* ed. Arthur Silver Morton (Toronto: Macmillan, 1929), 31.

6   Jean Baptiste Trudeau, "Trudeau's Journal," *South Dakota Historical Collections* 7 (1914): 461.

7   Joseph Jablow, *The Cheyenne in Plains Indian Trade Relations, 1795–1840* (Seattle: University of Washington Press, 1966), 32.

8   Charles MacKenzie, "Missouri Indians: A Narrative of Four Trading Expeditions, 1804–06," in *Les Bourgeois de la Compagnie du Nord-Ouest,* vol. 1, ed. L.R. Masson (New York: Antiquarian Press, 1960), 331, 377.

9   François Antoine Larocque, *Journal of François Antoine Larocque from the Assiniboine to the Yellowstone, 1805,* ed. with notes by L.J. Burpee, Publications of the Canadian Archives 3 (1805; Ottawa: Government Printing Bureau, 1910), 168–91.

10   Paul C. Phillips, *The Fur Trade* (Norman: University of Oklahoma Press, 1961), 262.

11   Hiram Martin Chittenden, *The American Fur Trade of the Far West* (1902; Stanford: Academic Reprints, 1954), 1:146–51.

12   John C. Ewers, *The Blackfeet: Raiders on the Northwestern Plains* (Norman: University of Oklahoma Press, 1958), 55.

13   MacKenzie, "Missouri Indians," in Masson, *Les Bourgeois,* 1:342.

14   Edward S. Curtis, *The North American Indian,* 20 vols. (1907–30; New York: Johnson Reprint, 1970); Ewers, *Blackfeet;* Frank Raymond Secoy, *Changing Military Patterns on the Great Plains* (Seattle: University of Washington Press, 1953); Arthur Silver Morton, *A History of the Canadian West to 1870–71* (Toronto: University of Toronto Press, 1973).

15   J.G. Nelson, *The Last Refuge* (Montreal: Harvest House, 1973), 170.

16   Ewers, *Blackfeet,* 32.

17   Mackenzie, *Voyages from Montreal,* 49.

18   Morton, *History of the Canadian West;* Nelson, *Last Refuge.*

19   Nelson, *Last Refuge,* 188.

20   Ray, *Indians in the Fur Trade,* 11.

21   Arthur Dobbs, *An Account of the Countries Adjoining to Hudson's Bay in the Northwest Part of America* (1744; London: S.R. Publishers; Johnson Reprint, 1967), 35.

22   In L.J. Burpee, ed., *Journal and Letters of Pierre Gaultier de Varennes de La Vérendrye and His Sons* (Toronto: Champlain Society, 1927), 301.

23   McGillivray, *Journal,* 34.

24   Henry, "Henry's Journal," in Coues, *New Light,* 2:723–24.

25   Henry in Coues, 2:737, 512–13.

26 R. Grace Morgan, *An Ecological Study of the Northern Plains as Seen through the Garratt Site*, Occasional Papers in Anthropology 1 (Regina: Department of Anthropology, University of Regina, 1979); Boyd Wettlaufer and William J. Mayer-Oakes, *The Long Creek Site*, Anthropological Series 2 (Regina: Department of Natural Resources, 1960); Brian J. Smith, "The Lebret Site" (MA thesis, University of Saskatchewan, 1986).

27 Wilfred M. Husted, *Bighorn Canyon Archaeology*, Smithsonian Institution River Basin Surveys, Publications in Salvage Archaeology 12 (Lincoln: University of Nebraska Press, 1969).

28 William Mulloy, *A Preliminary Historical Outline for the Northwestern Plains*," University of Wyoming Publications 22 (Laramie: University of Wyoming, 1958).

29 Nelson, *Last Refuge*, 171.

30 Ewers, *Blackfeet*, 32; Umfreville, *Present State of Hudson's Bay*, 88.

31 Richard Lancaster, *Piegan* (Garden City, NY: Doubleday, 1966), 188.

32 Clark Wissler, *Ceremonial Bundles of the Blackfoot Indians*, Anthropological Papers of the AMNH, vol. 8, pt. 2 (New York: American Museum of Natural History, 1912), 168–69; Clark Wissler and D.C. Duvall, *Mythology of the Blackfoot Indians*, Anthropological Papers of the AMNH, vol. 2, pt. 1 (New York: American Museum of Natural History, 1908), 75–78.

33 Curtis, *North American Indian*, 70–71.

34 A.L. Kroeber, "Cheyenne Tales," *Journal of American Folklore* 13, no. 50 (1900): 161–90.

35 Alice Marriott, "Osage Indian II," in David Agee Horr, ed., *American Indian Ethnohistory: Plains Indians* (New York: Garland, 1974).

36 Marvin Harris, *Culture, People, Nature: An Introduction to General Anthropology* (New York: Harper and Row, 1985), 459.

37 George Bird Grinnell, *The Cheyenne Indians: Their History and Ways of Life*, 2 vols. (Lincoln: University of Nebraska Press, 1972), 104.

38 MacKenzie, "Missouri Indians," in Masson, *Les Bourgeois*, 1:378

39 Ernest Wallace and E. Adamson Hoebel, *The Comanches: Lords of the South Plains* (Norman: University of Oklahoma Press, 1952), 175.

40 Curtis, *North American Indian*, 6:183; Wallace and Hoebel, *Comanches*, 175.

41 T.R. Fehrenbach, *Comanches: The Destruction of a People* (New York: Knopf, 1974), 108.

42 R. Grace Morgan, "Bison Movement Patterns on the Canadian Plains: An Ecological Analysis," *Plains Anthropologist* 25, no. 88 (1980): 157.

43 Eugene P. Odum, *Fundamentals of Ecology* (Philadelphia: W.B. Saunders, 1959), 201.

44 Steven W. Seagle, S.J. McNaughton, and Roger W. Ruess, "Simulated Effects of Grazing on Soil Nitrogen and Mineralization in Contrasting Serengeti Grasslands," *Ecology* 73, no. 3 (1992): 1105–23.

45 T.A. Day and J.K. Detling, "Grassland Patch Dynamics and Herbivore Grazing Preference following Urine Deposition," *Ecology* 71, no. 1 (1990): 180–88.

46 Harris, *Culture, People, Nature*, 459.

47 David Thompson, *David Thompson's Narrative, 1784–1812*, new ed., ed. Richard Glover (1916; Toronto: Champlain Society, 1962), 95.

48 Thompson, *David Thompson's Narrative*, 83.

49 Morgan, *Ecological Study*. See also the appendix in this volume.

50 Morgan, *Ecological Study*, 180.

51 Ewers, *Blackfeet*, 17.

52 Robin Ridington, "Technology, World View, and Adaptive Strategy in a Northern Hunting Society," *Canadian Review of Sociology and Anthropology* 19, no. 4 (1982): 478.

53 Henry T. Lewis, "Why Indians Burned: Specific versus General Reasons," in *Proceedings: Symposium and Workshop on Wilderness Fire*, ed. J.E. Lotan et al., General Technical Report INT-182 (Ogden, UT: Intermountain Forest and Range Experiment Station, Forest Service, US Department of Agriculture, 1985), 75.

54 Henry T. Lewis, *A Time for Burning*, Occasional Publication 17 (Edmonton: Boreal Institute for Northern Studies, University of Alberta, 1982), 47.

55 Lewis R. Binford, introduction to *For Theory Building in Archaeology*, ed. Lewis R. Binford (New York: Academic Press, 1977), 8.

56 Michael Treshow, *The Human Environment* (New York: McGraw-Hill, 1976), 69.

57 William H. Rutherford, *The Beaver in Colorado: Its Biology, Ecology, Management, and Economics*, Beaver Investigations, Project W-83-R, Technical Publication 17 (Denver: Colorado Game, Fish, and Parks Department, 1964).

58 John H. Livingston, *One Cosmic Instant* (Toronto: McClelland and Stewart, 1973), 19; see also Amos Turk, Jonathan Turk, and Janet T. Wittes, *Ecology, Pollution, Environment* (Philadelphia: W.B. Saunders, 1972).

59 Paul R. Ehrlich, Anne H. Ehrlich, and John P. Holdren, *Human Ecology: Problems and Solutions* (San Francisco: W.H. Freeman and Company, 1973), 4.

60 See Francis C. Evans, "Ecosystems as the Basic Unit in Ecology," in *Conservation Ecology*, ed. George W. Cox (New York: Appleton-Century-Crofts, 1969), 4.

61 D.W. Moodie and Arthur J. Ray, "Buffalo Migrations in the Canadian Plains," *Plains Anthropologist* 21, no. 71 (1976): 45.

62 S. Raby and T. Richards, "Water Resources," in *Atlas of Saskatchewan*, ed. J.H. Richards and K.I. Fung (Saskatoon: University of Saskatchewan, 1961), 61.

63 Morgan, *Ecological Study*, 186.

64 George Knudson, *Relationship of Beaver to Forests, Trout, and Wildlife in Wisconsin*, Technical Bulletin 25 (Madison: Wisconsin Conservation Department, 1962), 32.

65 Ewers, *Blackfeet*, 17.

66 Mandelbaum, *Plains Cree*, 52.

67 C.B. Blyth and R.J. Hudson, "A Plan for the Management of Vegetation and Ungulates: Elk Island National Park" (MSc thesis, University of Alberta, 1987), 25.

68 Nelson, *Last Refuge*, 188.

69 Alice B. Kehoe, *North American Indians: A Comprehensive Account* (Englewood Cliffs, NJ: Prentice-Hall, 1981), 276–80.

70 Arthur J. Ray, "History and Archaeology of the Northern Fur Trade," *American Antiquity* 43, no. 1 (1978): 26.

Chapter 1: The Regional Setting

1 See Morgan, *Ecological Study*, 9–10.

2 I. Dyck, "The Prehistory of Southern Saskatchewan," in *Tracking Ancient Hunters: Prehistoric Archaeology in Saskatchewan*, ed. H.T. Epp and I. Dyck (Regina: Saskatchewan Archaeology Society, 1983), 68. See also Terri-Anne Lang and Ken Jones, *A Comparison of the Meteorological Conditions during the Droughts of the 1930s and the 1980s for the Prairie Provinces* (Ottawa: Atmospheric Environment Service, Environment Canada, 1988).

3 Morgan, *Ecological Study*, 182.

4 Morgan.

5 Robert T. Coupland, "A Reconsideration of Grassland Classification in the Northern Great Plains of North America," *Journal of Ecology* 49, no. 1 (1961): 137.

6 *Stipa-Bouteloua* is spear grass–blue grama, and *Bouteloua-Agropyron* is blue grama–wheat grass. Morgan, *Ecological Study*, 30.

7 Coupland, "Reconsideration," 164–65. *Agropyron-Koeleria* is wheat grass–June grass, and *Stipa-Agropyron* is spear grass–wheat grass. Morgan, *Ecological Study*, 29, 27.

8 Henry A. Wright and Arthur W. Bailey, *Fire Ecology and Prescribed Burning in the Great Plains: A Research Review*, General Technical Report INT-77 (Ogden, UT: Intermountain Forest and Range Experiment Station, Forest Service, US Department of Agriculture, 1980), 23.

9 R.T. Coupland and J.S. Rowe, "Natural Vegetation of Saskatchewan," in *Atlas of Saskatchewan*, ed. J.H. Richards and K.I. Fung (Saskatoon: University of Saskatchewan 1969), 73.

10 Morgan, *Ecological Study*, 32.

11 Wright and Bailey, *Fire Ecology*, 24.

12 The term was coined by Coupland and Rowe, "Natural Vegetation."

13 Coupland, "Reconsideration," 138.

14 A.K. Chakravarti, "The Climate of Saskatchewan," in Richard and Fung, ed., *Atlas of Saskatchewan*, 60.

15 E.A. Christiansen, *Geology and Ground-Water Resources of the Regina Area*, Saskatchewan Report 2 (Regina: Geology Division, Saskatchewan Research Council, 1961), 14.

16 Robert T. Coupland, "Ecology of Mixed Prairie in Canada," *Ecological Monographs* 20, no. 4 (1950): 278.

17 Richmond W. Longley, *The Climate of the Prairie Provinces*, Climatological Studies 13 (Toronto: Atmospheric Environment, Environment Canada, 1972), 25.

18 Christiansen, *Geology and Ground-Water Resources*, 12.

19 Coupland, "Reconsideration," 138.

20 Longley, *Climate*, 44.

21 Blyth and Hudson, "Vegetation and Ungulates," 13.

22 Coupland, "Ecology of Mixed Prairie," 279.

23 Chakravarti, "Climate of Saskatchewan," 60.

24 Coupland, "Reconsideration," 140.

25 Longley, *Climate*, 52.

26 Lang and Jones, *Comparison*, 1.

27 Lang and Jones, 7.

28 Lang and Jones, 3–7.

29 Canada, Historical Hydrometric Data Search, Station 05JF011, "Cottonwood Creek near Lumsden," last modified February 3, 2020, https://wateroffice. ec.gc.ca/search/historical_e.html.

30 Canada, Historical Hydrometric Data Search, Station 05JE001, "Moose Jaw River above Thunder Creek," last modified February 3, 2020, https:// wateroffice.ec.gc.ca/search/historical_e.html.

31 Raby and Richards, "Water Resources," 61.

32 Coupland and Rowe, "Natural Vegetation," 74.

33 Coupland and Rowe.

34 M.A.G. Ayyad and R.L. Dix, "An Analysis of a Vegetation-Micro-Environmental Complex on Prairie Slopes in Saskatchewan," *Ecological Monographs* 34, no. 4 (1964): 433–34.

35 S. Charles Kendeigh, *Animal Ecology* (Englewood Cliffs, NJ: Prentice-Hall, 1961), 124.

36 Canada, Saskatchewan, and Manitoba, *Report of the Qu'Appelle Basin Study Board* (Regina: Queen's Printer, 1972), 9; J.S. Rowe, "Nicolle Flats–Moose Jaw Creek," International Biological Programme, Section CT: Conservation of Terrestrial Biological Communities, Department of Plant Ecology, University of Saskatchewan, 1971; Rowe, "East Qu'Appelle Valley Natural

Area," International Biological Programme, Section CT: Conservation of Terrestrial Biological Communities, Department of Plant Ecology, University of Saskatchewan, 1973; Coupland, "Ecology of Mixed Prairie," 308.

37 Morgan, *Ecological Study*, 51.

38 Coupland, "Ecology of Mixed Prairie," 277.

39 Morgan, *Ecological Study*, 61.

40 Morgan, 63.

41 Coupland, "Reconsideration," 150.

42 Morgan, *Ecological Study*, 64–65.

43 Canada, Saskatchewan, and Manitoba, *Report*, xi.

44 D.M. Kent, "The Glacial History of the Regina–Qu'Appelle Valley Area" (unpublished paper, Department of Geology, University of Regina, 1968), 4.

45 Christiansen, *Geology and Ground-Water Resources*, 25.

46 Kent, "Glacial History," 4.

47 Canada, Saskatchewan, and Manitoba, *Report*, 6–7.

48 Canada, Saskatchewan, and Manitoba, *Report*, 8.

49 Morgan, *Ecological Study*.

50 George Bird Grinnell, *Blackfoot Lodge Tales* (1892; Lincoln: University of Nebraska Press, 1968), 234.

51 Henry Youle Hind, *Narrative of the Canadian Red River Exploring Expedition of 1857 and of the Assiniboine and Saskatchewan Exploring Expedition of 1858*, 2 vols. (1860; Edmonton: M.G. Hurtig, 1971), 2:108.

52 W.T. Hornaday, "The Extermination of the American Bison, with a Sketch of Its Discovery and Life History," in *Annual Report, 1887, Smithsonian Institution* (Washington, DC: Smithsonian Institution, 1889), 424.

53 Morgan, "Bison Movement Patterns," 152.

54 Morgan, 153, 151.

55 Morgan, 157.

Chapter 2: Human-Animal Relationships

1 Michael Stephen Kennedy, *The Assiniboines* (Norman: University of Oklahoma Press, 1961), 63.

2 George W. Arthur, "An Introduction to the Ecology of Early Historic Communal Bison Hunting among the Northern Plains Indians" (Archaeological Survey of Canada Paper 37, Mercury Series, National Museum of Man, Ottawa, 1975), 88.

3 Mandelbaum, *Plains Cree*, 68.

4 Frank Gilbert Roe, *The North American Buffalo: A Critical Study of the Species* (Toronto: University of Toronto Press, 1972), 643.

5 Harris, *Culture, People, Nature*, 459–60.

6   A. Radclyffe Dugmore, *The Romance of the Beaver* (London: William Heine-
     mann, 1914), 178–79; Wissler, *Ceremonial Bundles*, 168–69.
7   Ewers, *Blackfeet*, 17.
8   John C. Ewers, *The Horse in Blackfoot Indian Culture*, Bureau of American
     Ethnology Bulletin 159 (Washington, DC: Smithsonian Institution, 1955),
     32; Lancaster, *Piegan*, 188.
9   Grinnell, *Cheyenne Indians*, 1:94.
10   Nelson, *Last Refuge*, 171.
11   Curtis, *North American Indian*, 6:69.
12   Lancaster, *Piegan*, 188.
13   Curtis, *North American Indian*, 6:70–71.
14   On these other versions of the story, see Wissler and Duvall, *Mythology*,
     75–76 (Blood), 77–78.
15   Grinnell, *Cheyenne Indians*.
16   Frank B. Wire and A.B. Hatch, "Administration of Beaver in the Western
     United States," *Journal of Wildlife Management* 7, no. 1 (1943): 91.
17   Dorothy Bergstrom, "Beavers: Biologists 'Rediscover' a Natural Resource,"
     Forestry Research West, October 1985, 2; Morrell Allred, "A Re-emphasis
     on the Value of the Beaver in Natural Resource Conservation," *Journal
     of the Idaho Academy of Science* 16, no. 1 (1980): 3; Knudson, *Relationship of
     Beaver*, 32.
18   D. Sherratt and D. Hatch, *Qu'Appelle Mammalian Inventory*, Wildlife Technical
     Report 77-37 (Regina: Saskatchewan Tourism and Renewable Resources,
     1977).
19   Morgan, R. Grace, Beaver Cache Survey, October 22, 1979.
20   Ray, *Indians in the Fur Trade*, 118.
21   Nicolas Denys, *The Description and Natural History of the Coasts of North
     America*, ed. William F. Ganong (Toronto: Champlain Society, 1908), 429;
     Thompson, *David Thompson's Narrative*, 152.
22   Morgan, *Ecological Study*.
23   Hind, *Narrative*, 1:328.
24   For examples, see Arthur, "Introduction to the Ecology"; Kenneth F. Hig-
     gins, *Interpretation and Compendium of Historical Fire Accounts in the Northern
     Great Plains*, Resource Publication 161 (Washington, DC: Fish and Wildlife
     Service, Department of the Interior, 1986).
25   R. Daubenmire, "Ecology of Fire in Grasslands," *Advances in Ecological Research*
     5 (1968): 209–67; William T. Penfound and R.W. Kelting, "Some Effects of
     Winter Burning on a Moderately Grazed Pasture," *Ecology* 31, no. 4 (1950):
     554–60.
26   Arthur, "Introduction to the Ecology," 24; Higgins, *Historical Fire Accounts*;
     Henry T. Lewis, "Fire Technology and Resource Management in Aborig-
     inal North America and Australia," in *Resource Managers: North American*

and Australian Hunter-Gatherers, ed. N.M. Williams and E.S. Hunn, AAAS Selected Symposium 67 (Boulder, CO: Western Press, 1982), 49.

27 Arthur, "Introduction to the Ecology," 23.

28 Morgan, "Bison Movement Patterns," 151.

29 Thompson, *David Thompson's Narrative*, 51.

30 McDonnell, "Red River," in Masson, *Les Bourgeois*, 1:268.

31 Hind, *Narrative*, 1:331–32.

32 Morgan, *Ecological Study*, 182.

33 George C. Frison, *The Piney Creek Sites, Wyoming*, University of Wyoming Publications 33 (Laramie: University of Wyoming, 1967), 32.

34 Morgan, *Ecological Study*, 179.

35 Isaac Cowie, *The Company of Adventurers on the Great Buffalo Plains* (Toronto: William Briggs, 1913), 207.

36 Canada, Historical Hydrometric Data Search, Station 05JF011, "Cottonwood Creek near Lumsden"; Station 05JE001, "Moose Jaw River above Thunder Creek."

37 Knudson, *Relationship of Beaver*, 43.

38 Wire and Hatch, "Administration of Beaver," 91.

39 Morgan, *Ecological Study*, 180.

40 David I. Bushnell, *Villages of the Algonquian, Siouan, and Caddoan Tribes West of the Mississippi*, Bureau of American Ethnology Bulletin 77 (Washington, DC: Smithsonian Institution, 1922), 202.

41 Kennedy, *Assiniboines*, 117.

42 Wallace and Hoebel, *Comanches*, 15.

43 Richard I. Dodge, *Our Wild Indians: Thirty-Three Years' Personal Experience among the Red Men of the Great West* (Hartford, CT: A.D. Worthington and Company, 1959), 242.

44 John C. Ewers, *Ethnological Report on the Blackfeet and Gros Ventre Tribes of Indians Lands in Northern Montana*, Pocket 279–A, Indian Claims Commission, May 1, 1888 (New York: Clearwater, 1973), 17.

45 Edwin Thompson Denig, *Five Indian Tribes of the Upper Missouri: Sioux, Arickaras, Assiniboines, Crees, and Crows*, ed. John C. Ewers (Norman: University of Oklahoma Press, 1961), 67.

46 Thompson, *David Thompson's Narrative*, 167.

47 Alexander Henry, *Travels and Adventures in Canada and the Indian Territories*, ed. James Bain (1809; Edmonton: M.G. Hurtig, 1969), 303.

48 Morgan, *Ecological Study*, 178.

49 Ewers, *Blackfeet*, 76; Mandelbaum, *Plains Cree*, 56.

50 Ewers, *Horse in Blackfoot Indian Culture*, 154.

51 Canada, Historical Hydrometric Data Search.

52 Joseph G. Hall, "Willow and Aspen in the Ecology of Beaver on Sagehen Creek, California," *Ecology* 41, no. 3 (1960): 487. See also Stephen H. Jenkins,

"A Size-Distance Relation in Food Selection by Beavers," *Ecology* 61, no. 4 (1980): 742; Arlen W. Todd, *Methodology Used for Alberta Land Inventory of Furbearers* (Edmonton: Alberta Fish and Wildlife Division, Department of Recreation, Parks, and Wildlife, 1978), 19.

53 Glenn W. Bradt, "A Study of Beaver Colonies in Michigan," *Journal of Mammalogy* 19, no. 2 (1938): 156; Hall, "Willow and Aspen," 487; Kenneth W. Hodgdon and John H. Hunt, *Beaver Management in Maine*, Game Division Bulletin 3 (Augusta, ME: Department of Inland Fisheries and Game, 1955), 432; William H. Longley and John B. Moyle, *The Beaver in Minnesota*, Technical Bulletin 6 (Minneapolis: Division of Game and Fish, Minnesota Department of Conservation, 1963), 35; Rutherford, *Beaver in Colorado*, 17; Paul Isaac Vincent Strong, "Beaver-Cottonwood Interactions and Beaver Ecology in Big Bend National Park" (MSc thesis, Oklahoma State University, 1982), 49.

54 Arthur, "Introduction to the Ecology," 121.

55 Ewers, *Horse in Blackfoot Indian Culture*, 124.

56 Merrill C. Hammond, "Beaver on the Lower Souris Refuge," *Journal of Wildlife Management* 7, no. 3 (1943): 317.

57 Morgan, *Ecological Study*, 125.

58 Hind, *Narrative*, 2:106.

59 Mandelbaum, *Plains Cree*, 52.

60 Mackenzie, *Voyages from Montreal*, 51.

61 Henry, *Travels and Adventures*, 286.

62 Arthur, "Introduction to the Ecology," 121, 96.

63 Rudolph F. Kurz, *Journal of Rudolph Friedrich Kurz, 1846–1852*, trans. Myrtis Jarrell, ed. J.N.B. Hewitt, Bureau of American Ethnology Bulletin 115 (Washington, DC: Smithsonian Institution, 1937), 146; John McDougall, *Saddle, Sled, and Snowshoe: Pioneering on the Saskatchewan in the Sixties* (1896; Toronto: Ryerson Press, 1900), 282; Nelson, *Last Refuge*, 151.

64 Morgan, *Ecological Study*, 113.

65 Sherratt and Hatch, *Qu'Appelle Mammalian Inventory*, 14.

66 Morgan, *Ecological Study*, 137.

67 Lang and Jones, *Comparison*; Canada, Historical Hydrometric Data Search.

68 Morgan, *Ecological Study*, 136, 183.

69 Thomas C. Collins, "Stream Flow Effects on Beaver Populations in Grand Teton National Park," in *Proceedings of the First Conference on Scientific Research in the National Parks*, vol. 1, ed. Robert M. Linn, National Park Service Transactions and Proceedings Series 5 (Washington, DC: US Department of the Interior, 1979), 351.

70 David A. Dary, *The Buffalo Book: The Saga of an American Symbol* (New York: Avon Books, 1975), 34.

71 Thompson, *David Thompson's Narrative*, 153.

72 J.L. Retzer et al., *Suitability of Physical Factors for Beaver Management in the Rocky Mountains of Colorado*, Technical Bulletin 2 (Denver: Department of Game and Fish, State of Colorado, 1956), 25.

73 Alexander Henry, "Henry's Journal," pt. 1, "The Red River of the North," in *New Light on the Early History of the Greater Northwest: The Manuscript Journals of Alexander Henry and of David Thompson, 1799–1814*, vol. 1, ed. Elliott Coues (1897; Minneapolis: Ross and Haines, 1965), 371..

74 Morgan, *Ecological Study*, 138, 184; A.T. Semple, *Grassland Improvement*, Plant Science Monographs, ed. Nicholas Dolunin (London: Leonard Hill Books, 1970), 128; J.T. Sarvis, "Grazing Investigation on the Northern Great Plains" (North Dakota Agricultural Experiment Station Bulletin 308, 1941), 67.

75 Environment and Climate Change Canada (ECCC) climate archive online, data from Lumsden and Lumsden 3 stations.

76 Thompson, *David Thompson's Narrative*, 98.

77 Morgan, *Ecological Study*, 139.

78 Linda Maddock, "The 'Migration' and Grazing Succession," in *Serengeti: Dynamics of an Ecosystem*, ed. A.R.E. Sinclair and M. Norton-Griffiths (Chicago: University of Chicago Press, 1979), 127.

79 Dary, *Buffalo Book*, 33.

80 Dodge, *Our Wild Indians*, 246; Kennedy, *Assiniboines*, 21; Grinnell, *Blackfoot Lodge Tales*, 185; MacKenzie in Masson, *Les Bourgeois*, 1:338; George Catlin, *Letters and Notes on the Manners, Customs, and Conditions of the North American Indians*, vol. 1 (New York: Dover, 1973), 121.

81 Henry, "Henry's Journal," in Coues, *New Light*, 2:724; Clark Wissler, *Material Culture of the Blackfoot Indians*, Anthropological Papers of the AMNH, vol. 5, pt. 1 (New York: American Museum of Natural History, 1910), 31.

82 Wissler, *Material Culture*, 31.

83 Henry, "Henry's Journal," in Coues, *New Light*, 2:724.

84 Wissler, *Material Culture*, 31.

85 Henry, "Henry's Journal," in Coues, *New Light*, 2:724.

86 Grinnell, *Cheyenne Indians*, 1:65.

87 Grinnell, *Blackfoot Lodge Tales*, 230.

88 Mandelbaum, *Plains Cree*, 54.

89 Henry, "Henry's Journal," in Coues, *New Light*, 2:518.

90 Ewers, *Horse in Blackfoot Indian Culture*, 40.

91 Treshow, *Human Environment*, 98, 102.

92 Odum, *Fundamentals of Ecology*, 225.

93 Peter Grant, "The Sauteux Indians," in *Les Bourgeois de la Compagnie du Nord-Ouest*, vol. 2, ed. L.R. Masson (New York: Antiquarian Press, 1960), 2:341.

94 Grant in Masson, 2:345.

95 Alanson Skinner, *Notes on the Eastern Cree and Northern Saulteaux*, Anthropological Papers of the AMNH, vol. 9, pt. 1 (New York: American Museum of Natural History, 1911), 134.

96 Thompson, *David Thompson's Narrative*, 91, 94, 152.

97 Skinner, *Notes*, 25.

98 Edward S. Rogers, *The Hunting Group–Hunting Territory Complex among the Mistassini Indians*, National Museum of Canada Bulletin 195, Anthropological Series 63 (Ottawa: National Museum of Canada, 1963), 32–33.

99 Daniel Williams Harmon, *Sixteen Years in the Indian Country: The Journal of Daniel Williams Harmon, 1800–1816*, ed. W. Kaye Lamb (1820; Toronto: Macmillan, 1957), 209.

100 Ray, *Indians in the Fur Trade*, 27.

101 Grant, "Sauteux Indians," in Masson, *Les Bourgeois*, 2:345; Rogers, *Hunting Group–Hunting Territory*, 33; Skinner, *Notes*, 27.

102 Father Louis Hennepin, *A Description of Louisiana*, ed. John Gilmary Shea (New York: J.G. Shea, 1880), 318; Rogers, *Hunting Group–Hunting Territory*, 32; Skinner, *Notes*, 27.

103 Grant, "Sauteux Indians," in Masson, *Les Bourgeois*, 2:343–44; Hennepin, *Description of Louisiana*, 318.

104 Ray, *Indians in the Fur Trade*, 46.

105 Thompson, *David Thompson's Narrative*, 151–52.

106 Thompson, 152.

107 Rutherford, *Beaver in Colorado*, 14; Ernest Thompson Seton, *Lives of Game Animals*, vol. 4 (Boston: Charles T. Branford Company, 1953), 493.

108 Denys, *Coasts of North America*, 429.

109 Denys, 429–30.

110 Skinner, *Notes*, 25.

111 Thompson, *David Thompson's Narrative*, 152–53.

112 Hennepin, *Description of Louisiana*, 320–21.

113 Henry, *Travels and Adventures*, 125; Denys, *Coasts of North America*, 429–30.

114 Grant, "Sauteux Indians," in Masson, *Les Bourgeois*, 2:342.

115 Denys, *Coasts of North America*, 432.

116 Thompson, *David Thompson's Narrative*, 154.

117 Castoreum is the secretion of the castor sacs of mature beaver, which they use to scent-mark their territory.

118 Thompson, *David Thompson's Narrative*, 156; Ray, *Indians in the Fur Trade*, 92; Hennepin, *Description of Louisiana*, 320; Harmon, *Sixteen Years*, 209.

119 Henry, *Travels and Adventures*, 125.

120 Harmon, *Sixteen Years*, 209.

121 Denys, *Coasts of North America*, 426.

122 Thompson, *David Thompson's Narrative*, 156.

123 Ray, *Indians in the Fur Trade*, 118.

124 In Burpee, *Pierre Gaultier*, 59.
125 Blyth and Hudson, "Vegetation and Ungulates," 142–54.
126 Wes Olson, "Beaver Pond Management Activities and Impacts" (unpublished report, Resource Conservation, Elk Island National Park, Parks Canada, 1987), 33.
127 Knudson, *Relationship of Beaver*, 8–9, 14.
128 Robert J. Naiman, Carol A. Johnston, and James C. Kelley, "Alteration of North American Streams by Beaver," *BioScience* 38, no. 11 (1988): 757.
129 Naiman, Johnston, and Kelley, "Alteration," 761.
130 Lewis, *Time for Burning*, 17.
131 Henry T. Lewis and Theresa A. Ferguson, "Yards, Corridors, and Mosaics: How to Burn a Boreal Forest," *Human Ecology* 16, no. 1 (1988): 73.
132 Lewis, *Time for Burning*, 19, 28.
133 Lewis, 31.
134 Lewis, 24, 26.
135 Mackenzie, *Voyages from Montreal*, 68.
136 Robert Hood, "Some Account of the Cree and Other Indians, 1819," *Alberta Historical Review* 15, no. 1 (1967): 8; Skinner, *Notes*, 33; Denys, *Coasts of North America*, 423.
137 Skinner, *Notes*, 33.
138 Lewis, *Time for Burning*, 37.
139 Denys, *Coasts of North America*, 402.

Chapter 3: The Ecological Evidence

1   Blyth and Hudson, "Vegetation and Ungulates," 25.
2   Naiman, Johnston, and Kelley, "Alteration," 753; Seton, *Lives of Game Animals*.
3   Kendeigh, *Animal Ecology*, 124.
4   Henry Youle Hind, "Observations on the Foraging Habits of Beaver," *Journal of Mammalogy* 19, no. 3 (1938): 317–19.
5   Rutherford, *Beaver in Colorado*, 17.
6   A.W. Allen, "Habitat Suitability Index Models: Beaver" (FWS/OBS-82/10.30, Fish and Wildlife Service, US Department of the Interior, Washington, DC, rev. April 1983), 1.
7   Bradt, "Study of Beaver Colonies," 153.
8   Todd, *Methodology*, 33–34.
9   Strong, "Beaver-Cottonwood Interactions," 69.
10 Rutherford, *Beaver in Colorado*, 28.
11 Naiman, Johnston, and Kelley, "Alteration," 756.
12 Naiman, Johnston, and Kelley, 757.
13 Allen, "Habitat Suitability"; Brian G. Slough and R.M.F.S. Sadleir, "A Land Capability Classification System for Beaver (*Castor canadensis* Kuhl)," *Canadian Journal of Zoology* 55, no. 8 (1977): 1324–35; Todd, *Methodology*.

14 Slough and Sadleir, "Land Capability Classification System," 1327.

15 Rutherford, *Beaver in Colorado*; Collins, "Stream Flow Effects."

16 Todd, *Methodology*.

17 LeRoy C. Stegeman, "The Production of Aspen and Its Utilization by Beaver on the Huntington Forest," *Journal of Wildlife Management* 18, no. 3 (1954): 348; Hodgdon and Hunt, *Beaver Management*, 411.

18 Hammond, "Beaver," 317.

19 Stephen H. Jenkins, "Problems, Progress, and Prospects in Studies of Food Selection by Beavers," in *Worldwide Furbearers Conference Proceedings*, ed. J.A. Chapman and D. Pursley (Frostburg, MD: Worldwide Furbearers Conference, 1980), 566–72.

20 Naiman, Johnston, and Kelley, "Alteration," 753.

21 See Wire and Hatch, "Administration of Beaver," 91.

22 Jeffrey E. Foss, *Beyond Environmentalism: A Philosophy of Nature* (New Jersey: Wiley, 2009), 60.

23 Canada, Saskatchewan, and Manitoba, *Report*, 7.

24 df = degree of freedom; t = t value; p = p value.

25 Water near the lodges at Campbell I and II was significantly deeper (X^2 = 24; p = < 0.00) than that in the overall waterway. Similarly, at Thompson III, water was significantly deeper around the lodges than in the overall waterway (df = 7; t = 2.532; p = 0.02).

26 Todd, *Methodology*.

27 Beaver Food Cache Survey, October 22, 1979.

28 Sherratt and Hatch, *Qu'Appelle Mammalian Inventory*, 12.

29 Blyth and Hudson, "Vegetation and Ungulates," 23–25; S.C. Zoltai, *Southern Limit of Coniferous Trees on the Canadian Plain*, Information Report NOR-X-128 (Edmonton: Environment Canada Forestry Service, Northern Forest Resources Center, 1975).

30 Blyth and Hudson, "Vegetation and Ungulates," 3.

31 R. Schwanke and Keith Baker, *The Beaver of Elk Island National Park* (Ottawa: Parks Canada, 1977), 1.

32 Blyth and Hudson, "Vegetation and Ungulates," 25.

33 Blyth and Hudson, 10–12.

34 Blyth and Hudson, 13.

35 Blyth and Hudson, 16–18.

36 Blyth and Hudson, 142–54.

37 Wes Olson, personal communication, spring 1989.

38 Olson, personal communication.

39 D.L. Skinner, "Selection of Winter Food by Beavers at Elk Island National Park" (MSc thesis, University of Alberta, 1984), 4.

40 Schwanke and Baker, *Beaver*, 25, 28.

41 Schwanke and Baker, 53.

42 Schwanke and Baker, x, 59.

43 Skinner, "Selection of Winter Food," 13.

44 Longley and Moyle, *Beaver in Minnesota*, 35.

45 Skinner, "Selection of Winter Food," 55. Graminoids are grass-like plants.

46 Skinner, 20.

47 S.E. Clarke and E.W. Tisdale, "The Chemical Composition of Native Forage Plants of Southern Alberta and Saskatchewan in Relation to Grazing Practices" (Canadian Department of Agriculture Technical Bulletin 54, Publication 769, Department of Agriculture, Ottawa, 1945), 20.

48 Skinner, "Selection of Winter Food," 36.

49 Skinner, 39.

50 Dave Flato, "Aerial Beaver Survey Results" (unpublished report, Resource Conservation, Elk Island National Park, Parks Canada, Ottawa, 1988), 4.

51 Schwanke and Baker, *Beaver*, xi.

52 Blyth and Hudson, "Vegetation and Ungulates," 16, 18.

53 Blyth and Hudson, 28.

54 Knudson, *Relationship of Beaver*, 9.

55 Schwanke and Baker, *Beaver*, 65.

56 Schwanke and Baker, 27, 58.

57 Knudson, *Relationship of Beaver*, 14.

58 S.A. Wilde, C.T. Youngberg, and J.H. Hovind, "Changes in Composition of Ground Water, Soil Fertility, and Forest Growth Produced by the Construction and Removal of Beaver Dams," *Journal of Wildlife Management* 14, no. 2 (1950): 125–26.

59 Knudson, *Relationship of Beaver*, 15.

60 Schwanke and Baker, *Beaver*.

61 D.S. Leach, "Carrying Capacity and Beaver Population Study at Elk Island National Park" (unpublished report, Elk Island National Park Files, 1986), 13.

62 Olson, "Beaver Pond Management," 33, 11.

63 Knudson, *Relationship of Beaver*, 15.

Chapter 4: The Historical Evidence

1 The information for this analysis is derived mainly from R. Grace Morgan, "Beaver Ecology/Beaver Mythology" (PhD diss., University of Alberta, 1991).

2 Ray, *Indians in the Fur Trade*, 12–13.

3 Arthur J. Ray, "Indian Adaptations to the Forest-Grassland Boundary of Manitoba and Saskatchewan, 1650–1821: Some Implications for Interregional Migration," *Canadian Geographer* 16, no. 2 (1972): 105.

4 Quoted in Dobbs, *Account of the Countries*, 35.

5   Arthur G. Doughty and Chester Martin, eds., *The Kelsey Papers* (Ottawa: Public Archives of Canada; Belfast: Public Records Office of Northern Ireland, 1929), 13.

6   Ray, *Indians in the Fur Trade*, 12.

7   Morton, *History of the Canadian West*, 112; Doughty and Martin, *Kelsey Papers*, 9.

8   Doughty and Martin, 113.

9   Thompson, *David Thompson's Narrative*, 239.

10 Doughty and Martin, *Kelsey Papers*, 17–18.

11 Morton, *History of the Canadian West*, 16–17.

12 Morton.

13 Robert H. Lowie, *The Assiniboine*, Anthropological Papers of the AMNH, vol. 4, pt. 1 (New York: American Museum of Natural History, 1909), 7.

14 Ray, *Indians in the Fur Trade*, 4.

15 Lowie, *Assiniboine*, 8.

16 Lowie, 10.

17 Arthur Silver Morton, "Hudson's Bay Company Diary of Fort Edmonton October 1854 to May 1856," 90, C511/2/2, fonds MG 437, A.S. Morton Manuscript Collection, Archives of the University of Saskatchewan, Saskatoon.

18 Stephen Return Riggs, *Dakota Grammar, Texts, and Ethnography*, ed. James Owen Dorsey, Contributions to North American Ethnology, vol. 9 (Washington, DC: Government Printing Office, 1893), 188.

19 Doughty and Martin, *Kelsey Papers*, 16.

20 Ray, *Indians in the Fur Trade*, 60, 59.

21 Burpee, *Pierre Gaultier*, 301.

22 Kennedy, *Assiniboines*, xxx.

23 Thompson, *David Thompson's Narrative*, 240–51.

24 Quoted in Thompson, *David Thompson's Narrative*, 241–42.

25 Morton, *History of the Canadian West*, 16.

26 Francis Haines, "The Northward Spread of Horses among the Plains Indians," *American Anthropologist* 40, no. 1 (1938): 435.

27 Robert F. Murphy and Yolanda Murphy, "Shoshone-Bannock Subsistence and Society," *University of California Anthropological Records* 16, no. 7 (1960): 294.

28 Ewers, *Blackfeet*, 6–7.

29 Kehoe, *North American Indians*, 276.

30 Grinnell, *Blackfoot Lodge Tales*, 177.

31 Wissler, *Material Culture*, 18.

32 Thompson, *David Thompson's Narrative*, 254.

33 Kehoe, *North American Indians*, 280.

34 Secoy, *Changing Military Patterns*, 47.

35 Morton, *History of the Canadian West*, 19.

36 Ray, *Indians in the Fur Trade*, 22.

37 Dodge, *Our Wild Indians*, 241.

38 Dodge, 380.

39 Morton, "Hudson's Bay Company Diary," 84.

40 L.J. Burpee, ed., "York Factory to the Blackfeet Country: The Journal of Anthony Henday 1754–55," *Proceedings and Transactions of the Royal Society of Canada*, 3rd ser., 1, sec. 2 (1907): 340.

41 Burpee, "York Factory," 344.

42 Ewers, *Blackfeet*, 25.

43 Morgan, *Ecological Study*, 182.

44 Thompson, *David Thompson's Narrative*, 158.

45 Morton, *History of the Canadian West*, 18.

46 Burpee, "York Factory," 344.

47 Burpee, "York Factory," 350, 351.

48 Burpee, 352.

49 Burpee, 345.

50 Morton, *History of the Canadian West*, 249.

51 Burpee, "York Factory," 353.

52 Burpee, 338.

53 Ray, *Indians in the Fur Trade*, 75.

54 Arthur, "Introduction to the Ecology," 93.

55 Ray, *Indians in the Fur Trade*, 90.

56 Morton, *History of the Canadian West*, 274–75, 257.

57 Morton, 283.

58 L.J. Burpee, ed., "An Adventure from Hudson Bay: Journal of Matthew Cocking from York Factory to the Blackfeet Country, 1772–1773," *Proceedings and Transactions of the Royal Society of Canada*, 3rd ser., 2 (1908): 106.

59 Burpee, "Adventure from Hudson Bay," 109–10.

60 Burpee, 111.

61 Secoy, *Changing Military Patterns*, 53.

62 Burpee, "Adventure from Hudson Bay," 111.

Chapter 5: The Archaeological Evidence

1 Lewis R. Binford, "Willow Smoke and Dogs' Tails: Hunter-Gatherer Settlement Systems and Archaeological Site Formation," *American Antiquity* 45, no. 1 (1980): 4.

2 Morgan, *Ecological Study*.

3 Sally Thompson Greiser, "Predictive Models of Hunter-Gatherer Subsistence and Settlement Strategies on the Central High Plains," Memoir 20, *Plains Anthropologist* 20, no. 110, pt. 2 (1985): i–134.

4   J. Michael Quigg, *The Belly River: Prehistoric Population Dynamics in a North-western Plains Transitional Zone*, Archaeological Survey of Canada Paper 23, Mercury Series (Ottawa: National Museum of Man, 1974), 39.

5   Quigg, *Belly River*, 33.

6   George W. Arthur, Ivan Sharp, and Dianne Wilson, *Qu'Appelle Basin Archaeological Project*, report prepared for the Department of Tourism and Renewable Resources and the Saskatchewan Museum of Natural History, 1975.

7   Michael J. O'Brien and Chad K. McDaniel, "Prehistoric Community Patterns: Surface Definition," in *The Cannon Reservoir Human Ecology Project: An Archaeological Study of Cultural Adaptations in the Southern Prairie Peninsula* (New York: Academic Press, 1982), 217.

8   Dennis E. Lewarch and Michael J. O'Brien, "The Expanding Role of Surface Assemblages in Archaeological Research," *Advances in Archaeological Method and Theory* 4 (1981): 320.

9   See, for example, Binford, "Willow Smoke and Dogs' Tails," 9–12.

10 Greiser, "Predictive Models," 47.

11 Greiser, 47–48.

12 Lewis R. Binford, "Organization and Formative Processes: Looking at Curated Technology," *Journal of Anthropological Research* 35, no. 3 (1979): 260.

13 Greiser, "Predictive Models," 48.

14 Quigg, *Belly River*, 51.

15 Gary Adams, "The Alkali Creek Sites," *Tipi Rings in Southern Alberta*, Archaeological Survey of Alberta Occasional Paper 9 (Edmonton: Archaeological Survey of Alberta, 1978), 106; Frison, *Piney Creek Sites*; Thomas F. Kehoe, *Stone Tipi Rings in North-Central Montana and the Adjacent Portion of Alberta, Canada: Their Historical, Ethnological, and Archeological Aspects*, Anthropological Papers 62, Bureau of American Ethnology Bulletin 173 (Washington, DC: Smithsonian Institution, 1960), 468; J. Michael Quigg, "The Lazy Dog Site," Occasional Paper No. 8, in *Tipi Rings in Southern Alberta*, prepared for Archaeological Survey of Alberta (Edmonton: Historical Resources Division, Alberta Culture, 1978), 30.

16 Binford, "Willow Smoke and Dogs' Tails."

17 O'Brien and McDaniel, "Prehistoric Community Patterns," 250.

18 Morgan, *Ecological Study*.

19 Binford, "Willow Smoke and Dogs' Tails," 10–12.

20 Quoted in Richard G. Forbis, "The Old Women's Buffalo Jump, Alberta," *National Museum of Canada Bulletin* 180 (1962): 63.

21 Joe Ben Wheat, "Olson-Chubbuck and Jurgens Sites: Four Aspects of Paleo-Indian Economy," in "Bison Procurement and Utilization: A Symposium," ed. Leslie B. Davis and Michael Wilson, special issue, *Plains Anthropologist* 23, no. 82 (1978): 89.

22 Symmes C. Oliver, "Ecology and Cultural Continuity as Contributing Factors in the Social Organization of the Plains Indians," *University of California Publications in American Archaeology and Ethnology* 48, no. 1 (1962): 54; Clark Wissler, *The Social Life of the Blackfoot Indians*, Anthropological Papers of the AMNH, vol. 7, pt. 1 (New York: American Museum of Natural History, 1911), 20; Wissler, *The Sun Dance of the Blackfoot Indians*, Anthropological Papers of the AMNH, vol. 16, pt. 3 (1918), 258.

23 Ewers, *Ethnological Report*, 17–18.

24 Arthur, "Introduction to the Ecology," 121.

25 Arthur, 111.

26 Henry, *Travels and Adventures*, 295.

27 Peter Fidler in Alice M. Johnson, ed., *Saskatchewan Journal and Correspondence: Edmonton House 1795–1800* (London: Hudson's Bay Record Society, 1967), 307.

28 Dodge, *Our Wild Indians*, 245.

29 Dodge, 242, 245.

30 Dodge, 50.

31 Ewers, *Ethnological Report*, 18.

32 Kehoe, *Stone Tipi Rings*, 433.

33 Grinnell, *Blackfoot Lodge Tales*, 234.

34 Arthur, "Introduction to the Ecology," 55.

35 Greiser, "Predictive Models," 46.

36 Morgan, *Ecological Study*.

37 Johnson, *Saskatchewan Journal and Correspondence*, 79.

38 Johnson, 235.

39 Henry, "Henry's Journal," in Coues, *New Light*, 1:163.

40 McGillivray, *Journal*, 43.

41 Thomas F. Kehoe, "The Boarding School Bison Drive Site," Memoir 4, *Plains Anthropologist* 12, no. 35 (1967): 70.

42 Morgan, *Ecological Study*, 93–95; Quigg, *Belly River*.

43 Kehoe, *Stone Tipi Rings*, 433.

44 Morgan, "Bison Movement Patterns," 151.

45 Morgan, "Bison Movement Patterns," 152; Morgan, *Ecological Study*, 176.

46 Longley, *Climate*, 67.

47 Adams, "Alkali Creek Sites."

48 Johnson, *Saskatchewan Journal and Correspondence*, 281, 302, 320, 321.

49 Adams, "Alkali Creek Sites," 48.

50 Adams, 41–42.

51 Morgan, *Ecological Study*, 183, 182.

52 Frison, *Piney Creek Sites*, 5.

53 For data from the Piney Creek sites that support the above inferences, see Frison, *Piney Creek Sites*.

54 Morgan, *Ecological Study*, 177.

55 Morgan, 182.

56 Arthur, "Introduction to the Ecology," 72.

57 Forbis, "Old Women's Buffalo Jump," 64.

58 Richard G. Forbis, "Some Facets of Communal Hunting," in "Bison Procurement and Utilization: A Symposium," ed. Leslie B. Davis and Michael Wilson, special issue, *Plains Anthropologist* 23, no. 82 (1978): 5–6.

59 Alanson Skinner, *Political Organization, Cults, and Ceremonies of the Plains-Ojibway and Plains-Cree Indians*, Anthropological Papers of the AMNH, vol. 11, pt. 4 (New York: American Museum of Natural History, 1914), 525–26.

60 Arthur, "Introduction to the Ecology," 64–67.

61 Binford, "Willow Smoke and Dogs' Tails," 12.

62 Lewis R. Binford, "Dimensional Analysis of Variance and Site Structure: Learning from an Eskimo Hunting Stand." *American Antiquity* 43, no. 3 (1978): 330.

63 Binford, "Dimensional Analysis," 331, 335, 330.

64 Arthur, "Introduction to the Ecology," 90.

65 Henry, "Henry's Journal," in Coues, *New Light*, 2:519.

66 Descriptions of the sites and artifact tables and descriptions of the artifact types are in Appendix 2 and 3, respectively, of Morgan's original dissertation entitled "Beaver Ecology/Beaver Mythology," which can be found at the University of Alberta, Library.

67 Dyck, "Prehistory."

68 Dyck.

69 Dyck, 115.

70 Arthur, Sharp, and Wilson, *Qu'Appelle Basin*.

71 Mary Weekes, "An Indian's Description of the Making of a Buffalo Pound," *Saskatchewan History* 1, no. 3 (1948): 14.

Chapter 6: Changing Lifeways on the Northern Plains

1 Oliver, "Ecology and Cultural Continuity," 68.

2 Oliver, 68.

3 Haines, "Northward Spread of Horses," 436; Ewers, *Horse in Blackfoot Indian Culture*, 19.

4 Ewers, 18.

5 Diamond Jenness, *The Sarcee Indians of Alberta*, National Museum of Canada Bulletin 90, Anthropological Series 23 (Ottawa: National Museum of Canada, 1938), 263.

6 Clark Wissler, "The Influence of the Horse in the Development of Plains Culture," *American Anthropologist* 16, no. 1 (1914): 13; Frank Gilbert Roe, *The Indian and the Horse* (Norman: University of Oklahoma Press, 1955), 218.

7 Wissler, "Influence of the Horse," 17.

8   Ewers, *Horse in Blackfoot Indian Culture*, 339.

9   Morton, introduction to McGillivray, *Journal*, lxxiv.

10 Wallace and Hoebel, *Comanches*, 6–8, 39, 34–36.

11 Ewers, *Horse in Blackfoot Indian Culture*, 305.

12 Ewers, 304.

13 Ewers, 129, 304.

14 Arthur, "Introduction to the Ecology," 121–22.

15 Martin S. Garretson, *The American Bison* (New York: New York Zoological Society, 1938), 104.

16 Arthur, "Introduction to the Ecology," 94.

17 Henry, "Henry's Journal," in Coues, *New Light*, 2:520.

18 Ewers, *Horse in Blackfoot Indian Culture*, 304.

19 Morgan, *Ecological Study*, 189.

20 Moodie and Ray, "Buffalo Migrations," 50.

21 Arthur, "Introduction to the Ecology," 100.

22 Arthur, 121; Ewers, *Blackfeet*, 76; Mandelbaum, *Plains Cree*, 56.

23 Forbis, "Old Women's Buffalo Jump," 69.

24 Moodie and Ray, "Buffalo Migrations," 50.

25 Ewers, *Horse in Blackfoot Indian Culture*, 312.

26 Secoy, *Changing Military Patterns*, 58.

27 Mandelbaum, *Plains Cree*, 62.

28 Henry, "Henry's Journal," in Coues, *New Light*, 2:540.

29 Morton, introduction to McGillivray, *Journal*, lxxiv.

30 Oliver, "Ecology and Cultural Continuity," 53.

31 Ewers, *Horse in Blackfoot Indian Culture*, 41.

32 Norman Fergus Black, *A History of Saskatchewan and the Old Northwest*, 2nd ed (North West Historical Company, 1913), 94, quoted in Roe, *Indian and the Horse*, 176.

33 Hubert Howe Bancroft, *The Works of Hubert Howe Bancroft: The Native Races*, vol. 1 (San Francisco: History Company Publishers, 1886), 283.

34 Ray, *Indians in the Fur Trade*, 125–26.

35 Ray, 263–64.

36 Ray, 104.

37 Secoy, *Changing Military Patterns*, 48.

38 Mackenzie, *Voyages from Montreal*, 50; Secoy, *Changing Military Patterns*, 49.

39 Mackenzie, *Voyages from Montreal*, 50.

40 Mackenzie, 49.

41 Morton, introduction to McGillivray, *Journal*, lxiv, 34.

42 Harmon, *Sixteen Years*, 41.

43 McDonnell, "Red River," in Masson, *Les Bourgeois*, 1:281.

44 Thompson, *David Thompson's Narrative*, 157.

45 Burpee, "Adventure from Hudson Bay," 106.

46   Mackenzie, *Voyages from Montreal*, 50.

47   Henry, "Henry's Journal," in Coues, *New Light*, 2:512–13.

48   Morton, *History of the Canadian West*, 455.

49   John McDonald, "Autobiographical Notes," in *Les Bourgeois de la Compagnie du Nord-Ouest*, vol. 2, ed. L.R. Masson (New York: Antiquarian Press, 1960), 17.

50   McGillivray, *Journal*, 47.

51   McGillivray, 49.

52   McGillivray, 30, 31.

53   Thompson, *David Thompson's Narrative*, 45.

54   Johnson, *Saskatchewan Journal and Correspondence*, xviii; Morton, *History of the Canadian West*, 456.

55   Morton, *History of the Canadian West*, 456.

56   McGillivray, *Journal*, 62–64; Ray, *Indians in the Fur Trade*, 98.

57   Johnson, *Saskatchewan Journal and Correspondence*, lxxix.

58   Ray, *Indians in the Fur Trade*, 61–62.

59   Henry, "Henry's Journal," in Coues, *New Light*, 2:541.

60   Henry in Coues, 2:559.

61   Henry in Coues, 2:578.

62   Thompson, *David Thompson's Narrative*, 306.

63   Henry, "Henry's Journal," in Coues, *New Light*, 2:713.

64   Henry in Coues, 2:723–24.

65   Henry in Coues, 2:541.

66   Henry, in Coues, 2:721.

67   Morton, "Hudson's Bay Company Diary," 98.

68   Henry, "Henry's Journal," in Coues, *New Light*, 2:513.

69   Thompson, *David Thompson's Narrative*, 380.

70   Morton, "Hudson's Bay Company Diary," 98.

71   Johnson, *Saskatchewan Journal and Correspondence*, 312–14.

72   Thompson, *David Thompson's Narrative*, 392.

73   Ewers, *Blackfeet*, 50, 57.

74   Ray, *Indians in the Fur Trade*, 117, 118–21, 123.

75   McGillivray, *Journal*, 46–47.

76   Henry, "Henry's Journal," in Coues, *New Light*, 2:541.

77   Sutherland quoted in Johnson, *Saskatchewan Journal and Correspondence*, 132.

78   Johnson, *Saskatchewan Journal and Correspondence*, lxxxvi, 319.

79   Tomison quoted in Johnson, *Saskatchewan Journal and Correspondence*, xci–xcii.

80   Thompson, *David Thompson's Narrative*, 229.

81   McGillivray, *Journal*, 77.

82   Johnson, *Saskatchewan Journal and Correspondence*, 152.

83   McGillivray, *Journal*, 76.

84   Ray, *Indians in the Fur Trade*, 119.

85   Secoy, *Changing Military Patterns*, 62.

86   Quoted in Ray, *Indians in the Fur Trade*, 207.

87   Ray, *Indians in the Fur Trade*, 131.

88   Ewers, *Blackfeet*, 32.

89   Johnson, *Saskatchewan Journal and Correspondence*.

90   Ray, *Indians in the Fur Trade*, 195, 198, 204, 213, 205–7.

91   Ray, 210–11.

92   Ewers, *Blackfeet*, 64.

93   Cowie, *Company of Adventurers*, 280.

94   Ewers, *Blackfeet*, 54.

95   Ewers, 55.

96   Annie Heloise Abel, ed., *Chardon's Journal at Fort Clark, 1834–1839* (Pierre: Department of History, State of South Dakota, 1932), 253.

97   Chittenden, *American Fur Trade*, 335.

98   Ewers, *Blackfeet*, 58.

99   Reuben Gold Thwaites, ed., *Travels in the Interior of North America, by Maximilian, Prince of Wied*, vol. 2 (Cleveland: Arthur H. Clark, 1906), 159.

100 Oscar Lewis, *The Effects of White Contact upon Blackfoot Culture with Special Reference to the Role of the Fur Trade*, American Ethnological Society Monograph 6 (Seattle: University of Washington Press, 1942), 32.

101 Chittenden, *American Fur Trade*, 335–36.

102 Thwaites, *Travels in the Interior*, 96.

103 Ewers, *Blackfeet*, 55.

104 Thwaites, *Travels in the Interior*, 164–65.

105 Ray, *Indians in the Fur Trade*, 210.

106 Morton, "Hudson's Bay Company Diary," 107.

107 Ray, *Indians in the Fur Trade*, 182–83.

108 Ewers, *Blackfeet*, 64.

109 Ray, *Indians in the Fur Trade*, 212–13.

110 Pierre-Jean DeSmet, *Oregon Missions and Travels over the Rocky Mountains in 1845–46* (Fairfield, WA: Ye Galleon Press, 1978), 334.

111 Cowie, *Company of Adventurers*, 302.

112 Ray, *Indians in the Fur Trade*, 228.

113 Thwaites, *Travels in the Interior*, 162.

114 Henry, "Henry's Journal," in Coues, *New Light*, 2:643–65.

115 Henry in Coues, 2:657–71.

116 Abel, *Chardon's Journal*, 78–102.

117 Chittenden, *American Fur Trade*, 852.

118 Abel, *Chardon's Journal*, 85.

119 Thwaites, *Travels in the Interior*, 306.

120 Mackenzie, *Voyages from Montreal*, 45.

121 Henry, "Henry's Journal," in Coues, *New Light*, 2:737.

122 Henry in Coues, 2:649–59.
123 Henry in Coues, 2:663.
124 McGillivray, *Journal*, 47.
125 Chittenden, *American Fur Trade*, 335.
126 The use of fire in the historical period became an economic weapon but further disrupted bison movements. According to McGillivray at Fort George, "the Indians often use this method to frighten away the animals in order to enhance the value of their own provisions." McGillivray, *Journal*, 33.
127 Dodge, *Our Wild Indians*, 242.

Conclusion

1 Kent, "Glacial History," 5.
2 MacKenzie in Masson, *Les Bourgeois*, 1:331.
3 Grinnell, *Cheyenne Indians*, 1:104.
4 Marriott, "Osage Indian II," 5.
5 Murphy and Murphy, "Shoshone-Bannock Subsistence," 5.
6 Wallace and Hoebel, *Comanches*, 175–77.

Afterword

1 Cristina Eisenberg et al., "Out of the Ashes: Ecological Resilience to Extreme Wildfire, Prescribed Burns, and Indigenous Burning on Ecosystems," *Frontiers in Ecology and Evolution* 7 (2019): article 436.
2 James Daschuk, *Clearing the Plains: Disease, Politics of Starvation, and the Loss of Aboriginal Life* (Regina: University of Regina Press, 2014), 100–4.
3 Rasmus Nielsen et al., "Tracing the Peopling of the World through Genomics," *Nature* 541, no. 7637 (2017): 302–10; Jon M. Erlandson and Todd J. Braje, "From Asia to the Americas by Boat? Paleogeography, Paleoecology, and Stemmed Points of the Northwest Pacific," *Quaternary International* 239, no. 1–2 (2011): 28–37; Eline D. Lorenzen et al., "Species-Specific Responses of Late Quaternary Megafauna to Climate and Humans," *Nature* 479, no. 7373 (2011): 359; Jacquelyn L. Gill et al., "Pleistocene Megafaunal Collapse, Novel Plant Communities, and Enhanced Fire Regimes in North America," *Science* 326, no. 5956 (2009): 1100–3; Donald K. Grayson and David J. Meltzer, "A Requiem for North American Overkill," *Journal of Archaeological Science* 30, no. 5 (2003): 585–93.
4 Ann Garibaldi and Nancy Turner, "Cultural Keystone Species: Implications for Ecological Conservation and Restoration," *Ecology and Society* 9, no. 3 (2004).
5 Robert T. Paine, "A Note on Trophic Complexity and Species Diversity," *American Naturalist* 103 (1969): 91–93; Cristina Eisenberg, *The Wolf's Tooth:*

Trophic Cascades, Keystone Species, and Biodiversity (Washington, DC: Island Press, 2010), 33.

6   Michael E. Soulé et al., "Strongly Interacting Species: Conservation Policy, Management, and Ethics," *BioScience* 55, no. 2 (2005): 168–75.

7   Oswald Schmitz, "Enlisting Ecological Interactions among Animals to Balance the Carbon Budget," in *Biodiversity and Climate Change: Transforming the Biosphere*, ed. Thomas E. Lovejoy and Lee Hannah (New Haven: Yale University Press, 2019), 332–35.

8   Robert T. Paine, "Food Webs: Linkage, Interaction Strength and Community Infrastructure," *Journal of Animal Ecology* 49, no. 3 (1980): 667–85.

9   R. Grace Morgan and R.J. Hudson, "Dynamics of Fire and Grazing by Bison on Grasslands in Central Alberta" (paper presented at International Symposium on Bison Ecology and Management in North America, Bozeman, MT, June 4–7, 1997).

10 Garibaldi and Turner, "Cultural Keystone Species," n.p.

11 Ben Goldfarb, *Eager: The Surprising, Secret Life of Beavers and Why They Matter* (Hartford, VT: Chelsea Green, 2018), 40–43.

12 Garibaldi and Turner, "Cultural Keystone Species," n.p.

13 George D. Gann et al., "International Principles and Standards for the Practice of Ecological Restoration," *Restoration Ecology* 27, no. S1 (2019): S1–S46; Gregory Cajete, *Native Science: Natural Laws of Interdependence* (Santa Fe, NM: Clear Light Books, 2000), 78.

14 Cajete, *Native Science*, 60–64.

15 Cajete, 206.

16 Robin Wall Kimmerer, "Native Knowledge for Native Ecosystems," *Journal of Forestry* 98, no. 8 (2000): 4–9.

17 Cajete, *Native Science*, 186, 261; Gregory Cajete, "Native Science and Sustaining Indigenous Communities," in *Traditional Ecological Knowledge: Learning from Indigenous Practices for Environmental Sustainability*, ed. Melissa K. Nelson and Dan Shilling (Cambridge: Cambridge University Press, 2019), 16–17.

18 Dennis Martinez, "Redefining Sustainability through Kincentric Ecology: Reclaiming Indigenous Lands, Knowledge, and Ethics," in *Traditional Ecological Knowledge: Learning from Indigenous Practices for Environmental Sustainability*, ed. Melissa K. Nelson and Dan Shilling (Cambridge: Cambridge University Press, 2019), 140.

19 Morgan and Hudson, "Dynamics of Fire"; Cristina Eisenberg, "Revelations of the Kenow Wildfire," *About Place Journal* 5, no. 2 (2018); Christopher I. Roos et al., "Indigenous Impacts on North American Great Plains Fire Regimes of the Past Millennium," PNAS 115, no. 32 (2018): 8143–48.

20 Marvin Harris, *Cultural Materialism: The Struggle for a Science of Culture*, 2nd ed. (Lanham, MD: AltaMira Press, 2001).

21 Gann et al., "International Principles and Standards."

22 Robin Wall Kimmerer, "Restoration and Reciprocity: The Contributions of Traditional Ecological Knowledge," in *Human Dimensions of Ecological Restoration*, ed. Dan Egan and E.E. Hjerpe (Washington, DC: Island Press, 2011), 257–76; Victoria Reyes-Garcia et al., "The Contributions of Indigenous People and Local Communities to Ecological Restoration," *Restoration Ecology* 27, no. 1 (2018): 3–8; Roos et al., "Indigenous Impacts"; Eisenberg et al., "Out of the Ashes"; Robin Wall Kimmerer, "*Mishkos Kenomagwen*, the Lessons of Grass: Restoring Reciprocity with the Good Green Earth," in *Traditional Ecological Knowledge: Learning from Indigenous Practices for Environmental Sustainability*, ed. Melissa K. Nelson and Dan Shilling (Cambridge: Cambridge University Press, 2019), 27–56.

23 Morgan and Hudson, "Dynamics of Fire."

24 Walter McClintock, *The Old North Trail: Life, Legends and Religion of the Blackfeet Indians* (London: Macmillan, 1910), 41–44.

25 See Gerald. T. Conaty, ed., *We Are Coming Home: Repatriation and the Restoration of Blackfoot Cultural Confidence* (Edmonton: Athabasca University Press, 2014).

26 Cristina Eisenberg, "Walking the Wolf Trail," *Whitefish Review*, no. 17 (2015): n.p.

27 Gerald T. Conaty, "Niitsitapiisinni: Our Way of Life," in Conaty, *We Are Coming Home*, 75; Allan Pard, "Repatriation among the Piikani," in Conaty, *We Are Coming Home*, 126–27.

28 Glynnis A. Hood and David G. Larson, "Ecological Engineering and Aquatic Connectivity: A New Perspective from Beaver-Modified Wetlands," *Freshwater Biology* 60, no. 1 (2015): 198–208.

29 Ellen Wohl, "Landscape-Scale Carbon Storage Associated with Beaver Dams," *Geophysical Research Letters* 40, no. 14 (2013): 3631–36.

30 Eisenberg, "Revelations"; Eisenberg et al., "Out of the Ashes."

31 Morgan and Hudson, "Dynamics of Fire"; Roos et al., "Indigenous Impacts."

32 S.W. Barrett and S.F. Arno, "Indian Fires as an Ecological Influence in the Northern Rockies," *Journal of Forestry* 80, no. 10 (1982): 647–51; Nancy J. Turner, Marianne Boelscher Ignace, and Ronald Ignace, "Traditional Ecological Knowledge and Wisdom of Aboriginal Peoples in British Columbia," *Ecological Applications* 10, no. 5 (2000): 1275–87.

33 Matthew Boyd, "Identification of Anthropogenic Burning in the Paleoecological Record of the Northern Prairies: A New Approach," *Annals of the Association of American Geographers* 92, no. 3 (2002): 471–87.

34 Dale G. Brockway, Richard G. Gatewood, and Randi B. Paris, "Restoring Fire as an Ecological Process in Shortgrass Prairie Ecosystems: Initial Effects

of Prescribed Burning during the Dormant and Growing Seasons," *Journal of Environmental Management* 65, no. 2 (2002): 135–52.

35   E.A. Johnson and G. Fryer, "Historical Vegetation Change in the Kananaskis Valley, Canadian Rockies," *Canadian Journal of Botany* 65, no. 5 (1987): 853–58; Fred Samson and Fritz Knopf, "Prairie Conservation in North America," *BioScience* 44, no. 6 (1994): 418–21; Peter L. Achuff, M.L. Coleman, and R.L. McNeil, *Ecological Land Classification of Waterton Lakes National Park, Alberta* (Ottawa: Parks Canada, 2005); Kevin Hop et al., US *Geological Survey–National Park Service Vegetation Mapping Program: Waterton-Glacier International Peace Park* (La Crosse, WI: Geological Survey, Upper Midwest Environmental Sciences Center, 2007).

36   Floyd Larson, "The Role of Bison in Maintaining the Short Grass Plains," *Ecology* 21, no. 2 (1940): 113–21; Celina Campbell et al., "Bison Extirpation May Have Caused Aspen Expansion in Western Canada," *Ecography* 19, no. 4 (1994): 360–62; Alan K. Knapp et al., "The Keystone Role of Bison in North American Tallgrass Prairie: Bison Increase Habitat Heterogeneity and Alter a Broad Array of Plant, Community, and Ecosystem Processes," *BioScience* 49, no. 1 (1999): 39–50; Johnson and Fryer, "Historical Vegetation Change"; Turner, Ignace, and Ignace, "Traditional Ecological Knowledge."

37   Morgan and Hudson, "Dynamics of Fire"; see also chapter 6.

38   K. Aune, D. Jørgensen, and C. Gates, "American Bison," IUCN Red List of Threatened Species, 2017, https://www.iucnredlist.org/species/2815/123789863.

39   Morgan and Hudson, "Dynamics of Fire"; Soulé et al., "Strongly Interacting Species."

40   Donald G. Peden et al., "The Trophic Ecology of Bison bison L. on Short-grass Plains," *Journal of Applied Ecology* 119, no. 2 (1974): 489–97; Knapp et al., "Keystone Role of Bison"; Scott L. Collins et al., "Modulation of Diversity by Grazing and Mowing in Native Tallgrass Prairie," *Science* 280, no. 5364 (1998): 745–47.

41   Michael E. Soulé et al., "Ecological Effectiveness: Conservation Goals for Interactive Species," Conservation Biology 17, no. 5 (2003): 1238–50; Glenn E. Plumb et al., "Carrying Capacity, Migration, and Dispersal in Yellowstone Bison," Biological Conservation 142, no. 11 (2009): 2377–87; C. Cormack Gates et al., *American Bison: Status Survey and Conservation Guidelines 2010* (Geneva: International Union for the Conservation of Nature, 2010).

42   Larson, "Role of Bison"; Campbell et al., "Bison Extirpation"; Samson and Knopf, "Prairie Conservation"; Knapp et al., "Keystone Role of Bison."

43   Eric W. Sanderson et al., "The Ecological Future of the North American Bison: Conceiving Long-Term, Large-Scale Conservation of Wildlife," *Conservation Biology* 22, no. 2 (2008): 252–66.

44   Daschuk, *Clearing the Plains*, 182–83.

45 Dan Flores, "Bison Ecology and Bison Diplomacy: The Southern Plains from 1800–1850," *Journal of American History* 78, no. 2 (1991): 465–85.

46 Flores, "Bison Ecology."

47 Daschuk, *Clearing the Plains*, 37–38, 100–4.

48 Caroline C. Ng'weno, "The Restoration of Lions to a Human-Occupied Savanna" (PhD diss., University of Wyoming, 2017).

49 Okeyo Mwai et al., "African Indigenous Cattle: Unique Genetic Resources in a Rapidly Changing World," *Asian-Australasian Journal of Animal Sciences* 28, no. 7 (2015): 911–21.

50 Wes Olson, *A Field Guide to Plains Bison* (Calgary: Timbergulch Press, 2012); Wes Olson, personal communication, March 27, 2019.

51 Terry L. Hunt and Carl P. Lipo, "Late Colonization of Easter Island," *Science* 311, no. 5767 (2006): 1603–6.

Appendix

1   Wright and Bailey, *Fire Ecology*.

2   Meriwether Lewis and William Clark, *Original Journals of the Lewis and Clark Expedition, 1804–1806*, vol. 1, ed. Reuben Gold Thwaites (New York: Antiquarian Press, 1969); Trobriand quoted in Higgins, *Historical Fire Accounts*, 29–32; Dodge, *Our Wild Indians*.

3   Both quoted in Higgins, *Historical Fire Accounts*.

4   D.L. Coppock and J.K. Detling, "Alteration of Bison and Black-Tailed Prairie Dog Grazing Interaction by Prescribed Burning," *Journal of Wildlife Management* 50, no. 3 (1986): 452–55; James H. Shaw and Tracy S. Carter, "Bison Movements in Relation to Fire and Seasonality," *Wildlife Society Bulletin* 18, no. 4 (1990): 426–30; Mary Ann Vinton et al., "Interactive Effects of Fire Bison (Bison bison) Grazing and Plant Community Composition in Tallgrass Prairie," *American Midland Naturalist* 129, no. 1 (1993): 10–18.

5   R.J. Raison, "Modifications of the Soil Environment by Vegetation Fires, with Particular Reference to Nitrogen Transformations: A Review," *Plant and Soil* 51, no. 1 (1979): 75.

6   John T. Curtis and Max L. Partch, "Some Factors Affecting Flower Production in Andropogon Gerardi," *Ecology* 31, no. 3 (1950): 488–89; Sylvia M. Old, "Microclimate, Fire and Plant Production in an Illinois Prairie," *Ecological Monographs* 39, no. 4 (1969): 355–84; C.L. Kucera and John H. Ehrenreich, "Some Effects of Annual Burning on Central Missouri Prairie," *Ecology* 43, no. 2 (1962): 334–36.

7   Alan K. Knapp, "Effects of Fire and Drought on the Ecophysiology of Andropogon Gerardii and Panicum Virgatum in a Tallgrass Prairie," *Ecology* 66, no. 4 (1985): 1309–20; Old, "Microclimate," 380.

8   N. Thompson Hobbs and David S. Schimel, "Fire Effects on Nitrogen Min-
     eralization and Fixation in Mountain Shrub and Grassland Communities,"
     Journal of Range Management 37, no. 5 (1984): 402–5.

9   Ralph L. Dix, "The Effects of Burning on the Mulch Structure and Species
     Composition of Grasslands in Western North Dakota," *Ecology* 41, no. 1
     (1960): 49–56; S.E. Clarke, E.W. Tisdale, and N.A. Skoglund, "The Effects
     of Climate and Grazing Practices on Short-Grass Prairie Vegetation" (De-
     partment of Agriculture Technical Bulletin 46, Department of Agriculture,
     Ottawa, 1943); Dix, "Effects of Burning."

10   Macoun quoted in Higgins, *Historical Fire Accounts.*

11   Steven W. Seagle, S.J. McNaughton, and Roger W. Ruess, "Simulated Effects
     of Grazing on Soil Nitrogen and Mineralization in Contrasting Serengeti
     Grasslands," *Ecology* 73, no. 3 (1992): 1105–23.

12   M. Wright, "Le Bois de Vache II: This Chip's for You Too," in *Buffalo*, ed. J.E.
     Foster, D. Harrison, and I.S. MacLaren (Edmonton: University of Alberta
     Press, 1992), 225–44.

13   Walter Willms, "Foraging Strategy of Ruminants," *Rangeman's Journal* 5,
     no. 3 (1978): 72–74; G.M. Van Dyne et al., "Large Herbivore Subsystem,"
     in *Grasslands, Systems Analysis and Man*, ed. A.I. Breymeyer and G.M. Van
     Dyne (Cambridge: Cambridge University Press, 1980), 269–538; Old, "Mi-
     croclimate"; Knapp, "Effects of Fire and Drought"; Daubenmire, "Ecology
     of Fire"; W. Willms, A.W. Bailey, and A. McLean, "Effect of Burning or
     Clipping *Agropyron spicatum* in the Autumn on the Spring Foraging Behavior
     of Mule Deer and Cattle," *Journal of Applied Ecology* 17 (1980): 69–84.

14   Knapp, "Effects of Fire and Drought"; Old, "Microclimate," 365.

15   Seagle, McNaughton, and Ruess, "Simulated Effects of Grazing"; S.E. Clarke,
     "Pasture Investigations on the Short Grass Plains of Saskatchewan," *Scientific
     Agriculture* 10, no. 11 (1930): 732–49; Lyle A. Renecker and Robert J. Hudson,
     "Seasonal Quality of Forages Used by Moose in the Aspen-Dominated
     Boreal Forest, Central Alberta," *Holarctic Ecology* 11, no. 2 (1988): 111–18.

16   Blyth and Hudson, "Vegetation and Ungulates," 3.

17   Blyth and Hudson, "Vegetation and Ungulates," 23.

18   C.B. Blyth et al., "Ungulate and Vegetation Monitoring, Management, and
     Recommendations, 1990 and 1991" (Elk Island National Park, Canadian
     Parks Service, Environment Canada, Ottawa, 1991), 33.

19   Hobbs and Schimel, "Fire Effects."

20   Raison, "Modifications," 84; Daubenmire, "Ecology of Fire," 225.

21   Review by Raison, "Modifications," 81.

22   Daubenmire, "Ecology of Fire," 228; Raison, "Modifications," 81.

23   Raison, 81.

24   N.L. Christensen, "Fire and the Nitrogen Cycle in California Chaparral,"
     Science 181, no. 4094 (1973): 66–68.

25 Raison, "Modifications," 82.

26 Garretson, *American Bison*, 168–69.

27 Arthur, "Introduction to the Ecology."

28 Hal Riegger, *Primitive Pottery* (New York: Van Nostrand Reinhold, 1972).

29 Wright, "Le Bois de Vache II," 238.

30 Wright.

31 Metz, L.J., T. Lotti, and R.A. Klawitter, "Some Effects on Prescribed Burning on Coastal Plain Forest Soils" (US Forest Service, Southeastern Forest Experiment Station, Station Paper SE -133, November 1961), 8–9.

32 Z.N. Aref'yeva and B.P. Kolesnikov, "Dynamics of Ammonia and Nitrate Nitrogen in Forest Soils of the Transurals at High and Low Temperatures," *Journal of Soviet Soil Science* 3 (1964): 253.

33 Wright, "Le Bois de Vache II."

34 W.T. Hamilton and C.J. Scifres, "Prescribed Burning during Winter for Maintenance of Buffalograss," *Journal of Range Management* 35, no. 1 (1982): 10.

35 Blyth et al., "Ungulate and Vegetation Monitoring," 36.

36 Clarke, Tisdale, and Skoglund, "Effects of Climate and Grazing Practices," 23.

37 Coupland, "Reconsideration," 138.

38 Harold H. Hopkins, "Effects of Mulch upon Certain Factors of the Grassland Environment," *Journal of Range Management* 7, no. 6 (1954): 258; Old, "Microclimate," 381.

39 Coupland, "Ecology of Mixed Prairie."

40 Richard S. White and Pat O. Currie, "Prescribed Burning in the Northern Great Plains: Yield and Cover Responses of 3 Forage Species in the Mixed Grass Prairie," *Journal of Range Management* 36, no. 2 (1983): 182; Kling L. Anderson "Time of Burning as It Affects Moisture in an Ordinary Upland Bluestem Prairie in the Flint Hills," *Journal of Range Management* 18, no. 6 (1965): 311–16; Daubenmire, "Ecology of Fire."

41 Hopkins, "Effects of Mulch," 258; Dix, "Effects of Burning," 52–53.

42 P.J. Viro, "Effects of Forest Fire on Soil," in *Fire and Ecosystems*, ed. T.T. Kozlowski and C.E. Ahlgren (New York: Academic Press, 1974), 14.

43 Christensen, "Fire and the Nitrogen Cycle," 67; Daubenmire, "Ecology of Fire," 224.

44 Raison, "Modifications," 77; Daubenmire, "Ecology of Fire," 217.

45 Old, "Microclimate."

46 White and Currie, "Prescribed Burning."

47 D.L. Coppock et al., "Plant-Herbivore Interactions in a North American Mixed-Grass Prairie," *Oecologia* 56, no. 1 (1983): 1–9; April D. Whicker and James K. Detling, "Ecological Consequences of Prairie Dog Disturbances," *Bioscience* 38, no. 11 (1988): 778–85.

48 Viro, "Effects of Forest Fire," 21; Raison, "Modifications," 83.

49 E.M. White, F.R. Gartner, and R. Butterfield, "Blue Grama [*Bouteloua gracilis*] Response to Fertilization of a Claypan Soil in the Greenhouse," *Journal of Range Management* 36, no. 2 (1983): 232; P.O. Reardon and D.L. Huss, "Effects of Fertilization on a Little Bluestem Community," *Journal of Range Management* 18, no. 5 (1965): 238–40.

50 M.A. Vinton and D.C. Hartnett, "Effects of Bison Grazing on *Andropogon gerardii* and *Panicum virgatum*," *Oecologia* 90 (1992): 380.

51 Renecker and Hudson, "Seasonal Quality," 115.

52 Day and Detling, "Grassland Patch Dynamics."

53 Reardon and Huss, "Effects of Fertilization"; Charles W. Gay and Don D. Dwyer, "Effects of One Year's Nitrogen Fertilization on Native Vegetation under Clipping and Burning," *Journal of Range Management* 18, no. 5 (1965): 275.

54 Steven H. Sharrow and Henry A. Wright, "Effects of Fire, Ash, and Litter on Soil Nitrate, Temperature, Moisture and Tobosagrass Production in the Rolling Plains," *Journal of Range Management* 30, no. 4 (1977): 269.

55 Old, "Microclimate," 380; Knapp, "Effects of Fire and Drought," 1318.

56 Old, "Microclimate," 360.

57 I.F. Ahlgren, "The Effect of Fire on Soil Organisms," in *Fire and Ecosystems*, ed. T.T. Kozlowski and C.E. Ahlgren (New York: Academic Press, 1974), 51.

58 Ahlgren, "Effect of Fire," 49–50; Raison, "Modifications."

59 Aref'yeva and Kolesnikov, "Dynamics of Ammonia," 252.

60 Viro, "Effects of Forest Fire," 36; Aref'yeva and Kolesnikov, "Dynamics of Ammonia," 251–52; Selman A. Waksman and Robert L. Starkey, "Partial Sterilization of Soil Microbiological Activities and Soil Fertility: I," *Soil Science* 16, no. 3 (1923): 137–58.

61 Kaila et al. in Viro, "Effects of Forest Fire," 35.

62 Raison, "Modifications," 77.

63 Raison, 92.

64 Sharrow and Wright, "Effects of Fire."

65 Aref'yeva and Kolesnikov, "Dynamics of Ammonia."

66 F.E. Clark, C.G. Warren, and W.A. O'Deen, "Early Uptake of [15] N in Short Grass Prairie," *Geoderma* 13, no. 1 (February 1975): 61-66, quoted in F.E. Clark, C.V. Vole, and R.A. Bowman, "Nutrient Cycling," in *Grasslands, Systems Analysis and Man*, ed. A.I. Breymeyer and G.M. Van Dyne (Cambridge: Cambridge University Press, 1980), 671.

67 McLean et al., 1956, in Old, "Microclimate," 380.

68 Old.

69 Review by Raison, "Modifications," 88; J.D. Russell et al., "Thermal Decomposition of Protein in Soil Organic Matter," *Geoderma* 11, no. 1 (1974): 63.

70 Viro, "Effects of Forest Fire," 35; Christensen, "Fire and the Nitrogen Cycle," 67; Aref'yeva and Kolesnikov, "Dynamics of Ammonia," 250–51.

71 Hobbs and Schimel, "Fire Effects," 403–404.

72   Seagle, McNaughton, and Ruess, "Simulated Effects of Grazing."

73   Allan McGinty, Fred E. Smeins, and Leo B. Merrill, "Influence of Spring Burning on Cattle Diets and Performance on the Edwards Plateau," *Journal of Range Management* 36, no. 2 (1983): 175–78.

74   Willms, Bailey, and McLean, "Effect of Burning or Clipping."

75   Vinton et al., "Interactive Effects of Fire Bison."

76   Old, "Microclimate"; Knapp, "Effects of Fire and Drought."

77   Knapp, 1318.

78   Clark and Tisdale, "Chemical Composition of Native Forage Plants."

79   Clark, Vole, and Bowman, "Nutrient Cycling," 680.

80   Elmer B. Hadley and Barbara J. Kieckefer, "Productivity of Two Prairie Grasses in Relation to Fire Frequency," *Ecology* 44, no. 2 (1963): 391; Daubenmire, "Ecology of Fire."

81   Coupland, "Reconsideration," 138; Robert T. Coupland and T. Christopher Brayshaw, "The Fescue Grassland in Saskatchewan," *Ecology* 34, no. 2 (1953): 386–405.

82   Sharrow and Wright, "Effects of Fire," 268.

83   Seagle, McNaughton, and Ruess, "Simulated Effects of Grazing," 1118.

84   Desmond Vesey-Fitzgerald, "Fire and Animal Impact on Vegetation in Tanzania National Parks," *Fire Ecology Conference Proceedings* 11 (1972): 297–317.

85   Seagle, McNaughton, and Ruess, "Simulated Effects of Grazing," 1116.

86   Seagle, McNaughton, and Ruess, 1120.

87   Day and Detling, "Grassland Patch Dynamics," 186.

88   Seagle, McNaughton, and Ruess, "Simulated Effects of Grazing," 1118.

89   Penfound and Kelting, "Some Effects"; S. Clark Martin, "Responses of Semidesert Grasses and Shrubs to Fall Burning," *Journal of Range Management* 6, no. 5 (1986): 604–10; Hamilton and Scifres, "Prescribed Burning"; Willms, Bailey, and McLean, "Effect of Burning or Clipping."

90   Coppock and Detling, "Alteration"; Shaw and Carter, "Bison Movements"; Vinton et al., "Interactive Effects of Fire Bison."

91   Vinton et al.

92   Coppock and Detling, "Alteration."

93   Knapp, "Effects of Fire and Drought," 1318; Old, "Microclimate."

94   A.W. Bailey and M.L. Anderson, "Prescribed Burning of a Festuca-Stipa Grassland," *Journal of Range Management* 31, no. 6 (1978): 446–49; Dix, "Effects of Burning," 52.

95   P.D. Walton, R. Martinez, and A.W. Bailey, "A Comparison of Continuous and Rotational Grazing," *Journal of Range Management* 34, no. 1 (1981): 20.

96   E.H. Moss and J.A. Campbell, "The Fescue Grassland of Alberta," *Canadian Journal of Research* 25c, no. 6 (1947): 216.

97   P.J. Bowler, *The Fontana History of the Environmental Sciences* (London: Fontana Press, 1992), 6.

98 Review by Seagle, McNaughton, and Ruess, "Simulated Effects of Grazing."

99 R.G. Woodmonsee, I. Vallis, and J.J. Mott, "Grass-Land Nitrogen," in *Terrestrial Nitrogen Cycles*, ed. F. E. Clark and T. Rosswall (Stockholm: Royal Swedish Academy of Science, 1981), 443–62, in Seagle, McNaughton, and Ruess, "Simulated Effects of Grazing," 1109, 1120.

100 Seagle, McNaughton, and Ruess, "Simulated Effects of Grazing," 1120.

101 Day and Detling, "Grassland Patch Dynamics."

102 Old, "Microclimate"; Daubenmire, "Ecology of Fire."

103 White and Currie, "Prescribed Burning," 182.

104 Seagle, McNaughton, and Ruess, "Simulated Effects of Grazing."

105 Seagle, McNaughton, and Ruess, 1107.

106 Seagle, McNaughton, and Ruess.

107 Viro, "Effects of Forest Fire," 32.

108 Aref'yeva and Kolesnikov, "Dynamics of Ammonia," 252.

109 McGinty, Smeins, and Merrill, "Influence of Spring Burning."

REFERENCES

Abel, Annie Heloise, ed. *Chardon's Journal at Fort Clark, 1834–1839*. Pierre: Department of History, State of South Dakota, 1932.

Achuff, Peter L., M.L. Coleman, and R.L. McNeil. *Ecological Land Classification of Waterton Lakes National Park, Alberta*. Ottawa: Parks Canada, 2005.

Adams, Gary. "The Alkali Creek Sites." Occasional Paper No. 9. In *Tipi Rings in Southern Alberta*, prepared for Archaeological Survey of Alberta. Edmonton: Historical Resources Division, Alberta Culture, 1978.

Ahlgren, I.F. "The Effect of Fire on Soil Organisms." In *Fire and Ecosystems*, edited by T.T. Kozlowski and C.E. Ahlgren, 47–69. New York: Academic Press, 1974.

Allen, A.W. "Habitat Suitability Index Models: Beaver." FWS/OBS-82/10.30. Fish and Wildlife Service, US Department of the Interior, Washington, DC, revised April 1983.

Allred, Morrell. "A Re-emphasis on the Value of the Beaver in Natural Resource Conservation." *Journal of the Idaho Academy of Science* 16, no. 1 (1980): 3–10.

Anderson, Kling L. "Time of Burning as It Affects Moisture in an Ordinary Upland Bluestem Prairie in the Flint Hills." *Journal of Range Management* 18, no. 6 (1965): 311–16.

Aref'yeva, Z.N., and B.P. Kolesnikov. "Dynamics of Ammonia and Nitrate Nitrogen in Forest Soils of the Transurals at High and Low Temperatures." *Journal of Soviet Soil Science* 3 (1964): 246–60.

Arthur, George W. "An Introduction to the Ecology of Early Historic Communal Bison Hunting among the Northern Plains Indians." Archaeological Survey of Canada Paper 37, Mercury Series, National Museum of Man, Ottawa, 1975.

Arthur, George W., Ivan Sharp, and Dianne Wilson. *Qu'Appelle Basin Archaeological Project*. Report prepared for the Department of Tourism and Renewable Resources and the Saskatchewan Museum of Natural History, 1975.

Ayyad, M.A.G., and R.L. Dix. "An Analysis of a Vegetation-Micro-Environmental Complex on Prairie Slopes in Saskatchewan." *Ecological Monographs* 34, no. 4 (1964): 421–42.

Bailey, A.W., and M.L. Anderson. "Prescribed Burning of a Festuca-Stipa Grassland." *Journal of Range Management* 31, no. 6 (1978): 446–49.

Bancroft, Hubert Howe. *The Works of Hubert Howe Bancroft: The Native Races.* Vol. 1. San Francisco: History Company Publishers, 1886.

Barrett, S.W., and S.F. Arno. "Indian Fires as an Ecological Influence in the Northern Rockies." *Journal of Forestry* 80, no. 10 (1982): 647–51.

Bergstrom, Dorothy. "Beavers: Biologists 'Rediscover' a Natural Resource." *Forestry Research West,* October 1985, 1–5.

Binford, Lewis R. "Dimensional Analysis of Variance and Site Structure: Learning from an Eskimo Hunting Stand." *American Antiquity* 43, no. 3 (1978): 330–61.

———. Introduction to *For Theory Building in Archaeology,* edited by Lewis R. Binford, 1–13. New York: Academic Press, 1977.

———. "Organization and Formative Processes: Looking at Curated Technology." *Journal of Anthropological Research* 35, no. 3 (1979): 255–73.

———. "Willow Smoke and Dogs' Tails: Hunter-Gatherer Settlement Systems and Archaeological Site Formation." *American Antiquity* 45, no. 1 (1980): 4–20.

Blyth, C.B., and R.J. Hudson. "A Plan for the Management of Vegetation and Ungulates: Elk Island National Park." MSc thesis, University of Alberta, 1987.

Blyth, C.B., W. Olson, A.L. Horton, R. Fingland, M. Stromsmoe, and N.L. Cool. "Ungulate and Vegetation Monitoring, Management, and Recommendations, 1990 and 1991." Elk Island National Park, Canadian Parks Service, Environment Canada, Ottawa, 1991.

Bowler, P.J. *The Fontana History of the Environmental Sciences.* London: Fontana Press, 1992.

Boyd, Matthew. "Identification of Anthropogenic Burning in the Paleoecological Record of the Northern Prairies: A New Approach." *Annals of the Association of American Geographers* 92, no. 3 (2002): 471–87.

Bradt, Glenn W. "A Study of Beaver Colonies in Michigan." *Journal of Mammalogy* 19, no. 2 (1938): 139–62.

Brockway, Dale G., Richard G. Gatewood, and Randi B. Paris. "Restoring Fire as an Ecological Process in Shortgrass Prairie Ecosystems: Initial Effects of Prescribed Burning during the Dormant and Growing Seasons." *Journal of Environmental Management* 65, no. 2 (2002): 135–52.

Burpee, L.J., ed. "An Adventure from Hudson Bay: Journal of Matthew Cocking from York Factory to the Blackfeet Country, 1772–1773." *Proceedings and Transactions of the Royal Society of Canada*, 3rd ser., 2 (1908): 91–121.

———, ed. *Journal and Letters of Pierre Gaultier de Varennes de La Vérendrye and His Sons.* Toronto: Champlain Society, 1927.

———, ed. "York Factory to the Blackfeet Country: The Journal of Anthony Henday, 1754–55." *Proceedings and Transactions of the Royal Society of Canada*, 3rd ser., 1, sec. 2 (1907): 307–64.

Bushnell, David I. *Villages of the Algonquian, Siouan, and Caddoan Tribes West of the Mississippi.* Bureau of American Ethnology Bulletin 77. Washington, DC: Smithsonian Institution, 1922.

Cajete, Gregory. "Native Science and Sustaining Indigenous Communities." In *Traditional Ecological Knowledge: Learning from Indigenous Practices for Environmental Sustainability*, edited by Melissa K. Nelson and Dan Shilling, 15–26. Cambridge: Cambridge University Press, 2019.

———. *Native Science: Natural Laws of Interdependence.* Santa Fe, NM: Clear Light Books, 2000.

Campbell, Celina, Ian D. Campbell, Charles B. Blyth, and John H. McAndrews. "Bison Extirpation May Have Caused Aspen Expansion in Western Canada." *Ecography* 19, no. 4 (1994): 360–62.

Canada, Saskatchewan, and Manitoba. *Report of the Qu'Appelle Basin Study Board.* Regina: Queen's Printer, 1972.

Catlin, George. *Letters and Notes on the Manners, Customs, and Conditions of the North American Indians.* Vol. 1. New York: Dover, 1973.

Chakravarti, A.K. "The Climate of Saskatchewan." In *Atlas of Saskatchewan*, edited by J.H. Richard and K.I. Fung, 60. Saskatoon: University of Saskatchewan, 1969.

Chittenden, Hiram Martin. *The American Fur Trade of the Far West.* 2 vols. 1902; Stanford: Academic Reprints, 1954.

Christiansen, E.A. *Geology and Ground-Water Resources of the Regina Area.* Saskatchewan Report 2. Regina: Geology Division, Saskatchewan Research Council, 1961.

Christensen, N.L. "Fire and the Nitrogen Cycle in California Chaparral." *Science* 181, no. 4094 (1973): 66–68.

Clark, F.E., C.V. Vole, and R.A. Bowman. "Nutrient Cycling." In *Grasslands, Systems Analysis and Man*, edited by A.I. Breymeyer and G.M. Van Dyne, 659–706. Cambridge: Cambridge University Press, 1980.

Clarke, S.E. "Pasture Investigations on the Short Grass Plains of Saskatchewan." *Scientific Agriculture* 10, no. 11 (1930): 732–49.

Clarke, S.E., and E.W. Tisdale. "The Chemical Composition of Native Forage Plants of Southern Alberta and Saskatchewan in Relation to Grazing Practices." Canadian Department of Agriculture Technical Bulletin 54, Publication 769. Ottawa: Department of Agriculture, 1945.

Clarke, S.E., E.W. Tisdale, and N.A. Skoglund. "The Effects of Climate and Grazing Practices on Short-Grass Prairie Vegetation." Department of Agriculture Technical Bulletin 46. Ottawa: Department of Agriculture, 1943.

Collins, Scott L., Alan K. Knapp, John M. Briggs, John M. Blair, and Ernest M. Steinauer. "Modulation of Diversity by Grazing and Mowing in Native Tallgrass Prairie." *Science* 280, no. 5364 (1998): 745–47.

Collins, Thomas C. "Stream Flow Effects on Beaver Populations in Grand Teton National Park." In *Proceedings of the First Conference on Scientific Research in the National Parks*, vol. 1, edited by Robert M. Linn, 349–56. National Park Service Transactions and Proceedings Series 5. Washington, DC: US Department of the Interior, 1979.

Conaty, Gerald T. "Niitsitapiisinni: Our Way of Life." In Conaty, ed., *We Are Coming Home*, 71–117.

——, ed. *We Are Coming Home: Repatriation and the Restoration of Blackfoot Cultural Confidence*. Edmonton: Athabasca University Press, 2014.

Coppock, D.L., and J.K. Detling. "Alteration of Bison and Black-Tailed Prairie Dog Grazing Interaction by Prescribed Burning." *Journal of Wildlife Management* 50, no. 3 (1986): 452–55.

Coppock, D.L., J.K. Detling, J.E. Ellis, and M.J. Dyer. "Plant-Herbivore Interactions in a North American Mixed-Grass Prairie." *Oecologia* 56, no. 1 (1983): 1–9.

Coues, Elliott, ed. *New Light on the Early History of the Greater Northwest: The Manuscript Journals of Alexander Henry and of David Thompson, 1799–1814.* 2 vols. 1897; Minneapolis: Ross and Haines, 1965.

Coupland, R.T., and J.S. Rowe. "Natural Vegetation of Saskatchewan." In *Atlas of Saskatchewan*, edited by J.H. Richards and K.I. Fung, 73–75. Saskatoon: University of Saskatchewan, 1969.

Coupland, Robert T. "Ecology of Mixed Prairie in Canada." *Ecological Monographs* 20, no. 4 (1950): 273–315.

———. "A Reconsideration of Grassland Classification in the Northern Great Plains of North America." *Journal of Ecology* 49, no. 1 (1961): 135–67.

Coupland, Robert T., and T. Christopher Brayshaw. "The Fescue Grassland in Saskatchewan." *Ecology* 34, no. 2 (1953): 386–405.

Cowie, Isaac. *The Company of Adventurers on the Great Buffalo Plains.* Toronto: William Briggs, 1913.

Curtis, Edward S. *The North American Indian.* 20 vols. 1907–30; New York: Johnson Reprint, 1970.

Curtis, John T., and Max L. Partch. "Some Factors Affecting Flower Production in Andropogon Gerardi." *Ecology* 31, no. 3 (1950): 488–89.

Dary, David A. *The Buffalo Book: The Saga of an American Symbol.* New York: Avon Books, 1975.

Daschuk, James. *Clearing the Plains: Disease, Politics of Starvation, and the Loss of Aboriginal Life.* Regina: University of Regina Press, 2014.

———. "A Dry Oasis: The Canadian Plains in Late Prehistory." *Prairie Forum* 34, no. 1 (2009): 1–29.

———. "Who Killed the Prairie Beaver? An Environmental Case for Eighteenth Century Migration in Western Canada." *Prairie Forum* 37 (Fall 2012): 151–72.

Daubenmire, R. "Ecology of Fire in Grasslands." *Advances in Ecological Research* 5 (1968): 209–67.

Day, T.A., and J.K. Detling. "Grassland Patch Dynamics and Herbivore Grazing Preference following Urine Deposition." *Ecology* 71, no. 1 (1990): 180–88.

Denig, Edwin Thompson. *Five Indian Tribes of the Upper Missouri: Sioux, Arickaras, Assiniboines, Crees, and Crows.* Edited by John C. Ewers. Norman: University of Oklahoma Press, 1961.

Denny, R.N. *A Summary of the North American Beaver Management.* Current Report 28. Denver: Colorado Game and Fish Department, 1952.

Denys, Nicolas. *The Description and Natural History of the Coasts of North America.* Edited by William F. Ganong. Toronto: Champlain Society, 1908.

DeSmet, Pierre-Jean. *Oregon Missions and Travels over the Rocky Mountains in 1845–46.* Fairfield, WA: Ye Galleon Press, 1978.

Dix, Ralph L. "The Effects of Burning on the Mulch Structure and Species Composition of Grasslands in Western North Dakota." *Ecology* 41, no. 1 (1960): 49–56.

Dobbs, Arthur. *An Account of the Countries Adjoining to Hudson's Bay in the North-West Part of America.* 1744; London: S.R. Publishers, 1967.

Dodge, Richard I. *Our Wild Indians: Thirty-Three Years' Personal Experience among the Red Men of the Great West.* Hartford, CT: A.D. Worthington and Company, 1959.

Doughty, Arthur G., and Chester Martin, eds. *The Kelsey Papers.* Ottawa: Public Archives of Canada; Belfast: Public Records Office of Northern Ireland, 1929.

Dugmore, A. Radclyffe. *The Romance of the Beaver.* London: William Heinemann, 1914.

Dyck, I. "The Prehistory of Southern Saskatchewan." In *Tracking Ancient Hunters: Prehistoric Archaeology in Saskatchewan,* edited by H.T. Epp and I. Dyck, 63–139. Regina: Saskatchewan Archaeology Society, 1983.

Ehrlich, Paul R., Anne H. Ehrlich, and John P. Holdren. *Human Ecology: Problems and Solutions.* San Francisco: W.H. Freeman and Company, 1973.

Eisenberg, Cristina. "Revelations of the Kenow Wildfire." *About Place Journal* 5, no. 2 (2018). https://aboutplacejournal.org/article/revelations-of-the-kenow-wildfire/.

——. "Walking the Wolf Trail." *Whitefish Review*, no. 17 (2015). http://www.whitefishreview.org/.

——. *The Wolf's Tooth: Trophic Cascades, Keystone Species, and Biodiversity.* Washington, DC: Island Press, 2010.

Eisenberg, Cristina, Christopher L. Anderson, Adam Collingwood, Robert Sissons, Christopher J. Dunn, Garrett W. Meigs, Dave E.

Hibbs, Scott Murphy, Sierra Dakin Kuiper, Julian SpearChief-Morris, Leroy Little Bear, Barb Johnston, and Curtis B. Edson. "Out of the Ashes: Ecological Resilience to Extreme Wildfire, Prescribed Burns, and Indigenous Burning on Ecosystems." *Frontiers in Ecology and Evolution* 7 (2019): article 436. https://doi.org/10.3389/fevo.2019.00436.

Erlandson, Jon M., and Todd J. Braje. "From Asia to the Americas by Boat? Paleogeography, Paleoecology, and Stemmed Points of the Northwest Pacific." *Quaternary International* 239, no. 1–2 (2011): 28–37.

Evans, Francis C. "Ecosystems as the Basic Unit in Ecology." In *Readings in Conservation Ecology*, edited by George W. Cox, 3–5. New York: Appleton-Century-Crofts, 1969.

Ewers, John C. *The Blackfeet: Raiders on the Northwestern Plains.* Norman: University of Oklahoma Press, 1958.

———. *Ethnological Report on the Blackfeet and Gros Ventre Tribes of Indians Lands in Northern Montana.* Pocket 279-A, Indian Claims Commission, May 1, 1888. New York: Clearwater, 1973.

———. *The Horse in Blackfoot Indian Culture.* Bureau of American Ethnology Bulletin 159. Washington, DC: Smithsonian Institution, 1955.

Fehrenbach, T.R. *Comanches: The Destruction of a People.* New York: Knopf, 1974.

Flato, Dave. "Aerial Beaver Survey Results." Unpublished report, Resource Conservation, Elk Island National Park, Parks Canada, Ottawa, 1988.

Flores, Dan. "Bison Ecology and Bison Diplomacy: The Southern Plains from 1800–1850." *Journal of American History* 78, no. 2 (1991): 465–85.

Forbis, Richard G. "The Old Women's Buffalo Jump, Alberta." *National Museum of Canada Bulletin* 180 (1962): 56–123.

———. "Some Facets of Communal Hunting." In "Bison Procurement and Utilization: A Symposium," edited by Leslie B. Davis and Michael Wilson. Special issue, *Plains Anthropologist* 23, no. 82 (1978): 3–8.

———. "Some Late Sites in the Oldman River Region, Alberta." *National Museum of Canada Bulletin* 162 (1960): 119–64.

Foss, Jeffrey E. *Beyond Environmentalism: A Philosophy of Nature.* New Jersey: Wiley, 2009.

Frison, George C. *The Piney Creek Sites, Wyoming.* University of Wyoming Publications 33. Laramie: University of Wyoming, 1967.

Gann, George D., Tein McDonald, Bethanie Walder, James Aronson, Cara R. Nelson, Justin Jonson, James G. Hallett, Cristina Eisenberg, Manuel Guariguata, Junguo Liu, Fangyuan Hua, Cristian Echeverría, Emily Gonzales, Nancy Shaw, Kris Deceer, and Kingsley W. Dixon. "International Principles and Standards for the Practice of Ecological Restoration." *Restoration Ecology* 27, no. S1 (2019): S1–S46.

Garibaldi, Ann, and Nancy Turner. "Cultural Keystone Species: Implications for Ecological Conservation and Restoration." *Ecology and Society* 9, no. 3 (2004). https://www.jstor.org/stable/26267680.

Garretson, Martin S. *The American Bison.* New York: New York Zoological Society, 1938.

Gates, C. Cormack, Curtis H. Freese, Peter J.P. Gogan, and Mandy Kotzman. *American Bison: Status Survey and Conservation Guidelines 2010.* Geneva: International Union for the Conservation of Nature, 2010.

Gay, Charles W., and Don D. Dwyer. "Effects of One Year's Nitrogen Fertilization on Native Vegetation under Clipping and Burning." *Journal of Range Management* 18, no. 5 (1965): 273–77.

Gill, Jacquelyn L., John W. Williams, Stephen T. Jackson, Katherine B. Lininger, and Guy S. Robinson. "Pleistocene Megafaunal Collapse, Novel Plant Communities, and Enhanced Fire Regimes in North America." *Science* 326, no. 5956 (2009): 1100–03.

Goldfarb, Ben. *Eager: The Surprising, Secret Life of Beavers and Why They Matter.* Hartford, VT: Chelsea Green, 2018.

Grayson, Donald K., and David J. Meltzer. "A Requiem for North American Overkill." *Journal of Archaeological Science* 30, no. 5 (2003): 585–93.

Greiser, Sally Thompson. "Predictive Models of Hunter-Gatherer Subsistence and Settlement Strategies on the Central High Plains." Memoir 20. *Plains Anthropologist* 20, no. 110, pt. 2 (1985): i–134.

Grinnell, George Bird. *Blackfoot Lodge Tales.* 1892; Lincoln: University of Nebraska Press, 1962.

———. *The Cheyenne Indians: Their History and Ways of Life.* 2 vols. Lincoln: University of Nebraska Press, 1972.

Hadley, Elmer B., and Barbara J. Kieckefer. "Productivity of Two Prairie Grasses in Relation to Fire Frequency." *Ecology* 44, no. 2 (1963): 389–95.

Haines, Francis. "The Northward Spread of Horses among the Plains Indians." *American Anthropologist* 40, no. 1 (1938): 429–37.

Hall, Joseph G. "Willow and Aspen in the Ecology of Beaver on Sagehen Creek, California." *Ecology* 41, no. 3 (1960): 484–94.

Hamilton, W.T., and C. J. Scifres. "Prescribed Burning during Winter for Maintenance of Buffalograss." *Journal of Range Management* 35, no. 1 (1982): 9–12.

Hammond, Merrill C. "Beaver on the Lower Souris Refuge." *Journal of Wildlife Management* 7, no. 3 (1943): 316–21.

Harmon, Daniel Williams. *Sixteen Years in the Indian Country: The Journal of Daniel Williams Harmon, 1800–1816.* Edited by W. Kaye Lamb. 1820; Toronto: Macmillan, 1957.

Harris, Marvin. *Cultural Materialism: The Struggle for a Science of Culture.* 2nd ed. Lanham, MD: AltaMira Press, 2001.

———. *Culture, People, Nature: An Introduction to General Anthropology.* New York: Harper and Row, 1985.

Hennepin, Father Louis. *A Description of Louisiana.* Edited by John Gilmary Shea. New York: J.G. Shea, 1880.

Henry, Alexander. *Travels and Adventures in Canada and the Indian Territories.* Edited by James Bain. 1809; Edmonton: M.G. Hurtig, 1969.

Higgins, Kenneth F. *Interpretation and Compendium of Historical Fire Accounts in the Northern Great Plains.* Resource Publication 161. Washington, DC: Fish and Wildlife Service, Department of the Interior, 1986.

Hind, Henry Youle. *Narrative of the Canadian Red River Exploring Expedition of 1857 and of the Assiniboine and Saskatchewan Exploring Expedition of 1858.* 2 vols. 1860; Edmonton: M.G. Hurtig, 1971.

———. "Observations on the Foraging Habits of Beaver." *Journal of Mammalogy* 19, no. 3 (1938): 317–19.

Hobbs, N. Thompson, and David S. Schimel. "Fire Effects on Nitrogen Mineralization and Fixation in Mountain Shrub and Grassland Communities." *Journal of Range Management* 37, no. 5 (1984): 402–05.

Hodgdon, Kenneth W., and John H. Hunt. *Beaver Management in Maine.* Game Division Bulletin 3. Augusta, ME: Department of Inland Fisheries and Game, 1955.

Hood, Glynnis A., and David G. Larson. "Ecological Engineering and Aquatic Connectivity: A New Perspective from Beaver-Modified Wetlands." *Freshwater Biology* 60, no. 1 (2015): 198–208.

Hood, Robert. "Some Account of the Cree and Other Indians, 1819." *Alberta Historical Review* 15, no. 1 (1967): 6–17.

Hop, Kevin, Jennifer Dieck, Sara Lubinski, Marion Reid, and Stephen Cooper. US *Geological Survey-National Park Service Vegetation Mapping Program: Waterton-Glacier International Peace Park.* La Crosse, WI: Geological Survey, Upper Midwest Environmental Sciences Center, 2007.

Hopkins, Harold H. "Effects of Mulch upon Certain Factors of the Grassland Environment." *Journal of Range Management* 7, no. 6 (1954): 255–58.

Hornaday, W.T. "The Extermination of the American Bison, with a Sketch of Its Discovery and Life History." In *Annual Report, 1887, Smithsonian Institution,* 367–548. Washington, DC: Smithsonian Institution, 1889.

Hunt, Terry L., and Carl P. Lipo. "Late Colonization of Easter Island." *Science* 311, no. 5767 (2006): 1603–6.

Husted, Wilfred M. *Bighorn Canyon Archaeology.* Smithsonian Institution River Basin Surveys, Publications in Salvage Archaeology 12. Lincoln: University of Nebraska Press, 1969.

Jablow, Joseph. *The Cheyenne in Plains Indian Trade Relations, 1795–1840.* Seattle: University of Washington Press, 1966.

Jenkins, Stephen H. "Problems, Progress, and Prospects in Studies of Food Selection by Beavers." In *Worldwide Furbearers Conference Proceedings,* edited by J.A. Chapman and D. Pursley, 559–79. Frostburg, MD: Worldwide Furbearers Conference, 1980.

———. "A Size-Distance Relation in Food Selection by Beavers." *Ecology* 61, no. 4 (1980): 740–46.

Jenness, Diamond. *The Sarcee Indians of Alberta.* National Museum of Canada Bulletin 90, Anthropological Series 23. Ottawa: National Museum of Canada, 1938.

Johnson, Alice M., ed. *Saskatchewan Journal and Correspondence: Edmonton House 1795–1800.* London: Hudson's Bay Record Society, 1967.

Johnson, E.A., and G. Fryer. "Historical Vegetation Change in the Kananaskis Valley, Canadian Rockies." *Canadian Journal of Botany* 65, no. 5 (1987): 853–58.

Kehoe, Alice B. *North American Indians: A Comprehensive Account.* Englewood Cliffs, NJ: Prentice-Hall, 1981.

Kehoe, Thomas F. "The Boarding School Bison Drive Site." Memoir 4. *Plains Anthropologist* 12, no. 35 (1967): 1–165.

———. *Stone Tipi Rings in North-Central Montana and the Adjacent Portion of Alberta, Canada: Their Historical, Ethnological, and Archeological Aspects.* Anthropological Papers 62, Bureau of American Ethnology Bulletin 173. Washington, DC: Smithsonian Institution, 1960.

Kendeigh, S. Charles. *Animal Ecology.* Englewood Cliffs, NJ: Prentice-Hall, 1961.

Kennedy, Michael Stephen. *The Assiniboines.* Norman: University of Oklahoma Press, 1961.

Kent, D.M. "The Glacial History of the Regina–Qu'Appelle Valley Area." Unpublished paper, Department of Geology, University of Regina, 1968.

Kimmerer, Robin Wall. "*Mishkos Kenomagwen*, the Lessons of Grass: Restoring Reciprocity with the Good Green Earth." In *Traditional Ecological Knowledge: Learning from Indigenous Practices for Environmental Sustainability*, edited by Melissa K. Nelson and Dan Shilling, 27–56. Cambridge: Cambridge University Press, 2019.

———. "Native Knowledge for Native Ecosystems." *Journal of Forestry* 98, no. 8 (2000): 4–9.

———. "Restoration and Reciprocity: The Contributions of Traditional Ecological Knowledge." In *Human Dimensions of Ecological Restoration*, edited by Dan Egan and E.E. Hjerpe, 257–76. Washington, DC: Island Press, 2011.

Knapp, Alan K. "Effects of Fire and Drought on the Ecophysiology of Andropogon Gerardii and Panicum Virgatum in a Tallgrass Prairie." *Ecology* 66, no. 4 (1985): 1309–20.

Knapp, Alan K., John M. Blair, John M. Briggs, Scott L. Collins, David C. Hartnett, Loretta C. Johnson, and E. Gene Towne. "The Keystone Role of Bison in North American Tallgrass Prairie: Bison

Increase Habitat Heterogeneity and Alter a Broad Array of Plant, Community, and Ecosystem Processes." *BioScience* 49, no. 1 (1999): 39–50.

Knudson, George. *Relationship of Beaver to Forests, Trout, and Wildlife in Wisconsin.* Technical Bulletin 25. Madison: Wisconsin Conservation Department, 1962.

Kroeber, A.L. "Cheyenne Tales." *Journal of American Folklore* 13, no. 50 (1900): 161–90.

Kucera, C.L., and John H. Ehrenreich. "Some Effects of Annual Burning on Central Missouri Prairie." *Ecology* 43, no. 2 (1962): 334–36.

Kurz, Rudolph F. *Journal of Rudolph Friedrich Kurz, 1846–1852.* Translated by Myrtis Jarrell. Edited by J.N.B. Hewitt. Bureau of American Ethnology Bulletin 115. Washington, DC: Smithsonian Institution, 1937.

Lancaster, Richard. *Piegan.* Garden City, NY: Doubleday, 1966.

Lang, Terri-Anne, and Ken Jones. *A Comparison of the Meteorological Conditions during the Droughts of the 1930s and the 1980s for the Prairie Provinces.* Ottawa: Atmospheric Environment Service, Environment Canada, 1988.

Larocque, François Antoine. *Journal of François Antoine Larocque from the Assiniboine to the Yellowstone, 1805.* Edited with notes by L.J. Burpee. Publications of the Canadian Archives 3. 1805; Ottawa: Government Printing Bureau, 1910.

Larson, Floyd. "The Role of Bison in Maintaining the Short Grass Plains." *Ecology* 21, no. 2 (1940): 113–21.

Larson, Floyd, and Warren Whitman. "A Comparison of Used and Unused Grassland Mesas in the Badlands of South Dakota." *Ecology* 23, no. 4 (1942): 438–45.

Leach, D.S. "Carrying Capacity and Beaver Population Study at Elk Island National Park." Unpublished report, Elk Island National Park Files, 1986.

Lewarch, Dennis E., and Michael J. O'Brien. "The Expanding Role of Surface Assemblages in Archaeological Research." *Advances in Archaeological Method and Theory* 4 (1981): 297–342.

Lewis, Henry T. "Fire Technology and Resource Management in Aboriginal North America and Australia." In *Resource Managers: North American and Australian Hunter-Gatherers,* edited by N.M. Williams and E.S. Hunn, 45–67. AAAS Selected Symposium 67. Boulder, CO: Western Press, 1982.

———. *A Time for Burning.* Occasional Publication 17. Edmonton: Boreal Institute for Northern Studies, University of Alberta, 1982.

———. "Why Indians Burned: Specific versus General Reasons." In *Proceedings: Symposium and Workshop on Wilderness Fire*, edited by J.E. Lotan, B.M. Kilgore, W.C. Fischer, and R.W. Mutch, 75–80. General Technical Report INT-182. Ogden, UT: Intermountain Forest and Range Experiment Station, Forest Service, US Department of Agriculture, 1985.

Lewis, Henry T., and Theresa A. Ferguson. "Yards, Corridors, and Mosaics: How to Burn a Boreal Forest." *Human Ecology* 16, no. 1 (1988): 57–77.

Lewis, Meriwether, and William Clark. *Original Journals of the Lewis and Clark Expedition, 1804–1806.* Vol. 1. Edited by Reuben Gold Thwaites. 1904–1905; New York: Antiquarian Press, 1969.

Lewis, Oscar. *The Effects of White Contact upon Blackfoot Culture with Special Reference to the Role of the Fur Trade.* American Ethnological Society Monograph 6. Seattle: University of Washington Press, 1942.

Livingston, John H. *One Cosmic Instant.* Toronto: McClelland and Stewart, 1973.

Longley, Richmond W. *The Climate of the Prairie Provinces.* Climatological Studies 13. Toronto: Atmospheric Environment, Environment Canada, 1972.

Longley, William H., and John B. Moyle. *The Beaver in Minnesota.* Technical Bulletin 6. Minneapolis: Division of Game and Fish, Minnesota Department of Conservation, 1963.

Lorenzen, Eline D., David Nogués-Bravo, Ludovic Orlando, Jaco Weinstock, Jonas Binladen, Katharine A. Marske, Andrew Ugan et al. "Species-Specific Responses of Late Quaternary Megafauna to Climate and Humans." *Nature* 479, no. 7373 (2011): 359–64.

Lowie, Robert H. *The Assiniboine.* Anthropological Papers of the AMNH, vol. 4, pt. 1. New York: American Museum of Natural History, 1909.

Mackenzie, Alexander. *Voyages from Montreal on the River St. Laurence through the Continent of North America, to the Frozen and Pacific Oceans: In the Years 1789 and 1793 with a Preliminary Account of the Rise, Progress, and Present State of the Fur Trade.* New York: G.F. Hopkins, 1802.

Maddock, Linda. "The 'Migration' and Grazing Succession." In *Serengeti: Dynamics of an Ecosystem*, edited by A.R.E. Sinclair and M. Norton-Griffiths, 104–29. Chicago: University of Chicago Press, 1979.

Mandelbaum, David G. *The Plains Cree*. Anthropological Papers of the AMNH, vol. 37, pt. 2. New York: American Museum of Natural History, 1940. Reprinted and revised as *The Plains Cree: An Ethnographic, Historical, and Comparative Study*. Canadian Plains Studies 9. Regina: Canadian Plains Research Center, 1979.

Marriott, Alice. "Osage Indian II." In *American Indian Ethnohistory: Plains Indians*, edited by David Agee Horr. New York: Garland, 1974.

Martin, S. Clark. "Responses of Semidesert Grasses and Shrubs to Fall Burning." *Journal of Range Management* 6, no. 5 (1986): 604–10.

Martinez, Dennis. "Redefining Sustainability through Kincentric Ecology: Reclaiming Indigenous Lands, Knowledge, and Ethics." In *Traditional Ecological Knowledge: Learning from Indigenous Practices for Environmental Sustainability*, edited by Melissa K. Nelson and Dan Shilling, 139–74. Cambridge: Cambridge University Press, 2019.

Masson, L.R. *Les Bourgeois de la Compagnie du Nord-Ouest*. 2 vols. 1890; New York: Antiquarian Press, 1960.

McClintock, Walter. *The Old North Trail: Life, Legends and Religion of the Blackfeet Indians*. London: Macmillan, 1910.

McDougall, John. *Saddle, Sled, and Snowshoe: Pioneering on the Saskatchewan in the Sixties*. 1896; Toronto: Ryerson Press, 1900.

McGillivray, Duncan. *The Journal of Duncan M'Gillivray of the Northwest Company at Fort George on the Saskatchewan, 1794–1795*. Edited by Arthur Silver Morton. Toronto: Macmillan, 1929.

McGinty, Allan, Fred E. Smeins, and Leo B. Merrill. "Influence of Spring Burning on Cattle Diets and Performance on the Edwards Plateau." *Journal of Range Management* 36, no. 2 (1983): 175–78.

Metz, L.J., T. Lotti, and R.A. Klawitter. "Some Effects on Prescribed Burning on Coastal Plain Forest Soils." US Forest Service, Southeastern Forest Experiment Station, Station Paper SE-133, November 1961, 1–10.

Moodie, D.W., and Arthur J. Ray. "Buffalo Migrations in the Canadian Plains." *Plains Anthropologist* 21, no. 71 (1976): 45–52.

Morgan, R. Grace. "Beaver Ecology/Beaver Mythology." PhD diss., University of Alberta, 1991.

———. "Bison Movement Patterns on the Canadian Plains: An Ecological Analysis." *Plains Anthropologist* 25, no. 88 (1980): 143–59.

———. *An Ecological Study of the Northern Plains as Seen through the Garratt Site.* Occasional Papers in Anthropology 1. Regina: Department of Anthropology, University of Regina, 1979.

Morgan, R. Grace, and R.J. Hudson. "Dynamics of Fire and Grazing by Bison on Grasslands in Central Alberta." Paper presented at International Symposium on Bison Ecology and Management in North America, Bozeman, MT, June 4–7, 1997. Published as Appendix in R. Grace Morgan, *Beaver, Bison, Horse: The Traditional Knowledge and Ecology of the Northern Great Plains* (Regina: University of Regina Press, 2020).

Morgan, R. Grace, and W.J. Wood. "The Archaeology of the Alaska Highway Gas Pipeline (Zone 9) Southwestern Saskatchewan." Unpublished report, Foothills Pipe Lines, Saskatchewan, 1982.

Morton, Arthur Silver. *A History of the Canadian West to 1870–71.* Toronto: University of Toronto Press, 1973.

———. "Hudson's Bay Company Diary of Fort Edmonton October 1854 to May 1856." C511/2/2, fonds MG 437, A.S. Morton Manuscript Collection, University Archives and Special Collections, University of Saskatchewan, Saskatoon.

Moss, E.H., and J.A. Campbell. "The Fescue Grassland of Alberta." *Canadian Journal of Research* 25c, no. 6 (1947): 209–27.

Mulloy, William. *A Preliminary Historical Outline for the Northwestern Plains.* University of Wyoming Publications 22. Laramie: University of Wyoming, 1958.

Murphy, Robert F., and Yolanda Murphy. "Shoshone-Bannock Subsistence and Society." *University of California Anthropological Records* 16, no. 7 (1960): 293–338.

Mwai, Okeyo, Olivier Hanotte, Young-Jun Kwon, and Seoae Cho. "African Indigenous Cattle: Unique Genetic Resources in a Rapidly Changing World." *Asian-Australasian Journal of Animal Sciences* 28, no. 7 (2015): 911–21.

Naiman, Robert J., Carol A. Johnston, and James C. Kelley. "Alteration of North American Streams by Beaver." *BioScience* 38, no. 11 (1988): 753–62.

Nelson, J.G. *The Last Refuge.* Montreal: Harvest House, 1973.

Ng'Weno, Caroline C. "The Restoration of Lions to a Human-Occupied Savanna." PhD diss., University of Wyoming, 2017.

Nielsen, Rasmus, Joshua M. Akey, Mattias Jakobsson, Jonathan K. Pritchard, Sarah Tishkoff, and Eske Willerslev. "Tracing the Peopling of the World through Genomics." *Nature* 541, no. 7637 (2017): 302–10.

O'Brien, Michael J., and Chad K. McDaniel. "Prehistoric Community Patterns: Surface Definition." In *The Cannon Reservoir Human Ecology Project: An Archaeological Study of Cultural Adaptations in the Southern Prairie Peninsula*, edited by Michael J. O'Brien, Robert E. Warren, and Dennis E. Lawarch, 217–54. New York: Academic Press, 1982.

Odum, Eugene P. *Fundamentals of Ecology*. Philadelphia: W.B. Saunders, 1959.

Old, Sylvia M. "Microclimate, Fire and Plant Production in an Illinois Prairie." *Ecological Monographs* 39, no. 4 (1969): 355–84

Oliver, Symmes C. "Ecology and Cultural Continuity as Contributing Factors in the Social Organization of the Plains Indians." *University of California Publications in American Archaeology and Ethnology* 48, no. 1 (1962): 1–90.

Olson, Wes. "Beaver Pond Management Activities and Impacts." Unpublished report, Resource Conservation, Elk Island National Park, Parks Canada, 1987.

———. *A Field Guide to Plains Bison*. Calgary: Timbergulch Press, 2012.

Paine, Robert T. "Food Webs: Linkage, Interaction Strength and Community Infrastructure." *Journal of Animal Ecology* 49, no. 3 (1980): 667–85.

———. "A Note on Trophic Complexity and Species Diversity." *American Naturalist* 103 (1969): 91–93.

Pard, Allan. "Repatriation among the Piikani." In Conaty, ed., *We Are Coming Home*, 119–34.

Peden, Donald G., George M. Van Dyne, Richard W. Rice, and Richard M. Hansen. "The Trophic Ecology of Bison bison L. on Shortgrass Plains." *Journal of Applied Ecology* 119, no. 2 (1974): 489–97.

Penfound, William T., and R.W. Kelting. "Some Effects of Winter Burning on a Moderately Grazed Pasture." *Ecology* 31, no. 4 (1950): 554–60.

Phillips, Paul C. *The Fur Trade.* Norman: University of Oklahoma Press, 1961.

Plumb, Glenn E., P.J. White, Michael B. Coughenour, and Rick L. Wallen. "Carrying Capacity, Migration, and Dispersal in Yellowstone Bison." *Biological Conservation* 142, no. 11 (2009): 2377–87.

Quigg, J. Michael. *The Belly River: Prehistoric Population Dynamics in a Northwestern Plains Transitional Zone.* Archaeological Survey of Canada Paper 23, Mercury Series. Ottawa: National Museum of Man, 1974.

———. "The Lazy Dog Site." Occasional Paper No. 8. In *Tipi Rings in Southern Alberta,* prepared for Archaeological Survey of Alberta. Edmonton: Historical Resources Division, Alberta Culture, 1978.

Raby, S., and T. Richards. "Water Resources." In *Atlas of Saskatchewan,* edited by J.H. Richards and K.I. Fung, 61. Saskatoon: University of Saskatchewan, 1969.

Raison, R.J. "Modifications of the Soil Environment by Vegetation Fires, with Particular Reference to Nitrogen Transformations: A Review." *Plant and Soil* 51, no. 1 (1979): 73–108.

Ray, Arthur J. "History and Archaeology of the Northern Fur Trade." *American Antiquity* 43, no. 1 (1978): 26–34.

———. "Indian Adaptations to the Forest-Grassland Boundary of Manitoba and Saskatchewan, 1650–1821: Some Implications for Interregional Migration." *Canadian Geographer* 16, no. 2 (1972): 103–18.

———. *Indians in the Fur Trade: Their Role as Hunters, Trappers, and Middlemen in the Lands Southwest of Hudson Bay, 1660–1870.* Toronto: University of Toronto Press, 1976.

Reardon, P.O., and D.L. Huss. "Effects of Fertilization on a Little Bluestem Community." *Journal of Range Management* 18, no. 5 (1965): 238–41.

Renecker, Lyle A., and Robert J. Hudson. "Seasonal Quality of Forages Used by Moose in the Aspen-Dominated Boreal Forest, Central Alberta." *Holarctic Ecology* 11, no. 2 (1988): 111–18.

Retzer, J.L., Harold M. Swope, Jack D. Remington, and William H. Rutherford. *Suitability of Physical Factors for Beaver Management in the Rocky Mountains of Colorado.* Technical Bulletin 2. Denver: Department of Game and Fish, State of Colorado, 1956.

Reyes-Garcia, Victoria, Alvaro Fernandez-Llamazares, Pamela McElwee, Zsolt Molnar, Kinga Ollerer, Sarah Jane Wilson, and Eduardo Brondizio. "The Contributions of Indigenous People and Local Communities to Ecological Restoration." *Restoration Ecology* 27, no. 1 (2018): 3–8.

Ridington, Robin. "Technology, World View, and Adaptive Strategy in a Northern Hunting Society." *Canadian Review of Sociology and Anthropology* 19, no. 4 (1982): 469–81.

Riegger, Hal. *Primitive Pottery*. New York: Van Nostrand Reinhold, 1972.

Riggs, Stephen Return. *Dakota Grammar, Texts, and Ethnography*. Edited by James Owen Dorsey. Contributions to North American Ethnology, vol. 9. Washington, DC: Government Printing Office, 1893.

Roe, Frank Gilbert. *The Indian and the Horse*. Norman: University of Oklahoma Press, 1955.

———. *The North American Buffalo: A Critical Study of the Species*. Toronto: University of Toronto Press, 1972.

Rogers, Edward S. *The Hunting Group–Hunting Territory Complex among the Mistassini Indians*. National Museum of Canada Bulletin 195, Anthropological Series 63. Ottawa: National Museum of Canada, 1963.

Roos, Christopher I., María Nieves Zedeño, Kacy L. Hollenback, and Mary M.H. Erlick. "Indigenous Impacts on North American Great Plains Fire Regimes of the Past Millennium." PNAS 115, no. 32 (2018): 8143–48.

Rowe, J.S. "East Qu'Appelle Valley Natural Area." International Biological Programme, Section CT: Conservation of Terrestrial Biological Communities, Department of Plant Ecology, University of Saskatchewan, 1973.

———. "Nicolle Flats–Moose Jaw Creek." International Biological Programme, Section CT: Conservation of Terrestrial Biological Communities, Department of Plant Ecology, University of Saskatchewan, 1971.

Russell, Dale. *Eighteenth-Century Western Cree and Their Neighbours*. Ottawa: Canadian Museum of Civilization, 1991.

Russell, J.D., A.R. Fraser, J.R. Watson, and J.R. Parsons. "Thermal Decompostion of Protein in Soil Organic Matter." *Geoderma* 11, no. 1 (1974): 63–66.

Rutherford, William H. *The Beaver in Colorado: Its Biology, Ecology, Management, and Economics.* Beaver Investigations, Project W-83-R, Technical Publication 17. Denver: Colorado Game, Fish, and Parks Department, 1964.

Samson, Fred, and Fritz Knopf. "Prairie Conservation in North America." *BioScience* 44, no. 6 (1994): 418–21.

Sanderson, Eric W., Kent H. Redford, Bill Weber, Keith Aune, Dick Baldes, Joel Berger, Dave Carter, et al. "The Ecological Future of the North American Bison: Conceiving Long-Term, Large-Scale Conservation of Wildlife." *Conservation Biology* 22, no. 2 (2008): 252–66.

Sarvis, J.T. "Grazing Investigation on the Northern Great Plains." North Dakota Agricultural Experiment Station Bulletin 308, 1941.

Schmitz, Oswald. "Enlisting Ecological Interactions among Animals to Balance the Carbon Budget." In *Biodiversity and Climate Change: Transforming the Biosphere*, edited by Thomas E. Lovejoy and Lee Hannah, 332–35. New Haven: Yale University Press, 2019.

Schwanke, R., and Keith Baker. *The Beaver of Elk Island National Park.* Ottawa: Parks Canada, 1977.

Seagle, Steven W., S.J. McNaughton, and Roger W. Ruess. "Simulated Effects of Grazing on Soil Nitrogen and Mineralization in Contrasting Serengeti Grasslands." *Ecology* 73, no. 3 (1992): 1105–23.

Secoy, Frank Raymond. *Changing Military Patterns on the Great Plains.* Seattle: University of Washington Press, 1953.

Semple, A.T. *Grassland Improvement.* Plant Science Monographs, edited by Nicholas Dolunin. London: Leonard Hill Books, 1970.

Seton, Ernest Thompson. *Lives of Game Animals.* Vol. 4. Boston: Charles T. Branford Company, 1953.

Sharrow, Steven H., and Henry A. Wright. "Effects of Fire, Ash, and Litter on Soil Nitrate, Temperature, Moisture and Tobosagrass Production in the Rolling Plains." *Journal of Range Management* 30, no. 4 (1977): 266–70.

Shaw, James H., and Tracy S. Carter. "Bison Movements in Relation to Fire and Seasonality." *Wildlife Society Bulletin* 18, no. 4 (1990): 426–30.

Sherratt, D., and D. Hatch. *Qu'Appelle Mammalian Inventory.* Wildlife Technical Report 77-37. Regina: Saskatchewan Tourism and Renewable Resources, 1977.

Skinner, Alanson. *Notes on the Eastern Cree and Northern Saulteaux.* Anthropological Papers of the AMNH, vol. 9, pt. 1. New York: American Museum of Natural History, 1911.

———. *Political Organization, Cults, and Ceremonies of the Plains-Ojibway and Plains-Cree Indians.* Anthropological Papers of the AMNH, vol. 11, pt. 4. New York: American Museum of Natural History, 1914.

Skinner, D.L. "Selection of Winter Food by Beavers at Elk Island National Park." MSc thesis, University of Alberta, 1984.

Slough, Brian G., and R.M.F.S. Sadleir. "A Land Capability Classification System for Beaver (*Castor canadensis* Kuhl)." *Canadian Journal of Zoology* 55, no. 8 (1977): 1324–35.

Smith, Brian J. "The Lebret Site." MA thesis, University of Saskatchewan, 1986.

Smith, James G.E. "The Western Woods Cree: Anthropological Myth and Historical Reality." *American Ethnologist* 14, no. 3 (1987): 434–48.

Smyth, David. "Missed Opportunity: John Milloy's *The Plains Cree,*" *Prairie Forum* 17 (1992): 337–54.

Soulé, Michael E., James A. Estes, Joel Berger, and Carlos Martinez Del Rio. "Ecological Effectiveness: Conservation Goals for Interactive Species." *Conservation Biology* 17, no. 5 (2003): 1238–50.

Soulé, Michael E., James A. Estes, Brian Miller, and Douglas L. Honnold. "Strongly Interacting Species: Conservation Policy, Management, and Ethics." *BioScience* 55, no. 2 (2005): 168–75.

Stegeman, LeRoy C. "The Production of Aspen and Its Utilization by Beaver on the Huntington Forest." *Journal of Wildlife Management* 18, no. 3 (1954): 348–58.

Strong, Paul Isaac Vincent. "Beaver-Cottonwood Interactions and Beaver Ecology in Big Bend National Park." MSc thesis, Oklahoma State University, 1982.

Thompson, David. *David Thompson's Narrative, 1784–1812.* New ed. Edited by Richard Glover. 1916; Toronto: Champlain Society, 1962.

Thwaites, Reuben Gold, ed. *Travels in the Interior of North America, by Maximilian, Prince of Wied.* Vol. 2. Cleveland: Arthur H. Clark, 1906.

Todd, Arlen W. *Methodology Used for Alberta Land Inventory of Furbearers.* Edmonton: Alberta Fish and Wildlife Division, Department of Recreation, Parks, and Wildlife, 1978.

Trabert, Sarah. "Reframing the Protohistoric Period and the (Peri) Colonial Process for the North American Central Plains." *World Archaeology* 50, no. 5 (2018): 820–34.

Treshow, Michael. *The Human Environment.* New York: McGraw-Hill, 1976.

Trudeau, Jean Baptiste. "Trudeau's Journal." *South Dakota Historical Collections* 7 (1914): 403–74.

Turk, Amos, Jonathan Turk, and Janet T. Wittes. *Ecology, Pollution, Environment.* Philadelphia: W.B. Saunders, 1972.

Turner, Nancy J., Marianne Boelscher Ignace, and Ronald Ignace. "Traditional Ecological Knowledge and Wisdom of Aboriginal Peoples in British Columbia." *Ecological Applications* 10, no. 5 (2000): 1275–87.

Umfreville, Edward. *The Present State of Hudson's Bay: Containing a Full Description of That Settlement and the Adjacent Country; and Likewise of the Fur Trade.* Edited by W. Stewart Wallace. 1790; Toronto: Ryerson Press, 1954.

Van Dyne, G.M., N.R. Brockington, Z. Szocs, J. Duek, and C.A. Ribic. "Large Herbivore Subsystem." In *Grasslands, Systems Analysis and Man*, edited by A.I. Breymeyer and G.M. Van Dyne, 269–538. Cambridge: Cambridge University Press, 1980.

Vesey-Fitzgerald, Desmond. "Fire and Animal Impact on Vegetation in Tanzania National Parks." *Fire Ecology Conference Proceedings* 11 (1972): 297–317.

Vinton, M.A., and D.C. Hartnett. "Effects of Bison Grazing on *Andropogon gerardii* and *Panicum virgatum*." *Oecologia* 90 (1992): 374–82.

Vinton, Mary Ann, David C. Hartnett, Elmer J. Finck, and John M. Briggs. "Interactive Effects of Fire Bison (Bison bison) Grazing and Plant Community Composition in Tallgrass Prairie." *American Midland Naturalist* 129, no. 1 (1993): 10–18.

Viro, P.J. "Effects of Forest Fire on Soil." In *Fire and Ecosystems*, edited by T.T. Kozlowski and C.E. Ahlgren, 7–44. New York: Academic Press, 1974.

Waksman, Selman A., and Robert L. Starkey. "Partial Sterilization of Soil Microbiological Activities and Soil Fertility: I." *Soil Science* 16, no. 3 (1923): 137–56.

Wallace, Ernest, and E. Adamson Hoebel. *The Comanches: Lords of the South Plains.* Norman: University of Oklahoma Press, 1952.

Walton, P.D., R. Martinez, and A.W. Bailey. "A Comparison of Continuous and Rotational Grazing." *Journal of Range Management* 34, no. 1 (1981): 19–21.

Weekes, Mary. "An Indian's Description of the Making of a Buffalo Pound." *Saskatchewan History* 1, no. 3 (1948): 14–17.

Wettlaufer, Boyd, and William J. Mayer-Oakes. *The Long Creek Site.* Anthropological Series 2. Regina: Department of Natural Resources, 1960.

Wheat, Joe Ben. "Olson-Chubbuck and Jurgens Sites: Four Aspects of Paleo-Indian Economy." In "Bison Procurement and Utilization: A Symposium," edited by Leslie B. Davis and Michael Wilson. Special issue, *Plains Anthropologist* 23, no. 82 (1978): 84–89.

Whicker, April D., and James K. Detling. "Ecological Consequences of Prairie Dog Disturbances." *Bioscience* 38, no. 11 (1988): 778–85.

White, E.M., F.R. Gartner, and R. Butterfield. "Blue Grama [*Bouteloua gracilis*] Response to Fertilization of a Claypan Soil in the Greenhouse." *Journal of Range Management* 36, no. 2 (1983): 232–33.

White, Richard S., and Pat O. Currie. "Prescribed Burning in the Northern Great Plains: Yield and Cover Responses of 3 Forage Species in the Mixed Grass Prairie." *Journal of Range Management* 36, no. 2 (1983): 179–83.

Wilde, S.A., C.T. Youngberg, and J.H. Hovind. "Changes in Composition of Ground Water, Soil Fertility, and Forest Growth Produced by the Construction and Removal of Beaver Dams." *Journal of Wildlife Management* 14, no. 2 (1950): 123–28.

Willms, Walter. "Foraging Strategy of Ruminants." *Rangeman's Journal* 5, no. 3 (1978): 72–74.

Willms, W., A.W. Bailey, and A. McLean. "Effect of Burning or Clipping *Agropyron spicatum* in the Autumn on the Spring Foraging Behavior of Mule Deer and Cattle." *Journal of Applied Ecology* 17 (1980): 69–84.

Wire, Frank B., and A.B. Hatch. "Administration of Beaver in the Western United States." *Journal of Wildlife Management* 7, no. 1 (1943): 81–92.

Wissler, Clark. *Ceremonial Bundles of the Blackfoot Indians.* Anthropological Papers of the AMNH, vol. 8, pt. 2. New York: American Museum of Natural History, 1912.

———. "The Influence of the Horse in the Development of Plains Culture." *American Anthropologist* 16, no. 1 (1914): 1–26.

———. *Material Culture of the Blackfoot Indians.* Anthropological Papers of the AMNH, vol. 5, pt. 1. New York: American Museum of Natural History, 1910.

———. *The Social Life of the Blackfoot Indians.* Anthropological Papers of the AMNH, vol. 7, pt. 1. New York: American Museum of Natural History, 1911.

———. *The Sun Dance of the Blackfoot Indians.* Anthropological Papers of the AMNH, vol. 16, pt. 3. New York: American Museum of Natural History, 1918.

Wissler, Clark, and D.C. Duvall. *Mythology of the Blackfoot Indians.* Anthropological Papers of the AMNH, vol. 2, pt. 1. New York: American Museum of Natural History, 1908.

Wohl, Ellen. "Landscape-Scale Carbon Storage Associated with Beaver Dams." *Geophysical Research Letters* 40, no. 14 (2013): 3631–36.

Wright, Henry A., and Arthur W. Bailey. *Fire Ecology and Prescribed Burning in the Great Plains: A Research Review.* General Technical Report INT-77. Ogden, UT: Intermountain Forest and Range Experiment Station, Forest Service, US Department of Agriculture, 1980.

Wright, M. "Le Bois de Vache II: This Chip's for You Too." In *Buffalo,* edited by J.E. Foster, D. Harrison, and I.S. MacLaren, 225–44. Edmonton: University of Alberta Press, 1992.

Younging, Gregory. *Elements of Indigenous Style: A Guide for Writing by and about Indigenous Peoples.* Edmonton: Brush Education, 2018.

Zoltai, S.C. *Southern Limit of Coniferous Trees on the Canadian Plain.* Information Report NOR-X-128. Edmonton: Environment Canada Forestry Service, Northern Forest Resources Centre, 1975.

INDEX

A

Adams, Gary, 128
AGL Foundation, 194
agriculture, 75, 119, 141, 185, 189, 199
Alareak, Peter, 201
Alberta Forestry Lands and
    Wildlife: vegetation
    inventory system, 223
alcohol. *See* trade goods
Algonkian languages, 107
Algonquin people, 162, 170, 189
Alkali Creek, 128
Allen, A.W., 70, 234
American Fur Company,
    160, 165, 171, 182
American Prairie Reserve, 197
ammonium nitrogen, in soil,
    242–43, 251, 253–54
Anishinaabe people, 189
Apache people, 147
Arapaho people, 5, 108, 123
Archithinue people (Blackfoot
    tribes), 109–12
Aref'yeva, Z.N., 242–43, 256
Arthur, George, 33, 39, 45,
    111, 123, 125, 131, 150–51
artifacts: assemblages of, 119,
    133–35, 139; as cultural, 190–92;
    densities of, 121–22, 129, 133–34,
    136–38, 143; recovery of, 137;
    as surface collections, 118;
    types of, 121–22, 125, 143
ash deposits/residues, 233, 237, 239
Aspen Grove Region, 23–24,
    28–29, 31, 47, 236
Aspen Park Region, 245
aspen stands, 68, 88, 95, 179, 195–96;
    as burned for firewood, 66;

growth areas of, 22–23, 27, 46,
    65, 81–82, 87, 221–24; as preferred
    by beaver, 63, 71–72, 90, 93, 98;
    sheltering effect of, 28–29, 38
Assiniboine Cree people, 147, 154, 162
Assiniboine people (Assiniboils),
    18, 42, 44, 109, 123, 154, 158,
    163, 167–68, 171; as attacked
    by Blackfoot, 152; as canoe
    builders, 110; distinct language
    dialects of, 104–5; migrations
    of, 103–4, 108; as non-beaver
    hunters, 4; Plains/Woodlands
    distinction, 7, 103–6; as running
    bison drives, 54; settlement
    patterns of, 170; subsistence
    pattern for, 57; as supplier of
    furs, 3, 5, 102, 110–11. *See also*
    Plains Assiniboine people;
    Woodlands Assiniboine people
Assiniboine River, 4, 26, 29, 37,
    39, 104–5, 109, 153, 155, 170
Assiniboine River Valley, 160, 167
Athabascan people, 154
Athabasca River, 153
Atsina. *See* Gros Ventre
    people (Fall Indians)
Ayyad, M.A.G., 27

B

Badger–Two Medicine region
    (Montana), 198
Bailey, Arthur, 23, 244, 249
Baker, Keith, 92–93, 96–97
Bancroft, Hubert Howe, 153
Batt, Isaac, 111
Battle River, 108–9, 155

317

bear, 12, 155; as food source, 56
beaver/beaver populations, 18, 22, 72,
  100, 126, 190, 192, 196; activities
  of, 42, 54, 63, 66, 69, 75, 82,
  122, 202; as adaptable, 14, 70;
  as commodity, 157; diet/food
  requirements of, 71, 74, 88–89,
  94; distribution of, 13, 36, 63,
  68–70, 72, 74, 83, 87, 99, 175;
  effects of activities of, 17, 71–74,
  77, 86, 88, 91, 93, 97–98, 179,
  183–84; food resources/caches
  of, 72, 75, 77–79, 82–83, 85–88,
  92, 95, 97, 99, 145; foraging
  behaviour of, 45–46, 70, 77, 82,
  87, 92–93, 95; habitat for, 69–74,
  82–83, 85, 87, 90–91, 93, 98–99,
  146, 176; as having few natural
  predators, 59, 67, 100; impacts
  on, 67, 73, 179; as keystone
  species, 189, 192–93, 200, 202; as
  largely eliminated, 12, 37, 61, 67,
  161–62, 173, 185; macroclimatic
  conditions for, 70; migrations/
  movements of, 52, 86, 96, 99–
  100; protection of, 4, 34, 178, 182,
  190; as protector of human life,
  36, 54; as reduced by steel traps,
  179; as reduced during drought,
  176; restoration of, 191; sacred
  status of, 9, 34; selection of
  chokecherry by, 215; as source of
  food and clothing, 37, 56–57, 62,
  67, 178, 180; as stabilizing surface
  water, 9, 11, 14, 21, 25, 34, 36, 38,
  41, 48, 55, 68–69, 73–75, 89, 116,
  141, 147, 172, 175, 177, 182–83, 193
Beaver Ceremony, 9, 184
beaver dam-pond systems:
  abandonment of, 86, 142; as
  attracting a range of animals,

52, 176; components of,
  77; construction of, 52; on
  Cottonwood Creek, 216–17;
  effectiveness of, 74; as resistant
  to environmental disturbance,
  64; as retaining surface water,
  82–85, 99, 116, 123, 145, 178, 180;
  storehouse effect of, 11, 69
beaver dams, 49, 96; construction
  of, 45, 48, 50, 83, 86, 88–89, 95,
  99–100, 176; destruction of, 37,
  59, 61, 65, 68, 179; habitat for,
  14; quantity of, 61; as raising
  water level, 9, 35–36, 41, 54,
  58, 74, 84; sites of, 77–78
beaver ecology, 16, 72–73
Beaver Hills, 170, 221
beaver hunting, 155–56, 162, 169;
  aversion to, 6, 17–18, 33, 146,
  170–71, 175, 178, 184; prohibition
  against, 9, 19, 160, 171, 181;
  techniques for, 59, 65, 67–68,
  172, 176, 179; in winter, 60–62,
  67. See also trapping, of beaver
beaver lodges: abandonment of, 86;
  construction of, 45, 48, 60, 77,
  88, 94, 96–97, 145; destruction
  of, 61; habitat of, 9, 14, 55, 176;
  sites of, 37, 51, 72, 74, 78–79, 83–
  85, 87, 89, 92–93, 95, 98–99, 216
beaver meadows, 65, 68, 98, 100, 179
Beaver Medicine Bundle/bundle
  ritual, 34–35, 190–92, 194
Beaver Medicine Men, 9, 34
beaver pelts/fur, 5, 67, 164; as highly
  valued, 62, 175, 178; as price
  standard, 157, 181; seizing of,
  158, 171; trading of, 35, 62, 110–12,
  146, 160, 169–70, 188, 202
beaver ponds, 58, 164, 177, 184, 194,
  222; draining of, 37, 61, 65, 67–68,

76, 97, 179; during droughts, 49; as habitat, 19, 45; as product of beaver activity, 54, 71; as retaining surface water, 13–14, 36, 41, 50–51, 80, 93, 172; sites of, 78; toxicity of, 63, 97–98

Beaver River, 155

Belly River, 167

Belly River Valley, 116; settlement patterns in, 120; winter camp sites at, 127

Bergstrom, Dorothy, 36

Bering Land Bridge, 186

Besant point type (tool), 134–35, 138

Bighorn Canyon, 8

Binford, Lewis, 115, 120, 122, 131

biodiversity, 187, 189, 195, 197, 199

biomass, 196, 222, 225, 244, 247, 252; differences in, 227–28, 239, 254; production of, 236–37, 239, 245, 254; recovery of, 227–28, 232, 238, 240–41

biome, 11, 14, 21, 100, 179, 257

biophilia, 203

Bird, James, 126

Bison antiquus, 195

bison drives, 44, 54, 112, 141; ceremonies of, 33; conditions for, 46; as dangerous, 149; to jumps, 130–31, 176; and knowledge of bison behaviour, 47; methods for, 39, 123, 132; to pounds, 55, 140, 176; during rut, 124, 150, 248; scarcity of, 168, 183; as stabilized, 48; survival of, 50; use of horses with, 150–51. *See also* bison hunting; kill sites, of bison

bison grazing, 199, 238; in burned and non-burned areas, 231–32, 235, 239, 241; dynamics of,

198, 250; effects of, 223–25, 228, 230, 245, 248; effects on crude protein levels/soil nutrients, 220–21, 243–46, 255–56; effects on species composition, 249, 252; patterns of, 50; preferences for, 244, 247–48, 250; in relation to dung/urine deposits, 222, 233, 241, 246, 249, 251, 253, 256; role of beaver meadows in, 99; in summer or winter, 39

bison herds/populations: as abundant in Valley Complex, 10, 43, 46; behavioural patterns of, 44, 47, 55, 148, 172, 176, 183, 220, 256; as diminishing/facing elimination, 146, 167, 196–98; as disrupted by the horse, 150, 153; as disrupted by warfare, 152; during drought cycle, 21, 50, 177; as ecosystem engineer, 197; effects of grasslands and fire on, 219, 255; as food source, 202; habitat of, 190, 195; as increasing prairie biodiversity, 197; Indigenous knowledge of, 185; as inexhaustible resource, 33; as keystone species, 113, 192–93, 197, 200; life cycle of, 11, 22; locations of, 109, 224; mobility of, 110; restoration of, 191–93, 196–99. *See also* buffalo

bison hides/robes, 165–66; market for, 164, 182; trade in, 19, 167, 169, 171

bison hunting, 52, 73; as communal, 113; end of, 4, 19, 146, 168; on horseback, 68, 149, 151–52, 172, 183, 198; during the rut, 40, 44; techniques for, 146, 149–53, 168. *See also* bison drives; kill sites, of bison

bison jumps, 113, 125, 130–31,
    149, 151–52, 176, 180
bison migrations, between summer/
    winter ranges: as annual event,
    31, 125; archaeological evidence
    of, 138, 143; and camp sites,
    121–22, 127, 130, 141; controlling
    of, 148; disruption of, 151, 172, 183;
    during drought, 48–51, 55; and
    forage capacities, 10, 32, 39, 46,
    56; geographic areas of, 31; as
    influencing human movement,
    11, 13, 39–40, 45, 115, 120, 129,
    132, 135, 145, 150, 167, 176–77;
    as a two-field rotation, 32
bison pounds: construction/
    operation of, 54, 125, 128; as
    hunting technique, 40, 55,
    111–12, 122, 130–31, 151–52, 176;
    locations of, 15, 123, 131, 140, 144,
    149; as plains trait, 58, 112–13,
    155, 180, 182; time of use, 39, 178
Black, Norman F., 153
Blackfeet Reservation
    (Montana), 197
Blackfoot Confederacy, 185, 191,
    197; and buffalo hunting,
    195; spirituality of, 195;
    traditional ways of, 192
Blackfoot Nation, 7, 18, 101,
    113, 166–67, 182
Blackfoot people proper, 105–6;
    as acquiring horses, 147, 152;
    as averse to beaver hunting,
    3–8, 18, 55, 101, 110, 113, 169–71;
    as bison/buffalo hunters, 54,
    163–64; locations/territories of,
    42, 103, 107–9, 123, 125, 167–68;
    as preventing trapping, 159–60,
    182; and spiritual regard for
    beaver, 9, 34–35; as traders,

126, 128, 161, 180–81; tribal
    conflicts of, 154, 157–58, 165–66
Blood, Narcisse, 191–93
Blood people, 9, 18, 35, 156–57, 185;
    and beaver hunting, 5, 113,
    172, 182; location of, 106, 108,
    128, 167; as part of Blackfoot
    Nation, 101; as traders, 161,
    163, 165–66, 169, 171
Blood Ranch, 185
Blood Timber Limit, 185, 197
Blood Tribe Lands Department, 194
Blyth, C.B., 89–90
bomas (corrals), 199–200
bone tools, 125. See also
    steel axes; tools
Bow Fort, 159
Bow River, 108
Bradt, Glenn, 70
Briggs, John M., 244, 247
Bruised Head, Mike, 195–96
Buckingham House, 126, 161
buffalo, 8, 33, 155; hunting of, 163;
    scarcity of, 126; skins of, 7,
    106; in winter camps, 47. See
    also bison herds/populations
buffalo drives, 40, 124, 151
buffalo jumps, 195
Buffalo Pound Lake, 75
buffalo robes, 4, 159, 161, 164–65
burning, of grasslands: as attracting
    grazing herds, 177, 250, 257;
    effect on biomass, 228, 238, 241;
    effect on growth cycle, 199, 245;
    effect on herbivores, 219; effect
    on microbial populations, 242;
    effect on soil moisture, 237, 242;
    effect on species composition,
    249; grasslands' response to, 252;
    as increasing soil nutrients, 244,
    254–56; microclimatic changes

from, 220, 237, 242; microsite
alterations from, 236, 253;
physical effects of, 195, 226, 232;
residues from, 225, 227, 233, 235,
237, 239, 253, 255; as rotational
program, 257; timing of, 38,
55, 66; as traditional practice,
64–65, 179, 196, 202. *See also* ash
deposits/residues; grasslands
Bushnell, David, 42
butchering, of animals, 129, 143,
154; sites for, 119–21, 125, 127,
130, 136; tools for, 125, 136;
during winter, 126–27, 138

C

cairns, 120, 140, 144
Cajete, Gregory, 189
Campbell, J.A., 249
camp sites. *See* spring camp
sites; temporary camp
sites; winter camp sites
Canadian High Arctic: impact
of climate change on, 201
Canadian Pacific Railway
(CPR), 76, 117
Canadian Plains: bison movement
patterns on, 206; climatic
conditions of, 23, 30; grasslands
on, 28; precipitation rates in,
23–25, 28; snow cover in, 24;
vegetative communities in,
31. *See also* Northern Plains
canoes, 40, 112; abandonment of,
113, 180; use of, 105, 107, 111
capitalism, 185
caribou, 160, 201–2; as cultural
keystone species, 201; dung
and urine, as fertilizers, 201
Carrot River, 103
Catlin, George, 53

cattle, 247; dung, as fertilizer,
199; grazing of, 199
ceramics, 129, 134–35, 138, 143
Chardon's journal, 169–70
Chesterfield House, 123, 128, 159–61
Cheyenne people, 5, 123; beaver
regarded as sacred, 34, 36;
and firewood collecting, 53;
as not beaver hunters, 184;
traditional beaver stories of, 9
Chief Mountain area, 197
Chipped Stone tool category
(artifacts), 133–34, 136–38, 143
Chippewa people, 60, 106
Chittenden, Hiram Martin, 169, 172
chokecherry shrubs, 27,
77, 81, 87–89, 215
Christiansen, E.A., 24, 233
Circee people, 162
Clark, William, 170
Clarke, S.E., 95
climate, 201, 257; of Canadian
Plains, 23, 27, 29, 38, 71,
119; variability of, 255
climate change, 185–86, 194, 201;
mitigating impacts of, 198;
resiliency to, 187, 197, 200
clipping, of vegetation, 253;
microsite changes from,
254. *See also* vegetation
Cobble Stone Industry category
(artifacts), 133, 137–38, 143
Cocking, Matthew, 111–12, 155, 180
Collins, Thomas, 49
colonialism, 186, 188, 202; ecological
damage caused by, 185, 194, 203
Comanche people, 9, 42, 124, 148, 184
commensalism, 55
Coppock, D.L., 248
Cottonwood Creek: as
archaeological site, 133,

Cottonwood Creek (*continued*)
135–36, 175, 180, 211–12; beaver
populations in, 176, 216–17;
dam-pond system in, 75, 77,
86–88; during drought, 49, 51;
environmental conditions at, 17;
as migration corridor, 144, 146;
research areas in, 119, 207, 212;
surface water in, 26, 41, 79–80,
145; as tributary in Qu'Appelle
River Valley Complex, 16, 18, 69,
76, 82, 117, 141, 202; vegetation
surrounding, 29–30, 85
Coupland, Robert, 22–23, 27–28
Cowie, Isaac, 40, 164, 168
Cree people, 8, 18, 60, 106, 112,
152, 154, 158, 163; as bison
hunters, 54; locations of, 16,
33, 42, 102–4, 108–9, 167–68,
170–71, 181, 188; as middlemen
in trade, 3, 105; relationship
with the beaver, 7, 35, 123, 180,
182. *See also* Assiniboine Cree
people; Plains Cree people;
Woodlands Cree people
Crow people, 5, 152, 158, 168
cultural materialism, 190. *See
also* Harris, Marvin
Cumberland House, 101, 103
Cumberland House journals, 62
Currie, Pat O., 237, 253
Curtis, Edwards, 6, 9, 35
Custer, General George A., 123
Cypress Hills, 167

D

Dary, David, 50, 52
Daschuk, James, 3, 191
Daubenmire, R., 232
Davin Family Fund, 194
Day, T.A., 241, 247, 252

deer, 43, 57, 132, 144, 155, 177, 193, 247;
as food source, 106, 122, 145
Denig, Edwin, 43
Denys, Nicolas, 59, 61, 66
DeSmet, Pierre-Jean, 167
Detling, J.K., 241, 247–48, 252
Devon Island (Baffin Bay), 201
Dix, R.L., 27
Dodge, Richard, 42, 52,
109, 123–24, 172
drought, 83, 117, 144, 198; beaver
activity during, 11–12, 25, 36, 54,
69, 99–100, 146, 178, 193–94; as
causing ecological imbalances,
14–15, 29, 162; conditions of,
17, 25, 48, 50, 116; cycles of,
25–26, 29, 38, 48–50, 52, 55,
80, 85–87, 142, 176–77; effects
of, 21, 118–19, 141, 172; impact
on bison migrations, 10
dung deposits/patches, 220–21,
226, 230, 251; burning/
combustion of, 227, 229,
233–35, 237, 239–40, 253–54,
256; as creating an avoidance
area, 241, 248; distribution of
on grazed/non-grazed areas,
222; heat containment due to
burning, 235, 253; nutrients
from, 199–200, 225, 231, 246,
252, 254; size of, 232. *See also*
urine deposits/patches

E

Eagle Dance, 9
Eagle Hills, 106–7, 109
Eagle Hills Creek Nation, 103
Earthwatch Community
Conservation, 194
Earthwatch Institute, 185, 199
Easter Island, environmental
degradation of, 201

ecocultural relationships: as affected by arrival of horse, 198. *See also* horse
ecological keystone species, 188
ecological resiliency, 189, 193
ecological restoration, 190, 194; policies for, 257
ecological zones, 220
ecology, 189, 194, 200
ecosystem engineers, 187, 193, 197
ecosystems, 14, 17, 187–88, 190, 192–93, 197, 250
Edmonton House, 160
Edmonton House journals, 161, 163
elk, 132, 144, 177, 192; as food source, 122, 145
Elk Island National Park, 24, 92, 197, 202; beaver activity in, 95–96, 98; as beaver habitat, 63, 90–91, 93–94, 96, 179; bison activity in, 199; fires in, 190, 195–96; forage biomass production in, 236; precipitation in, 90; as research site, 11–12, 16–17, 70, 200, 209; species composition in, 223–24; vegetation in, 89–90, 98, 221
environmental conservation, global, 200
Environment and Climate Change Canada (formerly Environment Canada), 74–75
Europeans: arrival of, 18, 70, 145; in contact with Indigenous Peoples, 3, 48, 120; effect on Indigenous hunting practices, 5, 37, 44, 58, 61, 168, 194; as explorers and fur traders, 3–5, 17, 20, 44, 48, 146, 154, 184; and introduction of the horse, 17, 145
Ewers, John, observations: on beaver trapping, 166; on bison chases, 44, 149–50; on the

Blackfoot, 8, 34, 55, 107, 123, 147, 160, 163–65; as ethnographer, 6; on the horse, 148, 152; on trading, 167; on winter camp sites, 12, 15, 42, 46, 124

F

Fehrenbach, T.R., 9
Fenno-Scandia (California Chaparral), 243
Fescue Prairie, 23–24, 29, 31, 185
Fidler, Peter, 8, 122–23, 126, 128, 161
field camps, 121–22
Finck, Elmer J., 244, 247
fire, 14, 178, 193, 200, 226; as controlled, 64–65, 67, 100; dynamics of, 233, 257; ecology of, 64, 67–68, 179; effects on biomass, 239–40; effects on grassland ecosystem, 13, 199, 220, 230, 256–57; effects on species composition, 249; effects on ungulates, 38; elimination of, 90, 185, 197; Indigenous knowledge of, 185; as natural, 64–65, 67, 100; as prescribed, 190; relation to bison and grasslands, 255; return of, 192; setting of, 196, 219–20; as used to control herds, 12, 39, 116, 130–31, 148, 172, 183, 195, 221, 250; as wild, 194–96. *See also* Kenow wildfire
firewood, 17, 48, 52, 145, 176, 184; collecting of, 52–53, 66; as provided by beavers, 15, 34, 37, 42, 54–55, 66
fish, 57, 140, 189
Flathead people, 147, 152, 158, 171; as beaver hunters, 159. *See also* Kutenai people; Salish people
Flato, Dave, 96

flooding, 14, 37–38, 63, 73–74, 89–90, 125; as beaver induced, 93, 96–98, 100, 179–80

floodplains, 130, 139, 184; beaver activity on, 75, 82; as favourable to herbivores, 52; species destruction on, 63; as temporary sites, 15, 117, 136; tree/shrub species on, 27, 48, 81, 87–88, 97, 100, 132; as wintering sites, 45, 118, 122, 125, 137, 140, 142, 144, 181

Flores, Dan, 198

foliar crude protein content, 220–21, 231, 241–44, 247, 251–52; as caused by burning, 253; as different in burned/unburned areas, 229–30, 255; due to dung combustion, 254; effect of dung/urine deposits on, 246; effects of microbial activity on, 245

food-web relationships, 185, 187, 199–200

Forbis, Richard, 130–31, 151

Fort Alexandria, 155

Fort Belknap, 104

Fort Edmonton, 151

Fort Esperance, 155

Fort George, 5, 7, 155–56, 162–63

Fort McKenzie, 166

Fort Pelly, 168

Fort Piegan, 165–66, 172

Fort Qu'Appelle, 165, 168

Fort Vermilion, 66, 157–58, 161

Foss, Jeffrey, 73

Fox, Elliot, 194

foxes, 110, 126, 155

Frenchman River, 26

Frison, George, 40, 129

fur-bearing animals, 3, 5, 37, 62, 160, 162, 171, 202

furs: of beaver, as valuable, 5, 7, 111, 154, 157; of foxes, 112, 160–61, 169, 180; of lesser quality, 4, 56, 160, 169, 171, 180–81; suppliers of, 102, 110; trading of, 112, 163; trapping for, 8, 109, 155, 184; of wolf, 157. *See also* beaver pelts/fur; wolves

fur trade, 3–4, 10, 37, 102, 104, 164, 170–71; and access to canoes, 105; as affecting intertribal conflict, 154; and beaver hunting, 19, 59, 62, 67, 91, 175, 178–79, 184; changes caused by, 16, 54, 146, 169; collapse of, 201–2; and need for trading posts, 111; and provisions market, 153

fur trade companies, 160, 182. *See also* trade goods; trading posts

G

game animals: conditions for, 178–80; as declining, 3, 160, 167; as killed for meat, 63, 67–68; monitoring of, 131, 137

Garibaldi, Ann, 187–88

Garratt site: activity at, 127; as model of winter camp, 121; tool construction at, 125

Garretson, Martin, 149

gathering practices, 179, 189

General Debitage category (artifacts), 133–35, 137, 143

Glover, Richard, 155

Graham, Andrew, 111

Grand Coteau of the Missouri, 16

Grant, Peter, 56, 61

grasslands, 12, 21, 27, 42, 45–46, 76; curing of, 10, 32, 48, 88–89, 95; as declining, 196; ecological conditions of, 223–24, 243, 250, 254; effects on by fire and bison, 219; forage capacity of, 39; grazing on, 11, 220–21, 226, 231, 248–49, 251–53, 255;

as habitat, 10; importance of, 194; microsite changes to, 250; productivity of, 48, 250, 257; relation to bison and fire, 255; resiliency of, 197, 200; response to burning, 220, 236, 250, 252–53, 256; urine and dung deposits in, 253; vegetation on, 22, 27, 44, 71, 81, 249, 256. *See also* burning, of grasslands; vegetation

grazing. *See* bison grazing; grasslands, grazing on

Greiser, Sally Thompson, 116, 119–20

Grinnell, George Bird, 9, 36, 52–54, 107, 125

Gros Ventre people (Fall Indians): as fur traders, 112, 161, 164, 169–70, 180; as having horses, 147; intertribal conflicts of, 152, 157–60, 165, 181; location of, 102–3, 108–9; as non-beaver hunters, 4–5, 169, 171, 182; as not using canoes, 105; as part of Blackfoot Nation, 18, 101, 113; and provisions markets, 163; winter camps of, 42, 123, 128

guns/firearms. *See* trade goods; weapons, on the plains

H

Haines, Francis, 107, 147

Hall, Joseph, 45

Hamilton, W.T., 236

Hammond, Merrill, 46

Harmon, Daniel, 57, 61–62, 155

Harris, Marvin, 9, 11, 33–34

Hartnett, David C., 239, 244, 247

Henday, Anthony, 109–12, 180

Hennepin, Father Louis, 60

Henry, Alexander (the Elder), 44

Henry, Alexander (the Younger), observations: on the

Assiniboine, 54, 123; on beaver hunting, 62, 158; on bison hunting, 126; on bison winter behaviour, 47; on the Blackfoot, 4, 152, 161; on buffalo hunting, 132, 150; on the Chippewa, 60; on the Piegan, 7, 53; on the Sarcee, 8, 170; on trading, 157, 159, 169, 171; on water quality, 50

herbivores: as attracted to urine patches, 241, 252; behaviours of, 132, 144; diets of, 200; effects of fires on, 65, 70, 219; effects on vegetation, 90; grazing by, 11, 247, 250–51, 256; Indigenous knowledge of, 179; migrations of during drought, 52; requirements of, 257; in symbiosis with grasslands, 31, 38, 41, 45, 48

Hidatsa people, 5, 50, 52, 184

Hind, Henry Youle, 39, 46, 70

Hobbs, N. Thompson, 220, 244

Hodgdon, Kenneth, 72

horse: acquisition of, 19, 44, 47, 101, 107, 110, 145–46, 148, 155, 170; as altering pedestrian lifeways, 182, 198; arrival/introduction of, 10, 16–17, 147, 153, 198; as cultural keystone species, 198; as disrupting bison herds, 149–51; economic need for, 152; impact on Indigenous populations, 147–48, 173, 198; as providing mobility, 148, 152, 172–73, 182–83; raiding of, 152–53, 172, 183; trading of, 111–12, 159, 163, 169, 180–81; as used in battles, 106; as used in bison drives, 124. *See also* bison drives; bison hunting

Hovind, J.H., 97

Hudson, Robert J., 89–90, 241

Hudson Bay, 90, 110; fur trade at, 111, 201; trading posts on, 102, 104; use of canoes on, 105

Hudson House, 153

Hudson's Bay Company (HBC), 105, 110–12, 160–61, 163; establishment of, 102; inland trading posts of, 101, 153; as instigating tribal attacks, 165; merger with NWC, 4, 146; and sale of meat, 164, 169; and sale of pemmican, 167; as setting beaver pelt as the standard, 126, 157, 181

human-animal relationship, 10, 16, 32, 37, 145–47, 176, 186, 203

human-beaver relationship, 17, 22, 58, 69–70, 115

human populations, 124–25, 130; as affected by beaver populations, 67, 177; at camp sites, 38, 117; diets of, 39; habitat requirements of, 18, 21–22, 45, 48–49; movements of, 17, 39–40, 51–52, 120, 127, 186, 202; in relation to bison herds, 38, 109; survival of, 14, 187, 190, 193. See also Indigenous Peoples

Hunt, John, 72

hunter-gatherer societies, 119; environmental knowledge of, 55; settlement patterns of, 116

hunting techniques, 54, 60, 69, 124, 150, 176, 179, 189; as communal, 40, 47, 116, 148, 177, 180; as traditional, 37, 39–40, 47, 55, 61–62, 111, 150

I

Iinnii (buffalo) Initiative, 197

Indigenous knowledge, 185–86; of animal-human relationships, 203; of burning, grasslands, bison relationships, 219

Indigenous Peoples: distribution of, at contact, 211; occupations of women, 52–53, 66, 154; repatriation of, 198; as stewards of the land, 186; as using fire to manipulate herds, 250; worldview of, 34, 189. See also Northern Plains Indigenous Peoples; Plains Indigenous Peoples; Woodlands Indigenous Peoples

industrial forestry, 185

International Symposium on Bison Ecology and Management in North America, 219

International Union for the Conservation of Nature (IUCN): Red List of Threatened Species, 197

Inuit people, 201–2

Iroquois people, 160, 162, 181

J

Jablow, Joseph, 5

Jenkins, Stephen, 72

Jenness, Diamond, 147

Johnson, Alice M., 157

Johnston, Carol, 71–72

Judeo-Christian cosmology, 20

Jurgens site (Colorado), 122

K

Kabetogama Peninsula (Minnesota), 63

Kainai (Blood) First Nation, 185, 193–95; as reintroducing burning, 196

Kainai High School, 194

Kehoe, Alice, 18, 107–8

Kehoe, Thomas, 124

Kelley, James, 71–72
Kelsey, Henry, 102–3, 105, 108
Kendeigh, S. Charles, 70
Kennedy, Michael, 33, 42, 52, 106
Kenow wildfire, 194, 196
Kentucky bluegrass (Poa pratensis), 222–24, 227, 233, 247, 249
keystone species, 187, 192; as cultural, 187–90, 200, 202
kill sites, of bison: archaeological evidence at, 118; attributes of, 119–20, 134, 139–40; driving herds towards, 55, 122, 130, 150, 176, 183, 185; as located at/near winter camps, 117, 126–27, 131, 141–42, 144. See also bison drives; butchering, of animals
Kimmerer, Robin Wall, 189, 191
Kiowa people, 5, 42, 124
Knapp, Alan K., 244, 249
Knife River, 125
Knudson, George, 41, 63, 97–98
Kolesnikov, B.P., 242–43, 256
Ksisskstaki (beaver), 192. See also beaver/beaver populations
Kutenai people, 110, 147, 152, 158, 171, 182

L

La France, Joseph, 7, 102–3
Lake Diefenbaker, 29, 75
Lake Nipigon, 104
Lake of the Woods, 104
Lake Regina, 30
Lake Winnipeg, 104, 170
Lancaster, Richard, 8, 35
landscape mosaics, as increased by TEK practices, 189
Larocque, François, 5
Last Mountain Creek, 138, 140
La Vérendrye (Pierre Gaultier de Varennes), 7, 63, 105, 163

Leach, D.S., 98
Lebret (spring fishing camp), 142
Lewarch, Dennis, 118
Lewis, Henry, 13, 64–65
Lewis, Meriwether, 170, 219
Little Bear, Leroy, 190
Little Souris River, 46
Livingston, John, 14
Longley, Richmond, 24, 128
Longley, William, 94
Lowie, Robert H., 104

M

Mackenzie, Alexander, 4, 6, 46, 66, 154–55, 170
MacKenzie, Charles, 5, 9, 53, 184
Mackenzie River, 153
Maddock, Linda, 51
Mad Dog, Chief, 191
Mandan people, 43, 50, 52–53
Mandelbaum, David, 15, 33, 46, 54, 152
Marias River, 165
Marriott, Alice, 184
Martinez, Dennis, 189
Martinez, R., 249
Masai people (Kenya), 189, 199–200
Mask site (Nunamiut hunting stand), 132
Maximilian of Wied, 166, 169
McClintock, Walter, 191
McDaniel, Chad K., 121
McDonald, John, 155
McDonnell, John, 4, 39, 155
McGillivray, Duncan, 5, 126, 156, 160, 162, 171
McGinty, Allan, 244, 257
McKenzie, Kenneth, 165
McLean, A., 244
McNaughton, S.J., 244–47, 251, 256
meat processing sites, 119–21, 126, 154

medicine bundles, 8, 35, 193. *See also* Beaver Medicine Bundle
megafaunal extinction, 186
Merrill, Leo B., 244, 257
Mesic Mixed Prairie, 22–24, 29, 31
Métis people (freemen), 164, 168
Milk River, 26
Miller, Alfred Jacob, 5, 166
Mississippi River, 164
Missouri Fur Company, 160, 165
Missouri River, 5, 9, 43, 110, 121, 158, 160, 164–67, 170, 184
Mistassini Cree people, 57
Mi'kmaq people, 59, 66
Moodie, D.W., 151–52
moose, 12, 65, 155, 160, 178; as important food source, 56–57, 62, 67–68, 106
Moose Jaw Creek, 30, 75
Moose Jaw River: beaver activity on, 78, 85–88; beaver habitats on, 82–83; as part of Qu'Appelle River Valley Complex, 16–17, 29, 69, 175, 202; research areas on, 75–76, 208; role of in migrations, 41; spring runoff into, 124; water discharge rate of, 26, 51, 77, 79–80
Morgan, R. Grace, 3–4, 186–88, 190–91, 193–200, 202–3
Morley reserve (Alberta), 104
Morton, Arthur Silver, 6, 103, 106, 109–11, 148, 152, 157, 159, 167
Moss, E.H., 249
Mountainhorse, Alvine, 192–93
Moyle, John, 94

N

Nahathaway Indians (Woodlands Cree), 57. See also Woodlands Cree people
Naiman, Robert, 71–72

National Bison Legacy Act, 198
Native science (ecosophy), 189, 191–92, 195, 200
natural resources conservation, 194
natural world: ecological dynamics of, 20; Indigenous knowledge of relationships in, 186–87; kincentric view of, 189; living relationships in, 192
Navaho people, 147
Nelson, J.G., 6, 16
Nez Perce people, 147, 171
Ng'weno, Caroline, 199–200
Niisitapi (Blackfoot), 192. *See also* Blackfoot Confederacy
Nipissing people, 162
nitrogen, translocation of, 245
nomadism, 3, 151–52, 183
Northern Plains, 15, 145, 156, 163, 193; beaver dam-pond systems on, 55; beaver populations on, 8, 68; bison hunting on, 12, 120; bison migrations on, 31; drought conditions on, 48, 51; early fur trade in, 171; as ecosystem, 22, 38, 173, 176, 198, 203; environment (basin) of, 21, 29–30, 32, 40; grassland-bison-human subsystem in, 22, 31–32; reintroduction of the bison on, 197; settlement patterns on, 120; and use of fire on, 196; vegetation zones of, 206
Northern Plains Indigenous Peoples, 4, 146, 190–91; annual movement cycle of, 144, 176; as averse to beaver hunting/trading, 6, 17–20, 112–13, 175, 180–81, 202; distribution/settlement patterns of, 15, 36, 54, 109, 180; ecological knowledge of, 49, 148, 172–73, 176, 178–79; as hunter-gatherers,

13, 20, 119; hunting grounds
of, 109; as impacted by horse,
148; importance of beaver to,
184; and knowledge of bison
behaviour, 11, 172; non-use of
canoe, 113; traditional hunting
techniques of, 178; traditional
way of life, as ending, 168. *See
also* hunter-gatherer societies
Northern Saulteaux people, 56
North Saskatchewan River, 46,
103; as site of Elk Island
National Park, 90; trading
posts on, 4–5, 7, 153, 156, 160–61;
tribes residing on, 106–7, 155;
winter camp sites on, 126
North West Company (NWC),
4, 12, 146, 153, 157, 160–61
Nunamiut people, 132

O

Obama, President Barack, 198
observation posts, 131, 137, 142
Odum, Eugene, 10
Old, Sylvia M., 243, 249
The Old North Trail, 191
Oliver, Chad, 146–47
Olson, Wes, 98, 199–200
oral histories, 190–92, 194
oral traditions and literacies, 3, 191
Oregon Missions, 167
Osage people, 9, 184
Ottawa Indian-French trading
network, 7, 102
otter, 4–5, 8, 56, 59, 62
overgrazing, by herbivores,
10, 75, 119, 257
overhunting, of fur animals, 3, 186
Oxford University, 191
O'Brien, Michael, 118, 121
O'odham people, 189

P

Paine, Robert, 187
Parkland–Boreal Forest
transition zone, 16, 70, 89
Pawnee people, 5
Peabody Museum, 192
Peace River, 108
pedestrian peoples: as averse
to beaver hunting, 17, 101,
113, 172; hunting techniques
of, 47, 54, 176; importance
of conserving water by, 11,
36; in winter camps, 44
pemmican, 19, 129, 154, 163–64, 167
Pheasant Creek, 37, 87
Piapot Indian Reservation, 138
Piegan people: and beaver hunting,
5, 7–8, 157; as bison hunters, 39,
123; and fur trading, 165, 169, 171,
182; and intertribal conflicts,
106, 152, 158–60, 166, 181; location
of, 103, 108; as not using canoes,
107; as part of Blackfoot
Nation, 18, 101, 113, 167; and
taboo against killing beavers,
35; winter camps of, 126, 156;
and wood procurement, 53
Plains Assiniboine people, 101,
103, 105, 108–9, 111–13, 149,
155, 159; as not hunting
beaver, 112, 163, 170, 180, 182
Plains Cree people, 15, 54, 101,
108, 131, 147, 149, 152
Plains Indigenous Peoples, 3, 6, 12,
17, 42, 151, 153, 156–57; as averse
to beaver hunting, 33, 35, 37,
54, 69, 101, 146, 148, 154, 168, 188;
and beaver hunting, 8, 10, 58;
ecological knowledge of, 20,
32, 47, 49, 55, 65; hunting and
gathering strategies of, 64;

Plains Indigenous Peoples, (*continued*) importance of bison to, 33; importance of the beaver to, 34; knowledge of animal behaviours, 68, 116; patterns of distribution, 116–17; territorial claims of, 168; traditional burning practices of, 64

Plains of Eagle Hill, 106

pollinators, 192, 199

poundmaster (shaman), 33

pounds. *See* bison pounds

precontact period: agriculture during, 189; bison hunting during, 73, 168; bison movement patterns, 206; definition of, 4; ecological knowledge during, 172; human-animal relationship during, 20, 38, 145, 194; human settlement patterns during, 18, 44, 104, 108–9, 120; hunting techniques during, 47, 69, 124, 150; importance of beaver during, 178, 184; and non-use of beaver, 8; as prior to the fur trade, 16

provisions, dried, 4, 39, 46, 49, 129, 149, 159, 163

Q

Quigg, J. Michael, 116, 120

Qu'Appelle Basin Archaeological Project, 138

Qu'Appelle River: animal activity on, 144; as beaver habitat, 37, 86–87; and canoe use, 105; human settlements near, 155; as part of Qu'Appelle River Valley Complex, 16, 29, 69, 175; as research site, 75–76, 79, 117, 138, 183, 202, 214; water flow in, 14, 26, 30, 41, 48, 78, 82, 140, 145; as wintering site, 141, 181, 184

Qu'Appelle River Basin, 205

Qu'Appelle River Valley, 15, 88, 140, 167, 175; alluvial floodplains in, 30; glacial meltwaters in, 30; precipitation rate in, 24; settlement patterns in, 142; spring runoff in, 38; summer camp sites in, 130; wintering areas in, 142

Qu'Appelle River Valley Complex: beaver habitat in, 69, 71, 122, 146; climatic fluctuations in, 28–29, 36, 38, 48, 55; ecological conditions in, 13, 19, 21–22, 28, 45, 73, 98–99, 116, 121–22, 134; high degree of stability in, 29; human settlements in, 18, 51, 56, 69, 115, 122, 144–45; microclimatic conditions in, 27–28, 71, 76, 172, 183; as near bison winter range, 31; observation posts in, 132; precipitation rates in, 48–49; as research site, 16–17, 24, 27, 29, 68, 175, 202; surface water resources in, 26, 38, 41; topography of, 30; tree/shrub species in, 23, 45, 48; as wintering area, 15, 22, 42–43, 46, 125

Qu'Appelle River Valley Dam, 75

R

rabbit/hare, as food source, 57

Rainy Lake, 7

Raison, R.J., 220, 232

Ray, Arthur J., observations: on abandonment of canoe, 105; on beaver habitats, 37; on bison hunting, 151–52; on European contact, 18; on the

fur trade, 3, 7; on fur trade companies, 160; on intertribal conflicts, 154; on presence of game animals, 57, 162; on shift to provisions market, 163; on traditional hunting techniques, 111; on trapping, 62; on tribal alignments, 102–4, 109
Red Deer River, 108, 128, 159
Red River, 4, 103–5, 126, 153
Red River settlement, 163
reindeer, 12, 57
Renecker, Lyle A., 241
restoration ecology, 190
Ridington, Robin, 13
Riegger, Hal, 234
Riggs, Stephen Return, 104
riparian areas/zones, 71, 73, 193–94
riparian species, 28, 44–45, 63, 72, 81–82, 87–88
Rocky Mountain Fur Company, 165
Rocky Mountain House, 158–59, 169–71
Rocky Mountains, 22–23, 108, 110, 130, 156, 158, 184
Roe, Frank, 33, 147
Rogers, Edward, 57
Rowe, J.S., 27
Ruess, Roger W., 244–47, 251, 256
Rutherford, William, 59, 70

S

Sadleir, R.M.F.S., 72
Salish people, 181–82
Sarcee people, 4, 8, 18, 105, 108–9, 112, 123, 170, 181
Saskatchewan Museum of Natural History, 118
Saskatchewan River: ecological features of, 184; Indigenous settlement/migration on, 57, 102, 104, 149, 167; presence of buffalo near, 16, 46; traders' movement through, 153; trading posts on, 161; water flow in, 14, 26, 36, 41, 44
Saskatchewan River Valley, 107–8, 154, 175
Saskatchewan River Valley Complex, 183
Saukamappee, Chief, 106–7
Saulteaux people, 56, 61, 168
Schimel, David S., 220, 244
Schwanke, R., 92–93, 96–97
Scifres, C.J., 236
Seagle, Steven W., 244–47, 251, 256
sea stars (Pisaster), 187
Secoy, Frank, 6, 108, 152, 154
Seton, Ernest Thompson, 59
Shade, Alex, 195
Sharrow, Steven H., 241–42
Shoshone (Snake) people, 5, 103, 106–10, 112, 147–49, 158, 168, 184
Simpson, George, economic reforms of, 164, 182
Sioux people, 103–4, 110, 168
Sioux people (Minnesota), 60
site furniture, 134–35, 138, 143
Skinner, Alanson, 56, 60, 66, 92–95, 131
Slave Indians (Blackfoot), 156, 161
Slough, Brian, 72
smallpox epidemic, 3
Smeins, Fred E., 244, 257
Smith, Joseph, 111
Smoky Hill River, 52
Snake River (Wyoming), 49
snowmelt, 25, 30, 49, 51, 79, 90. See also spring runoff
soil moisture, 27–28, 235–37, 239–41, 243, 245–46, 250, 255; effects on microbial populations, 242

Solomon River, 50

Souris River, 43, 46, 105

Southern Plains Peoples, and
    acquisition of horse, 148

South Saskatchewan River, 109, 128,
    160; South Branch Houses, 157

South Saskatchewan Valley, 157

spring camp sites, 127–30,
    133–35, 138, 140, 142–43

spring runoff, 25, 38, 48–49, 51, 74,
    79, 83–85, 99, 124, 127, 177

steel axes, 37, 53–54. See also tools

steel traps, 61–62, 67, 162, 164, 179

Stoney people, 104

stream ecosystem, 71

Strong, Paul, 71

Strong Wood Assiniboine people,
    7, 156; as beaver hunters,
    155. See also Assiniboine
    people (Assiniboils)

Strong Wood Cree people, 8,
    156. See also Cree people

summer camp sites, 120, 128, 130, 202

Sun Dance, 191

sustainability, as kincentric
    view of nature, 189

Sutherland, George, 161

T

temporary camp sites, 121–22,
    133, 136, 141–43, 146, 180–81

Tewa people, 189

Thompson, David, 12, 39, 43, 51,
    57–61, 103, 106–8, 110, 157–61

tipis/tipi rings, 120–21, 124,
    127–29, 135, 140, 142, 144

Tisdale, E.W., 95

tobacco. See trade goods

Todd, Arlen, 70, 72

Tomison, William, 161

tools: for butchering, 136;
    maintenance of, 125, 129–30,

143; manufacture of, 120, 133–34,
    143; types of, 136–38, 143

Touchwood Hills, 46, 103, 109, 168

Trabert, Sarah, 3

trade goods: alcohol/liquor, 8, 19, 146,
    156, 158–59, 171–72, 182; firearms/
    ammunition, 19, 106, 108,
    110–12, 154–59, 162, 171, 180–82;
    as gifts to Indigenous Peoples,
    5; metal goods, 58, 111–12, 180;
    tobacco, 8, 35, 156, 158–59, 196

trading posts, 101, 110–11, 153, 156,
    158–59, 163, 167, 169, 171, 181,
    210. See also trade goods

Traditional Ecological Knowledge
    (TEK), 188–90, 194, 199–200

trapping: of beaver, 58, 109–10, 154,
    166, 171, 181, 188, 198, 202; of
    fur-bearing animals, 109, 111, 155,
    184, 202. See also beaver hunting;
    beaver pelts/fur; fur trading

Treaties 1 through 7, 168

Treaty of Paris, 4, 146, 153

tree and shrub species, 66, 68, 73–75,
    81, 83, 89, 92, 97–98, 100, 179

tree felling, by beavers, 52, 55,
    88, 93–94, 96–97, 100, 145

Treshow, Michael, 55

tribal conflicts, 112, 146, 153–54,
    156–60, 165, 167–68, 182;
    on horseback, 106, 152, 172.
    See also war/warfare

Trobriand, Philippe Régis de, 219

trophic cascades, 187, 191–92, 199–200

Trudeau, Jean Baptiste, 5

True Prairie (Tall Grass
    Prairie), 22–23

Turner, Nancy, 187–88

U

Umfreville, Edward, 4, 8

uniformitarianism, 13, 21

University of Alberta, 193
University of Lethbridge, 191
University of Regina, 118
Upper Qu'Appelle Valley, 102, 157
urine deposits/patches, 11, 220–21,
    253; as affecting crude protein
    levels, 241; as benefiting
    herbivores, 252; distribution of
    on grazed/non-grazed areas,
    222; effects on soil nutrients,
    197, 199, 225, 231, 246–47, 251.
    See also dung deposits/patches
Ute people, 147

V

vegetation: in beaver habitats, 44,
    70–72; in Cottonwood Creek,
    29–30, 85; curing of, 95; during
    drought, 52; effects of grazing
    on, 10; in Elk Island National
    Park, 89–90, 98, 221; factors
    affecting, 27, 81, 89–90, 96, 98,
    192, 202, 253; on grasslands, 21–
    22, 27, 44, 71, 81, 89, 221, 249, 256;
    as modified through burning,
    189, 256; near dung patches,
    220, 222, 231, 233, 246, 251–52.
    See also clipping, of vegetation;
    grasslands, vegetation on
Vesey-Fitzgerald, Desmond, 246
Vinton, Mary Ann, 239, 244, 247
Viro, P.J., 256

W

Walton, P.D., 249
war/warfare, 146, 158–59, 172;
    as disrupting bison herds,
    152; involving traders, 166.
    See also tribal conflicts
Wascana Creek: ecological
    conditions of, 29, 74; floodplain
    of, 144; as research site, 16,
18, 69, 75–76, 117–18, 175,
    202, 213; site description of,
    119, 136; winter camps on,
    137–38, 141–43, 146, 180
Washita River, 124
water conservation, 13–14
water resources, surface, 36, 44–46,
    124, 145; abundance of, 47, 84,
    93; availability of, 17, 38, 40,
    76, 79, 81–82, 87, 96, 99, 117,
    123, 140, 142, 173, 176–77, 183;
    major source of, 22, 26, 30, 79,
    90; as stabilized by beaver,
    9, 11, 21, 25, 36–37, 41, 50, 55,
    68–69, 73–75, 89, 116, 141, 147,
    175, 177, 180, 182–83, 193
Waterton Lakes National Park, 185,
    192, 194, 197; fire program of, 196
waterways: beaver presence on,
    39, 47, 49, 52, 69, 86–87, 175,
    180, 183; canoe use on, 105;
    ecological conditions of, 17,
    79, 134; human settlements on,
    46; in Qu'Appelle River Valley
    Complex, 16; as research site,
    117, 131; and surface water, 9, 15,
    76, 173; tree/shrub species on,
    81; and wintering areas, 18, 184.
    See also water resources, surface
weapons, on the plains: bows
    and arrows, 111–12; firearms/
    ammunition, 19, 106, 108,
    110–12, 154–59, 162, 171, 180–82
Western science, 20, 186–87,
    189–91, 199–200
Wheat, Joe Ben, 122
White, Richard S., 237, 253
white men, 5, 35, 103, 110, 158, 162,
    165–66, 168, 170–71, 182
Wilde, S.A., 97
wildfires. *See* fire
Wildlife Conservation Society, 197

Willms, Walter, 244

winter camp sites: artifacts at, 138; bison herds in, 109, 115; bison hunting at, 121, 131, 144, 149, 178; conditions for/traits of, 42, 44–46, 116–17, 123, 141, 143, 180, 183–84; definition of, 120; length of occupancy at, 124, 127; locations of, 12, 15, 38, 118, 126, 135, 137, 142, 153, 202; as research sites, 133; shelter types in, 43; tools used at, 129–30, 134. *See also* tools

Wissler, Clark, 9, 53, 107–8, 147

Wohl, Ellen, 194

wolves, 43, 109–10, 126, 155, 157, 161, 171, 193, 196; furs of, 112, 157, 160, 169, 180–81; Indigenous knowledge of, 185; as keystone species, 192; killing of, 185; restoration of, 192; trapping of, 111

Woodlands Assiniboine people, 154, 168, 181

Woodlands Cree people, 5, 12, 58, 65, 110–13, 154, 181; as beaver hunters,

155; occupations of women, 66; subsistence pattern of, 57

Woodlands Indigenous Peoples, 6, 64, 67, 111; and animal relationships, 178; and beaver hunting, 37, 161, 180, 188, 202; food resources in, 56; hunting-gathering strategies of, 58; knowledge of animal behaviours, 67, 179; westward migration of, 3

World Wildlife Fund, 197

Wright, Henry, 23, 241–42

Wright, M., 234–35

X

Xeric Mixed Prairie, 22–24, 28–29, 31

Y

Yellowstone River, 165

York Factory, 102–3, 111, 161

Youngberg, C.T., 97

Younging, Gregory, 3–4

A NOTE ABOUT THE TYPE

The body of this book is set in *Xaloc Text,* an asymetrical serif created by Ricardo Santos and published by Tiponautas. Designed for editorial use in books, magazines, and newspapers, Xaloc was based on Ricado Santos's *Tramuntana,* which has the same skeleton, proportions, and serifs with a more mechanical design. Xaloc is the Catalonian name from the Mediterranean wind that comes from the Sahara and reaches hurricane speeds in North Africa and Southern Europe.

The accents are set in *Knockout,* a family of sans serif typefaces inspired by a style of American wood type, which was first introduced in the mid-nineteenth century and remains popular to this day. Because its range of widths exceeds the usual classifications of 'compressed, condensed, narrow, and regular,' Knockout's nine different widths are named after the standards used in professional boxing, from the spindly 'Flyweight' to the gargantuan 'Heavyweight.' (The widest member of the range is named 'Sumo.')

ABOUT THE AUTHOR

R. GRACE MORGAN (1934–2016) was a life-long scholar and researcher. Trained in anthropology, Morgan brought a unique ecological understanding to her field, studying the patterns of sustainability that marked Indigenous Plains First Nations' relationships to beaver and bison resources.

www.ingramcontent.com/pod-product-compliance
Lightning Source LLC
Chambersburg PA
CBHW022135020426
42334CB00015B/900